NATIONAL GEOGRAPHIC
TRAVELER

brazil

NATIONAL GEOGRAPHIC
TRAVELER

brazil

by Bill Hinchberger

National Geographic
Washington, D.C.

CONTENTS

Pages 2–3: **The festival of Bumba Meu Boi Serrano, Maranhão state, Brazil**
Opposite: **Copacabana beach**

TRAVELING WITH EYES OPEN

Alert travelers go with a purpose and leave with a benefit. If you travel responsibly, you can help support wildlife conservation, historic preservation, and cultural enrichment in the places you visit. You can enrich your own travel experience as well.

To be a geo-savvy traveler:

- Recognize that your presence has an impact on the places you visit.

- Spend your time and money in ways that sustain local character. (Besides, it's more interesting that way.)

- Value the destination's natural and cultural heritage.

- Respect the local customs and traditions.

- Express appreciation to local people about things you find interesting and unique to the place: its nature and scenery, music and food, historic villages and buildings.

- Vote with your wallet: Support the people who support the place, patronizing businesses that make an effort to celebrate and protect what's special there. Seek out shops, local restaurants, inns, and tour operators who love their home—who love taking care of it and showing it off. Avoid businesses that detract from the character of the place.

- Enrich yourself, taking home memories and stories to tell, knowing that you have contributed to the preservation and enhancement of the destination.

That is the type of travel now called geotourism, defined as "tourism that sustains or enhances the geographical character of a place—its environment, culture, aesthetics, heritage, and the well-being of its residents." To learn more, visit National Geographic's Center for Sustainable Destinations at *www .nationalgeographic.com/travel/sustainable.*

brazil

ABOUT THE AUTHORS

Bill Hinchberger lived in Brazil for more than two decades. He worked as a foreign correspondent for media ranging from *The Financial Times* to *ARTnews* and served as president of the São Paulo Foreign Press Club. He founded the online travel guide *BrazilMax.com* and has contributed to several books. He now lives in Paris, where among other things he teaches a course about Brazil at CELSA, the Sorbonne's graduate school of communications.

Michael Sommers, author of the Rio de Janeiro chapter, has lived and worked in Brazil as a journalist for nearly 15 years, in the country's original capital of Salvador, Bahia. As a writer and photographer, he has contributed travel articles to the *New York Times,* the *Globe and Mail,* and the *International Herald Tribune.* He is the author of the new *National Geographic Traveler: Rio* guidebook.

São Paulo–born **Adriana Izzo-Ortolano,** research assistant, is a world traveler and teacher who speaks five languages. She can be contacted via the *www.globaldri.com* website, where she offers services for expatriates, travel advice, and research and administrative services.

Charting Your Trip

South America's largest nation could keep you exploring for decades. Brazil has the Amazon, the Pantanal, and São Paulo and Rio de Janeiro, just for starters. You'll also find an ethnically diverse culture, colonial architecture, remnants of mining and rubber boomtowns, and a rich artistic and musical heritage. With so much ground to cover—literally—you'll need to plan your trip carefully and be realistic about how much you can fit into your days in Brazil.

How to Get Around

Getting around in Brazil can be a challenge—the country is huge; bigger than the continental United States, and you could fit all of Western Europe into just the Amazon. In fact, a single national park in the Amazon rain forest is about the size of Maryland or Belgium. There are a lot of travel logistics to consider.

Air travel is generally the most efficient way to get around. Three major domestic air carriers fly to most of the country's major airports: Azul, Gol, and TAM. Colombia's Avianca operates domestic Brazilian flights to about two dozen places (see Travelwise p. 275). Unfortunately, traveler amenities in most of the country's airports remain less welcoming—crowded waiting areas and few VIP lounges—though several airports are being overhauled. Brazil's two major transportation hubs are São Paulo and Brasília. These cities offer the best connections to the rest of the country, and you will probably be routed through one of them if you are traveling to/from Rio de Janeiro or anywhere else. Do be aware that domestic air travel in Brazil is expensive by international standards.

Save for a couple of isolated lines, passenger train service in Brazil is nonexistent.

The interstate highway system is dominated by truckers, and their presence can make for stressful and even dangerous roadways. That aside, the distances you need to cover to get from place to place in Brazil often exceed comfortable driving range, and in many parts of the country rest stops and other roadside amenities are sparse. Wealthier states like São Paulo have roads that are generally in decent condition, but

A stylized Brazilian flag adorns a kite surfer's board on Prainha beach.

road maintenance elsewhere can be spotty. To top it off, car rentals are expensive: US$200 a day is not uncommon for a rental in major cities like Rio de Janeiro and Recife.

Brazil has a good network of bus lines (see Travelwise p. 275). If you have the time to take them, they can take you more or less anywhere. One company, Itapemirim *(www.itapemirim.com.br)*, serves 70 percent of Brazilian territory—including the nearly 1,850 miles (3,000 km) that separate São Paulo from Belém in the Amazon, a trip that takes three days. Although the quality of buses varies greatly, some can be quite comfortable, with reclining seats, adequate legroom, and other amenities like water, blankets, and pillows.

Huge distances and safety concerns make bicycle travel challenging; however, there is a good network of back roads, often dirt but reasonably well maintained. Signage is usually inadequate, however.

In the Amazon, boats take the place of buses. On longer routes, people bring hammocks and stretch them out on a lower deck, lounging and sleeping during what can be multiple-day journeys.

NOT TO BE MISSED:

Enjoying nature's contribution to Rio de Janeiro's beach scene 80–83

Stunning Iguaçu Falls 143, 147

Florianópolis's beach & surfing scene 150–151

Bird-watching in Pantanal wetlands 188–189

Afro-Brazilian culture in Salvador 200–204

One-of-a-kind attractions such as: Jalapão, Lençóis Maranhenses, & the Serra da Capivara 236–237, 239–240, 272

How to Visit

The most common mistake travelers to Brazil make is an overambitious travel agenda. Brazil is a large country with logistical challenges to boot, and travel can be slow. The best tactic for those for whom time is a constraint is to focus on a single region as travel time by air between destinations can use up a day. If you have two weeks, you might want to limit yourself to three destinations.

For first-time visitors to Brazil with only a few days at their disposal, two excellent destinations are **Rio de Janeiro,** the country's urban coastal postcard city, or **Foz do Iguaçu,** home of spectacular, soaring waterfalls (alas, you'll have to pick just one of these cities—they're close to 1,000 miles/1,600 km apart). If you allow three to four days for Rio, you can take an excursion to a beach resort like **Paraty** (155 miles/250 km W), or **Búzios** (112 miles/180 km E). Or if it's nature you're after and not the resorts, you can head another 93 miles (150 km) beyond Paraty to **Ilhabela,** an archipelago 4 miles

Visitor Information

The official Brazilian government tourism agency website *(www.visitbrasil.com)* provides a broad overview of the country and its attractions in English. The site also includes a link to a travel-planning app on Facebook that will give you access to information about travel services and providers in Brazil. Brazilian states and many cities also have their own visitor websites, some of which are in English, and many of which are very helpful (though this is not the rule). Another useful website with travel information in English is the Instituto EcoBrasil *(www.ecobrasil.org.br)*.

When to Visit

Brazil is in the Southern Hemisphere, so its summer is the U.S. winter, and vice versa. Most of the country falls within the tropics, and it never really gets bitterly cold anywhere, though summers are very hot across most of the country.

Heavy rainfall and seasonal high water affect some regions, making outdoor activities in those places less advisable at certain times of year. Check the seasonal conditions of the specific regions you plan to visit in advance of your trip.

The Brazilian high travel season is during the summer, especially from Christmas to Carnaval. Holiday weekends will find a deluge of Brazilians leaving the cities—most heading to beach resorts. If you want to avoid crowds and higher prices, plan around the Brazilian holiday calendar (see p. 52).

(6.5 km) off the coast of São Paulo state. Six hours to the north of Rio, there's **Ouro Preto,** a popular historic mining town in Minas Gerais. All of these are worthy excursions from the humming urban center of Rio.

If you want to explore the southern part of Brazil's coastline, **Florianópolis** is a great place to base yourself. Floripa, as Brazilians call it, offers a beach-and-party atmosphere without the megacity feel of Rio. Within a 50- to 300-mile (80–480 km) radius you will find the surfing village atmosphere at **Praia do Rosa,** rural tourism around **Lajes,** and top-notch national parks, including **São Joaquim, Serra Geral Aparados da Serra,** and **Superagüi.**

If You Have More Time

With more time, you can visit Brazil's famous and expansive natural attractions. A good itinerary for travelers on short time in Brazil starts with **Salvador,** the capital of Bahia state in Northeastern Brazil. The former colonial capital offers a mix of history, culture, and lively urban beaches. The city prides itself on its Afro-Brazilian heritage, which

Don't Forget to Get a Visa

As of early 2013, the list of countries whose passport holders needed tourist visas for Brazil included the United States, Canada, and Australia. In January 2013, the U.S. ambassador to Brazil was quoted in the Brazilian press as saying that the United States was working toward the elimination of the visa requirement for Brazilians. If this occurs, then in theory Brazil would end its visa policy for Americans. In the meantime, consult the Brazilian foreign ministry website for information about visa requirements.

To get a visa, you must consult the nearest Brazilian consulate for details about the application process. To find the location of the nearest consulate, visit Brazil's Consular Portal (*www.portalcon sular.mre.gov.br*).

If you need a visa and arrive in Brazil without one, you will not be allowed entry into the country, and there will be no way for you to obtain a visa. Some visa-less travelers have reported that they have been allowed to continue to a neighboring third country, such as Argentina, where they could then apply for a Brazilian visa, but in general you're much better off doing your homework and acquiring one before you leave.

Trekking along the Trilha do Ouro (Gold Trail) in Parque Nacional da Serra da Bocainak

you'll find on display at the Tuesday night open-air performances in the Pelourinho Centro Histórico section. Outdoor enthusiasts can head from Salvador to the **Chapada Diamantina** about 250 miles (400 km) inland, a stunning national park of plateaus and waterfalls. You can also visit splendid beaches backed by the Atlantic Forest along the southern coast of **Bahia. Recife** and its sister city **Olinda** are also good hubs for exploring the Northeast—from Recife you can visit the **Cariri region,** home of the haunting, drought-stricken *sertão*.

You'll need to build in a week to get to the Amazon Forest or Pantanal wetlands and explore those regions in earnest. If you're going to the **Amazon,** it will take one day after you arrive in Brazil to get to a gateway city— **Manaus** or **Belém.** From Manaus, taking a boat tour on the **Rio Negro** customarily takes about seven nights or more. Add a day of sightseeing in the old rubber boomtown of Manaus itself, and you've already been traveling for the better part of ten days. The same is true if you want to experience one of the better jungle lodges—by the time you arrive and pick your way to the hinterlands via transfers, you'll have been traveling for a week.

Many of Brazil's other main natural and archaeological attractions are relatively isolated from major urban centers, meaning you'll need extra travel time to reach them. These include **Lençóis Maranhenses** national park, a dune landscape that becomes pocked with blue and green freshwater lagoons after rainfall; **Jalapão,** a state park popular with outdoors enthusiasts for its white-water rafting; the **Delta do Parnaíba,** with river islands composed of sand dunes and mangrove swamps; and the **Serra da Capivara,** a World Heritage site and significant archaeological site that has changed the way paleoanthropologists think about the human settlement of the Americas. ∎

Currency

Though changing money in Brazil once entailed a rather cloak-and-dagger operation with shady figures called *doleiros* (dollar men), money changing today has become more straightforward. In large and medium-size cities, you will find ATMs linked to major international credit card networks. Most upscale establishments take credit cards. However, if you intend to travel to the outback, you may find yourself in a cash-only zone, so make sure you stock up on cash before you start out.

History & Culture

Catholic Mass at the Igreja do Mosteiro
de São Bento, Rio de Janeiro

Brazil Today

A multifaceted, multicultural society, Brazil is fraught with contradictions. Carnaval, capoeira, beaches, fashion models and soccer stars, all-you-can-eat steakhouses, caipirinhas, and hammocks are a visitor's dream, even as the country still contends with crime and poverty. As the legendary Bossa Nova composer Tom Jobim once put it: "Brazil is not for beginners." For all their society's complexities, Brazilians tend to be open and friendly toward visitors.

National Character

Brazilians are generally nonconfrontational, consensus oriented, tolerant, and informal. Personal relations generally matter more than institutional ones. These character traits help make the place pleasant to visit.

Nature has given Brazil a helping hand as well. With 18 distinct eco-regions and a wealth of cultural and outdoor activities, Brazil offers just about everything except winter sports.

> **With 18 distinct eco-regions and a wealth of cultural and outdoor activities, Brazil offers just about everything except winter sports.**

Brazil is a country that seems to grow on people, too. After a 1914 expedition to Brazil that took him across the tropical wetland expanse of the Pantanal, Theodore Roosevelt wrote of the experience, "The splendor of the sunset I never saw surpassed . . . The river ran, a broad highway of molten gold, into the flaming sky."

Elizabeth Bishop, a Pulitzer Prize–winning New England poet who arrived in Brazil a half century later, took another angle. "There are too many waterfalls here; the crowded streams/hurry too rapidly down to the sea," she wrote. Though she hated Rio de Janeiro, she fell in love with the country's orchids and hummingbirds. A stay that was supposed to last a few weeks extended into years.

Though Brazil is a country of beauty, fun, and carousing, Brazilians are not so easily defined. They have a melancholic streak they call *saudades*—a sense of loss and longing infused with a warm nostalgia for what has been lost. It's a condition so unique that it does not translate into any single English word. The country's fun-loving front disguises a complex national psyche and a society still grappling with social inequality and economic disparity.

Luiz Inácio Lula da Silva, arguably the most popular leftist politician of our generation, is a good instance of a figure at whom a closer look reveals much. He has a compelling rags-to-riches story and served two four-year terms as president, before stepping down at the end of 2010. Yet he wasn't really a leftist, not in the Che Guevara sense. Lula embodied his country's aversion to extremes—while still a labor leader in the 1970s, he was famously quoted as saying, "I am against radicalism on both the left and the right. I think that radicalism is a dead end."

If you want to "get" Brazil, you must dig deeply. When French sociologist Roger Bastide set foot in the country in the 1930s to study its Afro-Brazilian religions, he realized that he would have to abandon his old schools of thought and assume a new intellectual framework to grasp the country's character. For decades, Brazil seemed poised to come into its own, but never quite able to make the leap. Brazilians understood this and joked: "Brazil is the country of the future—and always will be," a saying derived from Austrian playwright Stefan Zweig's 1941 book, *Country of the Future.*

Visitors enjoy the view from the Cristo Redentor despite the crowds.

Flamengo vs. Vasco in Rio: You can't begin to understand Brazil until you take in a big soccer match.

A Country Emerging

Happily, times have changed, and Brazil enjoys a significant global presence today. It will host both the next soccer World Cup in 2014 and the Summer Olympics in 2016. Its military has been key in leading UN peacekeeping efforts in Haiti. And not least, Brazil is surging ahead economically. It set a record for foreign direct investment (FDI) for the second straight year in 2011, hitting $66.7 billion, from $48.5 billion the year before. Brazil represents the first letter in BRIC, a widely-used acronym that refers to a group of high-profile emerging economies—Brazil, Russia, India, and China.

Brazil has grown steadily, if not spectacularly, since the mid-1990s, thanks in part to consistently sensible macroeconomic fiscal and social welfare policies that helped it quell hyperinflation. Despite the debt crisis and the Lost Decade of the 1980s (when the nation defaulted on its foreign debt), Brazil registered one of the world's highest rates of growth in the 20th century. By 2011, Brazil passed the United Kingdom to become the world's sixth largest economy as measured by gross domestic product.

The country has finally started to close a legendary poverty gap, giving rise to a significant middle class for the first time in the nation's history. Standing at 95 million, the middle class now represents more than half the population. However, despite significant progress over the last two decades, Brazil's ranking on the World Bank's GINI index (which measures inequality) remains close to the bottom—even behind countries like Rwanda, Paraguay, and Zambia. These numbers are evidence that despite the presence of affluence and a rising middle class in the nation, staggering poverty still exists.

In June 2013, during the Confederations Cup, viewed as a tune-up for the World Cup, Brazilians flooded the streets of major cities to protest everything from bus fare hikes to political corruption. In sum, the middle class had become fed up with shelling out the lion's share of Brazil's world-class tax bill (36% of GDP) without receiving world-class services in return. Brazilians demanded "FIFA standards" for health, education, and transportation.

The extremes of wealth and poverty in Brazil can be jarring. Even as the poor exist in shantytowns and the murder rates climb, Brazil's shift toward a consumer-style economy has brought about some of the same ill effects that have plagued other developed nations.

Interpreting the Rules

Perhaps because of these tensions, Brazil can be a challenging place for visitors. The friendly demeanor of locals does not always translate into quality service. Brazil is conspicuously absent of clear, user-friendly signs—a hallmark of popular tourist destinations. Though the upper classes may speak English, few others do. Taxi drivers, bus drivers, hotel employees, and customer service representatives usually speak only Portuguese.

Some tourists adapt easily to Brazil, but the absence of clear standards of conduct confuses others. Many laws are ignored or selectively enforced. Permitted and prohibited, acceptable and unacceptable, legal and illegal, merge into a big mass of gray area. "What do I like most about Brazil?" a foreign businessman asked rhetorically. "The fact that there are no rules. And what do I like least about Brazil? The fact that there are no rules."

Even Elizabeth Bishop recognized that Brazil challenges the expectations of its guests. In "Arrival at Santos," the poet says of the port town, "Oh tourist/is this how this country is going to answer you/and your immodest demands for a different world/and a better life, and complete comprehension?"

The People

During Brazil's colonial period, which began around 1500 with the arrival of the Portuguese, the country's population was a mixture of indigenous people, Portuguese,

EXPERIENCE: Soccer the Brazilian Way

Soccer is more like Brazil's national passion than its national pastime. *Futebol* is so ingrained in the culture that conversations can be held using just soccer metaphors.

Even if you are not a sports fan, taking in a match can be exhilarating. Decked out in jerseys and team colors, fans set out early, filling the stadium well before game time, singing fight songs and chanting. When their team takes the field, pandemonium ensues. Chants and clapping accompany the action on the field until a team scores; then, jumping up and down in unison, fans enact a frenzied celebration.

São Paulo or Rio de Janeiro are the best places to try to catch a game—with multiple professional teams playing almost year-round in these cities, you'll have little trouble finding a match. A full set of listings is available at http://globoesporte.globo.com/futebol.

Unless you are familiar and comfortable with intense spectating, purchase a reserved seat somewhere away from the rooting sections; being opposite them provides a better view anyway. Women can be found at soccer games, but this is mostly a world of adult men and adolescent boys.

and Africans—respectively, the natives, the colonizers, and the laborers who were imported into the country against their will. As a result of this latter circumstance, Brazil still has the most people of African origin of any country in the world except Nigeria.

Beginning in the 19th century through the 1930s, large numbers of Europeans, especially Germans and Italians, immigrated to Brazil. In 1908, after a Japan-Brazil immigration treaty was established, huge numbers of Japanese immigrants began arriving in Brazil as well, and as a result, Brazil today boasts the largest number of people of Japanese origin in the world outside of Japan.

Race in Brazil has long been a murky issue. In the wake of the nation's history of conquest and slavery during Portuguese colonization, social relations were anything but ideal and abuses widespread. Even so, the people who inhabited Brazil mixed together somewhat more naturally than in places like the United States and South Africa. This phenomenon became a critical element in an influential 1933 book called *The Masters and the Slaves,* written by one of Brazil's most respected scholars of the 20th century, Gilberto Freyre. While Freyre's ideas were much more sophisticated and nuanced than the distilled version that became popularized, the concept of "racial democracy" associated with him came to symbolize the attitudes of an elite that preferred to pretend that racism did not exist. Almost no one calls Brazil a racial democracy anymore.

Though recent decades have seen a strong Movimento Negro (Black Movement) emerge to demand equal rights, and though specific legislation bans segregation in

Portuguese Is Not Spanish

When America's favorite cartoon family visited Brazil, Bart Simpson prepared by taking an audio course entitled Español for Dummies: "Get ready Brazil, I now speak fluent Spanish," the cartoon child noted, smugly crossing his arms. "Well done, Bart," responded his mother Marge. "But in Brazil they speak Portuguese."

It's a common misconception. Visitors to Brazil often assume that their Spanish will help, and they are usually disappointed. A different language and distinct colonial heritage have set Brazil off from the rest of Latin America. Indeed, when Brazilians use the term "Latin America," they mean everybody else—their Spanish-speaking neighbors.

If you want to learn Portuguese, there are a host of courses to choose from. In Salvador, Bahia, the **Diálogo Language School** *(tel 71/3264 0053, www.dialogo-brazilstudy.com, email: office@dialogo.tur .br)* has been offering intensive classes for

two decades. Students can choose from programs ranging from a week to a year. Extracurricular activities include classes in dance, capoeira (see sidebar p. 21), and Brazilian cooking. Diálogo helps support an NGO that works in a poor neighborhood where students can do volunteer work. It also sets up regular exchange meetings with Brazilian students of English. Housing options include homestays, apartments, guesthouses, and hotels.

Fast Forward *(tel 82/3327 5213, www.fastforward.com.br, email: info@ fastforward.com.br)* offers intensive, "super-intensive," and individual classes in Maceió, a beach town in the sunny, arid Northeast, and in São Paulo, Brazil's biggest and most important city. Students can stay with local families, in their own apartments, or in hotels or inns. The company organizes cultural excursions in both locations as part of its educational program.

cities like São Paulo and Rio de Janeiro, race remains a tricky subject in Brazil. One of the country's biggest icons, retired soccer player Pelé, is black. Nevertheless, even today, Brazil's mostly darker-skinned domestic servants are relegated to separate service elevators, forced to accept a sort of de facto apartheid in the apartment buildings where they work.

Religion

Although most Brazilians do not wear their religion on their sleeves, it is a country of believers. According to a 2009 poll, 97 percent of Brazilians believe in God, about three-quarters believe in the devil, and roughly two-thirds described themselves as Roman Catholics, giving Pope Francis I one of his largest legions of followers.

Children in São Luis, Maranhão

The first Catholic Mass in Brazil was celebrated on Easter Sunday, April 26, 1500, by Friar Henrique de Coimbra, soon after the Portuguese landed in what is today Porto Seguro, Bahia. During the colonial period, several magnificent churches were erected, notably in Minas Gerais state, often making use of the gold that was being extensively mined there. The country boasts several impressive museums of sacred art, the most notable of which are in Salvador and São Paulo. Mimicking the popular Road to Santiago in Europe, Brazilians engage in pilgrimages, such as one following the footsteps of the 16th-century Spanish Jesuit missionary Padre Anchieta in Espírito Santo and São Paulo states. Though the Brazilian constitution is secular, many Catholic feast days are public holidays.

Catholic culture in Brazil is characterized by a strong belief in miracles. Catholic pilgrims flock to the interior of São Paulo state to visit a gigantic but otherwise unexceptional basilica that holds a statue of the Virgin Mary believed to perform miracles. An impressive Miracle Room in the basilica displays objects left in gratitude for acts that the faithful believe have been performed on their behalf. Large numbers of believers also converge on Juazeiro do Norte, Ceará, home of the 19th-century priest Padre Cícero, who had a reputation for performing miracles. The grave of an early 20th-century rabbi in the city of Manaus in the Amazon is visited by Christians looking for divine intercession.

Missionaries have tried to convert Brazil's indigenous population over the centuries with varying degrees of success. Some indigenous practices still exist, but they are dwarfed by the ones imported by immigrants over the last five centuries. After Catholicism, other prevalent denominations include traditional Protestantism, evangelical Protestantism, Mormonism, and Jehovah's Witnesses. Evangelical Protestantism in particular is on the rise; adherents include top soccer stars, and the group is becoming increasingly influential in electoral politics.

Though the culture is devout, Brazilians today often demonstrate an exceptional degree of tolerance for those with different beliefs. In São Paulo, for example, it is common for Jews and Muslims to frequent the same butcher to satisfy their dietary requirements. In São Paulo, Muslims happily partake of the kosher *feijoada* (a black-bean stew customarily containing pork and pork sausage) that a local restaurant developed in conjunction with a neighboring synagogue.

Capoeira performers in Jericoacoara, Ceará, Brazil

EXPERIENCE: Getting the Hang of Capoeira

Fluid and (mostly) without contact, it is a sport too nice to be a martial art. Combative and aggressive, it is too rough to be dance. Some call it a "fight-dance game," though that is a rather unpoetic description of a dynamic art form.

It's called capoeira and it is performed by two dueling protagonists, who swing and lurch at each other seemingly in unison, if done well. Yet, any sense of collaboration is at least partly misleading: Somebody is getting the upper hand, and anyone who understands the ritual knows who it is. The duo does battle in the middle of a circle of participants in waiting. Instruments play distinctive capoeira songs. After a minute or two, someone from the circle relieves the person who has been inside the longest, and the ritual continues.

A legacy of slaves, capoeira is reminiscent of similar practices in Africa. Although often associated with the large Afro-Brazilian population in Bahia, it is practiced all over the country. Eduardo da Silva Areias, better known as Professor Kiduro, receives students at his **Acapoeira academy** in São Paulo *(Rua Cardoso Moreira, 110 Ari Bazão, tel 11/8149 7901 or 3539 2464, email: kidurocapoeira@ hotmail.com)*. Adult classes are on Mondays and Wednesdays from 7:30 p.m. to 9:00 p.m. Call or send an email in advance of your visit. In Salvador, **Diálogo Language School** *(see p. 18; tel 71/3264 0053, www.dialogo-brazilstudy.com)* offers a free capoeira workshop with its language classes. Lessons are in the afternoon, and you can try the basic steps—the *ginga* and *golpes* (leg swings)—yourself.

Traditions

Most religious traditions in Brazil are fairly standard, though some Brazilians subscribe to syncretism—the melding of seemingly contradictory beliefs. A classic example of Brazilian syncretism is the practice of Afro-Brazilian Candomblé, which emerged from the need for African slaves to disguise their true faith from their owners by hiding their beliefs behind a facade of Catholicism.

Brazilians also practice Santo Daime, a syncretic practice that emerged from the Amazon in the 1930s. Once popular among some members of Brazil's chic artistic class, its ritual includes such unorthodox practices as drinking psychoactive compounds called Ayahuasca, which can act as an emetic believed to bring about spiritual and physical cleansing.

Other less traditional spiritual practices of Brazil include Spiritism, a doctrine founded by French educator Allan Kardec and popularized by Brazilian disciple Chico Xavier; and Positivism, a philosophy developed in the 1800s by the "father of sociology," Auguste Comte.

Some indigenous practices still exist, but they are dwarfed by the ones imported by immigrants over the last five centuries.

A prominent and controversial Brazilian spiritual practitioner who has made forays into even American media and pop culture is faith healer João de Deus (John of God), a supposed medium who claims to channel the healing powers of God. ■

Food & Drink

Brazilian cuisine can be presented as a chronicle of the people who have inhabited the country, from the indigenous people to the wave of immigrants centuries later. Each group has brought something different to the mix, and newcomers have adapted their recipes to the local culture and integrated local ingredients.

Brazilian cuisine can be viewed through a geographic prism. The different climates, soils, and vegetation of Brazil's eco-regions, added to the varied cultural heritages of groups settled there, have produced a series of distinct regional culinary traditions. There are, however, commonalities.

Sugar Lovers

Centuries of sugarcane cultivation have left many Brazilians with a sweet tooth. Residents mark the progression of the day with a series of strong shots of black coffee laden with sugar, called *cafezinhos*. Sugar serves as a main ingredient (twice over) for the national drink, the caipirinha—a mixture of high-proof sugarcane spirit known as *cachaça* or *pinga*, superfine sugar (the most common kind available in Brazil), sliced limes, and ice. Caipirinhas often accompany Brazil's national dish, a black-bean stew called *feijoada*. Another popular item

loaded with sugar is the national soft drink *guaraná*, made from a bean of the same name that comes from a shrub native to the Amazon. Guaraná contains *guaranine*, a caffeine-like stimulant.

Brazil has a wide variety of fruit trees, and juice is a must at breakfast, a common accompaniment to meals, and a popular refreshment on a hot afternoon. Take your pick of juices: cashew, mango, passion fruit, acerola, pineapple, *cupuaçu*, and papaya, among others. You'll find juice bars on the streets of many cities.

Typical Meals

Elaborate meals are consumed in restaurants or on special occasions, but a typical meal in a typical home consists of something like rice and beans (black or brown), generally mixed together on the plate and often sprinkled with manioc meal, with grilled chicken, and perhaps a small salad. Pasta, especially

EXPERIENCE: Cooking Classes

Chef Gustavo Iglesias runs the **Viandier Casa de Gastronomia** *(Alameda Lorena, 558, Jardim Paulista, São Paulo, tel 11/3057 2987 or 3887 2943, www.viandier .br/index.php, email: casadegastronomia@ viandier.com.br)* as his grandmother would her kitchen. The cozy setting in São Paulo's upscale Jardins district is organized around what he calls traditional cooking—food designed to taste like it came from grandma's kitchen, albeit with a pinch of modern sophistication. In addition to housing a small restaurant, a gourmet

emporium with select ingredients, and a space for small private events, Viandier offers cooking classes. Class sizes are kept small (16 is capacity), and a group meal awaits at the end of the class. There are about a dozen different courses, each focusing on a different food group or specialty. The highlight of the course catalog is called Day Cook. Students meet in the morning to head en masse to a local farmers market, where they choose the ingredients for their class and ultimately, their lunch.

Acarajé **bean–flour patties are fried in** *dendê* **palm oil at a Copacabana beach celebration.**

spaghetti, might make an appearance. Budget eateries serve this kind of fare as part of a set menu *(prato feito)* at lunchtime during the week. The most common form of alcohol is beer. Brazilians often prefer their beer *estupidamente gelada*–stupidly cold.

Ethnic Traditions

Italian, German, Lebanese, and other immigrants each brought with them culinary traditions that have lasted. Brazil contains the largest population of Japanese outside of Japan, so you can find excellent sushi in places like São Paulo. However, what most people consider traditional Brazilian dishes are rooted in the cuisine of the natives and the first two groups to settle the country in large numbers, Portuguese and Africans.

The Natives: The first inhabitants left an enduring legacy on Brazil's culinary scene. They spent centuries adapting to their environment,

Brazilian *feijoada*, a stew of beans and meat

19th century, Brazilians continued the tradition and today imported codfish is still featured prominently on the menus of local restaurants of all stripes.

Portuguese habits of preparing food may have been their most significant contribution to Brazilian cuisine. These include stews, sautéing ingredients with spices over the stove, and marinating meat prior to cooking it.

Africans: Africans and their descendants often ran the kitchens of the well-to-do during Brazil's era of slavery, which lasted until 1888. Partly as a result, Brazil's cuisine has absorbed many elements of West African cooking. This is particularly evident in the Northeastern state of Bahia, where ingredients of African origin or derivation are commonplace, notably hot peppers and the reddish *dendê* palm oil.

Dendê is the defining ingredient of *moqueca*, a seafood stew that also includes fish and/or shrimp, onions, tomatoes, cilantro, coconut milk, and *malagueta* chile pepper. Another characteristic dish is *vatapá*, a paste sometimes served as a side dish or spread on bean fritters filled with shrimp to make a snack called *acarajé* that is sold as fast food in the streets of Salvador and other cities. The recipe for vatapá, celebrated in a song of the same name by the Bahian composer Dorival Caymmi, includes bread, dendê, dried shrimp, peanuts, cashew nuts, malegueta peppers, onions, garlic, and ginger.

and newcomers invariably had to learn from them in order to survive.

Perhaps their most important lesson was how to prepare and serve manioc, a tuber also known as the cassava root—a main staple that filled a niche occupied by wheat or corn elsewhere. For manioc to become edible, it must undergo an involved process to extract toxins from it. Manioc is also fried or boiled and served as a side dish to many recipes, including feijoada. It is known by different names in different parts of the country—for example, *aipim* in Rio de Janeiro, *macaxeira* in the Northeast, and *mandioca* in São Paulo.

Portuguese: On festive occasions in Brazil, people often serve something called *bacalhau*, the Portuguese name for dried, salted codfish. While the Portuguese were talented sailors and had a strong history as fishers, most of the waters off the coast of Brazil are notoriously poor fishing regions. But bacalhau had been the Portuguese national dish since the 16th century, so the colonists imported it. Even after Brazil's independence from Portugal in the

Regional Cuisine

North: In Belém, Manaus, and other cities of the Amazon region, the indigenous influence on dietary habits is unmistakable. One of the first things you notice are simple street vendors ladling out *tacacá*, a soup made with *jambu* (a variety of paracress), *tucupi* (manioc broth), dried shrimp, and small yellow peppers—served piping hot in a native gourd called a *cuia*. The leafy green jambu has an analgesic property that will leave your mouth numb.

Local freshwater fish are the cornerstone of any menu. The enormous *tambaquí*, which feeds on fruits and seeds and can weigh as much as 60 pounds (27 kg), is prized. Another popular species is the *tucunaré*, or peacock bass, with a taste akin to snapper when cooked. Fish is served every which way in the Amazon: in stews, boiled and served in broth, fried, and barbecued.

Northeast: Bahia is best known for the seafood abundant along the coastline. But when Brazilians think of the food typical of this region, they think of the meat-based dishes of the outback and that is what dominates the menus in Northeastern-style restaurants. This hearty fare hails from the parched backlands known as the *sertão*, populated by small farmers and cattle ranches and manned by cowboys known as *vaqueiros*. Sun-dried beef is a regular feature, and is often accompanied by mandioca, sweet potatoes, and a coarse mixture of toasted manioc and dried beef called *paçoca*. *Baião-de-dois* is a mishmash of rice, beans, and goat cheese generally served with sun-dried beef. Roasted goat is another regional favorite.

Queijo coalho, a regional cheese, is popular as an appetizer or a snack. Slices of the cheese are heated on the grill in restaurants or slightly roasted over coals by street vendors and then served on a stick.

Central-West: Tourists think of the Pantanal and region surrounding it mostly in terms of its wetland ecology, but it has long been an important cattle-ranching region. Not surprisingly, the wetlands serve up abundant amounts of fish, but steakhouses are just as plentiful as fish places. *Pintado*, a kind of catfish, is popular, particularly when it is barbecued *(pintado na brasa)*.

South-Central: The most distinctive cuisine from this region comes from Minas Gerais, a state with a long tradition in both mining and agriculture. These are the heavy, filling meals of people who spent their days burning through calories in the mines or fields. Pork is a mainstay, generally served with rice, black beans, shredded kale sautéed in oil, and pork rinds. The beans can be served as a thick paste called *tutu*, somewhat reminiscent of Mexican refried beans. Or the beans and rice can be substituted for *feijão tropeiro*, a mixture of rice, black beans, scrambled eggs, and bits of sausage and pork. The best known dish in neighboring Espírito Santo is a local kind of *moqueca* made without the dendê oil.

Feijoada

There are differing legends of the origin of Brazil's national dish. The more folkloric one is that the black-bean stew known as *feijoada* was concocted by slaves who made the most of the scraps left over from the Big House. Scholars have an alternate theory—they suggest that feijoada is more likely a hybrid descendant of the French cassoulet and the Portuguese *caldeirada*. Mixed in with the beans are sundry cuts of pork, sausages, and jerked beef. The stew is generally served with rice, kale sautéed in oil, fried manioc, pork chops, fried sausages, manioc flour called *farinha*, sliced orange pieces, and hot sauce. An aperitif made of a mixture of fruit juice, *cachaça*, and sugar, called a *batida*, is often served beforehand. (A song by Chico Buarque called "Feijoada Completa" narrates the procedure for making the storied dish.) Many restaurants offer feijoada on Saturdays and, in some cities, on one other day of the week. In São Paulo, it is Wednesday, while restaurants in Rio de Janeiro will often serve feijoada on Fridays. In major cities, some establishments specialize in feijoada and serve it daily.

Natural Brazil

With abundant biodiversity and diverse landscapes, Brazil is often touted as a natural paradise. Once overlooked in favor of the sun and surf, activities like bird-watching and wildlife spotting are becoming increasingly popular.

Fauna

Wildlife spotting is one of Brazil's greatest attractions. People traipse through the Pantanal wetlands in search of jaguars; through the Amazon rain forest to view monkeys, piranhas, and pink freshwater dolphins; and to the coast for whale-watching. Bird-watchers flock to all corners of the country to view some of its 1,700 species of fowl, 200 of which are endemic.

Brazil ranks first in the world for the number of amphibian species, third for birds, second for mammals, and fourth for reptiles, according to the United Nations Environmental Program (UNEP). The animals that inhabit Brazil today are descended from ancient animal populations (think primeval-looking anteaters, sloths, armadillos, and marsupials); relatively early immigrants like monkeys and cavy rodents like the capybara; and relative newcomers, like carnivores, hoofed animals, and rodents.

The puma rivals the jaguar as Brazil's most impressive feline mammal; other unusual terrestrial mammals you might catch a glimpse of include the maned wolf, the tapir, the giant anteater, and the giant armadillo. The country has monkeys galore, including howlers and capuchins. Caimans lurk in the waterways of certain parts of the Pantanal and the Amazon, and brightly-colored poison dart frogs are commonplace as well.

Fittingly for a country that was named after a tree (brazilwood), Brazil boasts more vascular plant species than any country in the world.

Brazil is debatably home to the world's biggest freshwater fish (the pirarucu in the Amazon), the world's largest snake (the anaconda), the world's largest river dolphin (pink dolphin), the world's largest surviving rodent (the capybara), and the world's second largest spider (the Goliath birdeater).

Bird species range from the miniscule hummingbird to the imposing harpy eagle. Colorful birds include parrots, toucans, and macaws. Curiosities include the hoatzin (an Amazonian bird whose chicks possess claws), the southern screamer (in southern Brazil and neighboring countries, whose courtship involves loud screeches that can be heard miles away), and nocturnal potoos that camouflage themselves during the day by sitting frozen on branches, resembling tree stumps.

Flora

Fittingly for a country that was named after a tree (brazilwood), Brazil boasts more vascular plant species than any country in the world, according to UNEP. With a knowledgeable guide, a simple walk through the Brazilian countryside can turn into a fascinating botany lesson.

Amazonian milk frog: one of the better known examples of Brazil's abundant biodiversity

There are magnificent trees: the kapok, which can reach up to 200 feet (61 m) in height; the mulateiro (used for herbal medicine), known for its ability to completely shed and regenerate its bark on a yearly basis; the jacaranda with its breathtaking floral display; and the cannonball tree, which grows fruits as large as its namesake. Look out—these woody fruits can come crashing down to earth with loud explosive bursts. Ornamental plants are commonplace in nature and often cultivated; these include orchids, bromeliads, palms, and cacti.

A trip to an open-air street market in almost any Brazilian town will reveal a generous offering of fruits and nuts. Depending on the region and season, these may include açaí, cocoa, cupuaçu, pequi, brazil nuts, jaboticaba, guava, and guaraná. Many can be consumed as juices or ice creams. You'll also find dozens of medicinal plants and herbs at the markets.

Impressive botanical gardens are open to visitors in many Brazilian cities, including Brasília, Curitiba, Manaus, Rio de Janeiro, and São Paulo. Several private reserves can also be visited, including the Kautsky Orchid Center in Domingos Martins, Espírito Santo; the Sítio Bacchus, with its orchid collection in the Atlantic Forest in Macaé, Rio de Janeiro; and the Sebuí Ecological Reserve on the coast of Paranáthe.

Land & Landscape: Bioregions of Brazil

A bioregion is defined as a place where certain flora, fauna, and physical conditions predominate. These are generally determined by factors like climate, geography, geology, and soil conditions. Brazil is divided into six main bioregions: Amazon Rain Forest, Cerrado, Pantanal, Caatinga, Atlantic Forest, and Pampas.

Amazon Rain Forest: Including the parts of it that cross into other countries, the world's largest rain forest covers more than 2,000,000 square miles (5,000,000 sq km) of

Açaí, a regional fruit of the Brazilian Amazon

which 80 percent is in northern Brazil. In the states of Acre, Amapá, Amazonas, Pará, Roraima, Rondônia, Mato Grosso, Maranhão, and Tocantins, more than a thousand rivers—accounting for one-fifth of the world's fresh surface water—run from the rain forest. Scientists estimate that it contains nearly one-third of the world's biodiversity, especially species of plants and insects. They also believe that only about half of the region's species have been identified so far. The climate is hot and humid, and even though rainfall may vary slightly by region, the heaviest deluges usually come between November and May. But rainfall is common all year—goes the old lighthearted adage, "There are two seasons in the Amazon: the

Rio São Francisco

If there is a waterway that captures the Brazilian imagination the way the Mississippi does the American, it is the São Francisco. Velho Chico (Old Chico), as it is popularly known, has its source in Minas Gerais, at an elevation of 3,900 feet (1,200 m) in the Serra da Canastra. It cuts through part of neighboring Bahia, and then runs to the sea, acting as the border between Bahia and Pernambuco and then Sergipe and Alagoas. Near its mouth, the river runs through magnificent canyons that can be viewed in the opening scene of the film *Baile Perfumado*. It runs primarily through Brazil's folklore-rich semiarid backlands and is the subject of legends of giant water snakes and even mermaids. Boats that ply the São Francisco invariably sport a fierce lion-man figurehead on the bow to ward off evil spirits.

However, more opportunistic interests are beginning to impact the river. Long considered a potential source of water for human use, it is finally being diverted for irrigation after decades of contentious debate over whom the project will truly benefit. Despite environmentalists' warnings that the diversion project will further deplete the river, which is already being drawn down by several dams, construction began in 2007. As of April 2013, though, not a single drop of water had yet been delivered anywhere.

period when it rains every day, and the period when rains all day." As is to be expected, water levels in the Amazon rise significantly during the periods of heavy rains, and some parts of the forest remain permanently under water, while others are temporarily flooded. Some remain permanently above the floodplain.

The rain forest is characterized by tall trees that create a canopy overhead, with a heavy understory beneath. So dense is the forest and the vegetative cover that uninitiated visitors may have a hard time spotting animals, birds, and interesting flowers—this is where a good guide can come in, to help draw out details and point out interesting elements.

Cerrado: Covering an area roughly equivalent in size to western Europe, the Cerrado, in the Central and Northeast, is sometimes called Brazil's heartland. It is considered one of the world's richest tropical savanna regions, and boasts an enormous variety of plant and animal biodiversity. Three of South America's most important river basins originate in the Cerrado: Tocantins, São Francisco, and Platina. Plains and plateaus streak the horizon, and here low-lying vegetation is normal. The climate is semihumid hot tropical, with alternating rainy and dry seasons, the latter running from May to September.

The Cerrado is becoming a magnet for outdoor enthusiasts, with opportunities for hiking, rafting, canoeing, rappelling, rock climbing, caving, and more. Among the more popular destinations in the Cerrado are Chapada Diamantina in Bahia, Chapada dos Veadeiros in Goiás, and Chapada dos Guimarães in Mato Grosso. They are all marked by expansive landscapes, cliff and rock formations, and waterfalls. Hikers will notice varied vegetation along their treks: flooded grassy areas called *veredas,* groves of trees that seem stunted, and fields speckled with wildflowers.

Rainbow across Foz do Iquaçu

Pantanal: In the middle of South America, in the states of Mato Grosso do Sul and Mato Grosso, lie the world's largest wetlands. Their extent lies almost entirely in Brazil, though a small section crosses into neighboring Bolivia and Paraguay. The region experiences an annual cycle of flooding. Following a period of heavy rains (Oct.–March), water gradually drains into the Paraguay River and its tributaries. Rich soil and ample rainfall ensure abundant vegetation, which in turn sustains a huge diversity of wildlife. Although many animals also inhabit other parts of the country, they are most readily spotted in the Pantanal. The Pantanal has one of the greatest concentrations of aquatic and *paludicola* bird species in the world. Among those most commonly seen are the jabiru stork, the wood stork, the roseate spoonbill, the neotropic cormorant, the heron, and the hyacinth macaw. Cattle ranches also occupy large swaths of the region.

The Pantanal is a prime destination for those looking to bond with nature. Ecolodges serve as outposts for visitors, who then make excursions into the wetlands on foot, on horseback, by boat, or in a four-wheel-drive vehicle. The Pantanal is also a popular destination for sportfishing—the season runs from March to October.

Caatinga: At 325,000 square miles (850,000 sq km) the Caatinga is the only bioregion that falls entirely within Brazil's boundaries. It is home to a large number of plant species that are not encountered in any other region in the country. In the native Tupi language, Caatinga means "white forest" or "white vegetation," an accurate description of the xeric shrubland, thorny trees, and arid-adapted grasses that survive in the parched heat that bakes the region for most of the year.

When the brief and often sparse rainfall begins in November, the landscape explodes into a verdant green before again blanching in the heat a few months later.

Atlantic Forest: Once a rival to the Amazon in size, the Atlantic Forest is left with an estimated 7 percent of its original cover and is one of the most threatened rain forests in the world. What's left can be visually stunning, with tree-covered rocks and outcroppings that sometimes jut out to the sea. There are waterfalls and orchids, and occasionally spottings of the golden lion tamarin monkey. Prime segments of the forest lie within easy reach of major urban centers like São Paulo, Rio de Janeiro, Curitiba, and Salvador. Well-equipped inns are set in the countryside or in colonial towns that populate the region. Popular activities include hiking, mountain biking, rappelling, rafting, canoeing, and horseback riding.

> Once a rival to the Amazon in size, the Atlantic Forest is left with an estimated 7 percent of its original cover.

Pampas: Located in the state of Rio Grande do Sul, this is Brazil's sliver of a bioregion typically associated with Argentina and Uruguay. Inland are open grasslands, while marshes along the coast serve as important way stations for migratory birds. Rainfall is abundant, generally coming from cold fronts from the south. Winters are colder than elsewhere in Brazil. Summers can be hot and humid, albeit milder in the foothills. Much of the region was developed long ago for agriculture, but several conservation areas allow for outdoor activities, from adventure sports to horseback riding. ∎

Sertão—the Backland of Legends

The Caatinga region has a mystique that has made it a popular backdrop for works of Brazilian literature and cinema. It doubles in popular parlance as the *sertão*, sparsely populated arid badlands that are dotted by traces of prehistory—rock paintings and carvings, and dinosaur and megafauna fossil sites. It was here the legendary early 20th-century bandit Lampião roamed. It was here, too, that the mystic Antônio Conselheiro organized a utopian community that was brutally destroyed by federal forces in the 1890s. And future Brazilian president Lula spent his early years in poverty in Caatinga before emigrating with his mother to a port town called Santos.

Classic books like *The Devil to Pay in the Backlands* by João Guimarães Rosa and *Barren Lives* by Graciliano Ramos were set here. The Caatinga region was also the setting for classic films like Nelson Pereira dos Santos's film version of *Barren Lives,* and *Black God, White Devil* by avant-garde director Glauber Rocha. *Baile Perfumado* by Paulo Caldas and Lírio Ferreira, and *Auto da Compadecida* by Guel Arraes are set here as well.

Brazilian History

Most accounts of Brazilian history tend to start in 1500 with the arrival of Portuguese explorer Pedro Álvares Cabral. Like Christopher Columbus in the Caribbean a few years earlier, Cabral was on a course to India when he stumbled entirely by accident upon a beach—what today is Porto Seguro in the state of Bahia in Northeastern Brazil.

After Cabral's discovery, the Portuguese arrived in what we now know as Brazil to find somewhere between 500,000 and 2,000,000 people, speaking hundreds of languages, already inhabiting the region. A wave of epidemics in the 16th century wiped out as much as half of this original population. Relatively little is known about these precolonial people. They seem to have fallen into one of two groups—nomadic hunters and

Pedro Álvares Cabral stumbled on the land that would later be known as Brazil.

Ancient Artifacts in Serra da Capivara

Evidence from Northeastern Brazil in recent decades has sent the archaeological world into a tizzy. For decades, scientists agreed that the first humans to inhabit the Americas came over the Bering Strait from Asia in around 10,000 B.C. But the spectacular rock paintings in Serra da Capivara National Park in the Brazilian state of Piauí have been dated by experts as reaching back 25,000 years ago or more. Other human artifacts include a series of hearths, the earliest of which has been dated to 46,000 B.C. In the face of this evidence, some paleoanthropologists now believe that humans may have migrated from Africa over the Atlantic Ocean as long as 60,000 years ago. For more about the Serra da Capivara, see page 236.

gatherers, and seminomadic tribes practicing slash-and-burn agriculture. They had no written forms of their languages, so what is known of them comes from early accounts of the Portuguese and relatively scanty archaeological evidence. Fortunately, archaeological work has accelerated in recent

decades, and tens of thousands of sites have been identified that contain rock paintings and carvings, native burial grounds, and stashes of artifacts.

When the Portuguese first arrived, the region was mostly covered by two rain forests of roughly equal size. The Amazon, while suffering from rampant deforestation remains largely intact today; the Atlantic Forest to the south, which once extended across an area that now includes megacities São Paulo and Rio de Janeiro, has been decimated.

Portuguese Colonization

Unlike the English who had a penchant for establishing settlements, the Portuguese cared mostly about commerce and preferred to establish trading posts in lieu of colonies. But to rebuff competing claims, first mostly by the French and later by the Dutch, they took a different tack in South America. The Portuguese crown established land grants that gave privileged nobles sway over vast expanses of territory and mandated the establishment of colonies. Two of them, São Vicente (which gave origin to today's state of São Paulo) and Pernambuco, were well managed and successful. Others languished.

Brazilwood, prized in Europe for the reddish dye derived from it and for its high-quality wood, gave the place its name. Colonial Brazil's export economy was powered largely by slave labor imported from Africa. The 16th century saw a series of boom-and-bust export cycles, starting with sugar in the Northeast. Sugar exports constituted the backbone of the Brazilian economy during the 16th and 17th centuries. Just as the international demand for sugar was waning, gold was discovered, and what is now the state of Minas Gerais (literally "general mines") became the center of extraction. By the end of the 18th century, the mines were depleted, and gold exports declined.

Inspired in part by the U.S. and French Revolutions, Brazil saw a number of uprisings in a quest for independence in the late

18th century. The most widely remembered is the Inconfidência Mineira, led by a man known as Tiradentes (Teethpuller), who was a dentist. The uprising was crushed and Tiradentes was executed, but he became a national hero in Brazil and the anniversary of his death is a national holiday.

Arrival of Royalty

Napoleon's army invaded Portugal in 1807, and in response, the Portuguese royal family fled under British protection to its South American colonial outpost in 1808.

Trade liberalization soon followed in Brazil, engendering a commercial boom in port cities Salvador and Rio de Janeiro. The latter was a backwater of 60,000 when the royal family arrived, but members of the court and hangers-on added thousands to the population. An influx of foreigners, including diplomats, gave the town a more cosmopolitan air. Universities were founded, and a library was built; printing presses were established, and the *Gazeta do Rio de Janeiro,* the country's first newspaper, appeared in 1808. Ironically, perhaps, given that the crown had fled a French invasion, a French cultural mission was established, launching a Brazilian love affair with French culture that would last well into the 20th century.

The Portuguese court stayed until 1821, when troubles brewing back home forced the king to return to Europe. He left behind his son, Dom Pedro, who a year later declared Brazil independent—and himself its emperor. Even though the changeover is often presented as bloodless, the newly independent government did in fact put down rebellions, notably in the Northeast and the South. The emperor's rule was considered liberal for its time, though there was no significant movement on the issue of slavery, which lasted for decades longer.

Baroque church in Minas Gerais state

Abolition of Slavery

It was not until 1888 that Brazil abolished slavery, though it had formally outlawed the foreign slave trade in 1850. In the 1830s, the British—who had by then replaced Portugal as the most prominent foreign player in Brazil—took it upon themselves to squelch seaborne slave trade. The Brazilians made a show of acquiescing, but quietly set up clandestine ports to receive transports, giving rise to the still popular term *para inglês ver* (for the English to see). The term referred specifically to aboveboard ports, with no slave trading, that were open, while the illicit human traffic was disembarked at alternative ports.

The Lost Community of Palmares

Over the centuries of the African slave trade, thousands of individuals escaped. They formed communities called *quilombos*. Many of these communities proved so successful that they exist to this day, often in isolated areas that make it difficult for them to gain access to social services and other modern amenities.

In large part, quilombos kept to themselves, but one community called Palmares seemed to pose a true threat to Portuguese rule. Located in what is now Alagoas state, it lasted throughout most of the 17th century. Historians believe that at its peak the population reached 20,000, divided among nine settlements. It outlasted the 1630–1654 Dutch occupation, but eventually succumbed to a series of Portuguese campaigns.

The last leader of Palmares was named Zumbi, and the anniversary of his death, November 20, 1695, is celebrated as Black Consciousness Day in Brazil. For the Portuguese, the destruction of Palmares was considered as great a victory in military terms as the expulsion of the Dutch from Pernambuco.

The site of the settlement has been made into a park that is open to visitation: Palmares Quilombo Memorial Park and Serra da Barriga *(tel 82/3281 3923 or 3181 3167, http://serradabarriga.palmares .gov.br)*. The best way to get there is by car: Take the BR-316 road to Satuba and then the PE-126 road; the trip takes about an hour and 20 minutes from Palmares. It is best to call ahead and organize a guided visit as the park lacks road signs.

After the defeat of the Confederacy in the U.S. Civil War, Brazil and Cuba remained the lone outposts of slavery in the Americas. Brazilian abolitionist movements began springing up, often led by society women. Presaging its growing influence, the Brazilian military set the stage for abolition in 1887 by formally refusing to any longer hunt down fugitive slaves. The Lei Áurea (Golden Law) that finally ended slavery in 1888 was signed by Princess Isabel, acting on behalf of her father the emperor.

From Monarch to Republic

Brazil found itself behind the political curve in more ways than one. As the world turned republican, Brazil remained a monarchy. The empire held onto power after subduing a handful of rebellions, notably the Cabanagem Revolt in the Amazon and the Farroupilha Revolution in the South, both of which began in 1835. Despite the lack of political progress, the 19th century brought significant economic changes. The Amazon experienced a rubber boom that would briefly make the region's most important city, Manaus, into one of the richest cities in the world. Foreign capital, especially from England, helped build railroads that laid the way for the coffee export boom.

The Paraguayan War (1864–1870) boosted pro-army sentiment and sparked interest among soldiers in abolitionist and republican causes. By the end of the century, two forms of thought were gaining ground among the educated classes, including young military officers: Republicanism and Positivism, the latter a humanist concept of orderly progress first developed by the French philosopher Auguste Comte. Compared to other countries of South America, the military in Brazil took longer to intervene in politics but intervene it eventually did, marching on the royal palace on November 15, 1889, to overthrow the emperor. For the next century, up to the end of the 1964–1985 dictatorship, soldiers remained intimately involved in the political realm.

Following the declaration of the republic in 1889, regional oligarchies gained the upper hand. Coffee was king: By the turn of the 20th century Brazil was producing nearly two-thirds of the world's supply of beans. Landholders who produced coffee exerted broad political influence, facilitated by a *café com leite* (coffee with milk) alliance, with coffee symbolizing São Paulo and milk Minas Gerais. Immigration helped meet the demand for extra labor, and the end of slavery encouraged capital formation that led to nascent industrialization. Under a decentralized federal system, richer states like São Paulo and Minas Gerais became in many ways more powerful than the central government in Rio de Janeiro. Rulers were all at least nominally liberal constitutionalists, and commercial interests gained wealth, power, and influence.

In the 1890s a messianic preacher named Antônio Conselheiro established a utopian community in the outback of Bahia state in the Northeast. Called Canudos, it boasted the second biggest congregation of people in Bahia after the state capital Salvador within a few years. The size and independence of the community, along with its pro-monarchy stance, were viewed as a threat by the new republic in Rio de Janeiro. Successive military expeditions to destroy the outpost were forced to retreat in defeat until a final, brutal attack destroyed the community in 1897. The episode was related in the book *Rebellion in the Backlands* by Euclides da Cunha, published in Portuguese in 1902. Canudos and da Cunha's book proved important to the development of Brazil's national identity.

A Call for Change

Marking the hundredth anniversary of independence, the year 1922 witnessed important developments that would help set the political and cultural trajectory for the coming century. In politics, the Tenente (Lieutenant) Revolt at Copacabana Fort in Rio de Janeiro

Put Some Love in the Flag

Foreigners sometimes wonder about the slogan "Ordem e Progresso" that is sprawled across a blue globe in the middle of the Brazilian flag against a gold and green background. It seems a little ironic—after all, the flag flies over chaotic streets and neighborhoods afflicted by poverty, and these would seem to belie the claim to Order and Progress.

The phrase's origin can actually be traced back to the 19th-century French philosopher Auguste Comte, a man who is sometimes called the father of sociology. Born during the turmoil that followed the French Revolution, Comte sought a theory that would allow for human progress without major disruptions. His concept of gradual change, led by technocrats, appealed to many up-and-coming Brazilians, including instructors and cadets at military schools, when the republic was proclaimed in 1889.

Called Positivism, this humanist philosophy is summed up by Comte's maxim, "Love as the Principle, Order as the Base, and Progress as the End."

Recently, Brazilian composer Jards Macalé has taken exception to the Brazilian flag. He isn't protesting the Positivist slogan it bears, but is instead lamenting that the flag's creators left out the Love (Amor) in Comte's maxim. The musician is on a mission to have the flag amended to read, "Amor, Ordem e Progresso."

Forte de Copacabana, Rio de Janeiro

ended with the deaths of 16 young officers, many of whom hailed from poor states that lacked political influence. They were protesting the political and economic dominance of plantation owners in the rich states. Some of the tenentes escaped and dispersed. A few hundred individuals joined the Coluna Prestes (Prestes Column), named for its leader Luis Carlos Prestes (who would later become Brazil's most important communist). Though defeated in 1927, the Coluna Prestes weakened the federal government and cleared the way for the Revolution of 1930 that brought strongman Getúlio Vargas to power.

Young artists and intellectuals, often educated in Europe, became increasingly interested in the modernist movements abroad. In 1917, Anita Malfatti returned to São Paulo after studying painting in Germany and New York. Her fauvist works were wholly misunderstood by establishment critics, but they caught the eye of contemporaries. Writers Mário and Oswald de Andrade (no relation) defended her, as did artists Victor Brecheret and Emiliano Di Cavalcanti. They would form part of a core group that organized the São Paulo Modern Art Week in 1922. Modeled after similar events in Europe, it featured not only art expositions but also conferences, poetry readings, and music, and included a recital of a composition by Brazil's icon of classical music Heitor Villa-Lobos. While they defended formal progress in the arts, these intellectuals were not content to merely copy foreign models. In 1928 Oswald de Andrade published the "Manifesto Antropófago" ("Cannibalist Manifesto"), referring to the ritual dietary habits of some Brazilian indigenous people, to suggest that the country's artists should absorb foreign influences and transform them to create

> **Coffee was king: By the turn of the 20th century Brazil was producing nearly two-thirds of the world's supply of beans.**

something uniquely Brazilian. The iconic line, riffing on both Shakespeare and the name of a native tribe, was "Tupi or not Tupi? That is the question." Cannibalist sensibilities would help shape the thinking of the Tropicalist movement in the 1960s and 1970s and remain influential to this day.

These calls for economic, political, and artistic change emerged in an era of budding industrialization, albeit one held back by the landed oligarchs who guided public policy. Many contemporaries may have missed their significance, but in retrospect we can view these manifestations as precursors to events that followed the 1930 presidential election.

Getúlio Vargas, president of Brazil from 1930 to 1945 and from 1951 to 1954

Vargas & Populism

The 1930 presidential campaign pitted a career politician from the southern state of Rio Grande do Sul named Getúlio Vargas against a candidate from São Paulo handpicked by the oligarchs. The results were disputed. Election officials declared the oligarchy's candidate the winner. The military took the matter into its own hands and installed Vargas in power. He would rule as a dictator until 1945, with the most serious effort to overthrow him coming from a constitutionalist revolt in São Paulo in 1932, which federal forces defeated easily. (The date that marked the beginning of the São Paulo uprising, July 9, is a public holiday in that state. A major thoroughfare in São Paulo is named for it, Avendia 9 de Julho.)

The populist style perfected by Vargas still serves as a model for Brazilian politicians, having been most recently and brilliantly updated by Luiz Inácio Lula da Silva (president, 2003–2010). Vargas's nationalist, protectionist, and centralizing policies also established the parameters for the country's economic debate throughout the rest of the 20th century. The Vargas approach essentially mimicked the corporativist model perused by Benito Mussolini in Italy. Privatization and trade liberalization in the 1990s reversed some Vargas-era policies, but others like the rigid labor code remain in place. Vargas was a pioneer in establishing social welfare policies, though their scope was limited. The Vargas regime, collaborating with the gestapo, deported Olga Benário, Prestes's Munich-born Jewish wife, pregnant at the time, to Germany in 1936. She was executed in a concentration camp. Despite his fascist tendencies, Vargas eventually gave in to the Good Neighbor Policy of the United States, including Uncle Sam's favorable loans, and Brazil finally joined the Allies in World War II.

Emerging Views

In 1945 a bloodless military coup put an end to the Vargas dictatorship and ushered in the way for elections. It had been two years since he had failed to keep a promise to hold elections, citing the wartime emergency. Vargas sat out the first democratic go-round, but five years later he ran and won. After pushing industrialization and nationalization of natural resources, including petroleum, he committed suicide while in office in 1954, under rather obscure circumstances. It seemed that Vargas allies might have been involved in an attempted assassination of an opposition political figure, and, as a result, army generals were demanding the president's resignation.

Demographic Shift

While all this was transpiring in the capital, the country was undergoing a not-so-silent demographic revolution. In 1940, Brazil was still a predominantly rural nation, with more than two-thirds of citizens living in the countryside. During the four decades from 1940 to 1980, some 41 million net migrants moved from rural areas to cities. They included future president Lula, taken by his mother at the age of seven from Garanhuns, Pernambuco, to the port town of Santos in São Paulo state. In popular culture, Northeasterners like Lula's mom are depicted as fleeing drought and its corresponding poverty. "A Triste Partida" ("The Sad Departure"), a song based on a poem by Patativa do Assaré and popularized by the iconic musician Luiz Gonzaga, tells of a family that abandons its parched farmland for a more promising, albeit tough, life in São Paulo. Push factors definitely played a role, but the appeal of greater access to employment and public services in the growing South-Central region that includes São Paulo probably played a larger role. Today Brazil is nearly completely urbanized: Roughly 80 percent of Brazilians live in cities.

Following a caretaker period after the ouster of Vargas, the newly elected President Juscelino Kubitschek took office in 1956. Kubitschek is revered by many Brazilians to this day—partly for good reason. He was the only Brazilian president between 1930 and Fernando Henrique Cardoso (1995–2002) to run, be elected, and serve a full term without any sort of military intervention before or after. And he presided over the first of Brazil's record five soccer World Cup victories in Sweden in 1958. This was also a period when Brazilians were being projected onto

The Birth of Organized Crime

Chalk up another victory for the Law of Unintended Consequences. During the 1964–1985 dictatorship, the military regime threw political prisoners together with leading common criminals. This happened at a penitentiary on Ilha Grande island, off the coast from Angra dos Reis in Rio de Janeiro state.

During military rule, university-educated political prisoners did what might be expected: They organized study groups, and not only on politics. Many of the political prisoners had received paramilitary training and knew how to properly rob banks and kidnap people. They offered tutorials in those skills as well.

Eventually the political prisoners were released or amnestied. The common criminals, however, put those lessons in bank robbery and kidnapping to effective use, forming Brazil's first successful organized crime syndicate, Commando Vermelho (Red Command). The Red Command was able to ensure discipline from within penitentiary walls: Step out of line on the outside, suffer the consequences on the inside.

Other groups adopted Commando Vermelho's model. Brazil's elevated rates of homicides and other crimes can in large part be attributed to that group and rivals like the Terceiro Comando Puro (Pure Third Command).

Pelé and his former Santos teammates in 2012 during the centennial anniversary celebration of the team—one of the most successful in soccer

the world stage without any outside help. A decade earlier Carmen Miranda had been a Hollywood phenomenon. Bossa nova's hip, cool, jazzy style needed little assistance in capturing global tastes. Less than two years after the end of Kubitschek's term in office, "The Girl from Ipanema" would start (according to legend, from a napkin containing scrawls by Tom Jobim and Vinicius de Moraes) its trajectory to become one of the world's most recognizable tunes. When Pelé took the field against the USSR in the 1958 World Cup, he was the youngest player to date to appear in the international soccer extravaganza.

Kubitschek's adage, "Fifty years of development in five," appealed to Brazilians impatient with their country's lack of progress. But his megalomania left a legacy of lingering problems that plague the country to this day. His two main achievements were to create the new capital Brasília and to encourage the automobile industry. Many people dislike Brasília's sterility, and the endeavor proved to be a costly one for a poor developing nation. Kubitschek inaugurated Brasília as the new capital in 1960, a few months before his term ended. Planned by Lúcio Costa, with monumental buildings designed by Oscar Niemeyer, Brasília's utopian project has come to represent one of the worst failures of social engineering in human history. As for the boost to the auto industry, all you need to do is spend a few minutes stuck in traffic in your favorite Brazilian city to see the downsides of that—not to mention the damage to the environment and quality of life.

Political Changes

In 1960, voters elected right-wing populist Jânio Quadros as their next president. Given an unusual split-ticket voting system, Quadros's political opponent, leftist populist João Goulart, became vice president. When Quadros resigned after just months in office for reasons that remain unclear, conservative forces, including the military, tried to block Goulart's inauguration. Eventually he was allowed to take office.

Given the prevailing Cold War ambience, Goulart's left-wing policies provoked predictable opposition among generals. In 1964 they overthrew him and took power themselves. Much is made of support by the U.S. Central Intelligence Agency and President Lyndon Johnson, but their backing seems to have been peripheral. The Brazilians were entirely capable of running their own coup.

The 1964–1985 dictatorship was relatively tame compared to the brutal regimes in neighboring Argentina, Chile, and Uruguay, but the period was nevertheless marked by stories of the suppression of civil rights, censorship, exile, imprisonment, torture, and death. Moderate opponents organized themselves into a legally recognized party which took part in elections for congress and local offices. Though they never proved a serious threat to the regime, leftist groups formed guerrilla movements. The biggest was based in Araguaia, in today's Tocantins state, and was put down by the military in the early 1970s. Dozens of guerrillas were killed. The most daring and successful effort by Brazilian urban guerrillas was the 1969 kidnapping of American ambassador Charles Burke Elbrick, who was released in exchange for a group of political prisoners. The episode is described in a book written by one of the kidnappers, Fernando Gabeira. After a period in exile he became a politician with the Brazilian Green Party. The book was made into a movie entitled *Four Days in September.* During the dictatorship, an independent labor movement emerged with Lula as its standard-bearer. In reaction to restrictions on freedom of speech, composers, writers, and journalists devised creative ways to fool the censors. The lyrics of songs by Chico Buarque stand out in this regard.

The most daring and successful effort by Brazilian urban guerrillas was the 1969 kidnapping of American ambassador Charles Burke Elbrick.

Economic Growth

From the late 1960s to the early 1970s, Brazil's economy grew at rates similar to those of today's China. The period was denominated "the economic miracle." Thanks to an embargo on soybean exports from the United States in 1973, a Cold War move designed to keep the Soviet Union from purchasing cheap foodstuffs, Brazil began for the first time to invest heavily in that crop—at the time to satisfy Japanese demand but also setting the stage for the current boom. With the oil crisis and higher petroleum prices, the military government began to invest heavily in ethanol production from sugarcane, leading to Brazil's leadership today in biofuels. Yet the economy could not withstand the double whammy of excessive public borrowing to finance megaprojects like the Itaipú hydroelectric dam and the oil crisis. In 1982 it defaulted on the country's foreign debt, leading to a period of high inflation and low growth called the Lost Decade.

Having already begun a process of liberalization, weakened by economic realities, and facing a wave of popular protests demanding direct presidential elections, the military government agreed to indirect balloting in 1985, hoping to install a civilian of its own choosing. But some of its erstwhile allies in congress rebelled against the chosen candidate and cut a deal with the legal opposition. That led to the election of the latter's candidate, Tancredo Neves. But the 75-year-old Neves took sick, was forced to have an operation, and died without taking office. The vice president–elect, José Sarney, one of those last-minute dissenters, took his place.

The dictatorship was over, but it marked the formative years of each of Brazil's last three presidents. Current president Rousseff was an anti-dictatorship activist who backed urban guerrilla groups and was jailed and tortured. As a union leader, her predecessor and political godfather Lula spent a brief stint in jail for leading labor strikes. Lula's predecessor, sociologist Fernando Henrique Cardoso, was forced to abandon his job as a college professor and go into exile. All this helps explain why polls show Brazilians broadly support democracy even if it has not always ensured social and economic progress.

Fuel for Thought

In late 2007, when international oil prices soared, Brazil became the envy of many countries when the nation's oil giant, Petrobras, tapped into deepwater reserves off Rio de Janeiro state's northern coast. It's estimated that the Tupi reserve contains as much as eight billion barrels of oil—although it's not as if Brazil is prey to a nasty oil habit. In the aftermath of the 1973 oil crisis, the government's inspired solution was to convert sugarcane into ethanol as an inexpensive, less-polluting fuel for all vehicles. As a result, today Brazil is the world's top producer of sugarcane alcohol, and all Brazilian vehicles are flex-fuel models that run on gas, alcohol, or a blend of both.

Economic Instability

The late 1980s and early 1990s were marked by economic stagnation and hyperinflation. A series of unorthodox "plans" implemented by Sarney and his successor Fernando Collor de Mello proved woefully unsuccessful. Still, Brazil managed to host the Earth Summit in Rio de Janeiro, putting the country back on the international diplomatic map. Privatization of state-owned companies, trade liberalization, and the opening of the domestic stock market to foreign investors began to make the country relevant to the global economy again. Collor resigned in an effort to derail impeachment proceedings on corruption charges in 1992.

Hyperinflation continued apace, twice topping 2,000 percent a year during this period. In 1994, Itamar Franco, Collor's vice president who had taken the presidential reins, named Cardoso as finance minister. Putting together a crack team of academic economists, he was able to quell inflation and voters elected Cardoso as president later that year. During his two terms, he would implement sensible macroeconomic policies that were quietly maintained by his successors. Hyperinflation left its mark on everyone who lived through it, including politicians, economists, and voters. Concern for economic stability, like democratic principles, has become a prerequisite for successful political candidates in Brazil.

21st-Century Changes

After winning an all-time record fifth World Cup soccer championship in 2002, Brazil made history again that year by electing an immigrant from the poor backlands of the Northeast with a fourth-grade education, former labor leader Lula, as president. Markets reacted fiercely, fearing instability, but they soon took a liking to the working-class president. Lula maintained pro-stability economic policies and expanded and amplified a cash transfer program for the poorest Brazilians. Taking advantage of a commodities export boom, he was able to raise the minimum wage. The Brazilian economy bounced back quickly from the 2008 economic shock. The middle class continued to grow, keeping Brazil on track to becoming a U.S.-style consumer economy.

Brazilian former president Luiz Inácio Lula da Silva (left) and President Dilma Rousseff (center)

Corruption scandals rocked the Lula administration. One led to the conviction of members of his inner circle by the Supreme Court after he had left office. Lula has enjoyed a Reaganesque Teflon reputation, and attempts to associate him with wrongdoing have been unsuccessful. Parallels with Reagan do not end there. Like Reagan, he left office with his popularity intact. Like Reagan with Americans, his great achievement was to make Brazilians feel good about themselves. He managed to convince the rest of the world as well, as evidenced by the winning bids for the 2014 World Cup and the 2016 Summer Olympics. Lula's crowning achievement, perhaps, was his swan song: He chose an electoral neophyte, his then chief of staff, Dilma Rousseff, to run as his successor. When she won, Dilma (Brazilians refer to her by her first name) became the first woman president in Brazilian history. ■

The Arts

Brazil's cultural heritage and effervescent contemporary artistic scene strike visitors from all angles. In Recife or João Pessoa, guitar-wielding duos called *repentistas* serenade passersby with improvised verse. In São Paulo, art galleries hold openings and exhibitions of contemporary Brazilian art. Street fairs sell manually printed little booklets called *cordels* that tell popular stories, while chain megastores stock classic literature by the likes of João Guimarães Rosa.

The indigenous people who inhabited today's Brazil obviously had their own traditions when the colonizers arrived. Though it is hard to generalize about hundreds of tribes, they often produced elaborate headdresses made of colorful bird feathers or impressive cloth masks. From the western tradition, the most enduring art from the early colonial period came from European visitors like the Dutch painters Albert Eckhout and Frans Post who went to Brazil in the 17th century to document the landscape and its inhabitants. The Instituto Ricardo Brennand in Recife displays a permanent exhibition of Post's work.

A landmark exhibition at the Guggenheim Museum in New York in 2001–2002 provided an extraordinary retrospective of Brazilian art, architecture, and cinema since the colonial era. It followed a similar show in Brazil the year before, one that marked the 500th anniversary of European contact. Called "Body and Soul," the Guggenheim exhibition divided Brazil's artistic history into two: the baroque and the modern. Although this division is both arbitrary and overly simplistic, something the exhibition curators understood, it is nevertheless useful as a way to organize an overwhelming volume of output influenced by traditions from across the globe.

> **Brazilian culture got a jolt from the installation of the Portuguese court in Rio de Janeiro early in the 19th century.**

Baroque

Most artworks from the colonial period are religious in nature. Some can still be viewed in colonial churches, notably in Bahia and Minas Gerais. There are also museums of sacred art in many cities. The best of the bunch are probably in Salvador and São Paulo.

Many of the artists of this period are anonymous, and it is assumed that at least some of them were of African descent. The emblematic figure of Brazil's baroque period is known as O Aleijadinho ("the little cripple"), a nickname that refers to the effects of an unidentified degenerative disease that struck Antônio Francisco Lisboa. His dramatic life-size soapstone images of Old Testament prophets dating from the late 18th century stand guard outside the Bom Jesus de Matozinhos church in Congonhas do Campo, Minas Gerais. His colorful, equally life-size, and sometimes eerie wood carvings depicting the stations of the cross can be found in adjacent chapels.

Premodern

Brazilian modernism is normally dated from 1922 and the historic Modern Art Week in São Paulo, or perhaps more accurately to 1917 and painter Anita Malfatti's then shocking exhibition. But some historians identify seeds of modernism in the 19th century. Brazilian culture got a jolt from the installation of the Portuguese court in Rio de Janeiro early in the century. And although it remained a monarchy, the country did gain a new mind-set from independence in 1822. Also influential was a French artistic mission installed in Rio de Janeiro in 1816. While those elements were themselves premodern, they did serve to shake up what had been a fairly mundane and derivative artistic environment.

Aleijadinho's sculptures in Congonhas, Minas Gerais: iconic works by Brazil's baroque master

Candido Portinari depicts the coffee plantations of the mid-20th century (1935).

Music

The first manifestation of what we recognize today as characteristically Brazilian music dates to the mid-19th century. As told by musician and historian Henrique Cazes, it starts with polka in Rio de Janeiro in 1845. Brazilian bands phrased polka oddly, reminding people of weeping, leading to the name of a new genre, *choro,* which means "cry." Others attribute it to what scholar John Murphy calls melancholic low-register guitar counterlines. By the 1870s and 1880s, pianists and composers Chiquinha Gonzaga and Ernesto Nazareth were pumping out this newfangled music, sometimes also called *chorinho,* along with their regular polkas and tangos. The most illustrious choro composer and performer was without a doubt Pixinguinha (1897–1973). If you do nothing else, check out his song "Carinhoso."

Architecture

The economy was expanding during these decades, especially in São Paulo, and building had to keep pace. In Rio de Janeiro, a neoclassical style inspired by the French architect Grandjean de Montigny took hold. The Foreign Ministry building, Itamaraty Palace, is a striking example. In São Paulo, art nouveau became popular—note the downtown Santa Ifigênia Overpass.

Literature

Brazil's greatest writer of all time came from this period. In 1881 Joaquim Maria Machado de Assis published his fifth book, *Epitaph for a Small Winner.* The book is not important because it was written by a mulatto (as mixed-race people are sometimes called in Brazil), or because it offers an incisive look into the oligarchy of the time—it is simply great literature. Inspired by the likes of Laurence Sterne, Machado de Assis has been called a forerunner of Latin American giants like Gabriel García Marquez and Jorge Luis Borges.

20th-Century Modernism

Brazilian art history would never be the same following the events of February 13–18, 1922, Modern Art Week, in São Paulo. Over four centuries, Brazil had hardly produced a single world-class artist, with the exception of O Aleijadinho and Mestre Valentim. Then a single generation brought forth dozens.

Painting & Sculpture

Women led the way in this genre. The main precursor to the 1922 extravaganza was Anita Malfatti's exhibition in 1917. Alas, she allowed conservative critics to bully her into a much more conventional style, which she followed for the rest of her life. Another woman, Tarsila do Amaral, took up the mantle. In 1928 she produced "Abaporu," depicting a stylized nude figure with an oversize foot, a cactus, a bright sky, and the sun. In the Tupi-Guarani indigenous language, *abaporu* means "the man who eats people." The painting was a gift to her then husband, the writer Oswald de Andrade, a leading thinker in the Cannibalist movement to use modern techniques to create art that was identifiably Brazilian. "Abaporu" sold at auction in 1995 for $1.4 million, the most ever fetched by a Brazilian painting. Tarsila (she is generally referred to by her first name) produced other iconic works, including "A Negra" ("The Black Woman") and "Operários" ("Workers").

Tarsila was not alone. The best known Brazilian painter of her generation, internationally speaking, was probably Cândido Portinari. His murals "War and Peace" were produced for the entrance hall of the UN General Assembly building in New York. Art buffs can visit the Museu Casa de Portinari, the house where the painter lived as a child, in his hometown, Brodowski, in the interior of São Paulo state. The museum's collection includes several important works by the artist. (The museum was closed for renovations in 2012, and no date had been set for reopening, so check first before making a trip.) Other important Brazilian modernists included Lasar Segall, Cícero Dias, Rego Monteiro, Di Cavalcanti, and Brecheret. The latter's colossal sculpture "Monumento às Bandeiras," a tribute to the pioneers who opened São Paulo state to settlement, can be seen in Praça Armando Salles de Oliveira, near one of the entrances to Ibirapuera Park. The Rio de Janeiro Museum of Modern Art lost pretty much its entire collection to a fire in 1978, but when Gilberto Chateaubriand donated his collection to the institution, it once again became the best place to see Brazilian modern art.

(continued on p. 50)

Art Deco Brazil

During the 1930s, Brazil's economic growth coincided with the emergence of art deco architecture. Surviving examples of the ornate, geometric style remain scattered throughout Brazil—including Bahia, Goiás, and Rio Grande do Sul—and are particularly dominant in Rio de Janeiro. Northeast Brazil has an art deco all its own. Characterized by some as "Art Deco Sertanejo" for its distinct features and countryside locale, most of these buildings are found in Campina Grande.

Music

Brazil is an extremely musical country. Its composers and performers have produced high-quality music in a wide variety of styles and genres. Most Brazilians know the lyrics to dozens of classic popular songs and will often quote a line from a song to emphasize an idea or emotion. While Brazilian music reflects what happens in the rest of society, its development often seems to run independent of trends in the rest of the art world.

Live music at the Carioca da Gema club in Rio de Janeiro

The best way to understand Brazilian music is to listen to it. Below are some of the major genres of Brazilian music.

Axé—From Bahia, Afro-Brazilian percussion combined with basic melodies. Exponents: Carlinhos Brown, Olodum, Margareth Menezes, Daniela Mercury, and Ivete Sangalo.

Bossa Nova—A sophisticated chill-out samba style that emerged in the 1950s and gave the world "The Girl from Ipanema." Exponents: Tom Jobim, João Gilberto, Carlos Lyra, Nara Leão, Roberto Menescal, and Marcos Valle.

Brazilian Blues—Brazilians play the blues. Exponents: Blues Etílicos and Flávio Guimarães.

Brazilian Classical—The music of composer Heitor Villa-Lobos (1887–1959) was influenced by both Brazilian folk music and European classical tradition. In the 1970s, the Quinteto Armorial pioneered chamber music with Brazilian roots. Exponents: Heitor Villa-Lobos, Quinteto Armorial, and Quarteto Romançal.

Brazilian Hip-Hop—Much Brazilian rap has maintained a focus on social commentary. Exponents: Gabriel O Pensador, MV Bill, and BNegão.

Brazilian Rock—Brazilians rock to a variety of genres, from punk to heavy metal and beyond. Exponents: Os Mutantes, Raul Seixas, Titãs, Ratos do Porão, and Sepultura.

Choro—A sambaesque genre with long, syncopated melodies. Exponents: Pixinguinha, Jacob do Bandolim, Paulo Moura, Raphael Rabello, and Hamilton de Holanda.

Forró—Northeastern dance music featuring the accordion, a bass drum called the *zabumba,* and the triangle. Often used to generically describe a whole range of Northeastern sounds. Exponents: Luiz Gonzaga, Jackson do Pandeiro, Dominguinhos, and Elba Ramalho.

Funk *Carioca*—Rhythms produced by electronic percussion devices are reminiscent of America's Miami Bass. Exponents: Bonde do Tigrão and MC Créu.

Manguebeat—A fusion of traditional Northeastern rhythms with rock-and-roll. Exponents: Chico Science & Nação Zumbi, Mestre Ambrósio, and Mundo Livre S/A.

Maracatu—An Afro-Brazilian style from the Northeastern state of Pernambuco. Exponents: Mestre Salustiano and Siba.

MPB—The Brazilian acronym for Brazilian Popular Music, born in the 1960s. Scholar John P. Murphy called it "popular music of high artistic achievement that drew from Brazilian musical traditions." Exponents: João Bosco, Jorge Ben Jor, Elis Regina, Caetano Veloso, Gilberto Gil, Chico César, Zeca Baleiro, and Seu Jorge.

Música Caipira—Literally "hillbilly" music, this rural folk music often features duos playing acoustic guitars. Exponents: Renato Teixeira, Millionário & Zé Rico, Pena Branca & Xavantino, Helena Meirelles, and Almir Sater.

Música Gaúcha—A catchall phrase for roots music from the South of Brazil. Exponents: Renato Borghetti and Yamandú Costa.

Pagode—There are two versions: a rootsy version sprung from backyard gatherings and a more commercial style with often banal or lewd lyrics. Those listed come from the first. Exponents: Zeca Pagodinho, Fundo de Quintal, and Beth Carvalho.

Samba—Brazil's national sound, of Afro-Brazilian origin. Exponents: Cartola, Zé Kétti, Paulinho da Viola, Noel Rosa, Martinho da Vila, Bezerra da Silva, Nei Lopes, and Nelson Sargento.

Sertanejo—A Nashville-inspired version of Brazilian country music that evolved from música caipira. Exponents: Chitãozinho & Xororó and Zezé di Camargo & Luciano.

Forró, Not For All

If you are an American, some Brazilian will soon ask, "Do you know the origin of the term *forró*?" Read on and you can answer, "Yes, and it isn't what you think."

Forró refers to a popular musical and dance style rooted in the Brazilian Northeast and to the parties where it was played. The local who has just buttonholed you is about to tell a widely believed yet patently false story of how the name is derived from the balls held by U.S. soldiers stationed in Rio Grande do Sul during World War II. According to legend, they organized dances that were "for all"—open to everyone—and that "forró" is a bastardization of that phrase based on its Brazilian pronunciation.

There is an identically tall tale told exactly the same way about British engineers building a railroad in Pernambuco in the early 20th century.

Philologists (who study the development of language) have traced the term to the Galician-Portuguese *forbodó,* in turn related to *farbodão* and ultimately to the French *faux-bourdon,* which had a connotation of musical dissonance. By the 19th century, popular balls in Pernambuco were called *forrobodó, forrobodança,* or *forrobodão*—eventually, *forró* for short. The word entered recorded musical history in 1937, five years before the U.S. military base, when Victor Records released "Forró na Roça" by Xerêm and Tapuya.

Architecture

The Swiss-born French architect Le Corbusier went to Brazil for the second time in 1936 as a consultant on the design of the headquarters of the Ministry of Education and Health (now known as the Palácio Gustavo Capanema) in Rio de Janeiro. His visit brought architectural rationalism to a group of young up-and-comers that included those who eventually drew up the blueprints for Brasília, Lúcio Costa, and Oscar Niemeyer. Niemeyer, who died in 2012 at the age of 104, is by far Brazil's most famous architect. He characteristically incorporated curves and open spaces into his buildings. He believed that architecture should leave people astounded, but critics counter that he concentrated too much on that aspect and not enough on functionality.

Pop Art & Abstractionism

Founded in 1951, the São Paulo Biennial of Art exerted a great deal of influence on Brazilian art during the second half of the 20th century. Examine the development of Brazilian Pop Art after the 1967 appearance of works by artists like Roy Lichtenstein and Claes Oldenburg, or the splash made by Germany's Anselm Kiefer in 1987. Brazilian informal abstractionism is another case in point. Led by Yolanda Mohali and Japanese-Brazilians Manabu Mabe and Tomie Ohtake, the movement was enriched by the biennials of the late 1950s that offered a close look at North American abstract expressionism and the tachism movement in Europe.

Intellectuals were often politically influential in the first half of the 20th century, and some suffered dearly as a result.

Cinema

Homegrown Brazilian cinema reached its peak during the 1950s, at least in terms of volume. Memorable films of the period included *O Cangaceiro* (1953), directed by Lima Barreto, and *Black Orpheus* (1959), based on a play by Vinícius de Moraes and directed by France's Marcel Camus. Vera Cruz studios, which produced *O Cangaceiro,* set new standards for Brazilian production values. Brazil's most influential film movement, Cinema Novo, got its start in 1955 with the premiere of *Rio 40 Graus (Rio 40 Degrees),* directed by Nelson Pereira dos Santos. It depicted the lives of Rio slum dwellers and featured amateur actors, including the samba composer Zé Kétti, whose emblematic song "Voz do Morro" ("Voice of the Hill") also opened and closed the film. Cinema Novo rejected Hollywood slickness, drawing its influences from Italian realism and the French New Wave. It also made a point of highlighting Brazil's social problems.

Literature

Brazilian literature also experienced a modernist boom. If there is such a thing as the Great Brazilian Novel, it would be either *Macunaíma,* published by Mário de Andrade in 1928, or *The Devil to Pay in the Backlands,* published by João Guimarães Rosa in 1956. Mário de Andrade was another of the leaders of the Modern Art Week and the intellectual fervor that followed. *Macunaíma* combines native Amazonian mythology and Afro-Luso Brazilian folklore to create a satirical comedy featuring "a hero without character" set in a fantastic world. Guimarães Rosa's book, described as psychological realism, is about a bandit in the backlands of the Brazilian interior. The Museu Casa Guimarães Rosa, which occupies the house where the writer grew up, can be visited in Cordisburgo, Minas Gerais. Manuel Bandeira and Carlos Drummond de Andrade ranked among the leading poets of the period.

Intellectuals were often politically influential in the first half of the 20th century, and some suffered dearly as a result. Writer Graciliano Ramos wrote a book called *Memórias do Cárcere* (still no English translation) about his experience in prison under dictator Getúlio Vargas. Patricia Galvão, popularly known as Pagu, an avant-garde writer and communist militant, was imprisoned and tortured by the Vargas regime.

Brazil's most popular novelist until Paulo Coelho, Jorge Amado, was also imprisoned by Vargas. Amado's early works, like *Captains of the Sands* (1937) about street urchins in Salvador, fit the political mold of socialist realism. Novels published in the 1960s and 1970s would focus more on manners and characters and often contained healthy doses of humor, sex, and local color from his home state of Bahia. Amado's works have been adapted to film and television dozens of times. One of the most entertaining adaptations is *Dona Flor and Her Two Husbands,* starring Sonia Braga and directed by Bruno Barreto. The Fundação Casa Jorge Amado in Salvador houses a permanent exhibition of artifacts of the writer's life.

Artistic Rebellion during the Military Dictatorship

After the 1964 military coup, intellectuals and artists suffered persecution, including censorship. Many were forced into exile. The musician and writer Chico Buarque wrote a play called *Roda Viva*, along with an accompanying musical score. The play was banned by the military, and Buarque was arrested before being allowed to leave for Italy. Like many exiles, Buarque returned as the dictatorship began to open up. Once back, he proved to be among the most skillful at confusing the censors. His song "Apesar de Você" ("In Spite of You") got past them to become an anti-dictatorship anthem.

Carmen Miranda (1939)

The performance artist, painter, and sculptor Hélio Oiticica spent most of the 1970s in New York. Oiticica's experimental drive helped pioneer installation art. He holds a "position in the cultural consciousness of Brazil analogous to that maintained by Andy Warhol in the United States or Joseph Beuys in Western Europe," according to art historian Eduard J. Sullivan. "Shaman" and "rebel" are two terms often used to describe him. The Centro Municipal de Arte Hélio Oiticica in Rio de Janeiro is dedicated to the preservation and dissemination of the artist's memory.

Oiticica's 1967 work "Tropicália" inspired and gave a name to a cultural movement called Tropicalism. Often identified chiefly with Bahian musicians Caetano

Brazil's Cultural Calendar

Brazil's calendar is chock-full of special dates and celebrations. Many people plan their visits to coincide with Carnaval, but there are major events year-round. The dates of many of these change every year according to the Catholic Church calendar.

January 6: Epiphany (Festa dos Reis), Minas Gerais—the Wise Men's Festival

Second Thursday after 6th: Washing of Bonfim (Lavagem de Bonfim), Salvador—A procession to the Catholic church culminates in the Afro-Brazilian "cleaning" of the stairway

January 16–19: Summer Festival, Salvador, Bahia—Music for all tastes

February 2: Yemanjá Festival, Salvador, Bahia—Honors the Afro-Brazilian goddess of the sea

February or March: Carnaval—The most popular street parties in Salvador, Recife, and Olinda, and many smaller towns

March or April: Easter—Impressive processions and manifestations organized locally

Late March: Lollapalooza—International Rock Festival in São Paulo

Late April–Early May: Amazonas Opera Festival—Held at the opera house

Late April: Formula Indy Automobile Race—São Paulo 300

May–June: Pentecost (Festa do Divíno)—Commemorations in cities including Alcântara, Paraty, Pirenópolis, and São Luis de Paraitinga

Mid-May: Avistar São Paulo—Conference of bird-watchers

June: São João Festival—Celebrations in honor of St. John held in Caruaru, Campina Grande, and elsewhere. The festival is most popular in Brazil's Northeast, where it is larger than Carnaval.

June: Parantins Festival—Amazon

June: GLBT Parade, São Paulo—The world's biggest gay pride parade

June: Gramado Film Festival, Rio Grande do Sul—Brazil's most important film festival

June 29–30: Parantins Festival—Two competing groups do battle in an Amazonian Carnaval-style extravaganza.

Mid-July: FLIP Literary Festival, Paraty—An international literary festival

Mid-August: Barretos Rodeo—Brazil's biggest rodeo

August weekends: Holy Mother of Achiropita Festival, São Paulo—Celebration of Italian immigration and culture

September 15: Mãe das Dores Procession, Juazeiro do Norte—Gathering of Catholics who believe in the miracle-working powers of Padre Cícero

Early October: Blumenau Oktoberfest, Blumenau, Santa Catarina—Organized by descendants of German immigrants

Late November: Formula 1, São Paulo—International Formula 1 race

End of November: Oyster Festival Floripa, Florianópolis—Consume oysters of every kind

December 31: New Year's Eve—A wish to the Afro-Brazilian goddess of the sea Yemanjá

Brazilian Public Holidays

Whether you want to join the fun or avoid the crowds, it is good to know when things shut down in Brazil.

Dates of Carnaval and Easter change annually according to the church calendar. States and some cities have additional holidays.

January 1—New Year's Day
April 4—Tiradentes Day
May 1—Labor Day
September 7—Independence Day
October 12—Feast Day of Our Lady of Aparecida
November 2—All Souls Day
November 15—Proclamation of the Republic
December 25—Christmas Day

The costumes, dances, and music of the Bumba-meu-boi Festival, São Luís, Maranhão

Veloso and Gilberto Gil, its influence reached beyond music to art, literature, film, and theater. It fused foreign cultures and Brazilian regional cultures. Among the most enduring manifestations of Tropicalism is the theatrical and experimental São Paulo rock band Os Mutantes.

Regions & the Future

As Brazil raises its profile on the international scene in other areas, its arts, music, and literature are gaining more attention. Britain's leading literary magazine *Granta* published a special issue focused on young Brazilian writers in late 2012, and a new magazine named after Machado de Assis and dedicated to Brazilian literature in translation has been launched by Brazil's National Library Foundation.

The focus has moved beyond the country's major centers, São Paulo and Rio de Janeiro—the end of the 20th century saw attention begin to shift to various other regions. One of the most important initiatives in this sense was the Armorial Movement in Recife, Pernambuco, in the 1970s. Inspired by Ariano Suassuna, one of Brazil's greatest playwrights, it aimed to encourage the creation of an erudite culture rooted firmly in Brazilian traditions. The movement engendered the Quinteto Armorial, which played chamber music with Brazilian roots. The quintet disbanded after a decade, but one of its members, Antonio Nóbrega, launched a success-ful solo career. He also heads the Instituto Brincante, a São Paulo–based school that offers courses in Brazilian percussion, dance, and music. Other leading figures associated with the Armorial Movement are the artists Gilvan Samico and Francisco Brennand. Brennand's magnificent workshop cum museum in Recife is open to the public. Suassuna has invented a new genre of performance called the *aula-espetáculo* (class-spectacle)—which, as the name implies, is part seminar and part stand-up comedy routine. ∎

A fusion of metropolis with natural paradise, offering getaways to historic towns, majestic mountains, and picturesque beaches

Rio de Janeiro

The bewitching view from Pão de Açúcar (Sugarloaf) of the sun setting behind Corcovado

Rio de Janeiro

Rife with contrasts and contradictions, Rio de Janeiro is mesmerizing and musical, complex and sometimes chaotic, but never, ever boring. Both the city and Rio state possess enough historical, cultural, and natural attractions to keep a visitor occupied for months—but don't forget that in Rio, relaxation is a serious art form.

Rio impresses even before one actually touches down in the Cidade Maravilhosa (Marvelous City). It's fitting that Rio's airport is named after Antonio Carlos Jobim, one of the creators of the quintessentially Carioca musical style known as the "bossa nova." Jobim's excitement infuses those who arrive in Brazil's second largest city of six million. Rio has been declared a UNESCO World Heritage site because of its natural landscapes: towering granite peaks, the lush Tijuca Forest, and glorious Guanabara Bay.

Although the settlement, founded by the Portuguese in 1503, began life as a mosquito-infested swampland, over time Rio blossomed into a major port city from which Brazil's riches—sugarcane, gold, and coffee—set sail around the world.

Along the way, it enjoyed increasing prominence as capital of colonial Brazil (1763), of the United Kingdom of Portugal, Brazil, and the Algarves (1815), of the independent Empire of Brazil (1822), and of Brazil's first democratic republic (1889), becoming more cosmopolitan, modern, and avant-garde as the centuries wore on.

When the federal capital moved to Brasília in 1960, Rio lost some of its political clout, but it never lost its zest for life and its place in the world's collective imagination. A city of paradoxes, Rio embraces high and low, nature and nurture, chaos and cool. It's a city where you stuff yourself on *feijoada* in a favela (shantytown) and then dine fine in swanky Leblon; where you can climb up—and hang-glide off—famous peaks such as Corcovado, Sugarloaf,

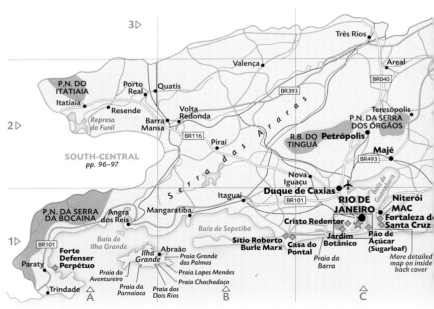

and Pedra Bonita and then samba in one of bohemian Lapa's clubs. Sure, the five-day frenzy of Carnaval will get you all riled up, but lying horizontal on Ipanema beach in the company of a caipirinha will relax you to the hilt.

Yes, the Cidade Maravilhosa is marvelous, but when you need a break, do as Cariocas (Rio natives) do and flee for the greener or bluer pastures of surrounding Rio de Janeiro state. Day trips can be made to Niterói—flush with colonial fortifications and Oscar Niemeyer–designed buildings—as well as the mountain town of Petrópolis. You'll be seduced by Búzios, where beaches and quasi-Mediterranean charms never go out of fashion and Paraty, a colonial gem surrounded by jungle-clad mountains and deserted beaches. For an ultimate getaway, there's Ilha Grande with its limpid waters and secluded coves framed by highly explorable native Atlantic Forest that will make it near impossible to return to civilization. ■

NOT TO BE MISSED:

Falling into hedonism during the world's most spectacular Carnaval 66–67

Sambaing the night away at clubs and bars in historic Lapa 71

The heights of—and gasping at the views from—Pão de Açúcar and Corcovado 77–79

Mellowing out amid Zona Sul's urbane yet über-relaxing beach culture 80–83

The alpine scenery and imperial finery of Petrópolis 89–91

The jungle-clad, beach-strewn island of Ilha Grande 92–94

Strolling the charming cobblestone streets of colonial Paraty 94–95

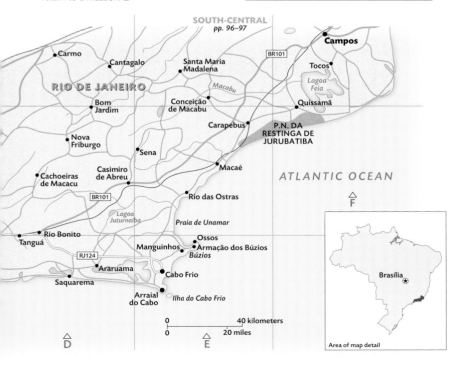

Centro

Rio's downtown is a busy and beguiling mishmash of cobblestone alleyways and traffic-clogged avenues, where baroque churches and neoclassical palaces vie for space with 20th-century skyscrapers. A commercial and cultural nexus, Centro is Rio's historic heart, and its pulse, spurred on by new projects, is more vibrant than ever.

Rio's Theatro Municipal, one of the most prestigious theaters in South America

Centro

⚅ 59 & Inside back cover (IBC) D6

Visitor Information

✉ Rio Tur, Rua Barão de Tefé 5, Saúde

☎ 1746

www.rioguiaoficial .com.br

Home to the city's port, Centro was where Rio first began, but aside from a handful of opulent churches, few colonial vestiges remain. In an attempt to live up to its prestigious role as capital of the Americas' sole empire, Rio strove to transform itself during the 19th century from a stagnant backwater into a cosmopolitan metropolis of tree-lined boulevards, elegant parks, and grandiose public buildings.

Centro's decline was sealed in the 1960s when the federal government moved to Brasília and São Paulo became the nation's financial center. In recent times, the area has been in the throes of a major revitalization. Former government palaces are now home to cutting-edge cultural centers. Historic streets shelter funky galleries and bistros as well as decades' old restaurants and bars. Meanwhile, as Rio prepares to host the FIFA World Cup and Olympic Games, the down-and-out area surrounding the historic port is getting a major makeover that promises to breathe new life into the region.

Castelo

Due to its strategic location at the entrance to Guanabara Bay, the hilltop known as Morro do Castelo was where the Portuguese decided, in 1567, to develop a settlement called São Sebastião do Rio de Janeiro. In the name of modernization, the *morro* itself was razed in the 1920s to make way for wide avenues and office buildings following in the style of Baron Haussmann's modern Paris.

Fortunately a few landmarks still survive. Among them is the complex that houses the **Museu Histórico Nacional** *(Praça Marechal Âncora, tel 21/2550 9220, www.museuhistoriconacional.com.br, closed Mon., $, Metrô: Cinelândia)*, a visit to which provides a great introduction to Brazil in all its fascinating complexity. The museum is installed in a gleaming white architectural complex that embraces a trio of historic buildings, the oldest—a fortress known as the Fortaleza

de Santiago—dates back to 1603. Reserve a couple of hours to tour the permanent collection, which earns high marks for providing descriptive explanations that are not only compelling, but also flawlessly translated into English (a rarity in Brazilian museums).

Of particular interest are the displays devoted to indigenous cultures (shark-tooth arrow tips and brilliant feather headdresses, not to mention a riveting description of cannibalism rituals), Brazil's African legacy (the iron gags used to prevent slaves from swallowing precious gold and gemstone are harrowing), and Brazilian baroque (a banquet of gold-doused cherubs and angels).

Cinelândia

Cinelândia sprang to life at the same time that the city's first grand boulevard, Avenida Central (today Avenida Rio Branco), was becoming Centro's new nerve center. The quartet of 1920s movie palaces that were built around **Praça Floriano** earned Cinelândia its name and

---

EXPERIENCE: Gafieiras & Ballroom Dancing

If you want to try dancing Rio style, on Praça Tiradentes stands Rio's last true *gafieira*, the name given to traditional dance halls, once magnets for fancy steppers and bohemians. Back in 1928, when Gafieira Estudantina first opened, there were upward of 450 salons devoted to ballroom dancing in the city. Today, the **Centro Cultural Estudantina Musical** *(Praça Tiradentes 79, tel 21/2232 1149)* is considered the last man standing, a feat that earned it heritage status in 2012.

Despite some restoration, much of the original décor (including signs prohibiting "scandalous" kissing and women dancing together) remains the same. However, to keep up with changing tempos, the Estudantina—like the **Elite** *(Rua Frei Caneca 4, 21/2232 3217)*, a nearby 1930 gafieira now completely given over to alternative *festas*—hosts samba, hip-hop, funk, and *bailes de charme*, with big band classics played by live orchestras on Saturday nights.

Theatro Municipal

- ✉ Praça Floriano
- ☎ 21/2332 9134
- 🕐 Guided tours: Tues.–Fri. noon–4 p.m., Sat. noon & 1 p.m.
- 💲 $
- Ⓜ Metrô: Cinelândia

www.theatro municipal.rj.gov.br

NOTE: Purchase tour tickets 30 min. before at box office on Av. 13 de Maio or reserve by phone (21/2332 9220).

Museu Nacional de Belas Artes

- ✉ Av. Rio Branco 199
- ☎ 21/2219 8474
- 🕐 Closed Mon.
- 💲 $
- Ⓜ Metrô: Cinelândia

Biblioteca Nacional

- ✉ Av. Rio Branco 219
- ☎ 21/2220 9484
- Ⓜ Metrô: Cinelândia

Largo da Carioca

- Ⓜ Metrô: Carioca

cemented its role as Rio's entertainment epicenter.

Although only one cinema has survived, Cinelândia is home to the splendid **Theatro Municipal** along with many outdoor bars. The theater, modeled after Paris's Opéra Garnier, is among the most eye-catching of the historic buildings surrounding Cinelândia—a shining example of the eclectic style that reigned in Brazil at the beginning of the 20th century.

Great Brazilian artists of the day such as sculptor Henrique Bernardelli (1858–1936) and painters Eliseu Visconti (1866–1944) and Rodolfo Amoedo (1857–1941) were summoned to embellish the facade and the interior using luxurious materials including bronze, Carrara marble, and gold. Since opening its doors in 1909, Brazil's premier theater has hosted some of the world's most renowned orchestras, theater, dance, and opera companies as well as icons including Isadora Duncan, Sarah Bernhardt, Vaslav Nijinsky, Igor Stravinsky, and Maria Callas. It is also home to reputed symphony and dance companies.

Across from the Theatro Municipal, the more somber, neoclassical **Museu Nacional de Belas Artes** was inspired by the Louvre. When completed in 1908, it housed the National School of Fine Arts before being converted into a fine arts museum, in 1937. Although there is a sprinkling of works by European masters, the real interest here is the national collection, which offers novices a useful historic overview of Brazilian painting with works by Pedro Américo (1843–1905) and

Victor Meirelles (1832–1903), and 20th-century artists such as Cândido Portinari, Anita Malfatti, Alfredo Volpi, and Emiliano Di Cavalcanti.

Next door, the **Biblioteca Nacional** is Latin America's largest library and another example of the eclectic style in vogue at the time it was built (1906). In the collection, you'll find every book ever published in Brazil along with rarities such as two Gutenberg Bibles from 1462. Free guided tours of the ornate interior are available.

INSIDER TIP:

If you'd like to bring home an authentic musical instrument, from curious African percussives to elegant Portuguese strings, visit the many shops of the music zone on Rua da Carioca, just to the west of the Largo da Carioca.

—SHAWN W. MILLER
Associate Dean, Brigham Young University & scholar of Rio de Janeiro urban street use

Largo & Rua do Carioca

Following Avenida Rio Branco north brings you to Largo da Carioca. This busy square was originally covered by a lagoon, which was drained in the early 1600s. Perched above the Largo are two of Rio's oldest colonial churches. On the left, the **Santuário e Convento de Santo Antônio** (*tel 21/2262 0129;*

closed Sat. p.m.–Sun.) dates back to the early 1600s. Since then, both church and convent have undergone numerous renovations, but much original artwork has been conserved along with the sacristy frescoes rendered in blue-and-white azulejos (ceramic tiles), depicting scenes from the life of Santo Antônio.

Next door, stepping inside the **Igreja da Ordem Terceira de São Francisco da Penitência** (tel 21/2262 0197, closed Sat.–Sun., $) is like walking into a jewel box. The last 30 years of the church's construction—which began in 1657 and lasted 115 years—were spent dousing the finely sculpted cedar altars and naves with 880 pounds (400 kg) of pure gold. One of the earliest examples of Brazilian baroque, the Igreja São Francisco was a prototype for many other churches across the country, although few ever matched its magnificence.

Breaking completely with baroque is the **Catedral Metropolitana.** Built between 1964 and 1976, it's devoted to the city's patron saint, St. Sebastian. The raw concrete, conical exterior may strike some as Blade Runner-esque. However, passing through the gigantic 60-foot-high (18 m) front doors and into the interior—vast enough to hold 20,000 souls—you can't help but be awed by the profusion of light and airiness. A small sacred art museum on the site, **Museu Arquidiocesano de Arte Sacra,** displays relics such as the baptismal fonts used to christen children of the imperial family and a throne belonging to Pedro II.

Running north from Rua da Carioca, along the narrow Rua Gonçalves Dias, is an unexpected treasure and a Carioca institution: **Confeitaria Colombo.** Open since 1894, this elegant art nouveau café offers a glimpse into how swank life must have been for Rio's turn-of-the-20th-century elites. Join workers chasing traditional pastéis de nata (custard tarts) with cafezinhos at the front bar or gaping tourists splurging for chá da tarde (afternoon tea).

Museu Nacional de Belas Artes

Praça XV

Some of Rio's most important landmarks flank the **Praça XV de Novembro,** including the former royal palace, the Paço Imperial. From the edge of Guanabara Bay, ferries depart from the Estação de Barcas to Niterói (see pp. 88–89) and Ilha de Paquetá. The praça's name refers to November 15, 1889—the date upon which Brazil's first president, Marechal

(continued on p. 64)

Catedral Metropolitana & Museu Arquidiocesano de Arte Sacra
- 🅰 IBC D5
- ✉ Av. República do Chile
- ☎ 21/2240 2669
- 🕐 Closed Sun.; museum open Wed. & Sat.–Sun. a.m.
- 🚇 Metrô: Carioca

Confeitaria Colombo
- ✉ Rua Gonçalves Dias 32
- ☎ 21/2505 1500
- 🕐 Closed Sun.
- 🚇 Carioca
- **www.confeitaria colombo.com.br**

Praça XV de Novembro
- 🚇 Metrô: Carioca or Uruguaiana

Walk: Following in João VI's Footsteps

On March 7, 1808, Portugal's King João VI arrived in Rio de Janeiro, accompanied by 15,000 royal followers. As capital of the Portuguese Empire, Rio was transformed from a colonial backwater to a world-class 19th-century city. This walk cleaves a path through Centro, showcasing the most important architectural legacies of the imperial era.

The splendid interior of the Biblioteca Nacional

Begin at **Praça Floriano,** also known as Cinelândia. In front of the Cinelândia Metrô station, the **Biblioteca Nacional ❶** (see p. 60) is the world's eighth-largest library. The books, manuscripts, and maps that João VI carried with him from Portugal—and made public in 1814—were the seed of the library's collection, which has expanded from 60,000 volumes to more than 9 million.

Next door, the **Museu Nacional de Belas Artes ❷** (see p. 60) also owes its origins to João VI. Artwork from the Portuguese Royal Collection that the prince regent brought to Brazil forms the core of the museum's European collection. Soon after arriving in Rio, João VI founded the Royal School of Sciences, Arts, and Crafts, which later became known as the National School of Fine Arts. This grand building housed the school from 1908 until

---

NOT TO BE MISSED:

Paço Imperial • Centro Cultural Banco do Brasil

1937, when it was converted into a fine arts museum.

Continue north along Avenida Rio Branco to Rua da Assembléia and take a right. A five-minute walk will bring you to **Rua Primeiro de Março.** Formerly known as Rua Direita (Main Street), this wide avenue runs parallel to Guanabara Bay and was the scene of major political and cultural happenings during Brazil's days of empire. Take a left, heading north on Rua Primeiro de Março, and almost immediately you're at **Praça XV de Novembro** (see

p. 61). This historic square is anchored by the **Paço Imperial 3,** (see p. 64) where João VI lived with his family upon arriving in Brazil. It was the seat of government throughout Brazil's imperial era.

Across Rua Primeiro de Março from Paço, Cândido Mendes University occupies the former **Convento do Carmo 4,** a Carmelite convent whose construction dates back to the early 1600s. The convent was appropriated by João VI as a residence for his mentally ill mother, Queen Maria I, known as Maria a Louca (Mad Maria). A plaque on the corner notes that from this spot passersby could hear Maria's frequent screaming. Across Rua Sete de Setembro, the **Igreja de Nossa Senhora do Carmo da Antiga Sé 5** (see p. 64), which formerly belonged to the convent, functioned as the Royal Chapel during João VI's reign.

Continue along the right side of Rua Primeiro de Março to No. 36, the **Igreja de Santa Cruz de Militares,** a church whose original 17th-century chapel was built by colonial soldiers as a place to bury their dead. The present incarnation dates from 1811 and was consecrated by João VI shortly after his arrival in Brazil. Inside, a magnificent organ is played during frequent recitals. Farther along, at No. 66, lies the main entrance to the **Centro Cultural Banco do Brasil 6** (see pp. 64–65). Before becoming one of Rio's premier cultural centers, this palatial building housed the seat of the country's first national bank, created by João VI in 1808.

After roaming the Centro Cultural Banco do Brasil, exit onto Praça Pio X and turn right where you'll see the **Casa França-Brasil 7** cultural center (see p. 65). Commissioned by João VI, Rio's oldest neoclassical building was

inaugurated on May 13, 1820, to coincide with his birthday. From here, follow the cobblestone Rua Visconde de Itaboraí and make a left onto **Rua do Rosário,** a charming old street lined with popular restaurants. Walk to the end and cross Avenida Alfred Agache to the **Espaço Cultural da Marinha 8,** where you can view João VI's namesake boat—in which the royal family went cruising around Guanabara Bay. It was built in 1808, the same year the prince regent created the Royal Naval Brigade (today the Brazilian Marine Corps), whose headquarters is located on adjacent Ilha das Cobras. If you schedule your walk accordingly, you too can hop a boat from the Espaço Cultural da Marinha and take a tour of Guanabara Bay.

🅰	IBC D5
▶	Praça Floriano
🕒	90 minutes
⬍	1.7 miles (2.8 km)
▶	Espaço Cultura da Marinha

The Man Who Gave Rio Away

In 1531, Martim Afonso de Sousa (1500–1571), a Portuguese explorer and childhood friend of King João III (1502–1557), was sent to Rio. His missions were to establish a colony and discover El Dorado, tales of which had been passed on to early explorers by Brazil's native peoples. He spent two years scouring the Brazilian interior for riches. During this time, the Spanish tumbled upon their own El Dorado in the form of the gold-drenched Inca Empire, while the hapless Portuguese were decimated by native attacks and diseases. By 1533, Afonso was disgusted with Brazil and journeyed to India, where spoils were guaranteed. Wanting nothing to do with the territory gifted to him by the king—including Rio—he happily gave the land away for free to other colonists, saying that whoever took it off his hands would be doing him "the greatest mercy and greatest honor in the world."

Paço Imperial

✉ Praça XV de Novembro 48, C

☎ 21/2215 2622

🚇 Metrô: Carioca or Uruguaiana

Igreja de Nossa Senhora do Carmo da Antiga Sé

✉ Rua Sete de Setembro 12

☎ 21/2242 7766

💲 $ (museum tours)

🚇 Metrô: Carioca or Uruguaiana

Igreja da Ordem Terceira de Nossa Senhora do Monte do Carmo

✉ Rua Primeiro do Março 14

☎ 21/2242 4828

🕐 Closed Sun.

🚇 Metrô: Carioca or Uruguaiana

Deodoro Fonseca, declared Brazil a republic.

The **Paço Imperial** dominates Praça XV. Completed in 1743, the palace served as the residence for Portugal's viceroys and governors before hosting the Portuguese royal family when João VI fled Napoleon in 1808. Among the historic events that occurred here were the coronations of King João VI and Emperors Pedro I and Pedro II and the signing of the Lei Áurea, which ended slavery, by Princesa Isabel, on May 13, 1888. Today, these cavernous rooms welcome some of the city's premier art exhibitions.

Baroque Churches: Across from Praça XV sits **Igreja de Nossa Senhora do Carmo da Antiga Sé**, which served as Rio's royal chapel as well as its former cathedral (antiga sé) until 1976. Following its completion in 1761, many of the city's most important religious commemorations were held here, including the baptism and marriage of Emperor Pedro II. Though the facade has undergone significant modifications, the interior is a rococo banquet, featuring altars dripping in silver and gold.

Next door, the **Igreja da Ordem Terceira de Nossa Senhora do Monte do Carmo** dates back to 1750. Its sober granite facade, completely unadorned, is rare and clashes with the gold-doused rococo interior.

Arco do Teles: Across Praça XV from the Paço Imperial, an imposing 1743 stone archway, the Arco do Teles, leads to a labyrinth of narrow pedestrian streets. Today this atmospheric maze shelters bars and restaurants, where workers gather for lunch and happy hour drinks. Open since 1884, **Rio Minho** (see Travelwise p. 280) is Rio's oldest restaurant still in operation.

Converted Palaces: A cluster of former administrative palaces have been converted into some of the city's most dynamic cultural centers. The most magnificent is the **Centro Cultural Banco do Brasil** (CCBB), former headquarters of Brazil's national bank. This eclectic-style edifice, built between 1880 and 1906, plays host to major international and national art exhibits and offers a quality selection of contemporary dance, theater, and music performances, along with film screenings, all of which are free or very affordable.

the **Igreja de Nossa Senhora da Candelária.** A coveted wedding venue, this large and ostentatious church is awash in multicolored marble and crowned by an enormous cupola. Construction lasted from 1775 to 1889—thus the fusion of Renaissance, baroque, and neoclassical elements.

Centro Cultural Banco do Brasil
- ✉ Rua Primeiro de Março 66
- ☎ 21/3808 2020
- ◷ Closed Mon.
- Ⓜ Metrô: Uruguaiana

The main rotunda of the Centro Cultural Banco do Brasil (CCBB)

Behind the CCBB are two other important cultural centers. Completed in 1922, the **Centro Cultural dos Correios** *(Rua Visconde de Itaboraí 20, tel 21/2253 1580, closed Mon.)* housed the headquarters of Rio's postal service until 1980. At the end of the same block, the **Casa França-Brasil** *(Rua Visconde de Itaboraí 78, tel 21/2332 5120, closed Mon.)* is Rio's earliest example of neoclassical architecture. Dating back to 1820, it originally served as a customs building.

Casa França-Brasil looks onto Praça Pio X, which is dominated by

From Praça Pio X, continue north along Rua Primeiro de Março to Rua Dom Gerardo Branco, and take the elevator up to the **Igreja e Mosteiro de São Bento.** The Benedictine monks who arrived in Rio from Bahia in the 17th century inaugurated this hilltop church and monastery in 1649. A contrast to the austere facade is the gasp-inducing interior, featuring carved columns and naves and altars decorated with clouds of angels and cherubs, smothered in gold. During Mass, the monks chant Gregorian hymns accompanied by the organ. ∎

Igreja de Nossa Senhora da Candelária
- ✉ Praça Pio X
- ☎ 21/2233 2324
- Ⓜ Metrô: Uruguaiana

Igreja e Mosteiro de São Bento
- ✉ Rua Dom Gerardo Branco 68 (elevator at No. 40)
- ☎ 21/2206 8100
- Ⓜ Metrô: Uruguaiana

Carnaval

Rio may not play host to the only Carnaval on the planet, but it's hard to dispute that the city's five-day, eye-popping, ear-exploding, mind-blowing extravaganza is the most spectacular—and fun—of them all.

Some samba schools may spend up to US$150,000 on a lavish *carro alegórico* (Carnaval float).

Desfiles

It's impossible to conjure up Rio without Carnaval. The city and the *festa* are joyously and inextricably linked. Most people associate Carnaval with the extravagant *desfiles* (parades) in which the city's top 12 *escolas de samba* (samba schools)—members of the Grupo Especial, the "special group"—strut their magnificent stuff down the main *avenida* of the Sambódromo. Designed by Oscar Niemeyer and opened in 1984, this giant concrete stadium can hold up to 75,000 people.

The desfiles take place on the Sunday and Monday nights of Carnaval. Starting at 9 p.m. and lasting until dawn, each of the 12 escolas have 90 minutes to parade down the 765-yard (700 m) stretch of Rua Marquês de Sapucaí. Along with bleachers full of shimmying spectators, there is a table of judges who award points for the strength of various performance elements, including floats, choreography, and the *samba de enredo* (theme song). Each year, inspired by dreams of championship, the escolas invest vast quantities of time, talent, hard work, and money. The glittery, gaudy-hued fruit of their labors is a spectacle on the grandest, most delirious scale imaginable.

Tickets & Seating: Most revelers purchase their desfile tickets in advance. Indeed, many snatch up the best seats when they first go on sale (usually in January). **Rio Services Carnival** *(www.rio-carnival.net)* and **Riotur** *(www.rioguiaoficial.com.br),* the city's tourist secretariat, are good sources. Sections 5, 7, and 9 offer the best views. You can also just go to the Sambódromo and purchase tickets from scalpers. If you take a page out of the Carioca playbook and arrive late, you can score a good deal—but make sure you receive a plastic card with a magnetic strip along with a paper slip. The best way to get to the Sambódromo is to take a taxi or the Metrô, which operates 24/7 during Carnaval, to Praça Onze (for even-number seating sectors) or Central (for odd-numbered sectors).

Banda da Ipanema, a traditional *bloco* (group) on the city streets during Carnaval

INSIDER TIP:

Take a stroll along what was Rio's fashionable colonial street, Rua do Ouvidor. Despite its extremely narrow dimensions, this was the first host of the now famous Carnaval.

—SHAWN W. MILLER

Associate Dean, Brigham Young University & scholar of Rio de Janeiro urban street use

Other Events

Although the Sambódromo desfiles are the best known of Carnaval events, many Cariocas prefer the street Carnaval. In recent years, *Carnaval da rua* has enjoyed a resurgence as revelers, or *foliões,* have flocked to see the neighborhood and resident association *blocos* and *bandas* (street bands), some of which have been making merry and music for

decades. Among the most traditional groups are those in Centro (Bafo de Onça, Cacique de Ramos, Cordão do Bola Preta), Santa Teresa (Carmelitas de Santa Teresa), Botafogo (Barbas, Bloco de Segunda, Dois Pra Lá, Dois Pra Cá), Copacabana (Bip Bip), and Ipanema (Símpatia é Quase Amor, Banda Ipanema, Banda Carmen Miranda).

To join the fun, show up at the blocos' headquarters on the days of their parades. (Riotur has online schedules.) Costumes aren't obligatory, but you might want to dress in a bloco's traditional colors or purchase a T-shirt on the spot. Complementing the street celebrations are the free shows and festivities organized by the city of Rio. Among the most popular are the festas held outside the Sambódromo at the Terreirão do Samba, the Baile da Cinelândia in Centro, and the alternative Rio Folia, which unspools beneath the Arcos da Lapa.

Meanwhile, the city's clubs and hotels host private *bailes* (balls) featuring live samba bands and guests whose extravagant costumes (usually obligatory) mask their inhibitions. The most lavish and expensive is the Magic Ball at the Copacabana Palace. Among the more affordable runners-up are the Baile Vermelho e Preto, where revelers honor the Flamengo soccer team by dressing in the team colors—red and black—and the gay-friendly, bacchanalian bashes held at the Scala Club's grand Cinelândia digs.

Port Zone & São Cristóvão

The port zone extending north from Praça Mauá comprises the overlapping neighborhoods of Saúde and Gamboa. Historically rich and increasingly cutting edge, this area is in the throes of an urban revolution for the upcoming events. Nearby São Cristóvão, a traditional working-class Zona Norte neighborhood close to Centro, has an imperial past (including a palace) and the most legendary soccer stadium on the planet, justifying a detour.

An impromptu *roda de samba* (samba jam), Pedra do Sal

Zona Portuária
🅰 IBC C6–D6

Fortaleza da Conceição
✉ Rua Major Daemon 81
☎ 21/2223 2177
🕐 Closed Sat.–Sun.; by appt. only
🚇 Metrô: Uruguaiana

São Cristóvão
🅰 IBC B6

Zona Portuária

Occupation of the areas of Saúde and Gamboa dates back to colonial times. The area's bucolic aspect was a draw for aristocrats who built elegant villas on the hills overlooking Guanabara Bay in the 1700s. In the 1770s, the Cais de Valongo (Valongo Docks) replaced Praça XV as the disembarkation point for the estimated one million African slaves who came to Rio. It was in these narrow streets that Carioca samba was born—a legacy kept alive with free jams held on Monday and Friday nights at the square known as **Pedra do Sal** (*Rua Argemiro Bulcão, Metrô: Uruguaiana*). To get a sense of this historic neighborhood, wander up Rua Jogo da Bola to the hilltop **Fortaleza da Conceição**, built in 1715 to thwart French invaders.

By the mid-1800s, the area began to decline as the port became increasingly industrialized.

Meanwhile, in 1897, lured to Rio by land promised to them by the government (a promise not honored), freed slaves from Bahia began settling on the Morro da Providência. Today, the hillside community is considered Rio's very first favela.

Until recently, the port zone had been abandoned. However, as part of a major US$33 billion city renovation project, the region is receiving a massive overhaul.

São Cristóvão

Now a public park, **Quinta da Boa Vista** (Av. Pedro II, tel 21/2589 4279, Metrô: São Cristóvão), the former royal estate, designed in English romantic style, is quiet on weekdays (when security can be sketchy). But on weekends, its sweeping lawns are blanketed with picnickers. The park shelters the **Jardim Zoológico,** also called the RioZoo—home to more than 2,000 mammals, birds, and reptiles.

A grand alleyway leads up to the Palácio da Boa Vista, where the royal family lived from 1817 until the declaration of the republic in 1889. Since 1892, it has housed the **Museu Nacional de História Natural** (aka Museu Nacional), Brazil's oldest scientific museum and the largest natural history museum in Latin America. Its collection includes a chunk of the Bendigo Meteorite—the largest metallic mass known to have crashed to Earth.

Ten minutes from the park is the **Feira de São Cristóvão.** This open-air market is a gathering point for Rio's residents from the Brazilian Northeast, many of whom migrated to the city in search of work but still get homesick for the food, culture, music, and vibrancy of their home states.

Taking the Metrô to Maracanã brings you to the most famous soccer stadium on the planet. **Maracanã** was originally built to host the 1950 World Cup, which Brazilians had high hopes of winning. Instead, fans witnessed Brazil's tragic defeat to Uruguay in the finals. In the hopes that history won't repeat itself, the stadium has been undergoing a massive renovation in preparation for the 2014 World Cup. You can take in a game as well as a guided tour, which includes a visit to the memorabilia-stuffed museum. ∎

Jardim Zoológico
- ⊠ Quinta da Boa Vista
- ☎ 21/3878 4200
- 🕐 Closed Mon.
- 💲 $
- 🚇 Metrô: São Cristóvão

Museu Nacional da História Natural
- ⊠ Quinta da Boa Vista
- ☎ 21/2562 6901
- 🕐 Closed Mon.
- 💲 $
- 🚇 Metrô: São Cristóvão

Feira de São Cristóvão
- ⊠ Campo de São Cristóvão
- ☎ 21/2580 5335
- 🕐 Closed Mon.
- 💲 $ Sat.–Sun.
- 🚇 Metrô: São Cristóvão

Maracanã
- ⊠ Rua Professor Eurico Rabelo, Portão 18
- ☎ 21/8871 3950
- 💲 $$$
- 🚇 Metrô: Maracanã

The New (& Improved) Port

Rio's Porto Maravilha project promises to revolutionize the city's port zone. Among the area's novelties are two cutting-edge museums. Opened in March 2013, the **Museu de Arte do Rio** (Praça Mauá 5, tel 21/2203-1235, closed Sun., $, free Tues., Metrô: Uruguaiana) fuses together a palace and a former bus terminal (located on Praça Mauá) into a museum featuring exhibits devoted to Rio de Janeiro artists. Slated to open in 2014 is the futuristic **Museu do Amanhã** (Museum of Tomorrow; Pier Mauá), located on the Mauá Pier. Green solutions, such as solar panels and the use of ocean water to cool the building, mirror the museum's sustainable mission—allowing visitors to imagine and experience what their lives, and life on Earth, will be like in the future.

Lapa & Santa Teresa

Synonymous with Carioca culture and identity, not to mention nightlife, Lapa is where icons of bohemia past and present mingle in bars, clubs, and on sidewalks while listening to off-the-charts musical offerings. Rising above it, hilltop Santa Teresa is often compared to Paris's Montmartre, due to its charm and its atmospheric old houses—haunted by artists and intellectuals.

Lapa

IBC D5

Metrô: Cinelândia

Lapa

Lapa has lived through its share of ups and downs. In colonial times, the region was covered by swampland, but in the 19th century it was drained and transformed into a wealthy residential neighborhood. In the early 20th century a colorful crew of tricksters, gangsters, prostitutes, sambistas, artists, and intellectuals, who created a legendary underground scene, replaced Lapa's well-to-do families. However, as the decades rolled by, the neighborhood fell on hard times. Increasingly dilapidated, it became disreputable and dangerous as crime levels escalated.

It wasn't until the late 1990s that a revival began to take hold of Lapa. Samba jams took place beneath the arches of the colonial aqueduct. Antique shops opened along Rua do Lavradio. And Cariocas from all walks of life began flocking to new and decades-old restaurants and clubs to eat, drink, and dance the night away.

Lapa's nexus is the square known as **Largo da Lapa.** Stretching across the square is the **Arcos da Lapa.** Built in the early 18th century to supply water to Rio's residents, the iconic aqueduct carried fresh water from the source of the Rio Carioca, in Santa Teresa, to a fountain in Largo da Carioca. In 1896, its original services no longer required, the aqueduct was transformed into a viaduct upon which bondes (trams) transported passengers from Centro to Santa Teresa. Come dusk on weekends, throngs gather beneath

Chatting and chilling out at the Parque das Ruínas

EXPERIENCE: Sambaing the Night Away

Although Lapa's famed brothels and gambling palaces are long gone, there are plenty of places where you can go to hear and dance to samba.

Opened in 1867 as a social club for abolitionists and Republicans, **Clube dos Democráticos** *(Rua do Riachuelo 91, Centro, tel 21/2252 4611, closed Sun.–Tues.)* lures all stripes of Carioca dancing fools to its humongous ballroom.

A pioneer of Lapa's revival movement, **Carioca da Gema** *(Av. Mem de Sá 79, tel 21/2221 0043, www.barcariocadagema .com.br)* offers high-caliber samba and *chorinho* performances.

One of Rio's most stunningly beautiful venues, **Rio Scenarium** *(Rua do Lavradio 20, tel 21/2147 9000, closed Sun.–Mon.)* boasts three floors stuffed with antiques (and tourists).

the 42 arches to listen and dance to improvised samba jams.

Behind Largo da Lapa, a staircase ascends to Santa Teresa, named after the convent founded here in the mid 1700s. The 215 eye-catching rising steps are paved in a multihued mosaic of ceramic tiles. Baptized the **Escadaria Selarón,** this Gaudí-esque piece of street art is the work of Chilean artist Jorge Selarón, who began this obsessive undertaking in 1994 as a gift to his adopted city, using dishes and ceramics sent to him by collaborators from all around the globe.

Santa Teresa

One of Rio's most charming neighborhoods, Santa Teresa is removed from the urban fray below, because it is relatively difficult to access. Strolling along its winding cobblestone streets is akin to meandering through a bucolic village, albeit a cosmopolitan one where local artists' ateliers and funky boutiques share sidewalk space with chic but understated bars and restaurants—many with bewitching views of the city splayed out below.

Built in 1954, the **Museu da Chácara do Céu** is the former home of wealthy industrialist Raymundo Castro Maya (1894–1968). Converted into a museum, the residence, with its streamlined elegance and modernist lines, provides an ideal backdrop for contemplating Maya's impressive art collection. The curators' refreshing approach mingles individual paintings, drawings, and engravings by European masters with work by Brazilian modernists. As enticing as the art is Castro Maya's home itself—furnished with an exquisite selection of antiques and furnishings from Brazil and around the world.

Adjacent to the museum is the **Parque das Ruínas,** a small park that once sheltered the mansion of Laurinda Santos Lobo (1878–1946), a patroness of the arts whose parties—packed with presidents and protégés—were as legendarily flamboyant as the hostess herself. Today, cleverly renovated ruins shelter a cultural center. The main attraction, however, is the fantastic views of the city afforded from its many terraces. ■

Escadaria Selarón
- ✉ Rua Joaquim Silva at corner of Rua Teotônio Regadas
- Ⓜ Metrô: Cinelândia

Santa Teresa
- ⒩ IBC C5–D5

Museu da Chácara do Céu
- ✉ Rua Murtinho Nobre 93
- ☎ 21/3970 1126
- ⏲ Closed Tues.
- 💲 $, free Wed.
- 🚌 Bus: 006, 007, or 014

Parque das Ruínas
- ✉ Rua Murtinho Nobre 169
- ☎ 21/2215 0621
- ⏲ Closed Mon.
- 🚌 Bus: 006, 007, or 014

Glória, Catete, & Flamengo

Largely overlooked by tourists, these traditional Carioca neighborhoods have lost some of their original splendor, but it's worth visiting the Igreja Nossa Senhora da Glória do Outeiro and the Palácio and Parque do Catete.

Igreja Nossa Senhora da Glória do Outeiro with Cristo Redentor in the background

Glória
🅰 IBC D5–E5

Igreja Nossa Senhora da Glória do Outeiro
✉ Praça Nossa Senhora da Glória
☎ 21/2557 4600
🕐 Closed Mon.
💲 $ (museum)
🚇 Metrô: Glória

Glória

The main attraction in Glória, an extension of Centro, is the **Igreja Nossa Senhora da Glória do Outeiro,** perched upon the steep Morro da Glória. In 1567, Portuguese soldier Estácio da Sá (1520–1567) succeeded in taking this strategic hilltop from French invaders, thus ensuring Portuguese control of Rio de Janeiro. Completed in 1739, this is one of Rio's earliest baroque churches, not to mention one of its most unusual: Its floorplan consists of two intersecting octagons. A favorite

of the royal family, various princes and princesses were baptized here, among them Pedro II and his daughter Princess Isabel.

From the Glória Metrô station, it's a steep walk up the Ladeira da Glória to the church. A less challenging alternative is a ride up the 1945 **funicular** (Rua do Russel 300). The church's exterior is a striking exercise in contrasts, with the gleaming white of its facade set off by somber stone pillars. Inside, splendid frescoes in Portuguese blue-and-white azulejos (tiles) depict biblical scenes. At the back of the church, a small museum displays a collection of sacred art.

Glória is only one Metrô stop north of Catete, but you can easily walk the distance between them—either by going south along Rua da Glória, which turns into Rua do Catete, or by following Rua do Russel, which segues into Avenida Beira Mar. This latter route passes the neoclassical **Hotel Glória** (*Rua do Russel 632*). Built in 1922, the Glória, designed by French architect Joseph Gire (1872–1933), was one of Rio's oldest luxury hotels. It reigned supreme for a year before being eclipsed by the Copacabana Palace, also designed by Gire. Having lost its former cachet, in 2008, the Hotel Glória was snatched up by local billionaire Eike Batista. After a complete overhaul, the revamped hotel is slated to reopen in 2014 as the Glória Palace.

Catete

Catete was originally swampland fed by a branch of the Rio Carioca as it wound its way down from Corcovado to Flamengo beach. In the 18th century, the abundance of fresh water led to the creation of farms along the main road of Rua do Catete. In the 19th century, wealthy coffee barons built mansions along what was becoming an increasingly urban thoroughfare. The most magnificent of them, the Palácio do Catete, belonged to the Baron of Nova Friburgo (1795–1869), who spared no expense in the construction of an eclectic-style building, inspired in part by the aristocratic palaces of Venice and

Florence. Following the baron's death, the palace was purchased and enlisted as the seat of government in the new republic. Between 1897 and 1960, when the capital moved to Brasília, 17 Brazilian presidents resided here.

It was the 18th president, Juscelino Kubitschek (1902–1976), who came up with the idea of transforming the Palácio do Catete into the **Museu da República.** Apart from exhibits that focus on various aspects of the Brazilian republic, you're treated to the full force of the Baron of Nova Friburgo's over-the-top extravagance in salons such as the lavish banquet room and exotically

INSIDER TIP:

Catete has an excellent buffet restaurant— Estação República (*Rua do Catete, 104*) across from the Museu da República. With its large selection, it's great for vegetarians.

—KELLY E. HAYES
Scholar of Brazilian religion,
Indiana University

adorned Pompeiian and Moorish rooms, in which ladies and gentlemen retired after dinner to gossip, play chess, and smoke pipes and cigars. More macabre is the bedroom of President Getúlio Vargas (1882–1954), where, at 9 a.m. on August 24, 1954, he died after shooting himself through the heart. Amid the retro effects in

Catete
🅰 IBC D4

Museu da República (Palácio do Catete)
✉ Rua do Catete 153
☎ 21/3235 5236
🕐 Closed Mon.
💲 $, free Wed. & Sun.
🚇 Metrô: Catete

Flamengo
 IBC D4–E4

Museu de Arte Moderna

✉ Av. Infante
Dom Henrique
85, Parque do
Flamengo

☎ 21/3883 5600

🕐 Closed Mon.

💲 $

🚇 Metrô:
Cinelândia

the museum are Vargas's suicide note and gun as well as his blood-stained, striped pajama top.

The former palace gardens are now the **Parque do Catete**. Designed by French landscape artist Paul Villon (1841–1905), the park features an artificial lake complete with a cascade and grotto and serpentine pathways punctuated with 19th-century French sculptures. The park often plays host to cultural events.

Flamengo

Flamengo is an attractive neighborhood of wide avenues and leafy side streets, lined with art deco apartments and palaces that once served as embassies. According to competing legends, the *bairro* of Flamengo earned its name from the *flamengo* (Dutch) prisoners held captive

here by the Portuguese in the 17th century—or from the pink flamingos that (poetically, but improbably) frequented its long, curvaceous shoreline. In the early to mid-20th century, Flamengo was one of Rio's most fashionable addresses, and to this day, it retains a certain cachet.

Its most notable and popular feature is **Parque do Flamengo** *(tel 21/2265 4990, Metrô: Cinelândia on the north or Flamengo on the south)*, a vast green park that runs along Guanabara Bay. It is one of the city's most popular playgrounds for Cariocas of all ages, providing jogging, biking, and skateboard paths, along with numerous playing fields, a children's park, and an area for flying model planes. It is also home to the **Marina da Glória,** from which yachts and schooners depart for points up and down the coast. The park is packed on Sundays when Avenida Infante Dom Henrique is closed to traffic and sporting events and other activities take place.

Two museums here are worth a peek. The **Museu de Arte Moderna** (MAM) occupies a somewhat bleak but beguiling modernist structure; its glass-and-concrete exterior offers a striking contrast to the soft colors and organic forms of the surrounding gardens, designed by landscape architect Roberto Burle Marx. Completed in 1958, the building is supported by thrusting V-shaped columns and is considered to be the masterpiece of architect Affonso Eduardo Reidy (1909–1964). Inside is one of Brazil's

---

Carmen Miranda

Although she was born in Portugal, Maria do Carmo Miranda da Cunha (1909–1955) was raised in Rio, where her rise to fame as a singer in the 1930s coincided with the birth of Brazil's recording industry and explosion of radio. In 1939, she was "discovered" by impresario Lee Schubert while performing in the Urca Casino and whisked off to Broadway. After taking New York by storm (the windows of Saks Fifth Avenue displayed Carmen-inspired platform shoes and turbans), the "Brazilian Bombshell" went to Hollywood, where she starred in 14 movies between 1940 and 1953. At the time, her over-the-top celluloid "Brazilian-ness" was met with ambivalence by Brazil's elites, but today Carmen is beloved in Rio, particularly when Carnaval rolls around and Carmen look-alikes take to the streets.

Skateboarders love to cruise the wide paths of Parque do Flamengo.

most significant collections of 20th-century art with choice works by such international artists as Alberto Giacometti, Henry Moore, and Jackson Pollock sprinkled amid pieces by national figures such as Tarsila do Amaral (1886–1973) and Anita Malfatti (1889–1964). The permanent collection on display provides an excellent overview of Brazilian modernism.

Rounding the tip of Flamengo beach brings you to the end of the park and the beginning of Botafogo. Amid the traffic racing along Avenida Infante Dom Henrique sits a squat concrete building by Affonso Eduardo Reidy that is truly at odds with the extravagance of the Brazilian bombshell to whom the **Museu Carmen Miranda** pays homage. Fans of Hollywood's golden age can get a quick glitz fix by ogling the appetizing tutti-frutti hats and sky-high platform shoes worn by the diminutive entertainer in the Technicolor musicals that made her Hollywood's top earning female star in the mid-1940s. There are plans to move the museum's collection to the soon-to-be-opened Museu de Imagem e Som in Copacabana.

A block up from the Parque do Flamengo and a block over from bustling Largo do Machado, **Oi Futuro** is one of Rio's most dynamic cultural centers. Operated by Oi, a major Brazilian telecommunications company, this cutting-edge multimedia center takes the future seriously. Within the cleverly renovated building, once inhabited by a phone company, multiple floors host exhibits of contemporary visual art, many of which incorporate technology. There are also spaces for concerts, film screenings, and dance performances. The rooftop terrace provides good views of the park. ■

Museu Carmen Miranda
- ✉ Av. Rui Barbosa 560
- ☎ 21/2334 4293
- 🕐 Closed Mon.
- 🚇 Metrô: Flamengo

Oi Futuro
- ✉ Rua Dois de Dezembro 63
- ☎ 21/3131 3060
- 🕐 Closed Mon.
- 🚇 Metrô: Largo do Machado

Corcovado & Sugarloaf

Two of Rio's oldest residential neighborhoods—Laranjeiras and Cosme Velho—are low-key, verdant, pretty *bairros* that provide a delightful area to stroll through. But by far the most significant attractions are Corcovado and the Cristo Redentor statue as well as Pão de Açúcar or Sugarloaf.

Staring down at Guanabara Bay from Corcovado

Laranjeiras

IBC C4–D4

Palácio das Laranjeiras & Parque Guinle

✉ Rua Paulo César de Andrade 407, Laranjeiras

🚇 Metrô: Largo do Machado

Laranjeiras

Laranjeiras dates back to the 17th century, when the area was known for the cultivation of *laranjeiras* (orange trees). Off the main tourist track, Laranjeiras retains a pleasant neighborhood atmosphere. Its main thoroughfare, Rua Laranjeiras, spools its way up from Largo do Machado before turning into Rua Cosme Velho, the main street of Cosme Velho, which leads all the way up to Corcovado.

Only two blocks from Largo do Machado and just off Rua das Laranjeiras is the **Palácio das Laranjeiras.** Formerly the residence of wealthy industrialist Eduardo Guinle (1846–1914), who modeled it upon the Monte-Carlo Casino, it was transformed into the official residence of Rio de Janeiro state's governor in 1947. The surrounding **Parque Guinle** is a lovely green oasis. Overlooking the park is an ensemble of residential buildings designed by architect Lucio Costa (who later planned Brasília) in the 1940s. Apart from the slender columns supporting the structures, other remarkable modernist features include the geometrically patterned ceramic sunshades in pastel hues.

Corcovado

The statue of **Cristo Redentor** (Christ the Redeemer) hovering gloriously atop Corcovado mountain is to Rio what the Statue of Liberty is to New York and the Eiffel Tower is to Paris. However, unlike these other landmarks, the Cristo is remarkable in that no matter where you happen to be in a 360-degree radius, the 98-foot (30 m) Christ—arms outstretched in a welcoming embrace—can be seen watching the city.

INSIDER TIP:

Catch the 8:30 train to the top of Corcovado to avoid the tour bus crowds and to get the best light for photos.

—LUIZ RENATO MALCHER
*Manager, Rio de Janeiro
Urban Adventures*

Rio's earliest Portuguese settlers ascribed spiritual significance to the mountain they called the Pico da Tentação (Peak of Temptation), an allusion to a biblical passage in which Jesus was tempted by the devil while atop a mountain. It wasn't until the 19th century that the 2,330-foot (710 m) granite pinnacle acquired the more secular, but no less poetic, name of Corcovado (hunchback).

Emperor Pedro II was fond of making the arduous journey to Corcovado's (statueless) summit by donkey. Wanting to share the sublime experience with his subjects, the altruistic emperor authorized the construction of a hill-climbing steam train. Inaugurated in 1884, the railway was considered an engineering feat.

Originally commissioned to coincide with the commemoration of Brazil's independence centennial in 1921, the statue of the Christ the Redeemer wasn't completed until 1931. Designed by French sculptor Paul Landowski (1875–1961), individual parts of the art deco monument were created separately and assembled upon their arrival in Rio.

The traditional way of reaching the Cristo is to take the Trem do Corcovado (Corcovado Train), which departs from the station on Rua Cosme Velho at 30-minute intervals. The ascent takes 17 minutes and includes a stop at Paineiras station, where you can get off and walk around, admiring the Tijuca Forest and the views. For the best vantage points while on the train, fight for a space at the back or at the right-hand side. You can also travel by taxi or car to Paineiras station, where certified vans offer transportation to the top, or you can choose to walk or take an elevator or escalator. Keep your eye on the weather; it might be best to delay a visit if it's overcast or rainy, as visibility will be poor.

Two minutes by foot from the Corcovado train station, at the base of the mountain, the **Museu Internacional de Arte Naïf** is home to the world's largest single

Corcovado
- ▲ IBC C3

Cristo Redentor
- ▲ 56 C1 & IBC C3
- ✉ Rua Cosme Velho 513 (train station), Cosme Velho
- ☎ 21/2558 1329
- 💲 $$$$ (train & adm.)
- 🚇 Metrô: Largo do Machado; Bus: 422, 498, integrated bus 580

www.corcovado .com.br

Museu Internacional de Arte Naïf
- ✉ Rua Cosme Velho 561, Cosme Velho
- ☎ 21/2205 8612
- 🕐 Closed Mon.
- 💲 $$
- 🚇 Metrô: Largo do Machado; Bus: 422, 498, integrated bus 580

EXPERIENCE:
Scaling Sugarloaf

In addition to walking to—and on top of—Sugarloaf (Pão de Açúcar), it's possible to walk around it, following the 1.5-mile (2.5 km) **Pista Claudio Coutinho,** an easy, paved trail. The route passes more difficult trails such as **Bem-te-vi,** which those spry of limb follow to Morro da Urca, and **Costão,** which rises to Pão de Açúcar and, because climbers ascend vertical rock, requires previous climbing experience. For guided outings as well as courses for beginners, contact **Climb in Rio** (tel 21/2245 1108, www.climbinrio.com) and **Companhia da Escalada** (tel 21/2567 7105, www.com panhiadaescalada.com.br), which also offer scaling experiences on more than 1,000 breathtaking routes throughout the city.

Botafogo
🅰 IBC D3

Fundação Casa de Rui Barbosa
✉ Rua São Clemente 134, Botafogo
☎ 21/3289 4600
🕐 Closed Mon. (museum)
💲 $ (museum), free Sun.
🚇 Metrô: Botafogo

Museu do Índio
✉ Rua das Palmeiras 55, Botafogo
☎ 21/3289 4600
🕐 Closed Mon.
💲 $, free Sun.
🚇 Metrô: Botafogo

Urca
🅰 IBC E3

collection of art naïf—defined as works created by artists with no formal training. Comprising 6,000 works, the vibrant ensemble offers an hour of delightful viewing. From the museum, continue up Rua Cosme Velho to **Largo do Boticário** (Rua Cosme Velho 822). Engulfed in jungly foliage, this charming square, framed by pastel-colored houses, resembles a 19th-century period movie set. The bucolic ambience is enhanced by the rushing of the Rio Carioca.

Botafogo

East of Corcovado, Botafogo's sweeping curve of a bay is as picturesque as it is polluted, but its tranquil side streets, stuffed with small museums, restaurants, and bars, offer a multifaceted taste of a traditional Carioca neighborhood.

For many tourists, Botafogo is the sprawling bairro they traverse en route to somewhere else, but this beach bairro is also one of Rio's most idyllic. The area closest to the waterfront is built-up and commercial, whereas inland, tree-lined streets are flanked by mansions that hint at the neighborhood's aristocratic past.

One of Botafogo's principal and grand avenues, **Rua São Clemente,** conserves a good number of stately mansions built by Rio's coffee barons, including the handsome mid-19th-century manor that houses the **Fundação Casa de Rui Barbosa.** The former residence of Rui Barbosa (1849–1923), an influential journalist, statesman, and abolitionist, the gracious bedrooms, ballrooms, and salons are immaculately preserved.

Farther west along São Clemente is the neighborhood of **Santa Marta.** Once one of Rio's most dangerous favelas, it was the first to receive its own Pacification Police Unit in 2008 and a *plano inclinado* (elevator) to shuttle residents up and down the steep hill. At the top, a lookout point affords magnificent vistas. A short walk through twisting alleyways brings you to an open plaza known as **Espaço Michael Jackson.** Here is where "the Gloved One" filmed the video to his controversial 1995 hit "They Don't Care About Us."

Back down on Rua São Clemente, across the street from Praça Corumbá, the **Museu do Índio** houses a modest but compelling ensemble of indigenous artifacts on display. Particularly noteworthy are the exquisite headdresses fashioned from the jewel-hued feathers of Amazonian toucans and parrots.

Urca

On March 1, 1565, Estácio de Sá landed at the tip of Urca and founded the tiny settlement of São Sebastião do Rio de Janeiro. It was only in the 1920s, however, that Urca began to emerge as a residential neighborhood. In the 1930s, the opening of the famous Cassino da Urca lured artists, celebrities, and bon vivants to the area and spurred the construction of villas and apartments, many in art deco and modernist styles.

Urca's most prominent feature is the 1,296-foot (395 m) block of granite known as **Pão de Açúcar** (Sugarloaf). Standing guard at the entrance to Guanabara Bay, this primitive sentry, cloaked in native Atlantic Forest, was called *pau-nh-acugua* (high pointed mountain) by Rio's original Tupi inhabitants. Both the Tupi term and the mountain itself reminded early Portuguese settlers of a *pão de açúcar,* a sugar loaf—a cone-shaped mound of sugar produced when cane juice is poured into a mold and solidifies. The name stuck—and today Sugarloaf is a symbol of Rio de Janeiro that is instantly recognizable around the world.

Sugarloaf actually consists of two twin hilltops: Morro da Urca and Morro Pão de Açúcar. Both can be visited by taking the cable car that departs from beside Praia Vermelha beach. Inaugurated in 1912, the cutting-edge *bonde* was the first cable car in Brazil and only the third in the world. Arrive a couple of hours before the sun descends behind the mountains and the city lights start to twinkle. If you want to interact with nature (see sidebar opposite), it's possible to follow steep, but short trails from Praça General Tibúrcio up to Morro da Urca (from where you can purchase a ticket to Morro Pão de Açúcar at reduced fare). ■

Pão de Açúcar

🅜 56 C1

✉ Av. Pasteur 520

☎ 21/2546 8400

💲 $$$$$ (cable car)

🚇 Metrô:
   Botafogo; Bus:
   511, 512, 513

www.bondinho .com.br

More than 50 climbing routes snake up Pão de Açúcar.

Zona Sul Beaches

Zona Sul's legendary beaches of Copacabana, Ipanema, and Leblon are what most people conjure up when they think of Rio. Long and languorous, they are the source of a compelling beach culture that radiates throughout these neighborhoods, casting a spell that is cool, carefree, and quintessentially Carioca.

Copacabana

△ IBC D2

Visitor Information

✉ Av. Princesa Isabel 183

Copacabana

Of the Zona Sul neighborhoods Copacabana is the largest, not to mention the most lively and socioeconomically diverse. Its majestic 2.5-mile (4 km) curvaceous crescent of a beach—which includes the 0.6-mile (1 km) expanse of Leme—is astonishingly full of life from dawn to dusk. However, it's worth exploring the rest of this compelling *bairro,* with its wealth of art deco architecture that in so many ways captures the essence of Rio de Janeiro. Despite its dissipated mid-20th century glamour, unpretentious Copa still seduces.

Leme: At Copacabana's north end, Leme's short, palm-lined stretch of beach is a favorite of local families due to its warm (and generally clean) waters. Beneath the looming rock known as Pedra do Leme, high waves lure surfers and a short trail leads partway around the hill's base. At the summit sits the **Forte Duque de Caxias.** Built in 1779, this fortress—and the Morro do Leme, a designated nature reserve—can be reached via a steep 25-minute ascent through tropical foliage. The views from the fort are terrific.

The adjacent hilltop of **Morro da Babilônia** is occupied by two of Rio's oldest favelas, Babilônia and Chapéu Mangueira. In 1959, Morro da Babilônia earned international renown for serving as the backdrop for a Carioca retelling of the myth of Orpheus

Afternoon shadows on Copacabana beach

INSIDER TIP:

Having breakfast at the Forte de Copacabana is an experience that opens your mind to a fantastic day at the beach.

—ARTURO SANCHEZ-AZOFEIFA

National Geographic grantee

in Marcel Camus's celebrated film *Black Orpheus*. Since 2009, both communities have received UPP forces (pacifying police forces), making security far less of an issue for the intrepid travelers who often venture up the hill to join the regular stream of residents, cab drivers, and cops who swear by the celebrated cooking at **Bar do David** *(Ladeira Ary Barroso 66, tel 21/7808 2200, closed Mon.).*

Praia de Copacabana:

Copacabana is one of the most instantly recognizable and splendid urban beaches on the planet, where Cariocas and tourists soak up the sun in rented beach chairs. Separating the sand from Avenida Atlântica is the iconic black-and-white mosaic *calçadão* (big sidewalk), designed by Roberto Burle Marx in the 1970s. Resembling a psychedelic sea of white (limestone) and black (basalt) waves, this boardwalk constitutes the world's biggest public mosaic. Cariocas are fond of walking and jogging along the calçadão and of hanging out at the many *quiosque* (kiosk) bars.

Copacabana beach was virtually deserted when the **Copacabana Palace** hotel (see Travelwise p. 282) opened its doors in 1923. International fame arrived a decade later, when it was featured in the 1933 film *Flying Down to Rio*. The glossy Hollywood musical not only catapulted Fred Astaire and Ginger Rogers to stardom, but also put Rio on the map as a romantic and glamorous destination. Over subsequent decades, moguls and movie stars, presidents and princesses have all checked in here.

The tip of Copacabana beach closest to Ipanema is guarded by the **Forte de Copacabana.** Built

Leme
- 🅰 IBC E2

Forte Duque de Caxias
- ✉ Praça Almirante Júlio de Noronha
- ☎ 21/3223 5076
- 🕐 Closed Mon.
- 💲 $
- Ⓜ Metrô: Cardeal Arcoverde

Praia de Copacabana
- 🅰 IBC D2

Forte de Copacabana
- ✉ Av. Atlântica, Posto 6
- ☎ 21/2521 1032
- 🕐 Closed Mon.
- 💲 $
- Ⓜ Metrô: Ipanema/ Gen. Osório or Cantagalo

Reveling in Réveillon

Praia de Copacabana is the stage of one of the biggest New Year's Eve (Réveillon) blowouts on the planet. As dusk falls, millions descend on the beach clad in white, symbolizing peace and new beginnings. White is also the color of Iemenjá, the popular Afro-Brazilian *orixá* (deity) known as the Queen of the Seas. To ensure a happy year, at the stroke of midnight, many Cariocas wade into the Atlantic and toss perfume, champagne, and flowers into the waves as offerings to Iemanjá. White gladioli are the most popular flowers, but those hoping for riches opt for yellow, while the lovelorn invest in red. Midnight also heralds a spectacular fireworks display and live music performances. After dancing and drinking until dawn, revelers rinse off the night's excesses with a dip in the sea.

Ipanema
🅰 IBC C1

in 1914, this fortress is occupied by the Museu Histórico do Exército, where a permanent exhibition provides some insights into the workings of a military fortress.

Ipanema

Idyllically situated between the open Atlantic and the Lagoa Rodrigo de Freitas, Ipanema encapsulates a highly seductive form of Carioca living—whiling away mornings on the beaches, afternoons in chic boutiques, and evenings at stylishly casual restaurants and bars.

music. Fringed by palm trees, framed by the gleaming hotels and residences that line Avenida Vieira Souto, and bookended by Pedra de Arpoador and Morro Dois Irmãos, it is an arresting sight.

At Ipanema's eastern extremity is **Praia do Arpoador,** a narrow 500-yard (500 m) strip of sand that is a mecca for surfers. To see the action, join the fishermen, lovers, favela kids, and other habitués who gather along the rocky promontory of Pedra do Arpoador to admire the sweeping views and ritually applaud summer sunset.

In the summer, crowds gather at Pedra do Arpoador to watch the sunset.

"Tall and tan and young and lovely"—these are the opening lyrics to the bossa nova classic "The Girl from Ipanema," but they also aptly describe the eternally sun-drenched, laid-back hedonists who frequent the beach bairro of the same name. It's not surprising that Ipanema beach is the source of so many myths and so much

Ipanema is punctuated by lifeguard *postos*, around which very different clans traditionally congregate. After Posto 7 at Arpoador's extremity, Posto 8 lures parents with small children and their nannies. Posto 9 remains the most famous spot among the beautiful Carioca youth. The area to the left of Posto 9, at the foot of Rua

Farme de Amoedo, is a magnet for gays, lesbians, and *simpatisantes* (sympathizers); the portion to the right draws an alternative crowd of students, artists, and neo-hippies that gathers round the Coqueirão (big coconut palm—actually the tallest on Ipanema). The beach also has its share of kiosks serving snacks and drinks and a **mosaic calçadão** designed by Burle Marx.

Two blocks back from the beach and parallel to Avenida Vieira Souto, **Avenida Visconde de Pirajá** is Ipanema's main commercial thoroughfare. It's lined with banks, bookstores, juice bars, chic boutiques, and *galerias*—micromalls sheltering hundreds of other chic boutiques. At the beginning of Avenida Visconde de Pirajá lies **Praça General Osório.** On Sundays, since the 1960s, the square has hosted the **Feira Hippie,** where vendors hawk a colorful but ragtag collection of handicrafts and souvenirs.

A block behind Praça General Osório, Morro de Cantagalo is home to the communities of Cantagalo and Pavão-Pavãozinho. These favelas were controlled by gangs and traffickers prior to the installation of a UPP station in 2009. Several months later, the **Complexo Rubem Braga** was inaugurated; its twin towers contain elevators that whisk residents between their hilltop homes and the Ipanema/General Osório Metrô station. This settlement can often feel spookily empty late in the day, even for locals, so it's best to visit earlier in the day. Tourists can also hop the free elevators, which ascend to the **Mirante da**

Beach Banquet

Reigning over the sands of the Zona Sul beaches are *barracas* (stands), whose employees rent chairs and umbrellas to loyal customers and keep them supplied with chilled beers, caipirinhas, and *água de coco*. Picking up any slack are legions of *ambulantes,* itinerant vendors who hawk everything from henna tattoos and transistor radios to *comidinhas* (little meals). Among the edible offerings are Globo's *biscoitos de polvilho,* crunchy, light-as-air cookies made of manioc flour, and Mustafá's *esfihas,* delicious meat and cheese stuffed Middle Eastern pastries, sold by a crew dressed up as sheiks. Wash these delicacies down with *cha-maté,* a chilled version of the traditional *gaúcho* beverage made from the leaves of the *erva-mate* plant.

Paz, a glassed-in lookout with mesmerizing 360-degree views.

Leblon

Separated from Ipanema by the Jardim de Alah canal, the bairro of Leblon is a little more chic, staid, and residential than Ipanema. Although lovely, its narrow beach is less popular than those of Copa and Ipanema. Its sands and shady streets tend to draw more locals, as do its sophisticated yet laid-back bars, boutiques, and delicatessens. It is home to some of the city's most innovative restaurants.

Leblon developed more gradually than Ipanema. Even today, its main commercial street, Avenida Ataulfo de Paiva, and side streets retain the feel of a village (albeit an upscale one) where local bakeries, cafés, delis, and *botecos* are interspersed between houses and low-slung apartment buildings. ∎

Leblon
🔼 IBC B1

Lagoa Rodrigo de Freitas, Jardim Botânico, & Gávea

The park-lined shores of Lagoa Rodrigo de Freitas offer a limitless number of sporting, leisure, and cultural activities amid a natural setting that encompasses Jardim Botânico along with the city's most iconic, rain-forest cloaked peaks.

Lago Rodrigo de Freitas
🅰 IBC C2

Fundação Eva Klabin
✉ Av. Epitácio Pessoa 2480, Lagoa
☎ 21/3202 8550
🕐 Closed Sat.–Mon.
🚇 Metrô: Cantagalo

Lagoa Rodrigo de Freitas

A saltwater lagoon, Lagoa Rodrigo de Freitas is connected to the Atlantic by the canal bisecting the Jardim de Alah, a narrow strip of land that separates Ipanema from Leblon. One of Rio's most attractive and popular playgrounds, the Lagoa's shoreline is ringed with verdant parks and sprinkled with piers, sports courts, private clubs, and pathways along which already toned and tanned Cariocas walk, jog, and cycle. To relax, they chill out at the numerous waterfront *quiosques*, with menus that range from simple to sophisticated.

Contrasting with the luxury high-rises that encircle the Lagoa is the early 1930s Norman-style villa of Eva Klabin (1903–1991). An heiress, she channeled her energies (and considerable fortune) into amassing a fantastic collection of fine art spanning five centuries and four continents. Today, the **Fundação Eva Klabin** operates as a museum; its treasure-laden rooms can be visited by guided tour.

A ten-minute walk north from the Klabin abode is the **Parque da Catacumba** (*Av. Epitácio Pessoa 3000, tel 21/2247 9949, closed Mon., $$$$–$$$$$ for activities, Bus: 157, 461*). Its upper reaches are covered with native vegetation, and the lower swatches are home to a sculpture garden. A 20-minute trail climbs to a lookout with spectacular views. Those seeking a shot of adrenaline can take advantage of the park's zip-lining circuits.

Jardim Botânico

Straddling the Lagoa's western shore, the affluent *bairro* of Jardim Botânico sprang up around the

Alley of Imperial Palms at the Jardim Botânico

city's botanical gardens. Rio's Jardim Botânico is unique in that its 356 acres (144 ha) unite native tropical forest and some 10,000 carefully cultivated species in verdant harmony—a feat that has earned it UNESCO Biosphere Reserve status. Compelling attractions include the Amazonian Garden, the Sensory Garden, and the Orquidário, a hothouse that shelters more than 600 species of strangely beautiful orchids. Irresistible to kids are the carnivorous plants, the lagoon topped with coffee-table size *Vitória regias* (water lilies), and the Jardim dos Beija-Flores's shrubs that attract tiny, iridescent hummingbirds.

Only five minutes from the Jardim Botânico, **Parque Lage** is a Romantic-style garden replete with lakes, islands, bridges, and artificial grottoes carved out of Parque Nacional da Tijuca (Tijuca National Park; see sidebar this page). Serpentine paths wind through the tropical foliage, including an arduous 1.4-mile (2.2 km) trail that leads up to the outstretched arms of Cristo Redentor.

Gávea

Gávea is squeezed between Leblon, Jardim Botânico, and the favela of Rocinha. Its steep well-to-do slopes, encrusted with mansions, rise up to the twin peaks of Morro Dois Irmãos. Among them is the splendid modernist residence designed in 1951 by architect Olavo Redig de Campos (1906–1984) for Walter Moreira Salles (1912–2001). A cultured diplomat and banker, Salles lived here with his family until 1992, when the house was converted into a private cultural center. Apart from a rich archive of books, photos, and musical recordings, the **Instituto Moreira Salles** (IMS) hosts cultural events and engaging art exhibits. Regardless of what's on, the residence is highly worth visiting. Designed by Roberto Burle Marx, the gardens—which merge with the surrounding forest—make use of homegrown species such as heliconia and anthuriums.

Gávea's nerve center is **Praça Santos Dumont.** Fanning out from this lively square, the traditional bars of the area known as Baixo (Lower) Gávea are a perennial lure for Zona Sul youngbloods. Also facing the praça is the **Gávea Jockey Club** *(Praça Santos Dumont 31, 21/3534 9000, closed Tues.–Thurs., Bus: Gávea).* Built in 1926, it's surely one of the world's most scenic racetracks. ∎

Jardim Botânico
- 🅰 56 C1 & IBC B2
- ✉ Rua Jardim Botânico 1008 & 920
- ☎ 21/3874 1808
- 💲 $
- 🚌 Bus: 161, 162, 570, 584

Parque Lage
- ✉ Rua Jardim Botânico 414
- ☎ 21/3257 1800
- 🚌 Bus: 161, 162, 570, 584
- www.eavparquelage .rj.gov.br

Gávea
- 🅰 IBC A1

Instituto Moreira Salles
- ✉ Rua Marquês de São Vicente 476
- ☎ 21/3284 7400
- 🕐 Closed Mon.
- 🚌 Bus: 150, 178

EXPERIENCE:
Tijuca National Park

Jardim Botânico includes patches of the Floresta da Tijuca (Tijuca Forest). The largest urban forest on the planet, it consists of 9,600 jungly acres (3,900 ha), much of which lies within the boundaries of the Parque Nacional da Tijuca, the most visited national park in Brazil. You can easily spend a few hours—or days—scaling the heights of Pico da Tijuca, plunging into waterfalls, picnicking in glades, and marveling at the view below from countless lookout points. To explore the hundreds of trails that weave through the park, contact **Rio Hiking** *(tel 21/2552 9204, www.riohik ing.com.br)* or **Jungle Me** *(tel 21/4105 7533, www.jungleme.com.br).*

São Conrado, Barra, & Recreio

Upscale, compact, and residential, São Conrado can be quickly taken in en route from the Zona Sul to Barra and Recreio—sprawling modern suburbs. The favela of Rocinha, a couple of fascinating *casa*-museums, and the beaches of Barra, Prainha, and Grumari make the trip west worthwhile.

São Conrado

IBC A1

São Conrado is a neighborhood of stark visual and socioeconomic extremes where inhabitants of swank modern high-rise apartments themselves gaze up at residents of Rocinha, whose cubist cluster of houses cover the Morro Dois Irmãos. São Conrado's beach attracts well-to-do residents along with kids from adjacent Rocinha; surfers are lured by the enormous waves. The far end of the beach, known as Praia do Pepino, is the landing spot for the daredevils who come hang gliding back down to Earth from Pedra Bonita.

The face of the New Rio, **Barra da Tijuca** is cluttered with megamalls, condo complexes, and hordes of vehicles whizzing up the main freeway-like arteries. Cars rule, but the beach is well served by buses from the Zona Sul.

The sweeping sands of **Praia da Barra** are cleaner than the sand at the Zona Sul's beaches, and it is never as crowded. The first 4 miles (6 km) are the most urbanized, with tons of kiosks for eating, drinking, and checking out the locals. The beginning—a perennially hip 1-mile (1.6 km) stretch known as **Praia do Pepê**—is a magnet for surfers, soccer players, and minor soap-opera stars. The entire length of Barra is beloved by surfers, windsurfers, and kite surfers.

A continuation of Barra, **Praia do Recreio** also beckons surfers, as does neighboring **Praia da Macumba.** From Recreio, the scenic Avenida Estado da Guanabara leads to Rio's wildest and most primitive beaches: **Prainha** and **Grumari.** Their unspoiled aspect

Kite surfers flock to Praia do Pepê.

EXPERIENCE: Appreciating the Favelas

Since 2010, the ousting of drug lords and implantation of permanent peacekeeping police (UPP) has encouraged a growth in "favela tourism." This phenomenon is not new. In existence for two decades is the pioneering **Favela Tours** *(tel 71/3322 2727, www.favelatour.com.br)*, which ferries small groups to Rocinha and Vila Canoas. According to founder Marcelo Armstrong, residents appreciate foreigners who want to see that there's more to their life than the clichés of poverty, drugs, and violence. **Favela Adventures** *(tel 21/8221 5572, www.favelatour.org)* offers a more personalized option. On these "adventures," outsiders accompany local guides as they drop by the homes of friends, neighbors, and *figuras* (neighborhood characters) in addition to bars, restaurants, and samba *festas*.

INSIDER TIP:

If you want to try tandem hang gliding, São Conrado is the place for you. Go early in the morning and avoid the afternoon's traffic jam.

—LUIZ RENATO MALCHER
Manager, Rio de Janeiro Urban Adventures

is guaranteed by their remoteness (only Prainha can be reached by bus; a taxi is needed for Grumari) and by their location within environmentally protected areas.

Casa do Pontal & Sítio Roberto Burle Marx

In the late 1940s, French art collector Jacques Van de Beuque began crossing Brazil and was amazed to encounter a rich folk-art tradition that seemingly nobody—not even Brazilians—knew existed. With the aim of preserving and promoting these neglected treasures, Van de Beuque constructed the **Casa do Pontal**

behind Praia do Recreio. Today, the more than 8,000 works created by more than 200 artists (many from the culturally rich Northeast) constitute the largest ensemble of Brazilian *arte popular* in the country. Despite its remote location, this museum is a must-see—as is the **Sítio Roberto Burle Marx.**

The lush legacy of Roberto Burle Marx (1909–1994), who was one of Brazil's greatest artists and one of the world's most influential landscapers, lives on in his country estate—situated in Barra da Guaratiba. Burle Marx purchased the former banana plantation in 1949 and lived here from 1973 until his death. The main colonial house functions as a museum; Burle Marx's former atelier showcases his drawings, murals, and engravings along with his impressive collection of Brazilian folk art. Even more impressive are the intricately laid-out gardens, in which multiple textures and gradations of green are combined to create living, growing tapestries comprising more than 3,500 tropical and semitropical species from all over Brazil and the world. ∎

Casa do Pontal
- 56 B1
- ✉ Estr. do Pontal 3295, Recreio
- ☎ 21/2490 3278
- 💲 $$
- 🕐 Closed Mon.
- 🚌 Bus: 703, S-20

**www.museucasa
dopontal.com.br**

Sítio Roberto Burle Marx
- 56 B1
- ✉ Estrada Roberto Burle 2019, Barra
- ☎ 21/2410 1412
- 🕐 Closed Sun.–Mon. (reserve guided tours in advance)
- 💲 $$
- 🚌 Bus: 387

Farther Afield

Cariocas know how to escape the city proper and enjoy the good life—whether they are across the bay from Rio in Niterói, visiting the mountain retreat of Petrópolis, savoring the beaches of Búzios and Ilha Grande, or surrendering to the charm of historic Paraty.

Oscar Niemeyer's Museu de Arte Contemporânea (MAC) overlooks Guanabara Bay.

Niterói

📍 56 C1

Museu de Arte Contemporânea

📍 56 C1
✉️ Mirante da Boa Viagem
☎️ 21/2620 2481
🕐 Closed Mon.
💲 $, free Wed.
🚌 Bus: 47B (from Estação das Barcas)

Niterói

Many Cariocas joke that the best thing about Niterói is its stunning view of Rio from the other side of Guanabara Bay. However, Rio's sister city possesses a handful of interesting attractions, including the largest collection of Oscar Niemeyer–designed buildings outside of Brasília, one of Brazil's oldest ensemble of colonial fortifications, and some alluring beaches.

Niterói is easily reached by bus or boat. Buses cross the Ponte Rio-Niterói, one of the longest bridges in the world; boats depart from Rio's Estação das Barcas (*Praça XV de Novembro, tel 0800/721 1012,*

Metrô: Carioca) at 15- to 30-minute intervals, docking at either the Estação das Barcas at Praça Arariboia in the center of town or the Estação Hidroviária at Charitas.

Niterói's most compelling attraction is the **Museu de Arte Contemporânea** (MAC), a futuristic structure perched on a cliff overlooking the bay that only Oscar Niemeyer could have dreamed up. The museum has minimal space to mount exhibitions of contemporary Brazilian art, which often take a backseat to the spectacular views of Rio.

Completed in 1996, MAC was the first of many constructions

comprised by the waterfront **Caminho Niemeyer** (Niemeyer Route), which extends from the center of Niterói to Boa Viagem, where the museum is located. Due to lack of financing, however, the original project remains incomplete; some buildings stand unfinished. Among the more interesting structures are the Teatro Popular, Praça JK, the completed (but not yet inaugurated) Centro Petrobras de Cinema, and the Fundação Oscar Niemeyer. **Neltur,** the municipal tourist agency, offers 40-minute bilingual tours of the Caminho Niemeyer.

In 1555, when Rio's colonial destiny was still up for grabs, the French sent a convoy led by Nicolas Durand de Villegaignon to stake a claim to what they hoped would become a strategic outpost for a future French Antarctica. With the goal of defending the entrance to Guanabara Bay, Villegaignon improvised a makeshift fortification—**Fortaleza de Santa Cruz.** Only two years later, it was captured by the Portuguese, who subsequently erected the Fortaleza de Santa Cruz da Barra. In 1831, it was converted into a prison, complete with gallows and torture chambers. Today, 45-minute guided tours (in Portuguese only) take visitors past rows of cannon, prison cells, and a firing wall pockmarked with bullet holes. The easiest way to get to the fort is to take a 15-minute taxi ride to the beach neighborhood of Jururuba.

The urban beaches in and around the center of Niterói tend to be crowded and too polluted for swimming. Vaunting its own mosaic

walkway replete with walkers and joggers, lively **Icaraí** is Niterói's version of Ipanema and its prettiest beach on the bay. The beaches along the open Atlantic are more appealing. One of the most popular is **Camboinhas**—increasingly developed but stunning nonetheless—located 10 miles (16 km) from the center of town. Several miles farther along is the even more captivating **Itacoatiara.** Set amid the Serra da Tiririca nature reserve, its rugged

---

Buy Your Fish & Eat It Too

In Niterói, get your fresh fish at the traditional **Mercado São Pedro** (Rua Visconde do Rio Branco, tel 21/2719 2600, closed Mon.), near the Estação das Barcas. From tiled stalls, fishmongers sing the praises (and prices) of fresh squid, lobster, shark, and sardines. The quality is so unbeatable that many restaurateurs buy their daily provisions here. However, mere laypeople need only make their purchase and head upstairs to the second-floor *botecos* where, for a small fee, you can have your catch fried or grilled while you enjoy an icy beer.

---

swells make it a surfer's delight. Access to all beaches is easy; from the ferry terminal, board any bus bound for Itacoatiara, where you'll find no shortage of *barracas* serving cool drinks and freshly grilled fish.

Petrópolis

When Cariocas can't take the heat, they beat a quick retreat to Petrópolis. Located only 44 miles (71 km) from Rio, the imperial family's summer refuge offers deliciously cooler temperatures as well as plenty of fine food, fresh air, and mountain scenery.

Neltur

Visitor Information

- ✉ Kiosk, Estação das Barcas, Praça Arariboia
- ✉ Kiosk, MAC, Boa Viagem
- ☎ 0800/282 7755

Fortaleza de Santa Cruz

- ⓜ 56 C1
- ✉ Estrada General Eurico Gaspar Dutra, Jurujuba
- ☎ 21/3611 1209
- 🕒 Closed Mon.
- 💲 $

Petrópolis

- ⓜ 56 C2

NOTE: Rio's Rodoviária Novo, **Única Fácil** (tel 21/2263 8792) provides bus service to Petrópolis.

Museu Imperial
- ✉ Rua da Imperatriz 220
- ☎ 24/2245 5550
- ⊘ Closed Mon.
- 💲 $$

Catedral de São Pedro de Alcântara
- ✉ Rua São Pedro de Alcântara 60
- ☎ 24/2242 4300

Palácio de Cristal
- ✉ Rua Alfredo Pacha
- ☎ 24/2247 3721
- ⊘ Closed Mon.

Back in the mid-1800s, when things got too hot (literally), Pedro II took to the fresher climes of the Serra do Mar mountain range, where he built a lavish pink summer palace and founded the town of Petrópolis in 1843. Counts and barons followed suit, constructing elegant mansions along bucolic canal-lined streets; immigrants from Germany, Austria, and Switzerland built Alpine-style chalets and opened breweries and delicatessens. Today this pretty historic town, with its Bohemian airs and architecture, remains a favorite weekend refuge for Cariocas.

Pedro II, Empress Teresa Cristina, and their two daughters, Isabel and Leopoldina, summered at the neoclassical Palácio Imperial. In 1943, it was transformed into the **Museu Imperial**, and now conjures up the life of the imperial family during Pedro II's impressively long reign (1840–1889). Among the most dazzling highlights on display are Pedro I's golden scepter and Pedro II's majestic crown—encrusted with 639 diamonds and 77 pearls—which he wore upon his coronation at the tender age of 15.

Around the corner and a block down from the museum, the imposing **Catedral de São Pedro de Alcântara** mingles French and German Gothic influences. Wrought out of marble, bronze, and onyx, the Imperial Mausoleum houses the remains of Pedro II, Teresa Cristina, Princesa Isabel, and her French husband, the Conde d'Eu.

Nearby, the delicate glass **Palácio de Cristal,** with its vertebrae of iron, was a gift to Princesa Isabel from her husband. Custom-built in France, it was transported across the Atlantic in pieces before being assembled on site in 1884.

According to Brazilians, the first person to fly in an airplane wasn't a Wright brother, but Alberto Santos Dumont (1873–1932). Santos Dumont became a national hero in 1906 upon completing the first unassisted flight in a fixed-wing aircraft of his own design and construction. This eccentric character

---

EXPERIENCE: Trekking in the Serra do Órgãos

Between Petrópolis and nearby Teresópolis, 36 miles (58 km) to the east, lies Parque Nacional da Serra dos Órgãos. Within this national park are 30,000 acres (12,000 ha) of Atlantic Forest threaded with trails that lead through a bizarrely shaped mountain range. Portuguese explorers noted its resemblance to a church pipe organ (hence the name Serra dos Orgãos). Rising 5,550 feet (1,692 m) above sea level, the equally aptly named Dedo de Deus (Finger of God) is the best known of all the peaks. The park's trails range from easy 30-minute strolls to the challenging but spectacular three-day, 26-mile (42 km) journey from Petrópolis to Teresópolis. **Trekking Petrópolis** *(tel 24/2235 7607, www.rioserra.com.br/ trekking)* organizes hiking, rappelling, and canyoneering excursions. The park's main entrance and headquarters are near **Teresópolis** *(Av. Rotariana, tel 21/2152 1100);* another entrance sits 10 miles (16 km) from Petrópolis's center on the Estrada União-Indústria.

Brazilian climber perched atop the Dedo de Deus (Finger of God)

was a passionate inventor whose many projects clutter the **Casa de Santos Dumont,** an Alpine-style chalet that he built on the slopes of Morro da Encantada.

Beyond the historic center, the Victorian-style **Casa da Ipiranga,** also known as the Casa de Petrópolis—and, among those critical of its asymmetrical facade, as the Casa de Sete Erros (House of Seven Errors)—was the home of José Tavares Guerra, a wealthy banker, industrialist, and abolitionist who created Brazil's first railroad (from Petrópolis to Rio). Guided tours are offered of the opulent interior with its walls hung in brocade, crystal chandeliers, and burnished jacaranda furniture.

Búzios

Búzios, poised upon the Costa do Sol, 105 miles (170 km) east of Rio, is one of Brazil's most internationally renowned beach resorts. It carries off the feat of being both utterly sophisticated and disarmingly casual with great flair.

Comparing Búzios to St.-Tropez is clichéd but surprisingly apt. This 5-mile (8 km) peninsula of

beckoning coves and rustic fishing settlements intrigued the jet set after its "discovery" by French actress Brigitte Bardot. Today, Búzios's limpid waters are sprinkled with yachts, and its cobblestone streets are lined with fashionable restaurants, boutique hotels, and plain old boutiques (selling international designer labels). Búzios attracts lots of pretty people and partiers (especially in the summer). Yet in off-season, its two dozen beaches and quasi-Mediterranean charms cast a seductive spell.

The peninsula of Búzios contains three main settlements. Nearest to the mainland, **Manguinhos** is the most urbanized and commercial. **Armação de Búzios** is the historic, touristic, and hedonistic center of Búzios. Many of the most fashionable boutiques, galleries, restaurants, hotels, and nightspots are located here, clustered on and around the main cobblestone drag of Rua das Pedras. Its picturesque seaside extension, baptized the Orla Bardot, winds along the waterfront. It's a 20-minute walk to the pretty fishing village of **Ossos.**

Casa de Santos Dumont
- ✉ Rua do Encanto 22
- ☎ 24/2247 5222
- ⌚ Closed Mon.
- 💲 $

Casa da Ipiranga
- ✉ Av. Ipiranga 716
- ☎ 24/2231 8718
- ⌚ Closed Tues.
- 💲 $$

Búzios
- ✉ 57 E1

Visitor Information
- ✉ Praça Santos Dumont, Armação
- ☎ 22/2623 2099
- **www.buziosonline.com.br**

NOTE: Viação 1001 (21/4004 5001, www.autoviacao1001.com.br) operates daily buses from Rio's Rodoviária Novo.

Ilha Grande

✉ 56 A1-B1

Visitor Information

✉ Ferry Dock

☎ 24/9922 9614

NOTE: Viação Costa Verde (tel 21/3622 3123) offers hourly bus service bet. Rio and Angra. If you're driving from Rio, follow the BR-101 south. The journey takes 2.5–3 hours.

Independent of Búzios's sophisticated trappings, it's impossible not to succumb to the lure of its beaches. On the north coast, **Praia de Manguinhos** and **Praia Rasa** lure sailors, windsurfers, and families. Traveling toward Armação, you'll be close to **Praia dos Amores, Praia das Virgens,** and **Praia da Tartaruga**—secluded beaches framed by lush foliage.

Armação's pretty beaches are really too polluted for bathing. Watched over by the 18th-century Igreja de Sant'Ana, the sugary sands of **Praia dos Ossos** beckon, but its calm seas are littered with boats. A five-minute walk brings you to the small, bewitching twin beaches of **Azeda** and **Azedinha.**

The Bardot Factor

In 1964, at the height of her fame, French actress Brigitte Bardot accompanied her Brazilian boyfriend for a two-month get-away to Búzios. The bucolic little fishing village was completely off the grid—until the international paparazzi got wind of their whereabouts and followed, hoping to capture the sultry starlet in a bikini. The stylish seaside walkway that bears her name—the Orla Bardot—is home to a bronze likeness of the actress (ca 1965) as she contemplates the colorful fishing boats.

From Ossos, another hilly road leads to **João Fernandes** and **João Fernandinho,** favorites of visiting Argentineans.

The extreme eastern tip of the peninsula hides some of the most remote and wildly windswept of Búzios's beaches. **Praia Brava** is the most surprising—with rose-colored sand backed by rugged cliffs. Smaller but equally enticing are **Praia Olho de Boi,** a tiny cove haunted by nudists, **Praia do Forno,** and **Praia da Foca,** whose transparent blue pools are framed by rocks sprouting sculptural cacti.

On the south side of the peninsula, the semicircular bay at **Praia da Ferradura** (Horseshoe Beach) is surrounded by mansions, condos, *pousadas* (guesthouses), and bars. Its wide beach and sheltered waters are ideal for families and sailing, kayaking, and windsurfing aficionados. Bigger and more developed, **Praia de Geribá** is popular with serious *surfistas* and young party animals. Toward the mainland is a trio of practically deserted beaches, **Praia dos Tucuns, Praia José Gonçalves,** and **Praia das Caravelas,** all of which compensate for their scant infrastructure with impressively rugged natural surroundings.

Want a break from walking? You can access most of Búzios's beaches by bus, taxi, rented buggy, or by sea. Daily schooner, catamaran, and speedboat excursions depart from Armação pier. If you don't appreciate crowded boats (or unlimited caipirinhas), consider renting one of your own. With room for up to seven people, *taxis marítimas* shuttle to and from the northern peninsula beaches.

Ilha Grande

Only 100 miles (160 km) south of Rio is **Angra dos Reis** (Bay of the Kings), a shimmering green-blue bay whose aquatic kingdom embraces some 1,000 beaches and 300 islands. The largest of them all, Ilha Grande, also happens to be the most escape worthy.

Ilha Grande's splendid isolation has determined much of its history. During colonial times, French, Dutch, and English pirates hid out in its coves, waiting to ambush gold-laden Spanish ships. In the 19th century, the island was a hideout for illegal traders selling slaves to sugar and coffee plantations. It also contained a leper colony, not to mention two prisons. It wasn't until the second prison's 1994 demolition that Ilha Grande started attracting tourists. Its immaculately preserved forests and beaches, coupled with the blissful absence of all motorized vehicles, have made this a favored getaway of nature lovers.

Ilha Grande is an 80-minute boat ride from the mainland towns of Angra and Mangaratiba, from which CCR Barcas (tel 0800/721 1012) offers daily ferry service. Another alternative is to take a high-speed catamaran from Angra. Since there are no bank machines on Ilha Grande, it's best to stock up on cash before you travel.

Ferries from the mainland dock at the colonial fishing village of **Abraão.** The island's "capital" of 3,000, with its pastel-hued houses and cobblestone streets, can be easily overwhelmed by tourists. Most of the island's rustic pousadas, eateries, and excursion agencies are located here.

One of the easiest walks from town is the 20-minute route to **Lazareto.** Here you can wander amid the daunting vestiges of a late 19th-century infectious disease hospital that was transformed

into a prison, which operated until 1964. Behind the ruins looms a striking 26-arch aqueduct, built in 1833. For refreshment, plunge into the nearby waterfall or the calm sea waters of **Praia Preta.** From the aqueduct, a 90-minute trail leads through the rain forest to the **Cachoeira da Feiticeira,** a 50-foot-high (15 m) waterfall that cascades into pools. Due to poor signage, it's best to go with a guide.

INSIDER TIP:

Try *caldo de cana*—very sweet but very refreshing sugarcane juice—sold in open markets. Add a *pastel,* a Brazilian filled pastry, for a perfect snack.

—ADRIANA IZZO-ORTOLANO
National Geographic contributor

Ilha Grande's beaches—many of them preserved, primitive, and utterly paradisiacal—are its main attraction. You could spend weeks exploring them all. If your days are limited, focus on the best of the best, most of which are open Atlantic beaches concentrated along the island's southern coast.

An hour's walk south from Abraão brings you to **Praia Grande das Palmas,** a small fishing village whose palm-fringed beach is lined with rustic bars. Continue for another 45 minutes to **Praia dos Mangues,** surrounded by mangroves. Only 20 minutes more separate you from the island's most worshipped

EXPERIENCE:
Going for the Gold

There is no shortage of hiking trails that weave up and down the jungly coastline and into the mountains of the **Serra da Bocaina.** A fascinating walk follows a small 1.5-mile (2.5 km) stretch of the historic **Caminho do Ouro**—a 746-mile (1,200 km) trail by which gold from Minas Gerais was transported to Paraty. A feat of engineering by the slaves who paved the mountainous route with irregular stones, the 90-minute trek can be undertaken with a guide from the **Centro de Informações Turísticas Caminho do Ouro** (*Estr. Paraty–Cunha, tel 24/3371 1222, closed Mon.–Tues., $$$*).

Paraty

🅰 56 A1

Visitor Information

✉ Av. Roberto Silveira 1

☎ 24/3371 3064

NOTE: Viação Costa Verde (tel 21/2233 3809) provides frequent bus service from Rio's Rodoviária Novo to Paraty. By car, follow the BR-101 south. The journey takes 3.5–4.5 hours.

Casa de Cultura

✉ Rua Dona Geralda 177

☎ 24/3371 2325

🕐 Closed Tues.

💲 $$

beach, **Praia Lopes Mendes,** regarded also as one of Brazil's top beaches. It's hard not to agree when faced with 2 miles (3 km) of firm white sand lapped by shimmery waves of jade and turquoise. The portion to the right is popular with surfers.

Other more remote beaches—accessible on foot or by boat—are also worth the effort. **Cachadaço** is a small gem nestled amid giant rocks and jungle; **Praia dos Dois Rios** is bracketed by two rivers. More remote, but equally captivating are **Praia da Parnaioca,** where the Rio Parnaioca forms a delicious lagoon with a small waterfall, and **Praia do Aventureiro,** located within a biological reserve.

The Baía da Ilha Grande is one of the best places in Brazil for both snorkeling and deep-sea diving, with more than 900 species of marine life and 15 sunken ships off the coast. **Elite Dive Center** (*tel 24/3361 5501*) offers lessons, equipment rental, and excursions.

Numerous hiking trails cut through the lush Atlantic forest that covers Ilha Grande. Among the most challenging but rewarding treks is the three-hour climb up to the summit of **Pico do Papagaio** (Parrot's Peak).

Paraty

Poised between green mountains and a diaphanous blue sea, Paraty is one of Brazil's most charismatic colonial towns. Its historic center, 160 miles (256 km) southwest of Rio, is filled with artists' ateliers, fine restaurants, and *cachaçarias* where you can sample the local produce.

Paraty's frequent comparison to a "colonial gem" is appropriate: In the late 17th century, the Portuguese needed a safe port from which to transport gold from neighboring Minas Gerais. Traders enlarged a trail that native Guaianá had carved through the Serra do Mar. Where the route encountered the sea, the founding stones of Paraty were laid. During the early 1700s, Paraty's remoteness made it difficult to defend from marauding pirates and bandits, so when a new gold route was built between Minas and Rio's port, it was abandoned—until the early 1970s, when the coastal highway linking Rio and Santos connected Paraty to the rest of the world.

Paraty's compact historic center lends itself to aimless wandering. The streets might be a challenge, however, because of the irregularly set stones. Although most of its white 18th- and 19th-century *sobrados* (mansions) are modest, one of the most striking is the **Casa**

da Cultura, built in 1758, now a cultural center with a permanent exhibit devoted to Paraty's history.

Paraty boasts a quartet of fetching churches, each of which reflects the communities that erected them. Built in 1800 on behalf of Paraty's wealthy doyennes, the **Igreja Nossa Senhora das Dores** was set where cooling breezes could reach local aristocrats during long services. More lavish is the **Igreja de Nossa Senhora dos Remédios,** where the city's bourgeoisie worshipped. Completed in 1725, the **Igreja de Nossa Senhora do Rosário** (aka Igreja da Matriz) is a simple church built by and for Paraty's slave population. Interestingly, it's the only church in town whose altars are covered with gold. The most photogenic is the **Igreja de Santa Rita dos Pardos Libertos,** built by freed slaves. Its lovely interior contains a small sacred art museum.

The beaches closest to Paraty aren't indicative of the paradisiacal options available farther afield. Every day, fleets of schooners, launches, and fishermen's boats offer tourists a small sampling of the 65 islands and 200 beaches located around the Bay of Paraty. **Paraty Tours** (*Av. Roberto Silveira 11, 24/3371 1327, www.paratytours .com.br*) organizes five-hour schooner trips, and you can also charter a boat from *barqueiros* at the quays.

Some of the region's most alluring and easily accessible beaches can be found at **Trindade,** a fishing village and former hippie haven. Only 16 miles (25 km) south of Paraty on the main Rio–Santos highway, it is served by local buses departing from Paraty's terminal. Another easily accessible beach is **Paraty-Mirim,** 11 miles (18 km) southwest of Paraty, that can be reached by municipal bus or driving along the BR-101. From here, it's only a quick 30-minute boat ride away from **Saco do Mamangua**—Brazil's only fjord. ■

Igreja Nossa Senhora das Dores
- ✉ Rua Fresca
- 🕐 Closed Mon.
- 💲 $

Igreja de Nossa Senhora dos Remédios
- ✉ Praça da Matriz
- 🕐 Closed Mon.
- 💲 $

Igreja de Nossa Senhora do Rosário
- ✉ Rua do Comércio
- 🕐 Closed Mon.

Igreja Santa Rita dos Pardos Libertos
- ✉ Largo de Santa Rita
- 🕐 Closed Mon.– Tues.

View of Paraty with Igreja de Santa Rita dos Pardos Libertos in foreground

A diverse region full of diversions both historic and modern, rural and urban, beach and forest

South-Central

The Octávio Frias de Oliveira Bridge over Rio Pinheiros in São Paulo illuminated at night

South-Central

The South-Central region is Brazil's richest, where services and infrastructure for travelers outshine those in the rest of the country. The locale offers a full gamut of attractions, from urban to rural and from radical to contemplative. There is much to explore in the area's history and heritage, including that of successive waves of immigrants.

This region's prosperity, relative to the rest of the country, reaches well back into history. In the early colonial period, São Vicente (roughly covering today's São Paulo state) was one of the Portuguese crown's only successful land grants, and Minas Gerais (literally "general mines") supplied mineral wealth. In the late 19th century, São Paulo state rode the coffee export boom to even greater riches. After the abolition of slavery, immigrants arrived, mostly from Europe but also from Japan, to supply extra labor. Industrialization drew domestic immigrants into the São Paulo metropolitan area. During the 20th century, the city's population surged again—from 250,000 to 10,000,000—sending ripples into the countryside. In the interior, agribusiness

expansion earned the region the nickname "the California of Brazil."

Paulistanos—as natives of the city are known (Paulistas are natives of the state)—like to compare São Paulo to New York City. São Paulo is home to more than its share of Brazil's best art galleries, museums, restaurants, and nightclubs, and certain districts stand as living monuments to immigrants' heritages.

The state is quite diverse. On holiday weekends, city residents descend on the state's beaches. Parque Nacional da Serra da Bocaina boasts many fascinating activities. The Vale do Ribeira is dotted by nature reserves, and PETAR, a state park, is Brazil's prime caving

NOT TO BE MISSED:

Street art at the Beco do Batman, in the city of São Paulo **109**

Scuba diving near, and hiking on, the island of Ilhabela **110–111**

Hiking and caving at the PETAR reserve **112–113**

Accessible adventures and activities in Socorro **115**

The world's biggest open-air art center in Minas Gerais **123**

Historic cities along the old gold trail, the Estrada Real **126–127**

Dramatic views of Pedra Azul in Domingos Martins **132**

region. The state's agricultural heartland to the west offers myriad activities and insights into the histories of coffee producers, cowboys, and immigrants. And the city of Socorro has proven itself a world leader in accessible tourism.

The main attractions in Minas Gerais are its historic mining towns. Foodies appreciate the state's home-style cooking, whereas readers

enjoy the homes of two literary giants: poet Carlos Drummond de Andrade and novelist João Guimarães Rosa. Minas Gerais also boasts the world's largest open-air contemporary art museum. Espírto Santo—surrounded by Rio de Janeiro, Minas Gerais, Bahia, and the ocean—has preserved large swaths of the Atlantic Forest and is especially popular with bird-watchers. ■

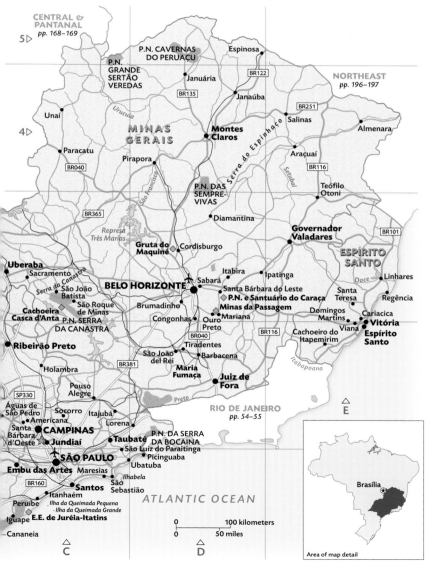

CENTRAL &
PANTANAL
pp. 168–169
5▷

P.N. CAVERNAS
DO PERUAÇU

Espinosa

P.N.
GRANDE
SERTÃO
VEREDAS

Januária

BR122

BR135

Janaúba

NORTHEAST
pp. 196–197

Unaí

Uruculu

MINAS
GERAIS

Montes
Claros

Salinas

BR251

Almenara

4▷

Paracatu

Piracatu

Pirapora

Araçuaí

BR116

BR040

Serra do Espinhaço

P.N. DAS
SEMPRE-
VIVAS

São Francisco

Sertubal

Teófilo
Otoni

BR365

Diamantina

Represa
Três Marias

Gruta do
Maquiné

Cordisburgo

Governador
Valadares

BR101

Uberaba

Sacramento

Itabira

Ipatinga

Doce

Linhares

ESPÍRITO
SANTO

Serra da Canastra

São João
Batista

BELO HORIZONTE

Sabará

Santa Bárbara do Leste

Santa
Teresa

Regência

Cachoeira
Casca d'Anta

São Roque
de Minas

P.N. SERRA
DA CANASTRA

Brumadinho

P.N. e Santuário do Caraça

Minas da Passagem

Domingos
Martins

Cariacica

Vitória

Congonhas

Ouro
Preto

Mariana

Viana

Espírito
Santo

Ribeirão Preto

BR040

Tiradentes

BR116

Cachoeiro do
Itapemirim

Holambra

São João
del Rei

Barbacena

BR381

Maria
Fumaça

Juiz de
Fora

Itabapoana

Pouso
Alegre

Preto

SP330

RIO DE JANEIRO
pp. 54–55

△
E

Águas de
São Pedro

Socorro

Itajubá

Santa
Bárbara
d'Oeste

Americana

Lorena

CAMPINAS

Taubaté

P.N. DA SERRA
DA BOCAINA

Jundiaí

São Luiz do Paraitinga

Picinguaba

SÃO PAULO

Ubatuba

Embu das Artes

Maresias

BR160

Ilhabela

Itanhaém

São
Sebastião

Santos

ATLANTIC OCEAN

Peruíbe

Ilha da Queimada Pequena
Ilha da Queimada Grande

Iguape

E.E. de Juréia-Itatins

Cananeia

△
C

△
D

Brasília
☆

0   100 kilometers
0   50 miles

Area of map detail

São Paulo City

Because São Paulo is by far Brazil's most important destination for business travelers, many international flights land here. Connections to the rest of the country are also better here than elsewhere. As a result, most visitors end up passing through São Paulo—a world-class city for nightlife, restaurants, galleries, and museums. If you have business or target attractions in the city, pick a conveniently located hotel, and use the Metrô to get around when possible.

São Paulo

🅜 99 C1

Visitor Information

✉ Airport: Departure areas of terminals 1 & 2

✉ República: Praça da República, Centro

✉ Mercado Municipal: Rua da Cantareira

www.cidadede saopaulo.com

Centro

For visitors with a sense of history and architecture, the Centro district offers a feast—one easily done on foot. São Paulo once had a unifying downtown, and it was here that Brazilian cultural history changed forever with the 1922 Modern Art Week (see p. 37) at the **Theatro Municipal de São Paulo** *(Praça Ramos de Azevedo, tel 11/3397 0300)*. Nearly six decades later, undaunted by military rule, a new generation of intellectuals would gather to the south at the

Italian restaurant **Gigetto** on Rua Avanhandava *(63, Bela Vista, tel 11/3256 6530)*. Patrons included sociologist Fernando Henrique Cardoso, later president, and comedian Jô Soares. **Avenida São João** appeared in popular songs: Paulo Vanzolini's "Ronda" (1953), Adoniran Barbosa's "Iracema" (1956), and Caetano Veloso's hymn "Sampa" (1978), which is set on the corner of Avenidas Ipiranga and São João.

The Centro drifted into disfavor as the 20th century drew to a

Bixiga

A compact neighborhood nestled between Avenida Paulista and the old city center, Bixiga is São Paulo's most accessible answer to Little Italy. Not that many people of Italian descent still live there, but a scattering of old cantinas remain—and of course there is the **Museu Memória do Bixiga** *(Rua dos Ingleses 118, Bela Vista, tel 11/3253 9338, www.museumemoriadobixiga .com)*. The district also boasts one of the city's most traditional samba schools, **Vai-Vai** *(Rua São Vicente 276, Bela Vista, tel 11/3266 2581)*; one of its oldest professional theaters, **Teatro Brasileiro de Comédia** *(Rua Major Diogo 311, Bela Vista, tel 11/3104 5523)*; and many bars.

As told by Armandinho do Bixiga—the late longtime curator, cofounder, and spirit behind the Bixiga museum who had a real surname but, like Brazilian soccer players,

never used it—the first cantinas were bring-your-own-food bars. Interminable card games determined who paid for drinks, and around 11 p.m. everybody unwrapped their sausage sandwiches (on Italian bread) and had a hearty snack.

The oldest remaining cantina was founded in 1907: **Capuano** *(Rua Conselheiro Carrão 416, Bela Vista, tel 11/3288 1460)*, the city's oldest public eatery of any kind.

Lined by theaters, Rua Rui Barbosa, nicknamed the "Broadway Paulista," drew intellectuals who spawned a bohemian ambience. Much of the sparkle is gone now, but you can still see a play or get a good Italian meal in the neighborhood.

Finally, don't let the maps fool you. Bixiga is part of an official municipal district called Bela Vista, but no city native would ever call it anything but Bixiga.

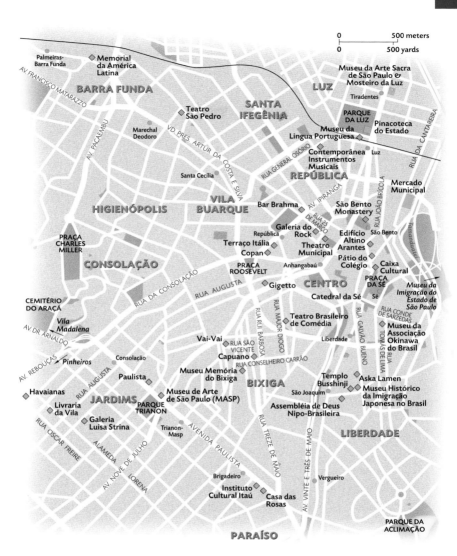

Palmeiras-Barra Funda
Memorial da América Latina
AV. FRANCISCO MATARAZZO
BARRA FUNDA
LUZ
Museu da Arte Sacra de São Paulo & Mosteiro da Luz
Tiradentes
SANTA IFEGÊNIA
Teatro São Pedro
PARQUE DA LUZ
Pinacoteca do Estado
Marechal Deodoro
AV. PACAEMBU
VD. PRES. ARTUR DA COSTA E SILVA
Museu da Língua Portuguesa
RUA DA CANTAREIRA
Santa Cecília
RUA GENERAL OSÓRIO
Contemporânea Instrumentos Musicais
Luz
REPÚBLICA
Mercado Municipal
HIGIENÓPOLIS
VILA BUARQUE
Bar Brahma
AV. IPIRANGA
RUA JOÃO BRICOLA
São Bento Monastery
PRAÇA CHARLES MILLER
República
Galeria do Rock
São Bento
Edifício Altino Arantes
São Bento
CONSOLAÇÃO
Terraço Itália
Theatro Municipal
Pátio do Colégio
Caixa Cultural
CEMITÉRIO DO ARAÇÁ
RUA DA CONSOLAÇÃO
Copan
PRAÇA ROOSEVELT
Anhangabaú
PRAÇA DA SÉ
Museu da Imigração do Estado de São Paulo
Vila Madalena
RUA AUGUSTA
Gigetto
CENTRO
Catedral da Sé
Sé
RUA CONDE DE SARZEDAS
AV. DR. ARNALDO
AV. REBOUÇAS
Pinheiros
RUA RUI BARBOSA
RUA MAJOR DIOGO
Teatro Brasileiro de Comédia
RUA GAIVÃO BUENO
Museu da Associação Okinawa do Brasil
Consolação
Vai-Vai
RUA SÃO VICENTE
Liberdade
RUA TOMÁS DE LIMA
Paulista
Capuano
RUA CONSELHEIRO CARRÃO
RUA AUGUSTA
Museu Memória do Bixiga
BIXIGA
Templo Busshinji
Aska Lamen
Havaianas
Museu de Arte de São Paulo (MASP)
São Joaquim
Museu Histórico da Imigração Japonesa no Brasil
Livraria da Vila
JARDIMS
PARQUE TRIANON
Assembléia de Deus Nipo-Brasileira
Galeria Luisa Strina
Trianon-Masp
RUA OSCAR FREIRE
ALAMEDA
AVENIDA PAULISTA
LIBERDADE
AV. NOVE DE JULHO
LORENA
RUA TREZE DE MAIO
AV. VINTE E TRÊS DE MAIO
Brigadeiro
Vergueiro
Instituto Cultural Itaú
Casa das Rosas
PARQUE DA ACLIMAÇÃO
PARAÍSO

0 — 500 meters
0 — 500 yards

close. The neighborhood dubbed "Crackolândia" pushed aside bohemian bars; and many company headquarters, hotels, and cafés closed. But today, the Centro is enjoying a revival, and establishments such as **Bar Brahma** (see Travelwise p. 288), at the intersection of Ipiranga and São João, are making a strong comeback. In a district nicknamed **Baixo Augusta,** surrounding Rua Augusta, new bars and nightclubs are crowding out streetwalkers. Hotels are cropping up or being renovated. Rua Avanhandava and the nearby Praça Roosevelt have received face-lifts.

Not far from the **Pátio do Colégio,** the city's founding place, the **São Bento Monastery** (Largo

The Catedral da Sé and the square before it have served as the epicenter of civic protests.

Embu das Artes
⚏ 99 C1

de São Bento, tel 11/3328 8799, Metrô: São Bento) and the **Catedral da Sé** (Praça da Sé, tel 11/3107 6832, www.catedraldase.org.br, Metrô: Sé) mark the presence of the Catholic Church. The square in front of the cathedral, **Praça da Sé,** has served as a stage for political demonstrations, notably a monumental 1984 anti-dictatorship rally for direct presidential elections.

In the financial district, north of Praça da Sé, take an elevator in the **Edifício Altino Arantes** (Rua João Brícola 24, tel 11/3249 7466, Metrô: São Bento), inspired by the Empire State Building and better known as the Banespa building, for an overwhelming bird's-eye view of the city. Or enjoy a similar view while dining or enjoying drinks on the top floor of a building a few blocks west at the **Terraço Itália** (Av. Ipiranga 344, República, tel 11/2189 2929, Metrô: República). Nearby is Oscar Niemeyer's **Copan** residential building (Av. Ipiranga 200, República, Metrô: República), with its towering, wavy facade.

Shopping: Shoppers will want to visit the teeming daily street

INSIDER TIP:

The weekend craft fair in Embu das Artes, just 19 miles (30 km) southwest of São Paulo, is great for a day of shopping and eating.

—RODRIGO NICOLETTE
Professor, University of São Paulo

fair on **Rua 25 de Março** (closed Sat. p.m.–Sun.), an oversize open-air shopping area that attracts bargain hunters. The **Mercado Municipal** (Rua da Cantareira 306, tel 11/3313 3365, www.mercadomunicipal.com.br), a bit farther afield on Rua da Cantareira, is a veritable emporium of food. Locals swear by the mortadella sandwich. There's also the **Galeria do Rock** (Rua 24 de Maio 62, República, www.galeriadorock.com.br, closed Sun.), a rock-and-roll shopping center and favorite hangout for rockers, skaters, tattoo artists, and sympathizers.

Music lovers should not miss the Saturday *choro* jam

session between 9 a.m. and 2 p.m. at the **Contemporânea Instrumentos Musicais,** to the north of the Galeria. A tradition since 1960, it has long attracted the likes of Elis Regina and Zeca Pagodinho during their visits to São Paulo.

Liberdade

Brazil has the highest concentration of people of Japanese descent outside of Japan. And São Paulo is the largest non-Nippon "Japanese" city in the world. For decades, Liberdade, located just south of Centro, was its Japantown. Japanese immigrants first took up in Liberdade in 1912. Their presence grew, and by 1967 the neighborhood received a landmark visit by Prince (and future emperor) Akihito.

After the Metrô arrived in 1973, local boosters erected the now emblematic "Suzuranto" streetlamps and required store owners to display names in Asian script. However, Asians who live in Liberdade now tend to be of Chinese or Korean descent.

Yet remnants of the Japanese immigrant world remain. Unlike many parts of São Paulo, Liberdade is easily explored on foot. Most people begin at the subway stop named after the neighborhood. On weekends from 8 a.m. to 6 p.m., this is the site of **Feira da Liberdade,** a popular crafts fair renowned for its Brazilian-style Asian street food. A short walk south grants a view of "São Paulo at its most massive and uncontrolled," as

(continued on p. 106)

Contemporânea Instrumentos Musicais
🅰 101
✉ Rua General Osório 46
☎ 11/3221 8477

Liberdade
🅰 101

Feira da Liberdade
✉ Praça da Liberdade
🕒 Closed Mon.– Fri.
🚇 Metrô: Liberdade

The Art World of São Paulo

Several very important galleries of Brazilian contemporary art are located throughout the city, and all hold regular exhibitions of leading contemporary Brazilian artists.

Galeria Luisa Strina *(Rua Padre João Manuel 755, Jardim Paulista, tel 11/3088 2471, www.galerialuisastrina.com.br, closed Sun.),* opened in 1974, is the grand dame, representing people like Marepe and Cildo Meireles. **Galeria Raquel Arnaud** *(Rua Fidalga 125, Pinheiros, tel 11/3083 6322, www.raquelarnaud.com, closed Sun.),* Strina's rival, was inaugurated in 1980 and represents artists such as Tunga and José Resende.

A child of the 1990s, **Galeria Fortes Vilaça** *(Rua Fradique Coutinho 1500, Pinheiros, tel 11/3032 7066, closed Sun.– Mon.)* represents Efrain Almeida and the street art twins dubbed Os Gêmeos. **Nara Roesler** *(Av. Europa 655, Jardim Europa, tel 11/3063 2344, www.nararoesler.com.br, closed Sun.)* was inaugurated in 1989 and represents artists like Karin Lambrecht and Laura Vinci.

Also in Jardim Europa, **Thomas Cohn** *(Av. Europa 641, tel 11/3083 3355, closed Sun.–Mon.),* a transplant from Rio de Janeiro that set up shop in 1997, focuses more on regional Latin American artists. Founded in 1997 and boasting a stable that includes Regina Silveira and Geraldo de Barros, is **Luciana Brito Galeria** *(Rua Gomes de Carvalho 842, Itaim Bibi, tel 11/3842 0634).* In 2012, renowned London gallery **White Cube** opened a São Paulo branch *(Rua Agostinho Rodrigues Filho 550, Vila Clementino, tel 11/4329 4474, whitecube.com, closed Sun.–Mon.).*

São Paulo by Metrô

Launched in 1974, São Paulo's Metrô ranks third in the world by number of daily users: four million. Nevertheless, it is limited for a city its size. Its midnight closing time (1 a.m. on Saturday) does not reflect São Paulo's vibrant nightlife, and the Metrô fails to serve airports, the "central park" Ibirapuera, major football stadiums, the Mercado Municipal, and other popular destinations. However, you can still enjoy a perfectly fine day of sightseeing by Metrô hopping—and the Metrô is great for people-watching.

Metrô Passes

A short-term Metrô pass, called *Bilhete Único Comum*, allows for one subway ride and three city bus rides (or four bus rides) in a three-hour window for a single fare. Passes can be purchased at Metrô stations, lottery outlets, newsstands, and many convenience stores known as *padarias*. (Padarias are bakeries, and, yes, they also sell fresh bread.) The minimum purchase is five trips, BRL 15 (US$7).

Line 1 Azul (Blue)
Villa Mariana Station

Born in Lithuania in 1891, Lasar Segall moved

to Brazil in 1923 and became one of the country's modernist pioneers. Following his death in 1957, his widow helped establish the **Museu Lasar Segall** (*Rua Berta 111, Vila Mariana, tel 11/2159 0400, www.museusegall.org.br, closed Tues.*) in the house where he lived and worked. Its collection includes more than 3,000 works.

Luz Station

The **Pinacoteca do Estado de São Paulo** (*Praça da Luz 2, Luz, tel 11/3324 1000, www.pinacoteca.org.br, closed Mon., $, Sat. free*) focuses on Brazilian art from the 19th century until today. Founded in 1905 by the state government, it is the city's oldest art museum. The building itself dates from the late 19th century, with original blueprints by Ramos de Azevedo and a major reform led by Paulo Mendes da Rocha a century later.

The **Parque da Luz** (*Rua Ribeiro de Lima 99, Praça da Luz, Luz*) is São Paulo's most elaborately landscaped park. At 28 acres (11 ha), its walkways are often populated by street musicians.

Opened in 1901, the **Estação da Luz** (*Praça da Luz 1, Luz, tel 0800/55 0121, www.cidadedesao paulo.com/sp/br/o-que-visitar/186-estacao-da-luz*)—which is an 80,730-square-foot (7,500 sq m) train station—features prefabricated cast-iron materials imported from England. It was a bustling center of activity during the first half of the 20th century. Opened more than a century later, in 2006, the **Museu da Língua Portuguesa** (*Praça da Luz, Centro, tel 11/3326 0775, closed Mon., $, Sat. free*) is an innovative museum of the Portuguese language. It is extremely popular with Brazilians.

Tours & Art

Turismetrô

On weekends, the Metrô runs a handful of guided tours of subway-accessible attractions. Sign-ups for all tours are at the central Sé station 20 minutes before the appointed hour. There is no additional fee—just a Metrô ticket. Guides are bilingual. The tour schedules are as follows: República, Sat. 9 a.m.; Sé, Sat. 2 p.m.; Luz, Sat. 2 p.m., Sun. 2 p.m.; Avenida Paulista, Sun. 9 a.m.

Metrô Art

If you get a chance, check out the panel at the República station by Antonio Peticov—**"Momento Antropofágico com Oswald de Andrade"**—and the large-scale exhibition of portraits of regular citizens by Alex Flemming at the Sumaré station.

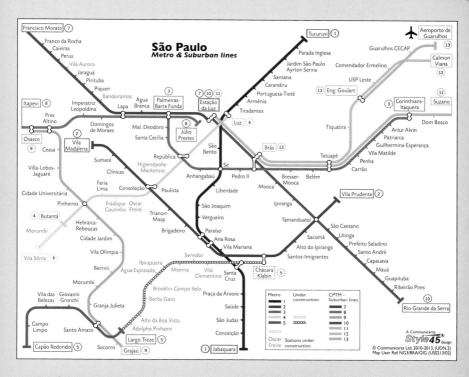

São Paulo
Metro & Suburban lines

Tiradentes Station

The **Museu de Arte Sacra de São Paulo** (*Av. Tiradentes 676, Luz, tel 11/3326 5393, closed Mon., $, Sat. free*), which makes its home in the **Mosteiro da Luz,** is one of Brazil's most important museums of Catholic religious art. Its collection was launched by Dom Duarte Leopoldo e Silva (1867–1938), São Paulo's first archbishop. As of 1907, it began pulling together images and artifacts from small chapels that were systematically demolished after the declaration of the republic in 1889.

Line 2 Verde (Green)
Santos–Imigrantes Station

The **Aquário de São Paulo** (São Paulo Aquarium; *Rua Huet Bacelar 407, Ipiranga, tel 11/2273 5500, www.aquariodesaopaulo.com.br, $$*), Latin America's only thematic aquarium, which opened in 2006, is also its biggest—with about 3,000 animals representing around 300 species.

Sumaré Station

At the **Centro da Cultura Judaica** (Jewish Cultural Center; *Rua Oscar Freire 2500, Sumaré, tel 11/3065 4333, closed Mon.*), visitors will find temporary exhibitions, music, theatrical performances, films, courses, and more.

Line 3 Vermelha (Red)
Palmeiras–Barra Funda Station

Designed by architect Oscar Niemeyer, the **Memorial da América Latina** cultural center (*Av. Auro Soares de Moura Andrade 664, Barra Funda, tel 11/3823 4600, closed Mon.*) features the art and culture of neighboring Latin American countries.

Marechal Deodoro Station

The **Theatro São Pedro** (*Rua Albuquerque Lins 207, Barra Funda, tel 11/3667 0499, www.theatrosaopedro.org.br, $–$$$$*), built in 1917 and renovated in 1998, has been dedicated exclusively to opera since 2006.

Museu da Associação Okinawa do Brasil

101

✉ Rua Tomás de Lima 72, 2nd fl., Liberdade

☎ 11/3106 8823

Aska Lamen

101

✉ Rua Galvão Bueno 466, Liberdade

☎ 11/3277 9682

🕐 Closed Mon.

Museu Histórico da Imigração Japonesa no Brasil

101

✉ Rua São Joaquim 381, 2nd fl.

☎ 11/3209 5465

🕐 Closed Mon.

Emory University historian Jeffrey Lesser puts it in "Um roteiro 'brasileiríssimo' pela bairro da Liberdade," from the Viaduto Guilherme de Almeida.

From there, it is about six blocks to **Rua Conde de Sarzedas,** a street overrun by a string of religious shops popularly known as the Evangelical Shopping Mall. But a century ago, it was where São Paulo's first Japanese immigrants settled. Some had arrived on the *Kasato Maru,* the first boat sent from Asia after a 1908 agreement between Japan and Brazil. The nearby **Museu da Associação Okinawa do Brasil** celebrates immigrants from that prefecture.

Then navigate south to Rua Galvão Bueno, on the other side of the highway, which sports one of the few remaining Japanese noodle joints in the area, **Aska Lamen.** From there, head toward the other end of the neighborhood. As you approach the São Joaquim Metrô stop, you will

find several gems. The Bunkyo, headquarters of the Brazilian Society of Japanese Culture and Social Assistance, houses the **Museu Histórico da Imigração Japonesa no Brasil** (Historical Museum of Japanese Immigration in Brazil), which presents the integration story. Emperor Akihito attended the building's inauguration in 1978.

Snatch a quiet moment at the **Templo Busshinji** (*Rua São Joaquim 285, tel 11/3208 4515, Metrô: São Joaquim*). Built by post–World

MASP ranks among Latin America's most impressive museums for modern and contemporary art.

War II Japanese immigrants, it is frequently open for meditation. Finally, you'll find that like many evangelical churches in Brazil, the **Assembléia de Deus Nipo-Brasileira** (*Rua São Joaquim 129*) occupies a former movie house; it was the Cine Tokyo, built in 1954 to specialize in Japanese films.

Paulista & Jardins

Everything happens along the 1.75 miles (2.8 km) of São Paulo's main drag, Avenida Paulista. When a local soccer team wins an important competition, fans converge on the street to commemorate—effectively blocking traffic for the interim. When activists wanted to protest the Belo Monte hydroelectric dam project in the Amazon, they marched on Paulista. And during the June 2013 protests—sparked by public transportation fare hikes—tens of thousands shut down this thoroughfare.

Cultural attractions line the street, with the epicenter at Brazil's most important art museum, the **Museu de Arte de São Paulo** (MASP). Just southeast of that is the **Instituto Cultural Itaú** (*Av. Paulista 149, Bela Vista, tel 11/2168 1777, closed Mon.*), an important cultural center that hosts sundry exhibits and events, and the **Casa das Rosas** (*Av. Paulista 37 Paraíso, tel 11/3285 6986, closed Mon.*), which occupies an old mansion and hosts art exhibitions. Across the street from the museum, **Parque Trianon,** an exuberant park, provides about the best

introduction possible to the Atlantic Forest within the confines of a concrete jungle.

Astride bustling Avenida Paulista, the Jardins neighborhood offers São Paulo's most fashionable shopping district—full of upscale boutiques, coffee

shops, and art galleries. Jardins (which means "gardens") is actually shorthand for four separate districts: Jardim Europa, Jardim Paulista, Jardim América, and Jardim Paulistano. As a whole, the region boasts more than a hundred top-notch restaurants, a couple hundred bars, and probably the highest concentration of hotels in the city. This is also prime residential real estate.

A must for shoppers, **Rua Oscar Freire** has been compared with Madison Avenue in New

---

Butantan Institute

Teddy Roosevelt might still be our best guide to Brazil. In *Through the Brazilian Wilderness,* **he writes that "On reaching São Paulo . . . we drove out to the 'Instituto Serum-thérapico,' designed for the study of the effects of the venom of poisonous Brazilian snakes. Its director is Doctor Vital Brazil, who has performed a most extraordinary work."**

That was 1913. A century later, you can visit the very same place—now called the Instituto Butantan (*Av. Vital Brasil 1500, Butantã, tel 11/2627 9300, closed Mon., $, Metrô: Butantã*) and set on a street named after the director who led Teddy around. Butantan remains one of the world's most important biomedical research institutions, and it is open to visitors, featuring a fascinating array of serpents.

Jockey Club de São Paulo

✉ Av. Lineu de Paula Machado 1263, Cidade Jardim

☎ 11/2161 8300

Paulista

🅰 101

Visitor Information

✉ Avenida Paulista 1853

Museu de Arte de São Paulo (MASP)

🅰 101

✉ Av. Paulista 1578, Bela Vista

☎ 11/3251 5644

🕐 Closed Mon.

💲 $, Tues. free

🚇 Metrô: Trianon-Masp

EXPERIENCE: Night Biking

Cycling in über-urban São Paulo would seem a severe challenge, with the city's ghastly air pollution and extreme traffic. And although city hall is extending its limited network of bike paths, it can be quite unpleasant to peddle around São Paulo. At night, when the cars are tucked away in their garages, lone cyclers often feel unsafe.

Enter night bike rides. Organized by dozens of diverse groups around the city, cycling excursions can be found on almost every night of the week. Starting around 9 p.m. and ending around midnight, these cover about 25 miles (40 km) at a rate of 9 to 11 mph (15–18 kmh). While the excursions are open to all comers, it is advisable to check first by email or telephone before simply showing up. (For instance, one group is for women only.) A cycling aficionado named Wadilson has compiled an excellent list of night-cycling options with contact details for each at his website (www.wde.com.br/bike/passeios.htm).

Visitors without bikes have two options. They can contact the organizers of their desired outing and (believe it or not) request a loaner—reports say that this works—or they can rent a vehicle from one of many outlets around the city. One interesting place is **Tag and Juice** (Rua Gonçalo Alonso 99, Vila Madalena, tel 11/2362 6888, closed Sun.–Mon.), a bike shop linked to the vibrant local graffiti community.

York and the Rue du Faubourg Saint-Honoré in Paris. A nine-block strip offers a gamut of upscale boutiques and shops including an outlet dedicated to Brazil's legendary **Havaianas** (Rua Oscar Freire 1116, Jardim Paulista, tel 11/3079 3415). These flip-flops are everybody's favorite gift, whether for themselves or their friends. This colorful shop—3,200 square feet (300 sq m) of nothing but flip-flops and accessories—was designed by the trending architect Isay Weinfeld.

Less than four blocks away, on the parallel street Alameda Lorena, you will find another Weinfeld creation, a whimsical branch of the **Livraria da Vila** (Alameda Lorena 1731, Jardim Paulista, tel 11/3062 1063) bookstore, which evokes the spirit of secondhand bookstores without looking out of place in an upscale shopping district.

Pinheiros & Vila Madalena

These adjacent neighborhoods, west of Jardins, enjoy a joint reputation as strongholds of São Paulo's bohemian culture. The real action is at night, when pubs and clubs light up, and on the weekends—especially at the vivacious Saturday street fair in **Praça Benedito Calixto,** which includes a choro jam session and food stands. Bar hoppers can run wild within the confines of an area of Vila Madalena bordered by four streets: Rua Fradique Coutinho, Rua Purpurina, Rua Harmonia, and Rua Luis Murat.

Rua Teodoro Sampaio is the go-to place for musical instruments; sometimes you can catch top musicians jamming as they try out new equipment.

Art Scene: During the day there are art galleries, streets,

and bookstores to prowl.
Galeria Raquel Arnaud (see sidebar p. 103), a venerated gallery of Brazilian contemporary art, launched its new location in Vila Madalena in 2011, putting it within walking distance of **Galeria Fortes Vilaça,** a pioneer in the neighborhood when it opened in the 1990s. These two represent many leading Brazilian contemporary artists.

Pinheiros also hosts the **Instituto Tomie Ohtake** *(Rua dos Coropés 88, Pinheiros, tel 11/2245 1900, closed Mon.),* named for the groundbreaking Japanese-Brazilian artist, in a building designed by her son Ruy, one of Brazil's most acclaimed architects. It hosts important temporary art exhibitions, with shows of everything from emerging Brazilian artists like Ana Prata to the American photographer Alfred Stieglitz.

Visit the **Beco do Batman** (Batman's Alley) for a taste of São Paulo's lively street art scene. The Beco formally consists of stretches of Rua Gonçalo Afonso and Rua Medeiros de Albuquerque. Vila Madalena is also home to **Galeria Choque Cultural,** a gallery for street art. About five blocks southwest of the Beco do Batman, you'll find the original branch of the **Livraria da Vila** *(Rua Fradique Coutinho 915, Pinheiros).*

Farther Afield: If you need to buy flowers, or if you want to just gasp at a marketplace full of them, visit the **Companhia de Entrepostos e Armazéns Gerais de São Paulo** (CEAGESP; *Av. Dr. Gastão Vidigal 1946, Vila Leopoldina, tel 11/3643 3700, open Tues.–Sun., hours vary)* in Pinheiros, about 4 miles (7 km) northwest of the Livraria da Vila. ∎

Galeria Fortes Vilaça

✉ Rua Fradique Coutinho 1500, Vila Madalena

☎ 11/3032 7066

🕐 Closed Sun.– Mon.

www.fortesvilaca .com.br

Galeria Choque Cultural

✉ Rua Medeiros de Albuquerque 250, Vila Madalena

☎ 11/2678 6600

This phone booth—located at Avenida Paulista—is part of Call Parade, a campaign to decorate a hundred phone booths in São Paulo with designs by local artists.

São Paulo State Coast & Interior

São Paulo city residents escape to the beaches, especially those on the Litoral Norte (North Coast). Much of the state's far eastern section is covered by the Atlantic Forest, where many cities retain a small-town atmosphere. The climate is pleasant at higher altitudes, even during summer. The southern region appeals to outdoor enthusiasts, while the agricultural western region sports everything from grand rodeos to the vestiges of U.S. Confederate culture.

Ilhabela is the best option for sandy leisure or rugged treks near São Paulo and Rio de Janeiro.

São Sebastião

⚠ 99 C1

Visitor Information

✉ Rua Sebastião Silvestre Neves 214, Centro

☎ 12/3891 2000

🕐 Closed Sat.–Sun.

North Coast

São Paulo city dwellers' favorite beaches are found about 125 miles (200 km) east of the city in **São Sebastião,** which offers 62 miles (100 km) of beaches and 1,350 square miles (350,000 ha) of protected Atlantic Forest in **Parque Estadual da Serra do Mar** (*Rod. Dr. Oswaldo Cruz km 78, São Luiz do Paraitinga, tel 12/3671 9266, closed Mon.*). Different stretches of shoreline appeal to different groups. For instance, **Maresias beach,** to the southwest, is known for

attracting a chic crowd, and surfing is popular there. If you don't yet know how to hang 10, you can take classes with an outfit called **EcoDynamic** (*Rua Olímpio Faustino 561, Praia de Camburi, São Sebastião, tel 12/3865 2545*), which also conducts ecotourism excursions.

Immediately off the coast, **Ilhabela** (Beautiful Island) boasts 21 scuba-diving spots—including nine shipwrecks—and is considered paradise by surfers and sailing buffs. Trekkers can choose from several day hikes. The trails are very much off the beaten path, so consider going with a guide. Guides from a reputable local firm **Ciribaí Turismo de Aventura** *(tel 12/3896 5202, email: alex@ciribai.com)* can lead groups, along the **Trilha do Bonete,** which passes by lookout points and waterfalls. They will also introduce visitors to locals (known as *caiçaras*) at an isolated fishing village. Leaving from downtown São Sebastião, ferries make the 4-mile (6 km) journey to Ilhabela every 30 minutes.

For quiet and seclusion, head northeast out of São Sebastião about 70 miles (115 km) to **Picinguaba,** where you can go hiking or scuba diving.

Vale do Paraíba & Serra da Bocaina

The Vale do Paraíba, a valley that takes its name from the Rio Paraíba do Sul—crucial to the coffee industry—runs between São Paulo and Rio de Janeiro. The Rodovia Presidente Dutra, or Via Dutra, runs across the valley, connecting the capital cities.

About 90 minutes out of São Paulo (80 miles, 130 km) on Via Dutra, you'll come upon the city of Taubaté. Here, the **Rota da Liberdade** offers several tours that promote the region's black history and culture. One multiple-day program offers visits to coffee plantations; another focuses on the religious syncretism devised by forced laborers from Africa.

Take this opportunity to explore the town of **São Luiz do Paraitinga**—one of the best representatives of traditional *caipira* (rural) culture. Its throwback Carnaval is legendary but still off the main radar. Founded by a French community in 1769, many of its citizens still have French names. To reach it, leave Taubaté and head toward the coast for 45 minutes (30 miles, 45 km). In a nearby village, an old coffee plantation has been transformed into a hotel: **Fazenda Catuçaba** (see Travelwise p. 285). The staff can

Ilhabela
⬛ 99 C1
Visitor Information
✉ Rua Prefeito Mariano Procópio de Araújo Carvalho 86, Perequê
☎ 12/3896 9200
🕐 Closed Sat.–Sun.

Ferry São Sebastião–Ilhabela
✉ Av. Antônio Januário do Nascimento, São Sebastião
☎ 12/3892 1576

Rota da Liberdade
✉ Rua Barão da Pedra Negra 500, sala 6, Centro, Taubaté
☎ 12/3621 9448
www.realitytour.com.br

Cunha Pottery

Mieko Ukeseki, a student of traditional ceramic techniques in her native Japan, arrived in Brazil in 1975. With the backing of local artists and art pottery makers, Ukeseki helped found a collective studio and kiln in **Cunha** (*Visitor information, Praça Cônego Siqueira 27, Cunha, tel 12/3111 2911*). After bouncing around a bit, Ukeseki returned to Cunha in 1981 and established her studio, **Ateliê Mieko e Mário** (*Rua Gerônimo Mariano Leite 510, Vila Rica, Cunha, tel 12/3111 1468*), where she continues to work.

Cunha has become a leading center of stonewood ceramics, with more than 20 studios and several Noborigama (multi-chamber) kilns. Most studios are open to visitors, and artists frequently organize openings. An annual festival is held in early October. The **Instituto Cultural da Cerâmica de Cunha** sometimes organizes intensive pottery courses, and many studios offer courses during the July school holidays. **Jotacê Carvalho** (*Rua Gerônimo Mariano Leite 190, Vila Rica, Cunha, tel 12/3111 2483 or 11/3742 0785, closed Mon.*) teaches year-round, though you must book in advance.

Barretos

Brazil's Liga Nacional de Rodeio (National Rodeo League) is a popular sport. The flagship competition is the annual **Festa do Peão de Boiadeiro** *(Parque do Peão Mussa Calil Neto, Rod. Brigadeiro Faria Lima km 428, tel 17/3321 0000, www .independentes.com.br),* held in a town of just over 100,000, located in the far northern end of the state. The 35,000-seat rodeo stadium in Barretos was designed by Brazil's most revered architect, the late Oscar Niemeyer. Attendance at the ten-day rodeo, held in

mid-August, hits the million mark, making it the largest rodeo in Latin America—and one of the biggest worldwide.

The rodeo's origin dates to 1955, when a group of locals planned a gathering with competitions—a "Peon Party." As anthropologist Alexander Sebastian Dent explains in *River of Tears: Country Music, Memory, and Modernity in Brazil,* peon was "the deliberately chosen archaic term for cowboy now universally employed in the designation of Brazil's 600-odd rodeos as 'Festas de Peão.'"

São Luiz do Paraitinga

🏔 99 C1

Visitor Information

✉ Praça Dr. Oswaldo Cruz 3

☎ 12/3671 7000

🕐 Closed Sat.–Sun.

Parque Estadual Turístico do Alto Ribeira (PETAR)

🏔 99 B1

✉ SP-165, 205 miles (330 km) southeast of São Paulo, bet. Apiaí & Iporanga

☎ 15/3552 1875

🕐 Closed Mon.

💲 $

🚌 Bus from São Paulo to Apiaí: Viação Transpen from Barra Funda station

help organize activities throughout the region.

Taubaté is about halfway between São Paulo and São José do Barreiro—host to **Parque Nacional da Serra da Bocaina** *(Rod. Estadual Francisca Mendes Ribeiro, SP-221, tel 12/3117 2143),* one of the largest nature reserves in the Atlantic Forest. São José do Barreiro—a three-hour drive on Via Dutra from São Paulo (70 miles, 270 km) but just 85 miles (140 km) from Taubaté—sits just outside the park. The main attraction of São José do Barreiro, located on the São Paulo–Rio de Janeiro border, is the **Trilha do Ouro,** an "alternative" road used by tax evaders in colonial times to transport (undetected) gold destined for Europe from Minas Gerais to the port in Paraty.

The **Cachoeira Santo Isidro** is the waterfall closest to the park entrance, about a mile (1.6 km) in. The best time to visit is May to August, when there is less rainfall—unless you want to hang out at the waterfalls, in which case

you should go during the Southern Hemisphere summer.

Vale do Ribeira

Large swaths of the Vale do Ribeira in the southeastern tip of São Paulo state are covered by state parks: PETAR, Intervales, Ilha do Cardoso, and Carlos Botelho. They protect some of the richest remaining sections of the Atlantic Forest, now reduced to 7 percent of its original size.

This region is also known as the "Northeast of São Paulo"—not for its geography, but as a reference to the poor northeastern region of Brazil. This is the poorest part of Brazil's richest state. Many residents are descendants of escaped slaves who established communities called *quilombos* hundreds of years ago (see sidebar p. 35).

PETAR: Parque Estadual Turístico do Alto Ribeira, universally called PETAR, is roughly 200 miles (322 km) southeast of São Paulo and contains some of Brazil's most important speleology sites, with more than 300 registered caves. Many of these are open to visitation, and there are caves for everyone, no matter your level of experience. One of the most interesting excursions involves a 5-mile (8 km) hike to the **Casa de Pedra Cave,** said to have the largest entrance in the world—at 705 feet (215 m). To get there, you cross the Rio Iporanga; on its banks you will find evidence of wildcat gold miners from the 17th and 18th centuries. As with many Brazilian public parks, you are required to hire a local guide to enter.

Three-quarters of the 40-plus quilombos in São Paulo state are located in the Vale do Ribeira. Founded hundreds of years ago, many of these rural communities still exist. In recent years, some of them have joined together to create the Circuito Quilombola (Quilombola Circuit) to facilitate tourism. For more information about PETAR, its mission, and the surrounding region, contact **Parque Aventuras.**

Other Parks: Parque Estadual Intervales, two hours north of PETAR, serves as a refuge for more than 300 species of birds. Bird-watching guru Bret Whitney of the bird-watching tour company Field Guides *(www.fieldguides.com),* includes Intervales in his Brazil Nutshell survey tour.

Parque Estadual Ilha do Cardoso protects 90 percent of the island covered by the Atlantic Forest on the state's border with Paraná. The main attractions are the beaches and the hiking trails. There is lodging on the island, which is accessible by boat from Cananéia; the trip takes between one and three hours, depending on the craft. **Parque Estadual Carlos Botelho,** which offers several nature hiking trails, is best known as home to about half of Brazil's known population of the

Parque Aventuras
- ✉ SP-165 km 13, Bairro da Serra, PETAR, Iporanga
- ☎ 15/3556 1485

Parque Estadual Intervales
- ✉ Estr. Municipal km 25, Ribeirão Grande
- ☎ 13/3542 1511

Parque Estadual da Ilha do Cardoso
- ✉ Av. Professor Wladimir Besnard, Cananéia
- ☎ 13/3851 1163

Parque Estadual Carlos Botelho
- ✉ São Miguel de Arcanjo, 137 miles (220 km) from São Paulo
- ☎ 15/3379 1477

Looking for the woolly spider monkey in Parque Estadual Carlos Botelho, Brazil

Americana

To encourage cotton production in Brazil following the U.S. Civil War, Emperor Dom Pedro II offered incentives to cotton farmers in the southern states who wanted to relocate. Several thousand took him up on his offer. The largest concentration settled in the interior of São Paulo state—many in the town of **Santa Bárbara d'Oeste**. Others started a settlement next door called **Americana** *(Visitor information, Av. Brasil 85, Centro, tel 19/ 3475 9000, open Mon.–Fri., p.m.)*.

A group called the Fraternidade Descendência Americana (Brotherhood of American Descent) takes care of the **Cemitério do Campo** *(Estr. dos Confederados, Antiga Estr. do Barreirinho, Santa Bárbara d'Oeste, tel 19/9783 8164)*, where many of the original settlers were buried. The cemetery, open by appointment, hosts the annual **Festa Confederada** in April. The **Museu da Imigração** *(Praça 9 de Julho, Centro, tel 19/3455 5082, closed Sun.–Mon.)* is dedicated to the memory of the American immigrants.

Although the Confederate flag flies here, the brotherhood has adopted the motto "Heritage! Not Hate."

**Estação
Ecológica da
Juréia-Itatins**
- 🅰 99 C1
- ✉ Estr. do Guaraú 4164, Peruíbe
- ☎ 13/3457 9243
- 🕐 Closed Sat.–Sun.

Peruíbe
- 🅰 99 C1

Visitor Information
- ✉ Rua Nilo Soares Ferreira 50
- ☎ 13/3451 1000
- 🕐 Closed Sat.–Sun.

endangered southern muriqui (woolly spider monkey). Visits here must be scheduled in advance.

South Coast

If the North Coast is for beach bums, then the Litoral Sul is for nature lovers and outdoor enthusiasts. A state nature reserve, the **Estação Ecológica da Juréia-Itatins** spans the coast between the towns of **Iguape** to the south and **Peruíbe** to the north, two hours southwest of São Paulo. The protected area encompasses nearly 198,000 acres (80,000 ha). Four main sections—roughly adjacent to one another along the same stretch of coastline—are open to visitors: Itinguçu, Vila Barra do Una, Canto da Praia da Juréia, and Praia do Guaraú.

Itinguçu, located inside the Iguape city limits, features a waterfall, the **Cachoeira do Paraíso,** and has a reception area with refreshment stands. You can camp at the **Núcleo Vila Barra do Una,** a fishing village with a 1.25-mile (2 km) stretch of beach. If you wish, locals will provide meals.

The **Núcleo Praia da Juréia** offers 4.5 miles (7 km) of shore, but hiking in the adjacent hillsides is prohibited. Juréia is popular with surfers, and the best waves are between November and April.

The calm, unpolluted waters of the **Núcleo Praia do Guaraú** beach are perfect for bathing. The **Rio Guaraú** reaches the sea here, ending in a waterfall. The **Praia do Arpoador,** also located within the ecological station, can be reached by a foot trail. The **Corredeira do Perequê** is a stream surrounded by a large area that is open to recreational activities and hiking.

Several trails run through the reserve or in adjacent areas. Among the more interesting longer hikes is the **Trilha do Abarebebê,** a 15.5-mile (25 km) path that links Peruíbe and the city of **Itanhaém,** once taken by Jesuit missionaries. Other trails pass near the **Aldeia Indígena Piaçaguera,** an indigenous village that recently won a battle against developers. Popular outdoor activities include canoeing, canyoning, rappelling, water trekking, hang gliding, zip-lining, and canopy walking.

Boat excursions both inland by river or by sea can be arranged with locals at the fishing villages. If you don't plan to visit the Amazon, a river trip by boat or canoe can provide a similar sensation. By sea, fishing boats can deliver you to one of several nearby islands.

INSIDER TIP:

Brotas is a rich place for eco-adventurers— with rafting, camping, climbing, canyoning on the Jacaré Pepira—and the downtown water- fall is stunning.

—RODRIGO NICOLETTE
Professor, University of São Paulo

Generally it is advisable to hire a local guide. You can find one through the **Associação dos Moni- tores Ambientais de Peruíbe.**

Itanhaém ranks among the best scuba diving spots in Brazil. Favorite destinations include two islands, **Ilha da Queimada Pequena** and **Ilha da Queimada Grande**, and the *Rio Negro* and *Tocantins* wrecks.

Interior

Some visitors to the inland region draw on its rural culture (this is rodeo country), others on the heri- tage of its immigrants. The region boasts great infrastructure for leisure travelers, making ecotourism

and adventure excursions comfort- able and stress free.

Given its proximity to São Paulo (85 miles, 135 km), the city of Socorro (pop. 37,000) is a great option for weekend leisure activities for business travelers. Set in a primarily rural area, **Socorro** is a national—indeed global—leader for accessible outdoor tourism, meeting the needs of persons with disabilities and restricted mobility. One local firm invented a new style of zip-lining, where you go horizontally, headfirst, as if laying on your stomach. Developed for people unable to use the normal sitting position, it has become popular with everyone.

About two hours north of Socorro, **Holambra**—a combina- tion of the first letters in *Holland, America,* and *Brazil*—was an agricul- tural collective founded by Dutch immigrants after World War II. In 1993, it became a municipality. Today, hundreds of small farmers have put the town on the map as a supplier of tulips, chrysanthe- mums, and other flowers. Visit the **Museu Histórico e Cultural de Holambra** and some of the flower farms. In September, the city hosts **Expoflora,** the biggest flower extravaganza in Latin America.

White-water rafting is the prin- cipal attraction in **Brotas**—110 miles (175 km) southwest of Holambra— but the region also offers trekking, mountain biking, and horseback riding. Other attractions include **Águas de São Pedro,** a health resort with hot mineral springs, and the city of **Bragança Paulista,** celebrated for the pork sausages served at local eateries. ∎

Associação dos Monitores Ambientais de Peruíbe

✉ Av. Padre Anchieta 1112, Centro, Peruíbe

☎ 13/3455 2456

Museu Histórico e Cultural de Holambra

✉ Alameda Maurício de Nassau 894, Holambra

☎ 19/3802 2053

🕐 Open Sat.–Sun. & holidays, daily in July

💲 $

www.museu holambra.com.br

Águas de São Pedro

🅰 99 C2

✉ Praça Prefeito Geraldo Azevedo 115, Centro, Brotas

☎ 19/3482 7100

Drive: São Paulo Highway of the Waters

Linking several interesting cities northwest of São Paulo, the Rodovia Engenheiro Constâncio Cintra (SP-360) is a state highway that runs for more than 62 miles (100 km) from Jundiaí, with its rich history linked to the coffee and railroad eras, to Águas de Lindóia, in a region known for its thermal hot springs, and beyond. The most interesting section runs to Amparo, another thermal hot springs resort, 44 miles (70 km) north of Jundiaí.

About 37 miles (60 km) northwest of the city of São Paulo, **Jundiaí** ❶ marks the starting point for the journey. Before taking off, check out some of the attractions in town. As you get onto SP-360 heading north, leaving the urban perimeter, you will find the **Fazenda Nossa Senhora da Conceição** (Rod. Engenheiro Constâncio Cintra km 72.5, tel 11/4535 1341, www.fnsc.com.br, open Sat.–Sun. & holidays) about 7.5 miles (12 km) north of downtown. A coffee plantation dating from 1810, it is now an open-air museum. Walk along trails that crisscross the farm's 7.5 acres (3 ha), take a buggy ride, or sample regional dishes at the restaurant. On weekends, guided tours include demonstrations of coffee production activities, and English-speaking guides are available.

If you want to visit Jundiaí without an automobile, you can ride the rails in renovated train cars from the 1950s. A regular Saturday tourism train, the **Trem Expresso Jundiaí** (tel 0800/055 0121) leaves from São Paulo's Estação da Luz in the morning and returns late afternoon.

Just about 15.5 miles (25 km) north of Jundiaí is **Itatiba** ❷, best known for its **Zooparque** (Sítio Paraíso das Aves, Rod. Dom Pedro I km 95, Bairro Paraíso das Aves, tel 11/9833 5328, $$), located within a stretch of Atlantic Forest. It contains a 2-mile (3 km) walking trail with displays of domestic and exotic animals—the former including monkeys and hyacinth macaws, the latter giraffes, tigers, and elephants. Zooparque is accessed via Rodovia Dom Pedro I (SP-065), about 12.5 miles

NOT TO BE MISSED:

Fazenda Nossa Senhora da Conceição • Zooparque • Morungaba's food shops • Amparo's historic buildings

(20 km) east of downtown Itatiba. Pass through town and head southeast on SP-065.

You will need to double back to Rodovia Engenheiro Constâncio Cintra (SP-360), so you may want to stop at Itatiba's central square, **Praça da Bandeira,** before or after you visit the Zooparque. There you will find the **Museu Histórico Municipal Padre Francisco de Paula Lima** (Praça da Bandeira 122, Centro, tel 11/4524 1264, closed Mon.), dedicated to the city's history; the **Basílica Menor de Nossa Senhora do Belém** (Praça da Bandeira, Centro, tel 11/4538 0208, closed Mon.), a 19th-century church; and a few other historic buildings. Back on SP-360, less than 2.5 miles (4 km) north of downtown Itatiba, you'll find the **Sete Voltas Spa Resort** (Rod. Engenheiro Constâncio Cintra km 93, Itatiba, tel 11/4534 7800), a health spa in a rural setting oriented toward people who want to lose weight or just relax. You'll need to book at least one night if you want to hang out.

Continuing on Rodovia Engenheiro Constâncio Cintra north about 12 miles (19 km) past Itatiba, you will reach **Morungaba** ❸ (pop. 12,000), home to—among other things—**Doces David,** a producer of quality home-style jams, jellies, ice creams, and more. There is a special outlet store downtown (*Rua Araújo Campos 533, Centro, tel 11/4014 7597*). The factory (*Rua Pedro Miguel 591, Parque Ecológico, tel 11/4014 7521*) itself is open to visitors Tuesday–Sunday, but only if you schedule in advance.

After the downtown shop, foodies will want to visit the nearby **Companhia das Ervas** (*Rua Felizardo Assis 260, tel 11/4014 1606, www .ciadaservas.com.br*), with its herbs, spices, and hot sauces, and the **Empório da Cana** (*Rua Araújo Campos 524 B, Centro, tel 11/7217 4382*), which sells *cachaça* (a sugarcane spirit) from around the country.

Continue on SP-360 north for another 17.5 miles (28 km) to **Amparo ④**, a bustling

place during the coffee boom, and view the many historic structures—especially around Praça Pádua Salles, a central square. A decommissioned train station dating to 1875, the **Estação Ferroviária da Companhia Mogiana** (*Praça Pádua Salles 160, Centro, tel 19/3807 7055, closed Mon.*), can be found on the Praça, where it houses cultural institutions. Like other towns of the region, the main attractions here are the spas with their thermal baths and other amenities. The most popular can be found in tranquil rural settings. A couple of choices here are **Lake Villas Charm Hotel** (*Estr. Antenor César km 10, tel 19/3817 5162 or 0800/778 0808, www.lakevillas.com.br, $$*) and **Hotel Sant'Anna** (*Bairro Córrego Vermelho, tel 11/3509 4252 or 19/3808 7527, $$*).

Map legend:
- Map pp. 98–99
- Jundiaí
- 1.5 hours
- 45 miles (71 km)
- Amparo

Minas Gerais

In the 18th century, Minas Gerais (General Mines) supplied Europe with gold and diamonds and reaped some of the benefits itself—as is evident in the spectacular baroque architecture of its historic mining cities. Combining the heritage of these historic mining cities, a section of the folklore-rich *sertão* to the north, and several national parks and nature reserves, Minas Gerais perhaps reflects "deep Brazil" better than any other state.

Belo Horizonte (Beautiful Horizon) and its surrounding hills

Belo Horizonte

🅰 99 D3

Visitor Information

✉ Av. Afonso Pena 1212, Centro

☎ 31/3277 1455

🕐 Closed Sat.–Sun.

Belo Horizonte

Belo Horizonte was planned and built in the 1890s to replace the colonial city Ouro Preto as the capital of Minas Gerais. The city as we know it today sports excellent urban amenities, especially top-notch restaurants and bars. As the capital of Brazil's third biggest state in economic terms, Belo Horizonte receives numerous business travelers and boasts several good hotels. For foreign visitors, its main attraction is probably as a base or way station for guests visiting the historic towns, national parks, and other attractions scattered about the rest of the state.

The **Savassi** district, found in the south-central section of Belo Horizonte, contains the city's best hotels, shopping, bars, restaurants, and nightlife. Try the **Amsterdam Pub** *(Rua dos Inconfidentes 1141, Savassi, tel 31/3262 0688, closed Sun.–Thurs.)* for live music and DJs, mostly rock and pop; the **Velvet**

Club *(Rua Sergipe 1493, Savassi, tel 31/3284 0836 or 31/9906 6613, closed Mon.–Tues.)* for new local bands and '80s, rock, and electronic theme nights; and **Up e.Music** *(Av. Getúlio Vargas 1423, Savassi, tel 31/3227 4012)* for electronic, hip-hop, and funk as well as a lesbian night.

On or near **Praça da Liberdade,** buildings that once housed state bureaucrats have been restored and opened to the public as cultural centers and museums. At the southern end of the square, mimicking the French architectural style of the period, is the **Palácio da Liberdade,** which was built in 1897 and served as the state capital building. A few blocks north of the square, an eclectic building—housing the **Arquivo Público Mineiro** (Minas Public Archives) and surrounded by gardens—hosts temporary exhibitions.

Continuing on the square in a northeasterly direction, you'll approach the **Espaço TIM UFMG do Conhecimento** *(tel 31/3409 8350, closed Mon.),* which belongs to the Universidade Federal de Minas Gerais (Federal University of Minas Gerais) and offers a link between town and gown: expositions and a planetarium. The **Museu das Minas e do Metal** *(tel 31/3516 7200, closed Mon., $, Wed. free)* tells the history of mining and metal and their roles in human history.

About a block west of the northwest corner of the square, the **Centro de Arte Popular–Cemig** features a permanent exhibition of popular art. The **Biblioteca Pública Estadual Luiz de Bessa,** or public library, was designed by the late Oscar Niemeyer, Brazil's famous architect.

Doubling back on the same street, Rua Gonçalves Dias, to the northeast corner of Praça da Liberdade, the **Memorial Minas Gerais–Vale** is dedicated to the history and culture of the state.

Arquivo Público Mineiro

✉ Av. João Pinheiro 372, Funcionários
☎ 31/3269 1060
🕐 Closed Sat.–Sun.

Centro de Arte Popular–Cemig

✉ Rua Gonçalves Dias 1608, Funcionários
☎ 31/3222 3231
🕐 Closed Mon.

Biblioteca Pública Estadual Luiz de Bessa

✉ Praça da Liberdade 21, Funcionários
☎ 31/3269 1166
🕐 Closed Sun.

Memorial Minas Gerais–Vale

☎ 31/3343 7317
🕐 Closed Mon.

Belo Horizonte's *Botecos*

A *boteco*, or *botequim*, is a down-home neighborhood bar. These establishments have served as the stage for sundry popular Brazilian songs, notably sambas by Zé Keti ("Diz que Fui por Aí") and Noel Rosa ("Conversa de Botequim"). Popular throughout Brazil, they have evolved into a local institution in Belo Horizonte—a city, it is said, with a bar on every corner.

A few years ago denizens of local culture decided to organize a kind of bake-off among local botecos, called **Comida di Buteco,** whereby each would prepare a special dish, something to accompany the beer and *cachaça*. Dozens of establishments take part every year from mid-April to mid-May. During the festival, locals hop from boteco to boteco. During the rest of the year, they hang at their favorite neighborhood joints. Some good ones? **Petisqueira do Primo** *(Rua Santa Catarina 656, Lourdes, tel 31/3335 6654, closed Sun.),* **Tip Top** *(Rua Rio de Janeiro 1770, Lourdes, tel 31/3275 1880),* **Café Palhares** *(Rua Tupinambás 638, Centro, tel 31/3201 1841),* and two at Mercado Central *(Av. Augusto de Lima 744):* **Casa Cheia** *(loja 167, tel 31/3274 9585)* and **Ronaldo Queijos & Cachaças** *(Cachaça Bar, loja 34 & 141, tel 31/3274 9611).*

Museu de Arte da Pampulha

- ✉ Av. Otacílio Negrão de Lima 16585, Pampulha
- ☎ 31/3277 7946
- 🕐 Closed Mon.

Casa do Baile

- ✉ Av. Otacílio Negrão de Lima 751, Pampulha
- ☎ 31/3277 7443
- 🕐 Closed Mon.

Igreja de São Francisco de Assis

- ✉ Av. Otacílio Negrão de Lima 3000, Pampulha
- ☎ 31/3427 1644

Itabira

- 🗺 99 D3

Visitor Information

- ✉ Av. Carlos de Paula Andrade 135
- ☎ 31/3839 2000

NOTE: For more information on the Caminhos Drummondianos walking tour, contact a local travel agent.

Taking Avenida João Pinheiro, the street perpendicular to the northern end of the square, for less than three blocks, you will find the **Museu Mineiro** (*Av. João Pinheiro 342, Lourdes, tel 31/3269 1168, closed Mon.*), which provides an overview of the state's art dating from the colonial period.

Pampulha is the name of an artificial lake built in 1940 and the surrounding neighborhood, which features three early works by Niemeyer: a former casino that houses the **Museu de Arte da Pampulha,** the **Casa do Baile** (now a cultural center), and **Igreja de São Francisco de Assis.** The surrounding green space reflects the talent of Roberto Burle Marx, Brazil's most venerated landscape artist. Inside the church, look for a series of panels representing the stations of the cross painted by another of Brazil's greatest artists—Cândido Portinari.

East of Belo Horizonte

Itabira, about 62 miles (100 km) east of Belo Horizonte, is the birthplace of Carlos Drummond de Andrade, Brazil's most influential poet of the 20th century. If you have been to Copacabana beach in Rio de Janeiro, perhaps you saw a life-size statue of a man wearing eyeglasses sitting on a bench on the strand with his back to the ocean. That's Drummond, the venerated poet. Among Drummond's best known works are the existentialist masterpieces "José," written for his brother, and "In the Middle of the Road," which ruminates about a stone on a pathway.

Casa de Drummond (*Praça do Centenário 135, Centro, tel 31/3835 3894*), the house where the poet spent his childhood—from the age of two until he turned 16—can be visited on Praça do Centenário. It has been altered, but it retains many of the spaces that inspired the 45 poems he wrote about it. A few blocks away is the **Memorial Carlos Drummond de Andrade** (*Encosta Leste do Pico do Amor, Campestre, tel 31/3835 2156*), designed by Niemeyer, a friend of the poet. The exhibit includes artifacts from his life and his hometown, including his typewriter. In a creative twist, the city has installed 44 plaques

INSIDER TIP:

Visit the historic cities of Minas Gerais to see 19th-century Brazil. The architecture preserves the authentic baroque heyday of the gold cycle.

—DENISE RAMBALDI
Vice President, Instituto Estadual do Ambiente

around town that contain poems related to the places where they have been placed. The **Caminhos Drummondianos** walking tour lasts a full day (see note).

Also east of Belo Horizonte is the **Parque Natural e Santuário do Caraça,** a private nature reserve that surrounds a 19th-century seminary. Accessed via the town of Santa Bárbara do Leste,

Galo da Campina (Paroaria Dominicana) or Rooster's Campina, a common species in Brazil

about 186 miles (300 km) east of Belo Horizonte, the park boasts two guesthouses that allow you to sleep in the nature reserve. The headquarters are set in a cluster of buildings that operated in the 19th century as a Catholic seminary and parochial school. At night a priest performs the ritual of calling maned wolves out of the wild. Using meat as bait, the priests have trained specimens of the largest canid of South America to walk right up to the middle of a patio near the church as visitors look on. A small farm on site supplies the *santuário,* which offers meals to guests. During the day you can hike one of the many trails that cross the nature reserve.

Ouro Preto

According to the late poet Manuel Bandeira, "Ouro Preto is a city that hasn't changed, and therein lies its incomparable charm." Hyperbole—but perhaps we should grant Bandeira his little exaggeration. The 20th-century modernist wrote that line not in one of his illustrious poems but in a 1938 guidebook he authored about the former gold-mining town in Brazil.

Four decades before Bandeira wrote his guidebook, Ouro Preto lost its status as state capital of Minas Gerais, after most of the gold had run out. Today, history is the commodity that draws visitors. They come to see the remnants of the 18th-century mining culture, notably the monumental churches with their gold-leaf interiors and baroque sacred art.

Early Portuguese explorers called the place Vila Rica (Rich Town). You can view what the miners were looking for, and

Parque Natural e Santuário do Caraça

🔺 99 D3

✉ Caixa Postal 12, Caraça, Santa Bárbara

☎ 31/3837 2698

www.santuariodo caraca.com.br

Ouro Preto

🔺 99 D3

Visitor Information

✉ Praça Barão do Rio Branco 12, Pilar

☎ 31/3559 3200

🕐 Closed Sat.–Sun.

www.ouropreto .org.br

Parque Estadual do Itacolomi

- ✉ Bet. Ouro Preto & Mariana
- ☎ 31/3351 6193 or 9891 9471
- 🕐 Closed Mon.

found, at the **Museu de Mineralogia** *(Praça Tiradentes 20, Centro, tel 31/3559 3119, closed Mon.)* on central Praça Tiradentes. Nearby is the **Igreja de São Francisco de Assis** *(Largo de Coimbra, Centro Histórico, tel 31/3551 3282, closed Mon., $)*, designed by the master of the Brazilian baroque, Aleijadinho (see sidebar p. 124). The town's rather steep streets hold about a dozen churches; but be sure to investigate São Francisco

in the historic center is the **Mina de Chico Rei** *(Rua Dom Silvério 108, Centro Histórico, tel 31/3551 1749, closed Sun., $)*, a mine with a mile (1.6 km) of tunnels that was abandoned in 1888.

As with the 1849 California gold rush, the deposits in Minas Gerais attracted free spirits quite happy with the scanty official presence on the frontier. In Brazil, most of the miners came from neighboring São Paulo state.

Street scene with typical architecture in the UNESCO World Heritage city center of Ouro Preto

de Assis, where almost all of the baroque statues inside were created by Aleijadinho.

Nearby, the **Museu da Inconfidência** *(Praça Tiradentes 139, Centro Histórico, tel 31/3551 1121, closed Mon., $)* commemorates an unsuccessful independence movement inspired by the American Revolution. Another attraction

When the Portuguese crown tried to crack down on miners' tax evasion in 1720, several days of "rage and death" swept Ouro Preto, according to an official report to authorities. Today, travelers to **Parque Estadual do Itacolomi** (Itacolomi State Park), just outside Ouro Preto, can visit the restored **Casa Bandeirista,** the tax collection station on the Estrada Real. Completed in 1708, it is considered to be the first public building in the state. From there you can hike to **Itacolomi Peak,** with views of both Ouro Preto and neighboring Mariana. The park is open to the public, but you must obtain permission from rangers to venture forth to the peak.

Mariana

About two-thirds of Parque Estadual do Itacolomi's area is within Mariana's city limits. There are several interesting hiking paths accessible from the Mariana side, including the **Trilha da Mina do Morro do Gogo,** a trail that runs past a mine that tapped into the same vein as the Minas da Passagem (see below). During the 2-mile (3 km) hike from downtown to the old mine, you can see the holes that provided ventilation for the tunnels below.

Mariana's most fascinating attraction is set 2.5 miles (4 km) outside of town: the **Minas da Passagem,** a mine that remained in operation until 1985. Billed as the largest gold mine open to the public in the world, it is accessible via a trolley that takes visitors down into the depths where tunnels run as deep as 394 feet (120 m). These you traverse on foot. Once back on the surface, you can visit the on-site **Museu da Mina,** with artifacts from the gold rush period, or have a traditional meal at the on-site restaurant.

If you get a different vibe from Mariana than from other historic cities like Ouro Preto, that's probably because it was the first planned city in Minas Gerais. Instead of twisted, organic alleyways, here you have wide streets and public squares that are truly square—or rectangular, at least. You can hire a buggy for a spin around these streets and, once a month, watch open-air reenactments of life from the gold-rush period.

The **Museu Arquidiocesano de Arte Sacra** (*Rua Frei Durão 49, Centro Histórico, tel 31/3557 2581, closed Mon.*), occupying a mansion dating from 1770, presents one of Brazil's richest collections of sacred art. Next door, the **Catedral Basílica da Sé** (Nossa Senhora da Assunção), completed

Mariana
🗺 99 D3
Visitor Information
✉ Praça Juscelino Kubitschek
☎ 31/3557 9000
🕐 Closed Sat.–Sun.

Minas da Passagem
🗺 99 D3
✉ Rua Eugênio Eduardo Rapallo 192, Passagem
☎ 31/3557 5000
💲 $$
www.minasda passagem.com.br

Inhotim

What's billed as the world's largest open-air contemporary art center can be found at the end of 37 miles (60 km) of sometimes dusty roads southwest of Belo Horizonte. Founded in 2005 in the town of Brumadinho *(Visitor information, Rua Doutor Victor de Freitas 28, tel 31/3571 3001, closed Sat.–Sun.),* the **Instituto Cultural Inhotim** (Inhotim Cultural Institute; *Rua B 20, Inhotim, tel 31/3571 9700, www.inhotim.org .br, closed Mon., $, Tues. free*) spreads out over farmland owned by the Brazilian mining magnate and art collector Bernardo Paz.

The institute's sculptures, paintings, drawings, photographs, videos, and installations include works by Brazilian artists like Tunga, Cildo Meireles, and Hélio Oiticica. Foreigners such as Doris Salcedo and Janet Cardiff are also represented. All told, about two dozen pavilions and galleries hold works by about 100 artists from some 30 countries. The grounds have been transformed into tropical botanical gardens, designed in part by Burle Marx.

Aleijadinho

The son of a slavewoman and a Portuguese architect, Antônio Francisco Lisboa championed the Brazilian colonial baroque style until his death in 1814. Nicknamed Aleijadinho ("little cripple") because of a degenerative disease that affected him late in life, he "exhibited a creative genius that has been compared with that of the great masters of the Italian Renaissance," according to Fábio Magalhães, curator of "Aleijadinho and His Times in Brazil," an exhibition in 2006–2007.

Aleijadinho's work can be seen throughout Minas Gerais's historic cities, including at the **Igreja de São Francisco de Assis** *(Largo de Coimbra, Centro Histórico, tel 31/3551 3282, closed Mon., $)* in Ouro Preto, where he was born. But he is best known for his soapstone sculptures of the Old Testament prophets that stand guard outside the **Basílica do Senhor Bom Jesus de Matosinhos** *(Praça da Basílica, tel 31/3731 1590)* in Congonhas,

an hour's drive from Ouro Preto. Nearby white chapels house Aleijadinho's equally interesting life-size wooden sculptures depicting the stations of the cross.

The church and its famous prophets were completed in 1803. Many people visit them as religious shrines—and indeed they are—but some scholars believe they also convey a political message.

A few years before the sculptor undertook this project, the Portuguese crown had cracked down on the Inconfidência Mineira, an anticolonial movement. Sympathetic to the rebels, the story goes, Aleijadinho included in each statue a symbol in homage to a dead or banished rebel.

Poets were overrepresented in the Inconfidência movement, and the prophets reflect this. The prophet Daniel, for example, is wearing a laurel crown—something more appropriate for a poet. Some scholars suggest that Daniel represents rebel-poet Tomás Antônio Gonzaga.

São João del Rei

 99 D2

Visitor Information

✉ Rua Hermílio Alves 234

☎ 32/3372 2758

🕐 Closed Sat.–Sun.

in 1750, offers a fine example of early baroque design in Minas Gerais. Equally impressive is its Arp Schnitger organ from Germany. Built in 1701, and the only one of its kind outside Europe, the organ can be heard during recitals on Fridays and Sundays. It is worth arriving early to get a pew slot near the altar. Other interesting secular buildings can be seen on **Rua Direita,** where a series of old mansions have been transformed into museums or cultural centers.

São João del Rei & Tiradentes

In line with many parts of the world, Brazil began to invest in railroads in the second half of the 19th century. Shortsighted leaders of the 20th century abandoned rail in favor of asphalt. As a result, rail transportation is almost nonexistent, even for industry, and there are virtually no long-distance passenger trains. However, a few old lines are maintained—mostly for the benefit of tourists. A steam locomotive, popularly known in Brazil as a *Maria Fumaça* (Smoking Mary), makes a 30-minute journey over the 7.5 miles (12 km) that separate São João del Rei and Tiradentes. It is a delightful way to take a detour from one city to the next, but you will have to plan ahead because it only makes a couple of runs a day.

Next to the Estação de Ferro Oeste de Minas—the train station in São João del Rei—you'll find the **Museu Ferroviário,** the railroad museum with its old equipment, photographs, antiquated railway cars, and a set of Baldwin steam locomotives from Pennsylvania. São João del Rei also sports a fine collection of old churches, but modern history buffs might prefer to visit the **Memorial Presidente Tancredo Neves** (*Rua Padre José Maria Xavier 7, São João del Rei, tel 32/3371 7836, closed Mon.–Thurs., $, www .memorialtancredoneves.com.br*), which tells the story of the city's favorite son, a politician who played a major role in the history of Brazil in the second half of the 20th century.

Near São João del Rei is the **Serra do Lenheiro,** an area popular with mountaineers and other outdoor enthusiasts. You can hike along several trails: One leads to prehistoric wall paintings; another takes you to a cavern called the **Gruta Casa da Pedra** (*Rod. São João del Rei/Tiradentes, BR-265 km 250*). It is worthwhile to go with a guide. For more information, contact the **Rede de Empresários da Estrada Real** (*tel 31/3241 7166*), a regional business tourism association.

Again with its own requisite set of colonial churches, the small town of Tiradentes tends toward the Zen end of the scale. Activities include horseback riding and hiking. The town has become a magnet for people in search of alternative lifestyles, and boasts more than its fair share of craftmakers and artists. The Serra do Lenheiro is also accessible via

Tiradentes: A trail called the **Trilha da Água Santa à Calçada dos Escravos** leads to natural hot mineral springs. A good place to make your base is the Pousada Solar da Ponte (see Travelwise p. 284).

Parque Nacional da Serra da Canastra

Set between the Cerrado and Atlantic Forest eco-regions more than 185 miles (300 km)

Aleijadinho's "Prophet Joel" in front of the Basílica do Senhor Bom Jesus de Matosinhos in Congonhas do Campo

west of Belo Horizonte, Serra da Canastra National Park is a hiker's paradise. The story of the national park starts with a group of local journalists and a 19th-century French

(continued on p. 128)

Maria Fumaça & Museu Ferroviário

🅰 99 D2

✉ Av. Hermílio Alves 366, São João del Rei

☎ 32/3371 8485

🕐 Closed Mon.

💲 $

NOTE: Train rides weekends & holidays: Departs São João del Rei 10 a.m. & 2:15 p.m.; returns 1 p.m. & 5 p.m.

The Estrada Real

Gold, diamonds, and other precious materials once moved along the 18th-century cobblestone and dirt highway known as Estrada Real, or King's Road, before being shipped to Portugal. Today, travelers are the "precious materials" moving along this route, which stretches from Minas Gerais to the coastal ports.

The UNESCO World Heritage city of Ouro Preto in Minas Gerais

In truth, there are two *estradas*. Explorers from the coastal village of Paraty created the **Caminho Velho** (Old Road) as they hacked their way through the rain forest of the Serra da Bocaina hills and then overland to the gold-rush town Vila Rica, known now as Ouro Preto. In the 18th century, this journey took three months, and travelers had to watch out for bandits on land and pirates once they set sail.

The **Caminho Novo** (New Road) left Paraty behind and sent the riches of Minas Gerais to Europe through Rio de Janeiro instead. In 1763, Rio replaced Salvador as the colonial capital. Meanwhile, in Minas Gerais, diamonds were discovered in what is now the city of Diamantina,

so the route was extended northward. The revised road map resembled a wishbone. On top was one straight shot from Diamantina to Ouro Preto—a stretch dubbed the **Caminhos dos Diamantes** (Path of Diamonds)—and below were two branches leaving Ouro Preto: the old one leading to Paraty and the new one to Rio de Janeiro.

In Their Footsteps

Many trails remain, or have been recovered, so contemporary travelers can follow one route or mix and match. Most people slice off a manageable section and stick to that. Because the main roads between major cities are paved, you can drive somewhere, hike along a stretch of the colonial road, and return to your lodgings at the end of the day.

One of the pioneers of the Estrada Real as a tourism concept, Tullio Marques *(tel 31/3344 8986)*, runs horseback trips at the Fazenda do Cipó near Belo Horizonte. He's traversed the entire route and suggests that visitors on horseback limit their time in the saddle to one day at a time. "Then they can do something else at night, like listen to a *congada* performance [Afro-Brazilian music from Minas Gerais], instead of sleeping in the bush," Marques says.

Like Route 66 in the United States, the Estrada Real has become popular with motorcyclists. American Glenn Cheney chose a different method of transportation: He walked the whole thing and wrote about it in *Journey on the Estrada Real: Encounters in the Mountains of Brazil.*

A Path Less Traveled

Another look at an Estrada Real map reveals a fourth path near the middle of the wishbone: the **Caminho do Sabarabuçu.** This 100-mile (60 km) stretch starts east of Belo Horizonte in a town called Cocais and takes a twisted, circuitous route southward to Glaura, near Ouro Preto. This extension to the Old Road was built after explorers noticed the shining peak of the Serra da Piedade hills (formerly known as the Pico de Sabarabuçu). They thought it might be gold shining on high, but it turned out to be sunlight reflecting on a deposit of iron ore.

This route runs in the vicinity of a river called the Rio das Velhas, but today it has become a road-less-traveled-by, passing through small towns—such as Caeté, Morro Vermelho, Sabará, Honório Bicalho, Rio Acima, and Acuruí—that, though charming, are not on most mainstream tourists' itinerary.

Known for the coconut trees that gave it its name, **Cocais** has been called a miniature Ouro Preto because of its colonial architecture. **Caeté** has also preserved much of its colonial-era architecture and the memory of a bygone era in its museums, houses, and churches. **Sabará,** just 30 minutes east of Belo Horizonte, was the state's first colonial settlement.

During your journey, you may find abandoned mines, exuberant vegetation, wildlife, and—if you pay close attention—remnants of the roadbuilding techniques used by the slaves who built the highway.

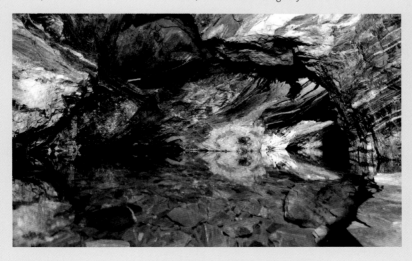

Explore the depths of the Minas da Passagem, an old gold mine, near Ouro Preto.

Parque Nacional da Serra da Canastra

🗺 99 C3

✉ Estr. MG-050, Piumhi

☎ 37/3433 1324

💲 $

São Roque de Minas

🗺 99 C3

Visitor Information

✉ Praça Alibenides Costa Faria 10

☎ 37/3433 1228

🕐 Closed Sat.–Sun.

naturalist painter. Pressured by journalists from Minas Gerais, the government established Serra da Canastra National Park in 1972 to protect the source of the country's "river of national integration," the Rio São Francisco.

A century and a half earlier, French artist Jean-Baptiste Debret had visited the region, immortalizing the park's most impressive waterfall, the **Cachoeira da Casca d'Anta**—at 610 feet (186 m), the biggest on the Rio São Francisco—in a painting that is considered a classic of the 19th-century naturalist style.

Hiking is the main activity inside the park, and one popular destination is the source of the river. Downstream are a series of natural pools that make for good swimming. The farther you hike, the more waterfalls and natural pools you'll encounter. Other popular attractions you might encounter inside the park are: the **Cachoeira dos Rolinhos,** another

waterfall; the **Curral de Pedras,** a collection of rocks that was used as a corral by cattle drivers during overnight stays; and the **Garagem de Pedras,** an old stone shelter used by travelers en route to and from the far eastern part of the state, a region called the Triângulo Mineiro (Minas Triangle).

If you are looking for something vigorous, you can take a 15.5-mile (25 km) trek to the **Cachoeira Antônio Ricardo,** a 262.5-foot (80 m) waterfall with a natural pool that is good for bathing. For that and several other trails, you must be accompanied by a licensed guide. In addition, roads that provide access to trails require a four-wheel drive. Local firms can provide transportation and guides. For more information, contact Maritaca Turismo (see sidebar below).

The main gateway town is **São Roque de Minas,** on the park's northern end. Other options include São João Batista to the west and Sacramento to the south.

EXPERIENCE: Discovering the Serra da Canastra

For a full experience of what the region has to offer, it might be worth checking in with **Maritaca Turismo** (*Av. Capitão Borges 301, tel 34/3351 5059, www .maritacaturismo.com.br),* an ecotourism operator in nearby Sacramento. Guides will lead you in and around the park during the usual activities, like wildlife spotting and bird-watching, and on excursions that focus on flowers and butterflies. Their specially reconditioned vehicle has seats on the roof, which changes your point of view and allows you to see more. They offer bicycle tours

through nearby communities, where you'll meet local characters—particularly interesting if you speak Portuguese.

Maritaca also offers courses in how to make the celebrated local cheese. The *queijo canastra,* as it is known, is a local tradition, said to date from colonial times. It is a distinctive version of *queijo minas* (Minas cheese), popular throughout Brazil. Hundreds of small producers make queijo canastra, but few have been authorized to distribute it through wider retail channels. So, even if you don't make any yourself, get some to take with you.

Minas Gerais supplied Europe with much of its gold in colonial days.

Northern Minas

Like eco-regions, heritage and culture have transition zones, and northern Minas Gerais is one of those places. It segues from the richer, more cosmopolitan South-Central region to the parched, folklore-rich badlands of the northeastern sertão. Minas Gerais compatriots sometimes jokingly call northerners honorary *baianos,* from neighboring Bahia state. Fans of Brazilian author João Guimarães Rosa and his legendary novel, *The Devil to Pay in the Backlands,* will certainly recognize the setting.

Cordisburgo: One of the highlights is Guimarães Rosa's hometown, **Cordisburgo.** The house where he lived during the first nine years of his life and where he began, at the age of seven, to teach himself French—the **Casa Guimarães Rosa**—serves as a museum and headquarters of the Contadores de Estórias Miguilim, a group of mostly poor local youngsters who recite sections of Guimarães Rosa's stories for anyone ready to listen.

Named after one of Guimarães Rosa's best known characters, the Miguilins also organize "eco-literary" walks through the adjacent countryside. These excursions must be booked in advance. The other main attraction in Cordisburgo is the **Gruta do Maquiné,** a commercially operated cavern. Explored by the Danish naturalist Peter Lund in 1834, it is considered the birthplace of Brazilian paleontology.

Diamantina: Set 174 miles (280 km) north of Belo Horizonte at the entrance to the **Jequitinhonha Valley,** Diamantina sticks out at the far northern end of the map of historic cities in Minas Gerais. It also sticks out, as the name implies, as a diamond center rather than as a gold-mining town. Its churches might not

Cordisburgo
🄰 99 D3
Visitor Information
✉ Rua São José 977
☎ 31/3715 1484
🕐 Closed Sat.–Sun.

Casa Guimarães Rosa
✉ Av. Padre João 744, Centro
☎ 31/3715 1425
🕐 Closed Mon.
💲 $

Gruta do Maquiné
🄰 99 D3
✉ Vila Alberto Ramos, MG-231 km 7, Cordisburgo
☎ 31/3715 1078
💲 $

Diamantina

⛰ 99 D3

Visitor Information

✉ Praça
  Conselheiro
  Mata 11

☎ 38/3531 9220

🕐 Closed Sat–Sun.

Garimpo Real

✉ BR-367 toward
  Belo Horizonte,
  6 miles (10
  km) from
  Diamantina

☎ 38/3531 1557

💲 $$

Casa de Chica da Silva

✉ Praça Lobo de
  Mesquita 266,
  Centro

☎ 38/3531 2491

🕐 Closed Mon.

be as opulent as those in Ouro Preto, but its colonial architectural heritage is nevertheless impressive.

If you understand Portuguese, perhaps the most absorbing attraction is the **Garimpo Real.** *Garimpo* basically means "wildcat mining." A local small-scale miner organizes visits to the river's edge, where he and other *garimpeiros* show and tell how diamond mining is done. Visits must be scheduled in advance, and tours are canceled if it is raining or has rained recently.

Black-heritage buffs will want to visit the **Casa de Chica da Silva,** the home of a freed slave who became rich and powerful. This is where she lived from 1755 to 1770 with her Portuguese partner—a diamond-mine owner, mining governor, and one of the richest men in colonial Brazil. Da Silva has become something

of a folk hero in Brazil. She was the subject of a feature length film called *Xica da Silva* (1976), directed by Cacá Diegues, and a 1996 telenovela seen around the globe. The actress who played the lead role in the latter, Taís Araújo, became the first black Brazilian to play the main protagonist in a Brazilian soap opera. Jorge Ben Jor's song "Xica da Silva" was on the soundtrack of the Diegues film and accompanied the opening credits of the telenovela.

The **Casa de Juscelino Kubitschek** is the house where the then future president (see pp. 39–40) lived from the age of 5 until he turned 18. Its exhibition features artifacts and photographs relating to both Kubitschek's life and his hometown.

For many people, the highlight of any visit to Diamantina is a meal at the **Restaurante O Garimpeiro,** "The Miner" (see

Giant anteater, Serra da Canastra National Park, Minas Gerais, Brazil

Artisanal *Cachaça*

Cachaça is a high-proof spirit made from sugarcane that is often mixed with sugar, lime, and ice to make a caipirinha or is served in shot glasses and imbibed straight. In his *Dicionário do Folclore Brasileiro* (1954), an indispensable mini-encyclopedia of Brazilian popular culture, Luís da Câmara Cascudo explains that during the colonial period, cachaça "became a national symbol with the pro-independence political movements."

In the 21st century, most cachaça is made in large factories and aged in stainless steel tanks. But Brazil never shook its tradition of small-scale cachaça producers, many of whom are happy to open the doors of their *alambiques* (stills) to visitors. Quality obviously varies, but the best use copper distillery equipment and special wooden casks for aging.

Cachaça is made countrywide, but *pinga* (a popular synonym) from Minas Gerais is often prized. The ones from the northern city of **Salinas** *(Visitor information, Praça Procópio Cardoso Araújo 7, tel 38/3841 1513)* enjoy a particularly good reputation. In Salinas, visitors can sample the merchandise, inspect the production facilities, and perhaps listen to a few tall tales by proud alambique owners before buying a bottle of their favorite stuff.

In July, Salinas hosts the annual **World Fair of Cachaça** *(Associação dos Produtores Artesanais de Cachaça de Salinas, Av. João Pena Sobrinho 341, Panorama, Salinas, tel 38/3841 3431).*

Travelwise p. 283), which is connected to a guesthouse, Pousada do Garimpo. Ask for the dish on the menu that was Chica da Silva's favorite.

Pirapora & Januária: A three-and-a-half-hour drive (about 185 miles, or 300 km) from Diamantina, the city of Pirapora boasts a truly singular attraction—a steamboat that once plied the Mississippi. Built in the United States in 1913 and billed as the world's only remaining operational steamboat, the ***Vapor Benjamim Guimarães*** now makes a regular 11-mile (18 km) excursion on the Rio São Francisco that starts in Pirapora, makes a loop, and returns. It is also possible to book a place on one of its periodic longer runs. While in Pirapora, visit the **Casa do Artesão,** a shop specializing in the wooden *carranca*

(literally, "scowl"), the devilish human-animal figureheads that were traditionally attached to the front of boats to ward off evil spirits.

Coincidentally, the town of **Januária** is also about 185 miles (300 km) from Diamantina, but it is farther north than Pirapora and sits along the banks of the river. (Guimarães Rosa is said to have immortalized Januária in print too, allegedly mentioning it 17 times in *The Devil to Pay in the Backlands*.)

Nearby is **Parque Nacional Cavernas do Peruaçu** *(MG-135, Praça Principal, Januária, tel 38/3623 1042 or 3613 1334),* with sundry caverns that can be explored, notably the Lapa do Malhador. The region features prehistoric rock inscriptions and a full range of outdoor activities, from trekking to horseback riding. You can also schedule boat trips on the river. ∎

Casa de Juscelino Kubitschek

✉ Rua São Francisco 241, Centro

☎ 38/3531 3607

🕐 Closed Mon.

Vapor Benjamim Guimarães

✉ Av. Salmeron 91, Centro, Pirapora

☎ 38/3743 9995

🕐 Closed Mon.–Fri.

💲 $$

Casa do Artesão

✉ Av. Jefferson Gitirana 270, Centro, Pirapora

☎ 38/3741 4491

Espírito Santo

Espírito Santo is jokingly called the beach of Minas Gerais. Its Atlantic Forest reserves are popular with bird-watchers and other outdoor enthusiasts. In other ways, it seems like a transition region between Rio de Janeiro and Bahia. The big debate, however, is whether its version of the traditional seafood stew *moqueca capixaba* is superior to the Bahian recipe.

A 17th-century baroque Catholic church near an Espírito Santo beach

Domingos Martins

M 99 E3

Visitor Information

✉ Rua Bernardino Monteiro 22, Centro

☎ 27/3268 1344

⊕ Closed Sat.–Sun.

www.domingos martins.es.gov.br

Parque Estadual da Pedra Azul

✉ Rota do Lagrato (Rod. Angelo Girardi) km 2

☎ 27/3248 1156

Domingos Martins

Just west of the state capital, Vitória, Domingos Martins offers ecotourism, rural tourism, and a taste of immigrant culture. The landmark and main attraction is the **Pedra Azul** (Blue Rock), a granite dome that surges out of the lush Atlantic Forest to reach its peak at over 5,900 feet (1,800 m). As the sunlight hits it from different angles over the course of the day, its glossy facade reflects changing hues—blue being among the most dramatic. The surrounding area, **Parque Estadual da Pedra Azul** (Pedra Azul State Park), offers several hiking trails. Visits should be scheduled at least 24 hours beforehand. For more information, contact the **Associação Turística de Pedra Azul** (ATPA), a local travel business association. If you want to go on horseback, go on the flagship ride of the specialized operator **Fjordland Cavalgada Ecológica Pedra Azul** *(Rod. Angelo Girardi/ Rota do Lagarto km 2.2, tel 27/3248 0076, www.cavalgada pedraazul.com.br),* which is an 80-minute trip to the Mirante do Lagarto. At the foot of the Pedra Azul, it is already 3,937 feet (1,200 m) above sea level.

The **Instituto Roberto Carlos Kautsky** *(Rod. João Ricardo Schorling km 2, tel 27/3268 2300)* is an environmental nonprofit dedicated to orchids. Its nature reserve, which covers about 74 acres (300,000 sq m) of Atlantic Forest, has been enriched by plants rescued from deforested foothills. Visits must be scheduled in advance. The reserve is closed if it is raining, or has rained a lot recently.

Italian and German immigrants settled this region, mostly in the late 19th century. Several circuits allow you to delve into the local culture. The **Circuito do Chapéu** runs along the **Estrada do Chapéu,** the road that gives the circuit its name. It highlights the lives of German immigrants. The **Circuito do Galo** will introduce you to rural life and offers options for outdoors enthusiasts, including hiking trails and waterfalls. The **Circuito do Vale da Estação** is centered on the Santa Isabel district, where the first settlers put down roots. It features home-style restaurants, homemade sweets, and rural farm-hotels. For more information about activities, contact the ATPA.

A train, the **Belo Horizonte–Vitória** (tel 31/3279 4389 or 0800/285 7000, $$), runs between Belo Horizonte, capital of Minas Gerais, and Cariacica, on the outskirts of Vitória, capital of Espírito Santo. Cariacica is about 31 miles (50 km) from Domingos Martins.

Santa Teresa, Linhares, & Regência

The central and northern parts of coastal Espírito Santo offer sundry opportunities to get in touch with nature and to experience the state's Italian immigrant culture. The Italian heritage is especially visible in the city of Santa Teresa, where the first 60 families came from Veneto, Italy, in 1875. The town's architecture, cuisine, festivals, and wine production reflect the influence of those and subsequent waves of immigrants. The **Casa Lambert** (Rua São Lourenço, tel 27/3259 1611, closed Mon.–Tues.), a house built by an immigrant family, has been transformed into a museum. Popularly known as Rua de Lazer, **Rua Coronel Bonfim Júnior** is a downtown street lined with houses from the early immigrant period. Today it hosts bars and restaurants.

The **Reserva Natural Vale** in Linhares—owned and operated by the Brazilian mining giant of the same name—has its own hotel (see Travelwise p. 283) and seven trails. Bird-watchers speak highly of the area: About 380 bird species have been cataloged, including a critically endangered Yellow-legged Tinamou. Also within the limits of the Linhares municipality, but 25 miles (40 km) away on the beach, in a village called Regência at the mouth of the Rio Doce, you will find an outpost of the **Tamar Project** (Caixa Postal 105, Linhares, tel 27/3274 1209, www.tamar.org.br), part of a joint government-NGO effort to protect endangered sea turtles. You can also visit the **Centro Ecológico de Regência** (Rua do Portinho, Regência, Linhares, tel 27/3274 1209), which has displays about the region's ocean fauna and a small aquarium. ∎

Associação Turística de Pedra Azul e Região

✉ BR-262 km 88, Domingos Martins

☎ 27/3248 0035

🕐 Closed Sat.–Sun.

www. pedraazul .com.br

Linhares

🔼 99 E3

Visitor Information

✉ Av. Governo Jones dos Santos Neves 1292, Centro

☎ 27/3372 6800

🕐 Closed Sat.–Sun.

Museu de Biologia Professor Mello Leitão

Naturalist Augusto Ruschi founded the Museu de Biologia Professor Mello Leitão in Santa Teresa (Av. José Ruschi 4, tel 27/3259 1182, closed Mon.) in 1949, naming it after Cândido Firmino de Mello Leitão, a legendary Brazilian zoologist and friend.

Ruschi has cataloged hundreds of species of animals and plants in the local stretch of the Atlantic Forest. The museum's collection of preserved hummingbirds (about 1,700 individuals) and bats (about 1,300) and its herbarium (about 7,000 plants) attract scientists from around the world. The orchids are a highlight.

The museum also operates the **Estação Biológica de Santa Lúcia**, a nature reserve for scientific research about 5 miles (8 km) outside of town. Visitation is open to groups of at least five people, although smaller groups or individuals can enter if they pay extra for the "missing people."

An underappreciated region where tourists escape to beaches, explore rain forest, delve into *gaúcho* culture, and marvel at Foz do Iguaçu's stunning waterfalls

South

Looking up the Iguaçu River toward the Garganta del Diablo, or Devil's Throat

South

Save for fly-in, fly-out Foz do Iguaçu and, increasingly, the surf-beach island city Florianópolis, the Brazilian South represents a part of the country largely ignored by foreign leisure travelers. As such, it offers unique opportunities to leave the crowds behind and escape into nature or history.

Florianópolis: Surf's always up in Floripa, even for kite surfers.

This is the land of cowboys, immigrants, farmers, winemakers, and surfers—a place where people take their traditions seriously. The calendar is dotted with events like Oktoberfest (Blumenau), a grape festival (Caxias do Sul), and Farroupilha Week (Porto Alegre and other cities of Rio Grande do Sul) that commemorates a 19th-century regional Republican rebellion against the imperial government in Rio de Janeiro. Rio Grande do Sul and its ranching culture gave Brazil its ubiquitous *rodízio*-style, all-you-can-eat *churrascaria* or steakhouse.

The spectacular and certainly not-to-be-missed Foz do Iguaçu and the beach-party and surf scenes in Florianópolis may get most of the attention, but the region offers sundry other options for visitors. Outdoor enthusiasts will marvel at a coastal region in Paraná called

Lagamar, a stretch of the Atlantic Forest on par with the Pantanal and parts of the Amazon in terms of natural beauty. Lagamar includes the Ilha do Mel, a carless island with sandy footpaths amid abundant vegetation, and Sebuí, an isolated private nature reserve.

To reach the coast from Curitiba, you can take the Serra Verde Express, a train that runs through a rugged, forest-covered mountain range. The canyons of Parque Nacional de Aparados da Serra provide a striking setting for hikers. Surfers and wannabes would do well to plan time for the Praia do Rosa, a well-structured surf village in Santa Catarina. From July to November, you can add whale-watching to the mix of activities.

Likewise ubiquitous is the Paraná pine, also known as the *araucária* or candelabra tree, with its characteristically outstretched branches. Immigrants are said to have survived mostly on its seeds until their crops were established. They remain a favorite snack among locals.

NOT TO BE MISSED:

The South is one of the richer parts of Brazil. As such, it tends to offer better infrastructure for travelers. As a general rule, national parks are notorious for their poor management and states of disrepair, but Aparados da Serra, straddling the border between Rio Grande do Sul and Santa Catarina, provides a counterexample. Tour operators and service providers are more likely to be well structured and focused on quality, and both owners and employees are more likely to speak English. It is not by chance that entrepreneurs from the region have become pioneers in niches like horseback riding, cycling, and rural tourism. In Bento Gonçalves, the wine-country tour and living museum of Italian immigration are on par with similar attractions in the United States and Europe. Though things might seem a little frayed at the edges, Curitiba has been held up for decades as a model of urban planning. ■

Paraná

Nature lovers and outdoor enthusiasts should note that Paraná hosts the lion's share of a breathtaking coastal stretch of the Atlantic Forest called Lagamar. The old mule-train commercial routes left an indelible mark on the state's culture, as have successive waves of immigrants. On the state's eastern edge, you'll find the Foz do Iguaçu, a natural wonder that cannot be described, even with multiple superlatives.

The glass and steel greenhouse of Curitiba's Jardim Botânico

Curitiba

📍 137 C3

Visitor Information

✉ Aeroporto Afonso Pena

☎ 41/3381 1153

www.aeroporto curitiba.net/en

Curitiba

Paraná's state capital, Curitiba, offers a broad range of cultural institutions, museums, and quality restaurants. Compared to other large Brazilian cities, it is easy to navigate. The downtown is pedestrian friendly, and a tourist bus takes you most anywhere else you will want to go.

Start on **Rua das Flores,** Brazil's most illustrious pedestrian street. It was created at the end of the

business day on Friday, May 19, 1972, when Mayor Jaime Lerner (see sidebar opposite) dispatched a team of municipal construction workers to this stretch of Rua Quinze de Novembro—from Rua Presidente Faria (aka Travessa da Lapa) to Rua Ébano Pereira (aka Travessa Oliveira Bello). Much to the consternation of some local merchants who opposed the initiative, the carless downtown street was complete by the following Monday.

The rest of downtown Curitiba can be explored on foot. Just a few blocks southwest of Rua das Flores is **Rua 24 Horas,** another pedestrian street. Shops line this city block, which is covered by a metal and glass structure, from Rua Visconde de Nacre to Rua Visconde do Rio Branco. Despite the name given to this street, shops here no longer stay open all night, but this is still a cool place to have a coffee and hang out.

If you instead want to explore the section of downtown that is north of Rua das Flores, start by walking five or so blocks north until you reach the **Largo da Ordem,** the hub of the old **Centro Histórico.** Curitiba's oldest church, the **Igreja da Ordem Terceira de São Francisco das Chagas** *(Rua Mateus Leme 1, Centro Histórico, Largo da Ordem, tel 41/3323 4190),* which gives the square its name, stands near historic buildings and the **Memorial da Cidade** *(Rua Claudino dos Santos 79, Centro Histórico, tel 41/3321 3313, closed Mon.),* a contemporary building with a theater and exhibition spaces. On Sundays, the Largo da Ordem also hosts a crafts fair.

For exploring the rest of the city, use the **Linha Turismo,** a classic double-decker, hop-on, hop-off tourism bus that makes regular stops at 24 locations. Tickets can be purchased at any of the pick-up points. Once on, you can get off and back on up to four times. Attractions visited include a train museum, the **Museu Ferroviário** *(Av. Sete de Setembro 2775, Rebouças, tel 41/2101 9202, closed Mon.);* stunning botanical gardens, the **Jardim Botânico** *(Rua Engenheiro Ostoja Roguski, Jardim Botânico, tel 41/3264 6994);* the **Museu Oscar Niemeyer** *(Rua*

Rua 24 Horas
- ✉ Rua do Comércio 24 Horas, Centro
- ☎ 41/3225 4336

Linha Turismo URBS
- ✉ Praça Tiradentes
- ☎ 41/3352 8000
- 🕐 Closed Mon.
- 💲 $
- **www.urbs.curitiba .pr.gov.br**

Urban Planner Jaime Lerner

"A nice place to visit is a nice place to live," goes the saying among responsible tourism advocates. Nowhere in Brazil is that more applicable than in Curitiba (pop. 1.8 million), which is regarded as a global leader in sustainable urban planning.

Kudos to world-renowned architect and urban planner Jaime Lerner, who has dedicated much of his professional life to re-creating the human-scale urban environment he enjoyed as a youth in Curitiba of the 1940s and 1950s. He served three terms as mayor of his hometown in the 1970s and 1980s before serving two terms as governor of Paraná, from 1995 to 2002.

His style of urban planning has been proposed as a model for rebuilding Kabul and New Orleans. Consider Curitiba's rapid transit bus system: With its trademark clear tubes for same-level preboarding, it is efficient, affordable, and solvent. His mark is also seen in expansive urban parks and on Brazil's first downtown pedestrian mall. Lerner's approach—he calls it "urban acupuncture"—involves pinpointed interventions that can be accomplished quickly to release energy and create a positive ripple effect. Another example, found in his book *Acupuntura urbana,* is the construction of Curitiba's Ópera de Arame theater at the site of an abandoned rock quarry.

As Curitiba's reputation as a livable city has spread, Brazilians have converged on the city, and some fret that Curitiba may be the victim of its own success.

Parque Nacional do Superagüi

▲ 137 C4

✉ Comunidade da Barra do Superagüi, Ilha do Superagüi, Guaraqueçaba

☎ 41/3482 7131

Marechal Hermes 999, Centro Cívico, tel 41/3350 4400, closed Mon., $), an art museum designed by its namesake to resemble an eye; the **Ópera de Arame** *(Rua João Gava, Parque Pedreira Paulo Leminski, Pilarzinho, tel 41/3355 6072, closed Mon.),* a theater with a tubular architectural structure in a lively park in a former rock quarry; and

Museu Oscar Niemeyer, renamed after the architect who designed it, also known as "the eye"

Santa Felicidade, Curitiba's Little Italy, known in part for cavernous trattorias that serve all-you-can-eat, set-menu Italian meals. One, **Madalosso** (see Travelwise p. 289), is said to rank among the world's largest eateries.

The city's culinary landscape is a mixture of regional *tropeiro* fare, traditional dishes brought over by immigrants, and some local inventions. Among the latter are the so-called *costelões,* set-price budget barbecues that specialize in buffets of beef ribs, potato salad, green salad, fried polenta, and more.

Lagamar

Two and a half hours east of Curitiba (100 miles/160 km) is the small coastal town of **Guaraqueçaba,** the gateway to the expansive Lagamar region, which boasts a national park and two important privately owned nature reserves.

In Guaraqueçaba you'll find boats to Superagüi or Sebuí and ground transportation to Salto Morato. While in town, take the half-mile (800 m) trail that starts behind **Igreja do Nosso Senhor Bom Jesus dos Perdões** *(Rua Coronel João Isidoro)* and continues up the **Morro do Quitumbê.** At the top, some 262 feet (80 m) above sea level, you will be treated to a bird's-eye view of the surrounding region.

In 1991, Lagamar—a 125-mile (200 km) stretch of coastline straddling the Paraná–São Paulo border—was declared the first Brazilian Biosphere Reserve by UNESCO. The Lagamar salt-water estuary ranks up there with other ecological paradises like the Pantanal and sections of the Amazon.

The **Parque Nacional do Superagüi**, which comprises several adjacent islands, protects one of the biggest remaining stretches of the Atlantic Forest. This rain forest has magnificent beaches and swamplands, and orchids stand out amid the trees. The endangered black-faced lion tamarin, also known as the Superagüi lion tamarin, was first discovered here in 1990. The park's guesthouses tend to be located in an area called Superagüi Barra.

Highlights of the 5,567-acre (2,253 ha) privately

EXPERIENCE: Riding the Trem da Serra do Mar

The Trem da Serra do Mar railway wends its way through some of the most rugged and striking territory in Brazil—a coastal mountain range covered by dense tropical rain forest. The trip takes passengers from Curitiba to the historic town of Morretes, founded in 1721, which sits in the hills next to the Rio Nhundiaquara.

After an early morning departure, it takes about three hours to reach **Morretes** *(Visitor information, Rua Conselheiro Sinimbú 62, Centro, tel 41/3462 1266, closed Sat.–Sun.)*. The return trip is in the mid-afternoon, allowing time for a leisurely lunch in Morretes, which bills itself as home of the *barreado,* Paraná's most traditional dish: a thick beef stew accompanied by rice, bananas, manioc meal, and banana-flavored *cachaça.* Find some at the riverside **Restaurante Madalozo** (see Travelwise p. 290).

Construction

The 68-mile (110 km) stretch of rail from the coast to the Paraná state capital went into service in 1885. An estimated 5,000 men—mostly Italians, Germans, and Poles—died on the job during the five years it took to finish the job. Most succumbed to regular maladies: snakebites, typhoid, malaria, and accidents. But on occasion workers faced more novel vocational hazards, including encounters with jaguars that had come to the riverside to drink.

Wildlife & Foliage

The now endangered jaguar enjoys in the Serra do Mar a rare chunk of preserved natural habitat. Other endangered species in the region include the giant anteater, the black hawk-eagle, and the black-fronted piping-guan. Even if you don't see any wildlife from your window, you will still have in view the spectacular **Serra do Marumbi**

INSIDER TIP:

In southeastern Brazil, look around for living fossils such as the *araucária* tree—a relic from the dinosaur era.

—PATRICIA H. KELLEY & CHRISTY VISAGGI
National Geographic researchers

mountain range. Take note of the Paraná state symbol: the flat-topped Paraná pine, also known as the *araucária,* or candelabra tree, with its tall, straight trunk and horizontal branches. This is a gendered tree, and only females produce the seeds that were once a staple of the natives' diet.

Historical Marker

At kilometer 65, down the embankment, there stands a lonesome cross. Such adornments are common along Brazilian roadsides, but this particular cross reveals where a political prisoner was assassinated. Following the declaration of the Brazilian republic in 1889, a wealthy businessman, the Baron Serro Azul, helped pay off unsatisfied, armed rebels and saved his hometown, Curitiba. This made him suspect to the Republicans. In 1894, he was arrested, taken to the middle of nowhere, pushed off the train, and shot. The cross marks the spot.

Excursions

This line was originally called the **Serra Verde Express,** but that moniker has been adopted as the umbrella name for the parent company *(Av. Presidente Affonso Camargo 330, Centro, Curitiba, tel 41/ 3888 3488, www .serraverdeexpress.com.br, $$$),* which is establishing similar tourist trains elsewhere— for example, the Trem do Pantanal (see p. 189). On weekends and holidays there is a Trem de Luxo (luxury train) to Morretes with leather seats and velvet sofas; a bar serves first-class food and drinks.

Longer stays and one-way tickets are also possible. On Sundays, the train continues to the port town of **Paranaguá** *(Visitor information, Rua Júlia da Costa 322, Centro Histórico, tel 41/3420 6029, closed Sat.–Sun.).*

Reserva Natural Salto Morato

⊠ PR-405 km 4, Guaraqueçaba

☎ 41/3381 9671

🕓 Closed Mon.

💲 $

www.fundacaobot cario.org.br

Reserva Ecológica de Sebuí

⊠ Reserva Particular de Patrimônio Natural (RPPN) do Sebuí

☎ 41/3566 6339

🕓 Closed Sat.–Sun.

NOTE: For reservations contact **Gondwana Brasil Ecoturismo** (www.gondwanabrasil .com.br).

Ilha do Mel

🗺 137 C3

www.ilhadomel-travel.com.br

owned **Reserva Natural Salto Morato** include **Salto Morato,** a 328-foot-high (100 m) waterfall, and the **Figueira do Rio do Engenho,** a fig tree that has put down roots on both sides of a river, which runs beneath it as it would under a bridge. You can also join the fish swimming in the clear waters of a natural pool called **the Aquarium** and scout for more than 300 bird species identified on the reserve. There is a well-equipped campsite, but you need an advance reservation to pitch your tent. The reserve is maintained by the Boticário Group Foundation.

The other private nature reserve on the mainland, **Reserva Ecológica de Sebuí,** is only reachable by boat, but once you're there, you can choose hiking, canoeing, zip-lining, and more. Seek out several waterfalls, or use the elevated wooden plank walk-way to comfortably explore the swamplands. A true retreat from civilization, the reserve's sustainably managed rustic but comfortable

ecolodge offers home-style meals, often featuring fresh local fish.

Ilha do Mel

A lighthouse! No cars! Pretty much the only way to get anywhere on Ilha do Mel is via sandy footpaths overgrown with vegetation. But there are plenty of guesthouses, campsites, and restaurants—and, of course, bars—on this small island.

If ferried over from the main-land by fishers from **Pontal do Sul** (a two-hour drive from Curitiba), you will arrive in short order. Or you can take a larger boat, and a longer trip, from **Paranaguá** (90 minutes from Curitiba; *Rua da Praia, $$*).

Most of the island is encom-passed by a nature reserve. State officials attempt to limit the num-ber of individuals on the island at any given time to 5,000. Once it reaches capacity, people might be turned away. (This is generally only a problem on holiday weekends and during vacation periods, but to be safe, check beforehand.)

Guesthouses and other amenities are concentrated in two

EXPERIENCE: Discovering Lagamar by Boat

Don't pass up the chance to explore the Lagamar region via boat with **Calango Expedições** *(Praça Rocha Pombo, Estação Ferroviária, Morretes, tel 41/3462 2600)*, an environmentally sensitive tour company run by locals. After casting off from Morretes, 45 miles (70 km) from Curitiba, your guide will head down the **Nhundi-aquara River** to **Paranaguá Bay,** passing by the Paranaguá port and several islands, including **Ilha do Mel** and **Ilha das Peças. Ilha do Superagüi** will appear on one side of the Canal do Varadouro, the man-made

channel that created it in 1953. You're likely to see dolphins at your final destination, **Ilha do Cardoso,** just across the São Paulo border. And on your return trip, you'll pass by the Sebuí reserve and go through the Baía de Guaraqueçaba.

During your outing, which lasts 10.5 hours, you'll make several stops to swim in the ocean, walk along deserted beaches, hike into bush, and just hang. Want the adventure to start even earlier? Take the Trem da Serra do Mar from Curitiba to Morretes (see p. 141).

sections of the smaller part of the island: **Nova Brasília** and **Encantadas.** There are also lodgings on the island's larger section in a village called **Fortaleza.** Assuming you have reservations, check the name of the guesthouse's district before you embark, as you want to be dropped off at the right place on the island—or you'll face a long walk to where your lodgings really are.

Farol das Conchas, a lighthouse built by an English firm in 1872, is about a 15-minute walk from the Nova Brasília jetty. The reward for climbing to the lighthouse lookout point is a formidable view of the rest of the island and the coastline. Not far off is the **Praia do Farol,** a beach popular with surfers. Farther south, in the vicinity of Encantadas, the **Gruta Encantada** (Enchanted Cave) is said to have been inhabited by mermaids. To facilitate access to all visitors, a ramp has been built along the coast to the cave entrance. Nearby, the **Praia do Fora** is replete with rustic bars.

On the larger section of the island, Fortaleza faces the Atlantic Ocean—unlike the spots mentioned above, which face inland. Named for the Fortaleza de Nossa Senhora dos Prazeres, this fort (completed in 1767) was built to protect the Paranaguá port. Just north of the fort is the **Ponta do Hospital,** apparently named for the layovers that slave ships would make here, where they secured an abundant supply of citrus fruits to help the human cargo recover from scurvy. Today, its beach is

Visitors to Foz do Iguaçu stand on the Brazil side and look across into Argentina.

one of the most popular on the western side of the island.

Caminhos do Sertão (see sidebar p. 154) offers a bicycle tour that includes a visit to the island.

Iguaçu Falls

With hundreds of individual waterfalls, the spectacular **Cataratas do Iguaçu** (Iguaçu Falls) are a natural wonder that you should go out of your way to see. As Brazilians love to tell Americans, when First Lady Eleanor Roosevelt got her first glimpse of Iguaçu Falls, she is said to have exclaimed, *(continued on p. 147)*

Foz do Iguaçu
 137 A3

Visitor Information

✉ Avenida Costa e Silva s/n Rodoviária

☎ 45/3522 1027

✉ Tourist Center, Foz do Iguaçu Airport, Rod. das Cataratas km 13

☎ 45/3521 42767

Drive: The Trilha do Tropeiro

Before freight trains took over, overland shipping was conducted by mule trains, and the men who operated these routes were called *tropeiros*. One of the many important trails through the outback ran from the city of Viamão—on the coast of Rio Grande do Sul and adjacent to today's state capital, Porto Alegre—to Sorocaba, in the interior of São Paulo. On the way, it crossed through Paraná. In terms of establishing settlements and influencing local culture, tropeiros made perhaps their biggest marks on a stretch just east of Curitiba.

Vila Velha, Paraná: Take a hike along what used to be the bottom of the sea.

Mules themselves helped established the route, and not just because they carried necessities. With the mineral discoveries in Minas Gerais, miners needed pack animals to transport cargo, and large numbers of mules happened to be roaming the ranges of Rio Grande do Sul. So they were commandeered for the mines and sent northward.

To get started on the drive, take BR-476 west out of **Curitiba,** and about 40 miles (70 km) later, you will reach **Lapa** ❶—a city founded by tropeiros around 1730 as a way station. Their culinary traditions are maintained by the **Restaurante Lipski** (see Travelwise p. 289), where the main dish is *quirera lapiana*, made of corn and pork ribs. The 14 blocks of

NOT TO BE MISSED:

Museu do Tropeiro • Parque Estadual de Vila Velha • Buraco do Padre • Rio Jaguaríaiva • Parque Estadual do Cerrado

the Centro Histórico resemble a Hollywood back-lot period set.

One of the oldest and best preserved buildings is the Casa Vermelha, which houses the **Museu do Tropeiro** (*Rua Barão do Rio Branco 1320, tel 41/3622 4387, closed Mon.*). Another, the **Theatro São João** (*Praça General Carneiro,* *tel 41/3911 1000),* a theater that opened in 1876, was pressed into service as an infirmary during the momentous 1894 stand by Republican troops against advancing Federalists from Rio Grande do Sul who were demanding more autonomy. Today, the theater, with its eclectic architecture—Italian-style stage, Elizabethan-style seating, and neoclassical facade—boasts a full schedule of plays, music, and dance.

Lapa has received religious pilgrims at the **Gruta do Monge** *(Av. Getúlio Vargas, tel 41/3547 8050),* where a 19th-century monk is said to have performed miracles.

Lapa Area Parks

From Lapa, take PR-427 north to Palmeira. and continue north on PR-151 to **Ponta Grossa ❷,** another stop on the Tropeiro Trail. Today it serves as a gateway to **Parque Estadual de Vila Velha** *(BR-376 km 28, Ponta Grossa, tel 42/3228 1138, closed Tues., $).* To reach the park take BR-376 southeast back toward Curitiba; at kilometer 28, take the Visconde de Mauá exit. This prairie region sports rock formations from millions of years ago, when it was covered by the ocean. The park is dotted with rock

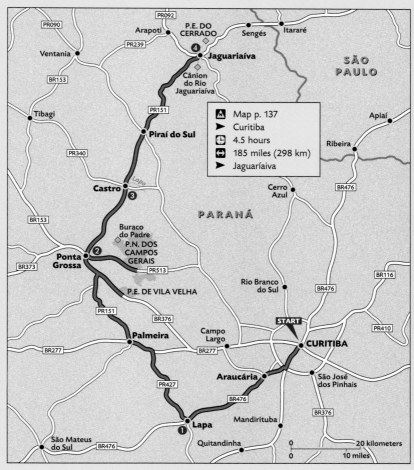

Map p. 137
► Curitiba
⏱ 4.5 hours
↔ 185 miles (298 km)
► Jaguaríaiva

Buraco do Padre in Campos Gerais National Park, Paraná

formations, like the emblematic Taça (which resembles a gigantic wine glass); vegetation-lined craters called *furnas* with groundwater at the bottom; and the **Lagoa Dourada,** a lake named for the golden light it reflects at sunset. Also nearby is **Parque Nacional dos Campos Gerais** *(Rua Monteiro Lobato 2625, Ponta Grossa, tel 42/3238 1515).* Its main attraction is the **Buraco do Padre,** a subterranean chamber about 98 feet (30 m) in diameter that contains a 148-foot (45 m) waterfall. Access to the Buraco do Padre is via PR-513, heading east out of Ponta Grossa. At kilometer 14, turn off on Estrada de Acesso ao Buraco do Padre. The whole trip is about 19 miles (30 km) from Ponta Grossa, partly on a dirt road.

River Stop

From Ponta Grossa, continue on PR-151 north to **Castro ❸**. Castro was an important rest stop along the Tropeiro Trail, in part because the Rio Lapo, the river bordering the town, was often flooded, forcing even the most hurried tropeiro to wait. Castro's **Museu do Tropeiro** *(Praça Getúlio Vargas 11, tel 42/3906 2179, closed Mon.)* is considered the best museum dedicated to the memory of the people who worked this trade route.

The **Casa de Sinhara** *(Praça Getúlio Vargas 6, tel 42/3906 2179, closed Mon.)* is a museum—its name being a play on the popular pronunciation of the word *senhora*—pays homage to colonial-era women. The **Fazenda Capão Alto** *(Estr. Castro Alto Caixa 119, tel 42/3232 5856, closed Mon., $ www.fazendacapaoalto.com.br)* marks the spot where the tropeiros used to camp. Later, the land was taken over by a rich rancher. Although undergoing restoration, 90-minute tours can be scheduled with advance notice.

Staying on PR-151, about 50 miles (80 km) northeast of Castro, just before the Tropeiro Trail slips across the border into São Paulo state, you'll find the world's eighth largest canyon by length. The **Cânion do Rio Jaguaríaiva** *(PR-151 km 7, tel 43/3535 7935)* is shaped by sandstone walls that reach up to 262 feet (80 m) high. The river that runs through it includes a 6-mile (10 km) stretch that is perfect for white-water rafting and canoeing. The gateway town, also called **Jaguaríaiva ❹**, was on the old tropeiro trail. Access to the canyon is 4.5 miles (7 km) south of downtown, at a traffic circle that is also the turnoff to two paper-mill companies.

Parque Estadual do Cerrado *(PR-092, Bairro Pesqueiro, Jaguaríaiva, tel 41/3213 3819),* a state park that protects the last vestiges of the *cerrado* eco-region in Paraná, is open to visitors, but you must schedule a visit beforehand. To reach the park from Jaguaríaiva, take PR-092 southeast toward Pesqueiro and look for the sign for the park. Turning off at the sign, it is another 1.2 miles (2 km) on a dirt road to the park entrance.

Although cowhands and old mule trains would probably continue north to Sorocaba, in the interior of São Paulo, before you finish the drive you should return to Jaguaríaiva and follow PR-151 as it continues to swing northeast, in the direction of Sengés, for about 2.5 miles (4 km). Here you'll come upon **Parque Ambiental Dr. Ruy Cunha Bosque do Tropeiro** *(Rua Porto Velho, Bairro Pedrinha, Jaguaríaiva, tel 43/9965 5752, closed Mon.–Tues.),* a nature reserve with a tropeiro museum as well as hiking trails.

"Poor Niagara! This makes it look like a kitchen faucet."

According to Brazilian history books, lobbying efforts by Alberto Santos Dumont, the "father of aviation," helped convince the government to create **Parque Nacional do Iguaçu** in 1939. Make no mistake about it—this mass-tourism destination has annual attendance figures topping one million.

INSIDER TIP:

There are facilities for tourists on both sides of Iguaçu Falls, including lodges, tours, hikes, and "run-the-falls" boating.

—ROBYN BURNHAM
National Geographic grantee

Veteran guides suggest three "can't miss" angles for viewing the falls, each of which must be approached from a different starting point. First, a spectacular panoramic view can be seen from the Brazil side. Second, a close-up of the literally breathtaking section called the **Devil's Throat** can be had only via the pedestrian ramp on the Argentina side. And third, outboard-powered rafts (accessible from either side of the border) ease you right up to the powerful showers as they smack the surface, giving you the impressive view from below. If you can afford a fourth, rather pricey helicopter tour, the view from on high is spectacular.

In the mid-2000s, a private firm called **Cânion Iguaçu** received the first concession to run adventure tourism activities inside a Brazilian national park—which means you can rappel down from a 180-foot-high (55 m) platform or go rock climbing in view of the falls. Cânion Iguaçu also offers a short river-rafting trip (Class III+) on the Rio Iguaçu and an obstacle course–style canopy tour.

Less than 12 miles (20 km) outside of town stands the **Usina Hidrelétrica de Itaipu**—the world's second biggest hydro-electric dam after China's Three Gorges. There are two tours for visitors: One covers the external section via buses; another slightly more expensive one descends into the belly of the beast, where you can feel the vibrations that run through the structure. On Friday and Saturday nights, there is a panoramic light show.

You can do everything in a few days. The town itself has little to offer. On the Argentina side of the falls, **Puerto Iguazú** harbors a handful of top-notch *parrillas,* or barbecues, and a few casinos. Brazilians like to skip over to the Paraguay side to buy cheap, duty-free consumer goods.

With few attractions in town, try to stay at the **Hotel das Cataratas** (see Travelwise p. 289), located inside the park—the only way to see the falls in the evening or at dawn, when the park is closed. The hotel also offers night excursions. A less-expensive option is the **Hostel Paudimar Campestre** (see Travelwise p. 289), a local affiliate of Hostelling International. ■

Parque Nacional do Iguaçu
✉ BR-469 km 18
☎ 45/3521 4400
www.cataratasdo iguacu.com.br

Cânion Iguaçu
✉ Rod. das Cataratas km 27.5, Parque Nacional do Iguaçu
☎ 45/3529 6040
www.campode desafios.com.br

Usina Hidrelétrica de Itaipu
🅼 137 A3–A4
✉ Av. Tancredo Neves 6731, Foz do Iguaçu
☎ 45/3520 5252 (Reservations recommended)
💲 $–$$
www.itaipu.gov.br /en/tourism-home

NOTE: Minimum age 14; check website for information on appropriate footwear

Santa Catarina

Surfing, whale-watching, and rural tourism are among the staples of what makes Santa Catarina attractive to visitors. The state capital, the island-city of Florianópolis, offers dozens of
beaches, lively nightlife, and an abundant supply of oysters. But it is worth getting out to the
countryside, where you might, for instance, enjoy a cycling trip through the rural outback.

There are scores of beaches in Florianópolis.

Florianópolis

🗺 137 C3

Visitor Information

✉ Rod. Rita Maria
(bus terminal)

✉ Av. Paulo Fontes
1101, Centro

☎ 48/3212 3100

Florianópolis

An island connected by bridge
to the mainland, Florianópolis—
roughly 45 miles (70 km) long
and 10 miles (18 km) wide—has
about 100 beaches, including
40 or so with easy access. These
beaches and the accompanying
nightlife constitute some of the
main attractions, though there are
opportunities to delve into the
culture of immigrants from the
Azores, oyster farming, and more.

You can view the island-city's
postcard image upon arrival:
a bridge, the **Ponte Hercílio**

Luz, closed since 1982, remains
Brazil's biggest suspension bridge.
Designed by the American firm
Robinson & Steinman and built by
the American Bridge Company, it
was the longest eyebar suspension
bridge in the world when built
in 1926. Much public money has
been poured into efforts to repair,
fortify, and reopen the bridge, but
no date has been projected for
reopening. Enjoy the bridge when
it is lit at night.

Near the bridge's island base
in Centro stands the **Mercado Público Municipal** *(Rua*

Conselheiro Mafra 255, tel 48/3225 8464, closed Sun.), the public market built in 1898 and expanded in 1915. With 140 kiosks that sell fish, fruits, vegetables, crafts, and more, it is a good place to try local finger food. The most animated hangout is, without a doubt, **Box 32** (see Travelwise p. 292), opened in 1984 by a former gas station owner, Beto Barreiros.

Many visitors come to Florianópolis, known as "Floripa" among the locals, in search of beaches and the attendant nightlife. (For an overview of surf spots, see p. 150.) Nightlife is centered around **Lagoa da Conceição** and beaches like Jurerê Internacional and **Praia Brava.** There are also some interesting bars downtown in the Centro district.

Portuguese Forts: Eleven forts were erected in the 18th century by the Portuguese to protect the island from Spanish forces. In partnership with the local university, Universidade Federal de Santa Catarina (UFSC), three of them have been renovated and are open to visitors: Completed in 1744, the **Fortaleza de Santa Cruz de Anhatomirim**—just off the mainland coast, near Floripa's northern end—has an impressive portico. The architecture of the **Fortaleza de São José da Ponta Grossa,** built on a hill opposite Anhatomirim and dating from 1740, was influenced by the Italian Renaissance. Just south of those fortresses, the **Fortaleza de Santo Antônio de Ratones** is also a starting point for walks on nearby trails through Ilha Ratones Grande's preserved section of the Atlantic Forest.

Art & Crafts: Offbeat and off the beaten path (just 10 miles/16 km south of the Mercado Público), the **Museu o Mundo Ovo de Eli Heil** *(SC-401 km 7, 7079 Santo Antônio de Lisboa, tel 48/3235 1076, www.eliheil.org .br)* is dedicated to the colorful and inventive work of Eli Heil, born in 1929. Untrained, she took up painting and drawing while recovering from a long illness. She became a leading exponent of outsider art, or art brut.

INSIDER TIP:

In Florianópolis, there is a path between Santinho beach and Moçambique beach— a 40-minute walk through the brush- wood in the cliffs— with a wonderful view. Bring water and food because Moçambique beach is almost virgin.

—RODRIGO NICOLETTE
Professor, University of São Paulo

More art can be found when you head to the northern half of the island. Don't miss the crafts shop and art gallery at **Casa Açoriana** *(Rua Cônego Serpa 30, Santo Antônio de Lisboa, tel* *(continued on p. 152)*

Fortaleza de Santa Cruz de Anhatomirim

✉ Ilha de Anhatomirim
☎ 48/3721 8302
$ $

Fortaleza de São José da Ponta Grossa

✉ Praia do Forte
☎ 48/3721 8302
$ $

Fortaleza de Santo Antônio de Ratones

✉ Ilha de Ratones Grande
☎ 48/3721 8302
$ $

Surfing Locales

Whether you are a hard-core surfer or an enthusiastic wannabe, Santa Catarina is the place to catch both waves and lessons.

Hard-core surfers flock to Florianópolis, Santa Catarina.

The origins of surfing in Brazil are linked to Osmar Gonçalves, who made a surfboard using instructions from an issue of *Popular Mechanics* that had been brought back from a trip to the United States. That was in the late 1930s, three decades after Hawaiian-born George Freeth introduced the sport to California. Tourists and airline employees had already introduced surfboards to Brazil, but Gonçalves and his friends made the sport stick with their homemade boards. When the mid-century California surf craze hit, and fiberglass boards came on the scene, surfing took off.

Brazil's best known surfer is perhaps international tennis star Gustavo "Guga" Kuerten, a three-time French Open winner. Not coincidentally, Guga was born in Florianópolis, Santa Catarina. While Brazil may have a vibrant beach culture all along the coast, the state of Santa Catarina is a revered pilgrimage destination for serious global surfers.

Florianópolis Island

Florianópolis is the capital of Santa Catarina state, but it is also an island just off the coast, adorned by beaches. You can hop from one beach to another, catching waves of 3 to 5 feet (1–1.5 m) depending on the season and conditions. (The best swells tend to be in the Southern Hemisphere's spring and summer.) Winds can be variable—favorable offshores (landside gusts) can quickly turn into swell-destroying onshores (seaside winds). But because the island is lined by craggy beaches, you can almost always find a place with suitable conditions.

Praia Brava stands out as one of the more popular of Florianópolis's beaches. Waves, here, break on a sandy seabed, creating a beach break. Good quality waves tend to crest between 1 and 8 feet (0.5–2.5 m) high. **Jurerê Internacional** and **Praia Mole** are also beloved spots. **Praia da Joaquina,** which has been dubbed the "Maracanã of Surfing"—a reference to the Rio football stadium that was the world's biggest when it first opened—hosts international surf competitions. Praia Mole and **Galheta** are close by, the latter being the only clothing-optional beach in the vicinity. For beginners, **Barra da Lagoa** is recommended.

Other Florianópolis beaches frequented by boarders include **Praia do Santinho** (ranked by surfers as the best spot on the northern tip of the island), **Praia do Moçambique** (to escape the masses), and **Praia do Morro das Pedras** (good but inconsistent wave activity). For a true surfin' safari, there's **Praia Lagoinha do Leste,** reachable only by foot or boat. Beware that in May and June, during mullet-fishing season—when fishers pull their catches out of the water and oxcarts replace surfboards—surfing is prohibited at a handful of spots.

On the Mainland

Surfing paradise **Praia do Rosa**—45 miles (70 km) south of São José—has become one of the best known secrets in Brazil (see p. 152). Only a couple decades ago, the Praia do Rosa was frequented by just a few odd hippies up from Rio Grande do Sul. The beach took its name from local resident Dorvino Manoel

INSIDER TIP:

Statues of the sea goddess Iemanjá, protector of fishermen and children, adorn many beaches, and celebrations in her honor may be held from December to February.

—PATRICIA H. KELLEY & CHRISTY VISAGGI,
National Geographic researchers

da Rosa. Although he didn't own the beach, he was the guy who lived in the house on a path that led to it. Locals disdained the land beyond Rosa's place on the seaward side of the hill overlooking the shore: It wasn't much good for growing manioc. Today, that seaside real estate is populated with guesthouses, bars, and other establishments, yet the area retains some of its old-time charm.

In addition to Praia do Rosa to the south, there are several other surfing outposts on the Santa Catarina mainland. Among them, **Balneário Camboriú,** 50 miles (80 km) north of Florianópolis, features an exposed beach break and pretty consistent waves.

Lounge on the sand or surf the waves at one of Florianópolis's beaches.

Whaling

Like many settlements along the Santa Catarina coast, **Garopaba** and **Imbituba** owe their histories—and not just their economic base—to whale blubber. Even that quaint church on the hill in Garopaba counted blubber extract among its construction materials.

Right whales were thus named because they were the "right" ones to hunt. They are slow swimmers, and their thick layers of blubber, the source of the valuable oil that once lit up the streets of Europe, ensured that the carcasses would float as fishermen towed them to shore.

Whalers bagged some 15,000 animals along the southern Brazilian coast between 1770 and 1950. Hunting ended after 1973 for the simple reason that nobody could find whales to kill anymore.

Around 1980, locals began to spot them again. A group of four volunteer biologists set out to confirm the rumors.

They founded the Projeto Baleia Franca (Right Whale Project) in 1981 to study and protect the animals. Meanwhile, global opposition to whaling increased, and Brazil prohibited hunting in its waters in 1985. A few years ago, the project convinced the federal government to declare this stretch of coast a nature sanctuary.

Whale season runs from July to November, when whales head to the area off the Santa Catarina coast for mating, calving, and nursing. A private firm, **Vida Sol e Mar** (see p. 153) runs whale-watching boat trips that leave from both Garopaba and Imbituba. The **Projeto Baleia Franca** *(Praia de Itapirubá Norte, Imbituba, tel 48/3255 2922)* provides orientation for observation from dry land; it also manages the **Museu da Baleia** *(Rua Itagiba 220, Praia do Porto, Imbituba, tel 48/3255 2922, closed Sun.–Mon., $)*, a museum located in an old whaling station.

Imbituba

 137 C3

Visitor Information

 Prefeitura de Imbituba, Av. Doutor João Rimsa 601, Centro

 48/3355 8100

48/3235 1262), which also has a café and restaurant.

Azores' Influence: The culture of immigrants from Portugal's Azores islands can be experienced in two places: in the **Ribeirão da Ilha district,** in the southwestern section of the island, and to the north in Santo Antônio de Lisboa and neighboring **Sambaqui.** These have become oyster-cultivation centers, and it is worth stopping at one of the local restaurants to try some—perhaps at **Ostradamus** *(Rod. Baldicero Filomeno 7640, tel 48/3337 5711, closed Mon., $)* in Ribeirão da Ilha or **Beira d'Água** *(Rod. Gilson da Costa Xavier, tel 48/3335 0194, $)* in Sambaqui.

After your visit to Floripa, you may want to spend the night somewhere more remote. Just south of Florianópolis by boat— but about 22 miles (35 km) by car from São José, the closest city on the mainland—is **Ilha do Papagaio,** an island with an upscale guesthouse and a tranquil beach surrounded by a preserved section of the Atlantic Forest.

Praia do Rosa, Garopaba & Imbituba

The Praia do Rosa stands out even among Santa Catarina's countless top-notch surf spots (see p. 151). Windsurfing and kite surfing are popular. Hikers can take trails to other beaches and nearby lakes, or they can just do a circuit for a day loop.

The beach has more than a dozen restaurants that serve up everything from pizzas and crepes to regional seafood dishes like squid with shrimp stuffing. A smattering of bars offers somewhere to relax during the day or party at night—often with live music.

During the August–November whale-watching season, Praia do Rosa offers quick access to land-side vista points. It is also halfway between two departure points for ocean excursions: Imbituba, 12 miles (20 km) to the south, and Garopaba, an equal distance to the north. For details, stop by the **Vida Sol e Mar Ecoresort** in Imbituba, which is owned by the same company that operates the whale-watching boats.

While you're in Garopaba, visit the **Dunas do Siriú** sand dunes, which are popular with sand boarders, and the **Praia da Ferrugem,** which is considered a prime surfing spot and sports lively nightlife.

Blumenau

Blumenau—an inland city approximately 90 miles (140 km) northwest of Florianópolis on the coast and a good 150 miles (250 km) south of Curitiba—hosts the biggest Oktoberfest beer bust outside of Germany, and its German immigrant culture and beer attract visitors 365 days a year.

Founded in 1850 by immigrants from the Old Country along the Rio Itajaí-Açu, Blumenau is an important regional commercial and industrial

center. Leisure travelers should begin their visit at **Parque Vila Germânica** (*Rua Alberto Stein 199, Bairro da Velha, 47/3381 7700, www.parquevilagermanica.com.br),* the epicenter of Oktoberfest, which stays open year-round. Half-timbered buildings typical of many German streets are filled with pubs, souvenir shops, and traditional restaurants.

Beer Tradition: Also downtown but closer to the river, you'll find a beer museum, the **Museu da Cerveja** (*Praça Hercílio Luz, Rua Quinze de Novembro 160, tel 47/3326 6791),* featuring

Vida Sol e Mar Ecoresort

✉ Estr. Geral da Praia do Rosa, Ibiraquera, Imbituba

☎ 48/3355 6111

www.vidasolemar .com.br

Shops line the streets of Blumenau, where descendants of German immigrants put on an annual Oktoberfest.

EXPERIENCE: Cycling

Brazil is slowly developing infrastructure for cycling tours, and most of the action is in Santa Catarina. Unlike in the United States and, especially, Europe, cycling tours never really caught on in Brazil. In some ways, it makes sense, since few urban areas offer extensive networks of bicycle paths. And Brazil's roadways can prove deadly: Its death rate is nearly double that for Argentina and more than three times higher than for bicycle-friendly France.

Bike touring in Santa Catarina

But Brazil is a country full of natural beauty, traditional cultures, and reasonably well-maintained (albeit often unpaved) country back roads that cry out to be explored. **Caminhos do Sertão** *(Rua Vento Sul 197, Campeche, Florianópolis, tel 48/3234 7712 or 8407 8103, www.caminhos dosertao.com.br, closed Sat.– Sun.)* has pioneered quality cycling tourism in Brazil since 2004. Guides are cycling enthusiasts—some of whom speak English, German, or Spanish. Support vehicles provide infrastructure.

The flagship tour runs from the hills of the Serra Catarinense to Florianópolis. The eight-day journey begins in the **Serra Geral** mountains, at 4,593 feet (1,400 m) above sea level, and wends its way through mountain paths and country roads—past cliff walls, rivers, waterfalls, farms, and hot springs. The trip passes by several interesting attractions, including a 5,978-foot (1,822 m) peak called the **Morro da Igreja** (see p. 156); the cliffs of the **Serra do Corvo Branco,** which reaches 4,822 feet (1,470 m); the "natural rock sculptures" of a mountain called the **Morro do Campestre;** the **Cascata do Avencal,** a 328-foot-high (100 m) waterfall; and the **Parque Nacional de São Joaquim** (see p. 156). Lodging is with local farmers, members of an association called Acolhida na Colônia, associated with the French Rede Accueil Paysan. The four-day rural tour also uses the Acolhida na Colônia network (see p. 157) and will put you in contact with local small farmers.

During the whale watching season (*July–Nov.;* see p. 152), cyclists follow the seagoing behemoths along a coastal route from Imbituba to Florianópolis. In addition to gazing at the whales, riders will pass along nine beaches; visit the **Projeto Ambiental Gaia Village** (Gaia Village Environmental Project), an alternative community focused on sustainable living; and have breakfast at a farm associated with the **Ponto de Cultura Engenhos de Farinha**—a group of small producers linked to the Slow Food movement.

A seven-day circuit, the **Vale Europeu,** explores a region of the state rich in natural beauty and German immigrant culture. Developed by **Clube de Cicloturismo do Brasil** (*www.clubedecicloturismo .com.br*), a cycling association, this was Brazil's first planned cycling route. The club has since developed a half-dozen more routes around the country.

Day trips (3–6 hours) in Florianópolis are always an option, too. Three different excursions of between 12 and 21 miles (20–35 km) will take you to beaches, fishing villages, and waterfalls.

brewing equipment from the old Cervejaria Feldmann and other artifacts.

Three local breweries offer tours of their facilities and an opportunity to taste their brews: **Cervejaria Bierland** *(Rua Gustavo Zimmermann 5361, Itoupava Central, tel 47/3337 3100, www.bierland .com.br, closed Mon.),* a 30-minute drive north of downtown; **Cervejaria Eisenbahn** *(Rua Bahia 5181, Salto Weissbach, tel 47/3488 7371, closed Sun., $),* 5 miles (10 km) west of downtown, on the river; and **Cervejaria Wunder Bier** *(Rua Frtiz Spernau 155, Fortaleza, tel 47/3339 0001, closed Sun.),* on the north side of the river, 4 miles (6 km) from the beer museum. If you plan to hit only one, Eisenbahn might be the best choice, but note that visits must

be scheduled in advance. Several breweries in neighboring towns are also open to visitors. And where would brewers be without a good source of clean water? The **Museu da Água** (Water Museum) is located in the city's old water-treatment plant.

Crafts & Museums: The town is a major center for handcrafted crystal, and there are several outlets in town. **Glas Park** *(Rua Rudolf Roedel 233 & 147, Salto Weissbach, tel 47/3327 1261, closed Sun.)* includes a small museum—the **Museu do Cristal**—and features demonstrations of crystal making.

The **Vapor** *Blumenau (Praça Juscelino Kubitschek de Oliveira, Prainha)* is an old, deactivated German-made steamship that

Museu da Água
✉ Rua Lages, Boa Vista
☎ 47/3340 3242

Anita Garibaldi & Laguna

Anita Garibaldi, the "heroine of two worlds," was born Ana Maria de Jesus Ribeiro da Silva in the Morrinhos district of Laguna, Santa Catarina, in 1821. By all accounts, this daughter of immigrants from the Azores was an independent young lady. A teen when her father died, she was soon, thereafter, married off by her mother. The marriage failed and her husband joined the army.

Around that time, a Republican uprising against the imperial government in Rio de Janeiro—known as the Farroupilha Revolution—broke out in southern Brazil. Giuseppe Garibaldi, an Italian revolutionary running from authorities back home, joined the rebel army and helped take Laguna in 1837. The rebels founded what would be a short-lived Juliana Republic with Laguna as its capital.

Anita met Giuseppe and soon was fighting at his side. Pregnant at the time, she was captured by imperial forces—escaping in a chase scene that would put Hollywood to shame. She rejoined the rebels and Garibaldi, and a few months later, their first child was born.

The couple went on to fight for causes in Uruguay and Italy, where Garibaldi emerged as the leader of an anticlerical Republican unification movement. Anita died in 1849, during the Italian uprising.

In Laguna, two sites pay homage to her legacy. The **Museu Anita Garibaldi** *(Praça República Juliana, tel 48/3646 2542, $)* houses mostly artifacts from the Farroupilha Revolution. And the **Casa de Anita** *(Rua Jerônimo Coelho, Centro)* is where she prepared for her first wedding. A small display tells her story.

Blumenau, Santa Catarina: Crystal makers at work

Parque Nacional de São Joaquim

⛰ 137 C3

✉ 16 miles (27 km) East of Urubici

☎ 49/3278 4994

embarked on its inaugural voyage in 1895 and plied the river from Blumenau to the port town of Itajaí. It now sits on the banks of that same river, the Rio Itajaí-Açu, and functions as a museum.

Oktoberfest: The city's annual festival (*www.oktoberfestblumenau .com.br*) runs for 18 days in October. On the eve of opening night, the Bierwagen circulates through the streets pouring free draft beer. Opening day is marked by a parade involving more than 2,500 participants divided into about 100 groups on the Rua Quinze de Novembro, a main drag downtown. All told, there are a

half dozen major parades during the festival.

There are also daily presentations of traditional German music and dance, food stands, and, of course, beer-drinking contests. Though some might question the wisdom of mixing alcohol and guns, local hunting culture is represented with the Rei do Tiro (King of the Shot) competition. Nearly 600,000 people passed through the turnstiles during the 2012 festival.

Parque Nacional de São Joaquim, Urubici, & Lajes

This section of south-central Santa Catarina is the coldest region of Brazil. Unheard of elsewhere in the tropics, snowfall is common here in wintertime. The main attractions are rural tourism and **Parque Nacional de São Joaquim,** created in 1961 to protect a section of southern Brazil's characteristic araucaria pine forest, threatened by deforestation. In winter, the snow-covered trees offer a landscape unequaled anywhere else in tropical Brazil.

Until July 2012, when new federal regulations laid down rules for permissible activities—contemplation, hiking, rock climbing, mountain biking, horseback riding, and hang gliding—the park had been closed to visitors. The park's main geological attractions are the **Pedra Furada**—as the name in Portuguese suggests, a rock formation with a hole seemingly punched through the middle—and a peak, **Morro da Igreja.** The weather station there registered

INSIDER TIP:

The little surfer town of Garopaba is a mix of beachgoers, surfers, yogis, and retirees. It is quiet and peaceful in comparison to the hustle and bustle of busy "Floripa."

—ROBYN BURNHAM
National Geographic grantee

the lowest temperature ever in recorded Brazilian history, −17.8°C (0°F), in June 1996.

Agritourism: Located about 90 miles (144 km) west-southwest of Florianópolis, Urubici is the town closest to the park entrance. It claims to be the vegetable-growing capital of Santa Catarina. For a real taste of the local culture, stay at one of the half dozen farms that operate guesthouses or rent rooms to travelers. They are members of an association called **Acolhida na Colônia** *(Santa Rosa de Lima, tel 48/3654 0186 or 3256 0131).*

Urubici's main attractions include **Vinhos Celestino** *(Rua Francisco Ghizoni 150, tel 49/3278 4169 or 8402 7877),* a family-run winery open for visitation and wine tasting; the **Café Colonia Sabor da Roça** (see Travelwise p. 292), where you can relish an enormous afternoon "snack" of cakes, jams, and more; and the **Propriedade Cascata Véu da Noiva** *(Morro da Igreja Urubici, tel 49/9134 3409 or 9135 2121, $),* with a trail that leads up to the Morro da Igreja—the waterfall that gives the place its name—a zip line, and a restaurant.

About 30 miles (50 km) southeast of Urubici, in the city of **São Joaquim,** a relatively new winery is producing award-winning vintages. **Villa Francioni** will take you beyond the normal tour and tasting experience: Its premises include an art gallery with works by such renowned artists as Camille Claudel and Luciano Martins.

Lajes, the birthplace of rural tourism in Brazil, is about 65 miles (105 km) east of Urubici. And another 28 miles (45 km) southeast from Lajes, the **Fazenda do Barreiro** counts among the pioneers. Founded in 1782, the farm is run by the eighth genera-tion of the founding family. The main house, a stone building, features a kitchen with a wood fire that remains lit throughout the cold winter days. Activities include hiking, fishing, helping with the farm chores, and, of course, horseback riding. ∎

Villa Francioni
- ✉ Rod. SC-438 km 70, São Joaquim
- ☎ 49/3233 8200
- $ $

Bolshoi

In 2000, Russia's Bolshoi Theatre estab-lished its only international outpost in **Joinville,** Santa Catarina—in the state's northeast corner. The initiative followed the company's 1996 Brazil tour, which included a stop at the Joinville Dance Festival. Any-one can audition for the **Bolshoi School of Ballet** (*Av. José Vieira 315, América, Joinville, tel 47/3422-4070, www.escolabolshoi.com.br, closed Sun., $*). Be sure to schedule your visit in advance.

Rio Grande do Sul

This is the land of the Pampas, reminiscent of Argentina and Uruguay with their characteristic open ranges. Even though much of Brazil's beef production has migrated elsewhere, cowboy culture remains strong in Rio Grande do Sul, as does the influence of immigrants.

Porto Alegre

🔺 137 B2

Visitor Information

✉ Largo Jornalista Glênio Peres s/n, ground floor Quadra 3, loja 99, Mercado Público

☎ 0800/517686 or 51/3211 5705

The Fundação Iberê Camargo in Porto Alegre, a world-class cultural and artistic institution

Porto Alegre

As capital of the state of Rio Grande do Sul, Porto Alegre offers a gateway to the region of the Pampas and a window on the culture of the *gaúchos,* as Brazilians from this part of the extreme south of the country are known. It also has lively bohemian and music scenes, and—drawing from the cattle-raising tradition—a number of excellent steakhouses.

Most of the major downtown attractions can be reached on foot in a single day. Several sit adjacent to the Praça da Alfândega. The **Museu Santander Cultural** *(Rua Sete de Setembro 1028, Centro Histórico, tel 51/3287 5500, closed Mon.)* offers a full program of art, cinema, and music. Set in an old post office dating from the early 20th century, the **Memorial do Rio Grande do Sul** *(Rua Sete de Setembro 1020, Centro Histórico, tel 51/3224 7210, closed Sun.–Mon.)* is dedicated to the state's culture and history. The **Museu de Arte do Rio Grande do Sul Ado Malagoli** (MARGS; *Praça da Alfândega, Centro Histórico, Porto Alegre, tel 51/3227 2311, closed Mon.)* boasts a collection of 2,800 international, national, and regional artworks.

A few blocks southwest, the **Casa de Cultura Mario Quintana** *(Rua dos Andradas 736, Centro Histórico, tel 51/3221 7147)* celebrates the memory of the 20th-century writer; set in the former Hotel Majestic, it offers a full range of diverse cultural activities. Also nearby is the **Mercado Público,** an eclectic 1869 building erected in the image of the Mercado da Praça da Figueira in Lisbon, with a second-floor add-on in the French neoclassical tradition.

Cultural Traditions

Southern Brazil probably has the best organized institutions to promote local roots culture of any region in Brazil. Many of the hundreds of centers in Rio Grande do Sul hold regular cultural activities that are open to the public. Held at various times of the year, they are aimed at preserving local traditions and heritage.

The oldest organization, **Centro de Tradições Gaúchas,** was founded in Porto Alegre in the 1940s and honors the *gaúcho.* Called CTG 35 in homage to the 1835 Farroupilha Revolution (see sidebar p. 155), it led to the creation of similar

centers throughout Rio Grande do Sul, the rest of Brazil, and indeed around the world. There are more than 1,600 in Rio Grande do Sul, more than 500 in neighboring Santa Catarina, and even 33 in the Amazonian state of Rondônia.

In Porto Alegre, the **Churrascaria Roda de Carreta** *(Av. Ipiranga 5200, tel 51/3336 0817, www.churrascariarodadecar reta.com.br, $),* next door to CGT headquarters, serves as a traditional steakhouse and cultural space offering its own cultural presentations on Monday to Saturday evenings and on Sunday at midday.

In the **Fundação Iberê Camargo** (Iberê Camargo Foundation), Porto Alegre boasts a state-of-the-art exhibition space and cultural center perhaps unrivaled anywhere in Brazil. Projected by the Portuguese architect Álvaro Siza, its award-winning design features curved outlines made of reinforced concrete. Landscaping chores were handed off to a local environmental group, the Gaia Foundation, which planted a native forest on the grounds behind the building. The institution—just 4 miles (7 km) south of the Praça da Alfândega—preserves the memory of local hero Camargo (1914–1994), one of Brazil's greatest expressionist painters, and features contemporary art.

Watching the sunset in the vicinity of the **Rio Guaíba** is popular with locals and visitors alike. One good spot is from the **Usina do Gasômetro** *(Av. Presidente João Goulart 551, Centro, tel 51/3289 8100, closed Mon.),* an old energy-generating plant astride

the river that has been converted to a cultural center that features plays, films, art expositions, a café, and a restaurant. You can also take a boat trip for the view.

The main nightlife district is **Cidade Baixa.** The centrally located **Bom Fim district,** an old-time haunt that had fallen into disrepute, is making a comeback. Locals might find it a bit over-the-top, but many foreigners enjoy the *rodízio* steakhouse **Galpão Crioulo** (see Travelwise p. 291). If you are in town on Sunday, the **Brique da Redenção** antique and crafts fair in the **Parque Farroupilha** *(Av. João Pessoa, Farroupilha, tel 51/3286 4458),* Porto Alegre's urban answer to Central Park, is worth a visit.

Serra Gaúcha: Gramado & Canela

The twin-cities Gramado and Canela, two hours north of Porto Alegre, provide a hillside escape popular with Brazilians—especially during the annual Christmas Festival, Natal Luz, which runs from

Mercado Público

- ✉ Largo Jornalista Glênio Peres, Centro Histórico
- ☎ 51/3289 4801
- 🕐 Closed Sun.

Fundação Iberê Camargo

- ✉ Av. Padre Cacique 2000
- ☎ 51/3247 8000
- 🕐 Closed Mon.

Gramado

 137 B2

Visitor Information

✉ Prefeitura de Gramado, Av. das Hortências 2029, Centro

☎ 54/3286 0200

Canela

 137 B2

Visitor Information

✉ Prefeitura de Canela, Rua Dona Carlinda 455

☎ 54/3282 4108

Gramado: German-style architecture and flower planters adorn the streets.

Mini Mundo

✉ Rua Horácio Cardoso 291, Planalto, Gramado

☎ 54/3286 4055

$ $

November 1 to January 13. Since 1973, Gramado has hosted Brazil's most important film festival, usually in August.

The towns are prime destinations for Brazil's mass tourism operators, but there are ways to beat the crowds and enjoy outdoor activities, culinary delights, and German immigrant culture.

Known as the Vale das Hortensias for the colorful flowers—known in English as hydrangeas—that bloom in the final months of the year, the region attracted German immigrants in the 19th century. They brought with them or developed traditions in timber-frame architecture, chocolate production, and the crafting of leather goods.

Gramado and Canela are just 4 miles (7 km) apart. Most of the urban attractions can be found in the former. You can take a pleasant downtown walk on the **Avenida Borges de Medeiros** and some of its cross streets, where you will be treated to German-style architecture and flower gardens. Shops feature colonial-style furniture, crafts, and chocolate shops. Several good restaurants figure in the downtown area. Not far, and popular with kids, is **Mini Mundo,** a miniature city theme park.

Chocolate hit the scene in the 1970s, when Jayme Prawer decided to mimic the small-scale production he found in an Argentinean ski resort. His factory, **Chocolates Prawer** *(Av. das Hortênsias 4100, Gramado, tel 54/3286 1580, factory closed Sat.– Sun.; store open daily)* welcomes visitors, as do some of his many competitors. Leave room for a *café colonial,* an abundant "more-than-you-can-eat" late afternoon "snack" of cakes, pies, sweets, jams and jellies, cold cuts, cheese, sausages, and more. The **Café Colonial Bela Vista** (see Travelwise p. 291) is the place to go.

Campofora (see sidebar p. 163) offers excellent excursions on horseback through the landscape of araucaria pines, waterfalls, streams, and pastureland. Regardless of your mode of locomotion, check out the **Caracol** waterfall in a nature reserve of the same name, the **Parque do Caracol,** 3 miles (5 km) north of Canela. For a different angle of the waterfall, visit the nearby **Parque da Floresta Encantada do Caracol** *(Estr. do Caracol, Banhado Grande 450, Canela, tel 54/3504 1405, $),* also known as the Teleférico. While out in that direction, stop by the **Castelinho Caracol,** which doubles as an immigrant museum and teahouse.

Bento Gonçalves

Although the Portuguese tried, not very successfully, to establish wineries over the centuries, it was not until immigrants started

INSIDER TIP:

A trip along BR-471 in southeastern Rio Grande do Sul will afford glimpses of the world's largest rodent, the capybara, wallowing in swampy areas.

—PATRICIA H. KELLEY & CHRISTY VISAGGI
National Geographic researchers

flowing from Italy in the 1870s that winemaking took hold. The conditions weren't the greatest, but the newcomers were determined. They achieved their greatest success around the city of Bento Gonçalves in the hills of the Serra Gaúcha, with its relatively temperate climate.

Today, the region around Bento Gonçalves is home to many wineries, and conditions for visitors have improved considerably in recent years. A tasting tour through Brazilian wine country offers an enjoyable window on the country's Italian immigrant heritage.

Wine Tours: Two main routes—Vale dos Vinhedos and Vinhos de Montanha—have been established to help wine buffs organize outings, and these can include lively Italian cantinas open for lunch and dinner. At some wineries, you can even prepare your own wine, crushing them the old-fashioned way with your feet.

Vale dos Vinhedos is the most extensive route, with more than 30 wineries and sundry other attractions. **Casa Valduga** *(RS-470–Linha Leopoldina, Vale dos Vinhedos, tel 54/2105 3122, www .casavalduga.com.br)* sports its own

Parque do Caracol
✉ RS-466 Canela
☎ 54/3278 3035
💲 $

Castelinho Caracol
✉ Estr. do Caracol km 3, Canela
☎ 54/3278 3208
www.castelinho caracol.com.br

Bento Gonçalves
🅰 137 B2
Visitor Information
✉ Prefeitura de Bento Gonçalves, Rua Marechal Deodoro 70, Centro
☎ 54/3055 7100

Linha Turismo

The **Linha Turismo** *(Travessa do Carmo 84, Cidade Baixa, tel 51/ 3289 0176, www .portoalegre.travel)* runs double-decker tour buses on two separate circuits through Porto Alegre. The main departure point for both lines is on a street called the Travessa do Carmo (no. 84), about three blocks south of the Parque Farroupilha.

The **Roteiro Centro Histórico** runs every hour during the day from Tuesday to Sunday through the historic downtown. It allows you to get on and off at five stops, including the Parque Farroupilha and the Fundação Iberê Camargo. On the Centro tour, you can get on at any stop as long as you already have your ticket.

The **Roteiro Zona Sul** (Southern District Route) operates once a day from Wednesday to Friday and twice on weekends and holidays. It runs along the shore and past several landmarks, including the soccer stadiums that house cross-town rivals Grêmio and Internacional. There are no stops on this circuit.

Vinícola Pizzato

137 B2

✉ Via das Parreiras, Vale dos Vinhedos

☎ 54/3459 1155 or 8136 4858

www.pizzato.net

Vinícola Marco Luigi

✉ RS-470—Linha Leopoldina—km 6, Vale dos Vinhedos

☎ 54/2621 1100

www.marcoluigi .com.br

Vinícola Aurora

✉ Rua Olavo Bilac, 500, Cidade Alta

☎ 54/3455 2051

🕐 Closed Sun. p.m.

guesthouses and restaurants. Once a month, Valduga hosts a **Dia da Vindima** (Vintage Day), during which visitors traipse into the vineyards to harvest grapes, prepare them, and stomp them in a barrel. The **Vinícola Pizzato** offers a similar experience. **Vinícola Marco Luigi** sports an attractive homespun cantina. The **Spa do Vinho Caudalie** (see Travelwise p. 290) specializes in vinotherapy.

Vinhos de Montanha heads in the direction of **Pinto Bandeira,** a town about 12 miles (20 km) outside of Bento Gonçalves. It features **Pousada Don Giovanni** (see Travelwise p. 290), which has its own guesthouse and restaurant, and awards for its sparkling wines. **Vinícola Aurora,** run by the Cooperativa Vinícola Aurora, a cooperative that gets its supplies from hundreds of small farmers, is on this route.

Caminhos do Sertão—one of Brazil's quality bicycle tour

operators (see sidebar p. 154)—offers a four-night package that explores the region, including the two main wine routes and the Caminhos de Pedra.

An old steam locomotive known in Brazil as *Maria Fumaça,* or *Smoking Mary,* makes a scenic 90-minute run from Bento Gonçalves to a neighboring town called **Garibaldi.** Folk dances and wine tasting are included.

Caminhos de Pedra: Adjacent to Brazil's wine country sits a living museum of Italian immigration called the **Caminhos de Pedra** (also known as the São Pedro district of Bento Gonçalves). The route can be visited by car, bicycle, or even on foot—independently or with the help of local guides.

The 7-mile (12 km) "itinerary," as the organizing body calls it, comprises dozens of visitation and observation points including:

Italian immigrants transformed Bento Gonçalves into Brazil's premier wine-producing region.

EXPERIENCE: Horseback Riding

More than half of the 21 gaúcho "articles of faith" listed in J. Simões Lopes Neto's classic 1912 book *Contos gauchescos (Gaúcho Stories)* refer to horses. One of the best ways to delve into the essence of the local gaúcho spirit is to mount one of Paulo Hafner's horses. Hafner, a former advertising executive, and his wife, Ângela, an engineer, abandoned the urban rat race two decades ago to start **Campofora** *(Passeio Caáguas 525, Boca da Serra, São Francisco de Paula, tel 54/ 3244 2993).*

Based about 20 miles (35 km) east of Canela, Campofora (Cross Country) offers excursions on horseback through the hills of the Serra Gaúcha, into the canyons of Parque Nacional de Aparados da Serra, and through the plains of the Pampas south toward Uruguay. While you're riding *crioulos* ("They're the same as the mustangs, the descendants of the horses brought to the Americas by Spanish settlers," says Hafner), you'll encounter waterfalls, rivers, and flat-topped Paraná pine tree forests. You will also see activities like roping, branding, and cattle driving—part of a mystique that permeates the entire region of the Pampas in Rio Grande do Sul. "The gaúcho is the South American cowboy," Hafner explains.

Dinner is prepared at one of the farmhouses where the group stops for the night. Midday grub is served somewhere along the trail—a picnic under a tree or beside a spring. Make reservations ahead of time and enjoy a few unhurried days on the range. As Hafner likes to say, "It's the journey, not the destination."

---

wineries and tasting rooms, restaurants and homes, small farms and artisans' workshops. Visitors are immersed in the region's traditional heritage along the route. A comprehensive map, with addresses and distances is available at the **Barracão Restaurante e Churrascaria** *(Estr. Do Barracão 580, tel 54/3454 9749)*—once a receiving center for arrivals awaiting their land assignments.

Any Brazilian wine connoisseur worth his grapes can relate the story of the Italian immigrants who arrived in the mountainous outback of Rio Grande do Sul in the late 19th century. But only enologist Silvério Salvati can offer a taste of the Italian varieties favored by those newcomers.

In the Vale dos Vinhedos, the wine tour route just to the east of Bento Gonçalves (see pp. 161–162), Cabernets and Chardonnays hold forth on both large estates and in little cellars. So fully have more recently imported varieties taken root that Salvati had to scrounge for surviving seedlings of Peverella and Barbera varieties once imported from the old country.

His winery was cobbled together with irregularly crushed basalt, the chief building material of early immigrants. The **Cantina Salvati & Sirena** *(Linha Palmeiro, tel 54/3455 6400)* stands in an "off Broadway" setting west of town. Wine casks line the walls of the octagon-shaped structure. By appointment, groups can partake of a traditional immigrant Sunday meal: bean soup, polenta, chicken stew, and frittata.

The area near Salvati's embodies the spirit of the Caminhos de Pedra, the Stone Trails, a name

Maria Fumaça

- ✉ Estr. Ferroviária, Rua Duque de Caxias, Bairro Cidade Alta
- ☎ 54/3455 2788
- 🕓 Closed Mon.– Wed.
- 💲 $$

www.mfumaca.com.br

Caminhos de Pedra

- ✉ Rua Henry Hugo Dreher 227, Planalto
- ☎ 54/3454 5702

www.caminhosdepedra.org.br

Museu do Imigrante

✉ Rua Henry Hugo Dreher 127, Planalto
☎ 54/3451 1773
🕐 Closed Mon.

derived from the remarkable stone buildings built by settlers—many of which survive.

During their first months and even years, many settlers survived thanks to the edible pine seeds that remain a popular snack in the Brazilian south. They used makeshift farm tools—hoes were often merely poles with handmade spikes at the end—which can be seen at the **Museu do Imigrante** in town. To protect staple crops from wild animals, settlers camped out in the fields.

The **Cantina e Casa Strapazzon** (Linha Palmeiro, tel 54/3455 6321, $), a stone structure dating from 1880, served as the setting for scenes in the 1995 Oscar-nominated film O Quatrilho. The Strapazzon complex is open to visitors for wine tasting and sampling locally produced cheese and salami. At the nearby **Casa da Ovelha** (Linha Palmeiro 400, tel 54/3455 6399, $), visitors can taste sheep-milk yogurt and learn about its health benefits. The

wooden structure, dating from 1917, flourished as the **Hotel Cavalet** (RS-453 km 109, tel 54/3458 7216), lodging travelers on the main road to Porto Alegre before a new highway bypassed by the community.

Other highlights include the **Casa do Tomate e Refrigerante Natural** (Linha Palmeiro, tel 54/3455 6292), in a structure designed by Júilo Posenato; the **Casa da Erva-Mate** (Santo Antônio, tel 54/3455 6427), where a mechanical mill powered by a waterwheel produces the chimarrão tea so dear to gaúchos; the **Casa Vanni** (Linha Palmeiro 795, tel 54/3455 6383, closed Fri.–Mon., $), where visitors can view traditional methods of pastamaking and weaving; and the **Casa Bertarello** (Linha Palmeiro 120, tel 54/3454 9756, closed Mon.–Tues.), where the Restaurante Nona Ludia serves Italian fare in the basement of a stone structure built by immigrant Giuseppe Dall'Acqua in 1880.

Chimarrão

Popular with the Guaraní, the region's original inhabitants, chimarrão—yerba-maté tea—was adopted by European settlers. Drinking it is often a group activity: A gourd of chimarrão is shared by people sitting in a circle and passed from hand to hand, often after meals.

The gourd is first stuffed with maté tea, made from a shrub called erva-mate; then it is filled with boiled water for each person in turn. Sipped from a metal straw, the gourd must be emptied before being passed along. Slurping is fine. It proves that you're done.

The **Rota da Erva Mate** is a 37-mile (60 km) circuit in the **Vale do Taquari** region dedicated to the history of maté in the Rio Grande do Sul. The main attraction is **Ilópolis** (Visitor information, Rua Expedicionários 930, Praça Itália, Centro, tel 51/3774 1537), 119 miles (192 km) northwest of Porto Alegre and 66 miles (106 km) from Bento Gonçalves. The town takes its name from the plant's scientific name. Its **Parque do Ibama** (Rua 7 de Abril, Centro, 51/3774 1322) showcases the history of the tea in Rio Grande do Sul, starting in 1509.

Internationally acclaimed gaúcho sculptor João Bez Batti lived and worked for a time in the **Casa Gilmar Cantelli** *(Linha Palmeiro, tel 54/3455 6254, closed Sat.–Sun.),* one of the region's best examples of a late 19th-century stone structure. Using basalt, in his case the red rock of the region, Bez Batti follows the traditions of Egyptians and pre-Columbian Indians. His painstaking process includes the application of three polishing rocks and eight grades of sandpaper. Visits to his new workshop, **Atelier João Bez Batti** *(tel 54/3455 6254),* should be scheduled in advance.

Cambará do Sul & Torres

On the extreme northeastern tip of Rio Grande do Sul, two small towns—Cambará do Sul (pop. 6,500) and Torres (pop. 35,000), which stand 43 miles (70 km) apart—offer access to natural attractions unparalleled in the region. Cambará do Sul serves as a base for exploring the two adjacent national parks that straddle the state border with neighboring Santa Catarina: Aparados da Serra and Serra Geral. Torres sits on the coast alongside the Parque Estadual da Guarita, a state park.

Parque Nacional de Aparados da Serra (Aparados da Serra National Park; *RS-429 km 18, Itaim-bezinho, 54/3251 1277, $*) contains some of the largest canyons in Brazil, reaching depths of up to 2,950 feet (900 m). The largest, **Itaimbezinho,** runs for nearly 4 miles (6 km), with a width of up to 6,550 feet (2,000 m). The park

features several impressive waterfalls, including **Cachoeira Véu da Noiva** and **Cachoeira das Andorinhas** (the latter named for the swallows, *andorinhas* in Portuguese, that make their nests behind the waters and can be spied darting in and out). Aparados da Serra ranks among the best of Brazil's national parks in terms of infrastructure for visitors.

Bento Gonçalves offers wine aficionados delightful opportunities for tasting, dining, and lodging.

Both parks are popular with hikers. A reputable local firm, **Cânion Turismo,** organizes several different excursions ranging from a four-hour waterfall walk to a daylong, 15-mile (24 km) trek in **Parque Nacional da Serra Geral** *(RS-429 km 18, Itaimbezinho, tel 54/3251 1277 or 3251 1262)* that takes you through araucaria forests, hills, and arroyos. Cânion Turismo also offers mountain-bike excursions through Itaimbezinho, a river trip in a small boat, and a visit to a local honey production center. Campofora (see sidebar p. 163) offers excursions through the area on horseback.

see sidebar p. 163

Cambará do Sul

🛆 137 C2

Visitor Information

✉ Prefeitura de Cambará do Sul, Rua Da Úrsula 641

☎ 54/3251 1174

Torres

🛆 137 C2

Visitor Information

✉ Prefeitura de Torres, Rua Júlio de Castilhos 707

☎ 51/3664 2202

Cânion Turismo

✉ Av. Getúlio Vargas 1098, Room 1, Cambará do Sul

☎ 54/3251 1027 or 8117 1017

Parque Estadual da Guarita

✉ Rua Caxias do Sul, Beira-Mar, Torres

☎ 51/3664 1411 ext. 247

$ $

Torres (towers) takes its name from the enormous blocks of basalt rock that jut out along the coast. Two of the largest towers are located inside the **Parque Estadual da Guarita**. There is a trail to the top of the **Torre do Meio,** and steps and railings on the seaside allow access to caves; there are steps to take you up to **Torre Sul.** The towers are popular with rock climbers, though you should be careful with the bolts—easily worn out due to their exposure to sprays of salt water. Torres has several

the Spanish crown in the 17th century. These 30 outposts are found in a region now split between Brazil, Argentina, and Paraguay. An estimated 140,000 Guaraní Indians ended up living in these centers of proselytization.

After the Treaty of Madrid in 1750—which gave the Portuguese legal title to a chunk of land previously claimed by Spain— seven of the missions changed hands. The Guaraní balked, partly because they associated the Portuguese with slave traders

Getúlio Vargas & São Borja

Getúlio Vargas, Brazil's most important 20th-century politician, was born in 1882 in a small town called São Borja on the edge of Rio Grande do Sul state, near the Argentina border. Initially a dictator (1930–1945) and then an elected president (1951–1954), Vargas set the tone for subsequent decades and remains influential today. The **Museu Getúlio Vargas** (Av. Presidente Vargas 1772, São Borja, tel 55/3430 4293) occupies the

house where Vargas lived with his wife and children, even as he built his political career. A mausoleum, designed by architect Oscar Niemeyer and inaugurated in 2004, is in the town's central square, Praça XV de Novembro.

The **Memorial Casa João Goulart** (Av. Presidente Vargas 2033, São Borja, tel 55/3431 5730, closed Mon.) honors another native son, João Goulart, who also rose to the presidency.

popular beaches, both inside and outside the park, and in late April, the city holds a four-day **Festival Internacional de Balonismo** (International Balloon Festival).

São Miguel das Missões

The ruins of **São Miguel das Missões** (founded in 1687) are considered to be the best preserved remnants of the 30 missions established by Catholic Jesuits in their effort to convert Guaraní Indians under

who customarily kidnapped their compatriots. This led to the Guaraní War (1754–1756), in which hundreds of natives were slaughtered by a joint Portuguese-Spanish force.

Though not entirely histori-cally accurate, the 1986 film *The Mission,* starring Robert de Niro, revolves around these events. Indeed, the set of the film re-created São Miguel das Missões.

Visitors can explore the ruins of the real mission, which are a

São Miguel das Missões: The most impressive remaining relic of the Jesuit and Spanish colonial efforts to convert Guaraní Indians to Catholicism

UNESCO World Heritage site, and get a sense of how imposing the stone church, **São Miguel Arcanjo,** must have been when it was completed in 1745. If you have time, catch the ruins in the light of sunset and then hang around or return later for the light show. Next door is the aptly named **Museu das Missões,** with a rich collection of mission-era artifacts, in a building designed by Lúcio Costa, one of the co-designers of Brasília.

From São Miguel das Missões, you can take an excursion to mission ruins at UNESCO sites in neighboring Argentina and Paraguay. Or consider visiting the three other sites in Brazil that hold modest vestiges of missions. At **São Nicolau,** in the town of the same name, a few walls from the 1687 mission and an old storage hut remain; at **São Lourenço**

Mártir, in São Luiz Gonzaga, you will find decayed walls of the 1690 mission; and **São João Batista,** in Entre-Ijuís, again, only a few walls remain, although tourist infrastructure helps visitors understand the mission's history and layout.

São Borja

São Borja is only 105 miles (170 km) from São Miguel das Missões by car, making it an attractive detour for anyone visiting the mission.

A 202-mile (325 km) walking path, **Caminho das Missões** (*www.caminhodasmissoes.com.br*), starts in São Borja and follows much of the old Guarnaí-Jesuit route near the Uruguay River and the Argentina border before turning inland to the city of **Santo Ângelo.** The entire walk takes about two weeks. ∎

Museu das Missões

🅼 137 A2
✉ Rua São Nicolau
☎ 55/3381 1291

NOTE: Light show times vary according to the time of year. Check when you are there.

Pantanal wetlands rife with wildlife, highland plateaus strewn with waterfalls, crystal clear rivers full of fish, and Brazil's capital, Brasília

Central & Pantanal

A jaguar in the Pantanal. These felines are notoriously hard to spot, but seeing one is an unforgettable experience.

Central & Pantanal

Central Brazil is a nature lover's paradise. The flagship destination for wildlife, birds, and fishing has to be the Pantanal wetlands, home to more than 80 species of mammals, 650 of birds, 235 of fish, and 1,000 of butterflies. Snuggled up against the Bolivian and Paraguayan borders, the central-western states of Mato Grosso and Mato Grosso do Sul eat up the jaguar's share of the Pantanal's 54,000 square miles (140,000 sq km).

The ebb and flow of the Pantanal floodwaters create an ecosystem that attracts nature lovers.

Known as the Serengeti of South America, the Pantanal is a patchwork of low-lying forests and marshes and dry, upland savannas inhabited by jaguars, giant anteaters, marsh deer, and giant otters. In the rainy season, rivers and streams overflow their banks and flood 80 percent of the Pantanal, covering an area more than ten times the size of the Florida Everglades. Lagoons swell with water lilies, while cattails sprout from marshes and palm trees grow along rivers. North American migratory birds such as the upland sandpiper and black-necked stilt rely on the Pantanal for seasonal respite. A variety of grasses feed wildlife and cattle, which have been raised in the region for more than 200 years.

The Pantanal can be explored by train, boat, or car. But the long distances, poor roads, and regular flooding make travel difficult. Most of the region's tourism infrastructure is based around autonomous ecolodges, which offer stress-free enjoyment of the region's exuberant natural beauty through organized activities for wildlife spotting, bird-watching, horseback riding, and more.

Many of the Pantanal's ecolodges are converted cattle ranches, and cattle pastures continue to dominate the landscape. In terms of percent of area dedicated to beef production, Mato Grosso and Mato Grosso do Sul rank first (15 percent) and third (12 percent), respectively, in Brazil. Only in recent decades has the region awakened to the potential of ecotourism.

Beyond the Pantanal

Just south of the Pantanal, in Mato Grosso do Sul, lies the Serra da Bodoquena, a snippet of the Atlantic Forest eco-region best known for the ecotourism destination Bonito. Mato Grosso boasts both the Chapada dos Guimarães, a prime example of the savanna-like Cerrado eco-region with its yellowish red sandstone cliffs, caves, rock formations, and waterfalls, and the relatively undiscovered Araguaia-Serra do Roncador region, a transition area between the Cerrado and Amazon eco-regions that offers everything from pristine fluvial beaches and freshwater dolphins to mysteries of lost explorers. Even farther east, Goiás's Chapada dos Veadeiros serves up magnificent scenery for hikers and good vibrations for mystics.

Rather incongruous amid this nature wonderland, Brasília is a planned city built from scratch in the 1950s and inaugurated in 1960. It is probably fair to say that its monumental modernist architecture is unmatched anywhere in the world. ∎

NOT TO BE MISSED:

The Niemeyer architecture, of Brasília, a World Heritage site **172–177**

Hiking and waterfalls in the Chapada dos Veadeiros or the Chapada dos Guimarães **180, 194–195**

Swimming with the fish along a river in the Serra da Bodoquena **184**

Wildlife spotting, bird-watching, and other outdoor activities at a Pantanal ecolodge **191–193**

A Pantanal fishing expedition aboard a yacht **193–194**

The untouched, mysterious Araguaia–Serra do Roncador region in eastern Mato Grosso **195**

Brasília

As Brazil's capital, Brasília offers good infrastructure for business travelers—comfortable hotels, good restaurants, and an ample supply of taxis. Leisure travelers have two main attractions: for denizens of modernist architecture, the city's monumental buildings, and, for political buffs, a glimpse into the buzz inside the halls of power. On the downside, the planned city seems to have a vendetta against pedestrians. You cannot really walk anywhere.

The Catedral Metropolitana Nossa Senhora Aparecida, a Catholic church designed by architect Oscar Niemeyer, is one of Brasília's most popular attractions.

Brasília

🅰 171 C2

Visitor Information

✉ Centro de Atendimento ao Turista, Praça dos Três Poderes

✉ Centro de Atendimento ao Turista, Brasília International Airport

www.brasil.gov.br/ brasilia-english/

Brasília is the consummate melting pot. Starting as a literal no-man's-land in the 1950s, it was populated first by construction workers, and then by bureaucrats, soldiers, politicians and hangers-on from across the country. For modernist architecture fans and urban-planning buffs, Brasília features numerous attractions. Some people refer to the city as an open-air museum of modernism. Oscar Niemeyer and Lúcio Costa headlined the group of architects, urban planners, land-scape architects, and assorted artists responsible for the look of the planned city.

Seeing the Sights

The best way to start your tour is to get an overview of the city from atop the **Torre da TV** (TV Tower; *Eixo Monumental, tel 61/3321 7944, closed Mon. a.m.*). The Costa-designed structure rises 735 feet (224 m), making it one of the world's highest television towers. The vista point rests at the 246-foot (75 m) mark, still high enough to give you a lay of the land and a spectacular view. You will notice that many points of architectural interest are spread about; to see more than a handful, you will need to rent a car or take taxis.

Key sights cluster around the Praça dos Três Poderes, a vast square, and along the 10-mile (16 km) Esplanada dos Ministérios, a mall lined with a few unique government buildings and 17 identical ones that hold various bureaucratic agencies (Niemeyer believed the sameness would cut down the one-upmanship and infighting among the agencies).

Praça dos Três Poderes:
Many people start their architectural tour at the Praça dos Três Poderes (Plaza of the Three Powers), the name a reference to the three branches of government, that sits at the head of the Esplanada dos Ministérios. Around the plaza you will find the **Palácio do Planalto,** a vision clad in white marble and the headquarters of the executive branch; the

Congresso Nacional (National Congress), featuring two domes, one concave and one convex; and the **Supremo Tribunal Federal** (Supreme Court), bearing arches similar to those adorning the Palácio do Planalto. In addition to admiring the lines of all three Niemeyer creations from the outside, you can tour the interiors; the Supreme Court has a small museum.

The plaza is adorned with an emblematic bronze sculpture

The Art of Athos Bulcão

While the names Lúcio Costa, Oscar Niemeyer, and Roberto Burle Marx pop up frequently in the Brasília narrative, painter and sculptor Athos Bulcão (1918–2008) seems to have been relegated to relative obscurity. But the master of tiles decorated many of Niemeyer's structures here, perhaps most dramatically at the Igreja Nossa Senhora da Fátima *(SQS 307–308, Asa Sul, tel 61/3242 0149)*, a chapel known as the Igrejinha, but also in the Congresso Nacional, Teatro Nacional *(Eixo Monumental, tel 61/3325 6153)*, Palácio da Alvorada, Palácio do Itamaraty, and more. The **Fundação Athos Bulcão** *(CLN 208, Bloco D, Entrada 49, Sala 111, Asa Norte, tel 61/3322 7801, closed Sat.–Sun.)* is a nonprofit foundation with a gift shop that sells items adorned with Bulcão designs.

by Bruno Giorgi. Formally named **"Os Guerreiros"** ("The Warriors"), its two figures are popularly known as "Os Candangos." Of African origin, *"candango"* was a derogatory term applied to the construction workers who moved here to build the city in the 1950s; *(continued on p. 176)*

Palácio do Planalto
✉ Praça dos Três Poderes, Esplanada dos Ministérios
☎ 61/3411 2317
🕐 Open Sun. a.m. only

Congresso Nacional
✉ Praça dos Três Poderes, Esplanada dos Ministérios
☎ 61/3318 5107 or 3311 3344

Supremo Tribunal Federal
✉ Praça dos Três Poderes, Esplanada dos Ministérios
☎ 61/3217 3000
🕐 Open Sat.–Sun. & banking holidays
www.stf.jus.br

Brasília by the Book

Many Brazilians swear by their capital, Brasília. They relish its designation as a UNESCO World Heritage site. But most have never been there. People who *have* visited often swear at it. A planned city built out of nothing in the middle of nowhere and inaugurated in 1960, Brasília can prove disconcerting to visitors. Many people have written about the city's design, trying to make sense of it.

Designed by Alexandre Chan and inaugurated in 2002, Brasília's Juscelino Kubitschek Bridge aesthetically complements the modernist architecture of the 1950s planned capital.

Brazilian journalist José Nêumanne Pinto traces Brasília's shortcomings to Swiss-born French architect Le Corbusier, mentor to the city's designers, Lúcio Costa and Oscar Niemeyer. "Speed, order and geometry were the priorities of an efficient city for the Swiss-Frenchman, and they predominated in the blueprints of Lúcio Costa's group, which reproduced in the arid Cerrado the outline of an airplane," Nêumanne wrote in his book *O Que Sei de Lula* (*What I Know About Lula,* available only in Portuguese). "Brasília was built at the height of the most broadminded administration in the history of the Brazilian Republic, but in line with a conception that was supremely anti-democratic . . . [It] attempts the impossible task of abolishing chance; for that very reason, it fails."

Marshall Berman, a political scientist who now teaches at the City College of New York, expressed similar observations and dissatisfaction with the city. "From the air, Brasília looked dynamic and exciting," he remarked in the preface to the 1988 edition of his book *All That Is Solid Melts Into Air: The Experience of Modernism.* "From the ground level, however, where people actually live and work, it is one of the most dismal cities in the world . . . one's overall feeling—confirmed by every Brazilian I met—is of immense empty spaces in which the individual feels lost, as alone as a man on the moon." Berman continues by saying, "There is a deliberate absence of public space in which people can meet and talk, or simply look at each other and hang around. The great tradition of Latin urbanism, in which city life is organized around a *plaza mayor* is explicitly rejected."

This fact is immediately evident to anyone staying in one of the city's three hotel districts, where all you get are hotels. There is virtually nothing worth doing or seeing within walking distance, and if you venture out on foot you must navigate roadways designed exclusively for vehicles, with no thought for pedestrians.

Aloneness

Some experts have looked to Brasília's isolation to explain the city's feel. "The journey to Brasília across the Central Plateau is one

of separation," wrote James Holston, professor of anthropology at the University of California, Berkeley, in his book *The Modernist City: An Anthropological Critique of Brasília.* "It confronts the traveler with the separation of modernist Brasília from the familiar Brazil: from the densely packed settlements along the coast to the emptiness of the interior; from layers of congestion and clutter in the big cities to the silent horizons of the plateau; from small town squares with their markets and conversations to the empty spaces of Brasília without squares or markets; from civilization to the frontier; from underdevelopment to the incongruously modern."

The late art critic and author Robert Hughes provides a global historical perspective in his book *Barcelona:* "The port is where the *ser autentic,* or 'essence,' of a country, as centralizing power imagines it, begins to fray. That is why Peter the Great's successors shifted the capital of Russia from Saint Petersburg to Moscow; why Mustafa Kemal Atatürk, inheriting one of the world's great port capitals in Istanbul, chose to create a new administrative center in Ankara; why the absurd and artificial Brasília, not Rio de Janeiro, is the capital of Brazil."

The light-filled interior of the spacious Catedral Metropolitana Nossa Senhora Aparecida

Espaço Lúcio Costa

- ✉ Praça dos Três Poderes, Esplanada dos Ministérios
- ☎ 61/3325 6163
- ⊕ Closed Mon.

Palácio do Itamaraty

- ✉ Esplanada dos Ministérios, Bloco H
- ☎ 61/2030 8051

Palácio da Justiça

- ✉ Esplanada dos Ministérios
- ☎ 61/3429 3401
- ⊕ Closed Sat.–Sun.

Catedral Metropolitana Nossa Senhora Aparecida

- ✉ Esplanada dos Ministérios, Lote 12
- ☎ 61/3224 4073
- ⊕ Closed Mon.

Memorial JK, honoring President Kubitschek, the father of Brasília

it evolved into a nickname for the natives of Brasília.

Underneath the plaza, with stairs at ground level leading down to the entrance, the **Espaço Lúcio Costa** features a model of Brasília's original urban design and other artifacts related to the work of the urban planner and architect whose vision brought about Brasília as we know it.

Esplanada dos Ministérios:

The **Palácio do Itamaraty** (Foreign Ministry), a block west of the Praça dos Três Poderes, displays some of Niemeyer's most inventive accessories: on the outside, a reflecting pool and a bridge over it; on the inside, a massive spiral staircase. Bulcão handled the marble walls. Roberto Burle Marx laid out the gardens. Giorgi signed the marble sculpture that seems to float in the pool. The Foreign Ministry has amassed an impressive collection of art over the years. You'll find works by

such icons as Victor Brecheret, Manabu Mabe, Maria Martins, Lasar Segall, and Alfredo Volpi. The palace contains the table that Princess Isabel used to sign the Lei Áurea, the decree that abolished slavery in 1888.

Opposite the Palácio do Itamaraty, on the other side of the Esplanada dos Ministérios, sits the remarkable **Palácio da Justiça** (Ministry of Justice), completed in 1958. This Niemeyer building appears to rise up out of a reflecting pool and waterfalls cascade off projections on the main facade.

Much farther down the mall stands the **Catedral Metropolitana Nossa Senhora Aparecida,** the cathedral's shape symbolizing Jesus' crown of thorns. Inside, expanses of bright white marble reflect the light let in by the glass ceiling, while three angels, the work of sculptor Alfredo Ceschiatti, float overhead, suspended from the ceiling.

At the far end of the mall is the **Memorial JK** (*Praça do*

Cruzeiro, Eixo Monumental, tel 61/3226 7860 or 3225 9451, www.memorialjk.com.br, closed Mon., $), a 1980 Niemeyer addition to the city and the resting place of Juscelino Kubitschek, the father of Brasília. It serves as a museum dedicated to his memory.

Beyond Brasília's Civic Center: Also worth a look are presidential residences past and present. The impressive **Palácio da Alvorada** (SPP Zona Cívico-Administrativa, tel 61/3411 2440, open Wed. 3–5 p.m.), on the shore of Paranoá Lake, is the official presidential palace. Its grounds were landscaped by Burle Marx and its rooms are decorated with artworks created by notable Brazilian artists. The palace's formal receiving rooms and residential quarters are open once a week to visitors. Maybe because of the palace's formalness, many Brazilian heads of state have preferred to spend most of their free time in Brasília at the

INSIDER TIP:

Look for the commemorative plaques on the apartment blocks, which were among the first buildings built in Brasília.

—CHRISTIAN BRANNSTROM
National Geographic grantee

Granja do Torto, a distinctly nonmonumental, ranch-style compound on the outskirts of town (closed to public).

Located outside Brasília, **Catetinho** (BR-040 km 27, tel 61/3338 8694, closed Mon.) is a simple two-story wooden structure designed by Niemeyer and erected in 1956. It was used by then President Kubitschek during his visits to accompany the city's progress before the Palácio da Alvorada was finished. It now functions as something of a period museum, featuring memorabilia and furnishings from Kubitschek's time. ■

Brasília Cultural Butcher

For something truly unique, visit the **T-Bone Açougue Cultural** (SCLN 312, Bloco B, Loja 27, Asa Norte, tel 61/3963 2069, www.t-bone.org.br, open Thurs. 6–11 p.m.): a local butcher shop that doubles as a cultural center. Luiz Amorim had nowhere to live when he was hired, so he slept out back and read books to pass his free time. Eventually he saved enough money to buy the little butcher shop where he worked. That was back in 1994. For the heck of it, he put a stand against the wall with a few books. People started to joke ironically about the Butcher Cultural Center. The books multiplied. Sanitary inspectors were not joking when they cited Amorim for violations related to the thousands of books that surrounded his racks of meat. Now the books are safely housed in a community library, and the T-Bone Açougue Cultural organizes regular cultural events from poetry workshops to presentations by nationally acclaimed acts like the composer and musician Lenine. And, yes, you can still get a T-bone steak.

Goiás

The central Brazilian state of Goiás, which surrounds Brasília, is a booming hotbed of agri-business and cattle ranching. The state capital, Goiânia, sits 130 miles (211 km) southwest of Brasília, but it offers little of interest. Visitors will find destinations like Pirenópolis, a colonial town; the former state capital, Goiás Velho; and two alluring national parks, Parque Nacional das Emas and Parque Nacional da Chapada dos Veadeiros, far more worthwhile.

Pirenópolis

Just 87 miles (140 km) west from the federal district, the historic city of Pirenópolis is a popular weekend destination

With its colonial architecture and proximity to waterfalls, Pirenópolis attracts people in search of rest and relaxation.

for people from Brasília, who love the easy access it provides to numerous outdoor activities. Pirenópolis can seem over-run on weekends and almost refreshingly desolate when the bureaucrats return to their cubicles in the capital. Pirenópolis has earned praise for neat and tidy appearance.

The historic downtown centers on Rua Direita, the street where its first mansions were built. Don't miss two churches of note: the **Igreja Matriz de Nossa Senhora do Rosário** (Praça da Matriz 2), inaugurated in 1732, and **Nosso Senhor do Bonfim** (Rua do Bonfim), which dates from 1754. For sustenance, head to **Rua do Lazer,** where a critical mass of bars and restaurants can be found.

The region surrounding Pirenópolis is known for its natural beauty and, especially, its numerous and often stunning waterfalls. On the outskirts of town, the **Santuário da Vida Silvestre Vagafogo** (Rua do Frota 888, tel 62/3335 8515 or 9222 0541, $), the first private reserve in Goiás, has a short hiking trail and an adventure obstacle course. The **Reserva Ecológica Vargem Grande** (turnoff from Estr. dos Pireneus, tel 62/3331 3071, $), 7 miles (11 km) northwest of town, includes two waterfalls: Cachoeira de Santa Maria and Cachoeira do Lázaro. The state park **Parque Estadual dos Pireneus** *(turnoff from Estr. dos Pireneus, tel 62/3331 2633)* is traversed by a trail that leads past waterfalls and natural pools to a vista point called the Mirante do Ventilador and then to the top of 4,544-foot (1,385 m) Pico dos Pireneus. If you are into river rafting or tubing, you can try the Rio Corumbá. For many of these outings, it is advisable to go with a local guide. Check with the Centro de Atendimento ao Turista information center or contact the local tour operator **Cerrado Aventuras** *(Praça do Coreto 45, Centro Histórico, tel 62/3331 3765).*

Goiás Velho

Sharing its name with the state, the 27,000-person-strong town of Goiás was founded in 1727 after gold was discovered nearby. The gold rush fueled growth, but the town was all but abandoned after losing its status as state capital in 1937. Partly as a result, it retained its historic architecture and unique culture. In 2001, UNESCO designated the town as a World Heritage site. To differentiate it from the state, the town sometimes goes by the name Goiás Velho.

The haphazard way that the original inhabitants settled the town makes its stone-paved streets complicated for cars to navigate and therefore all the more pleasant for pedestrians. The main sight is the home of the town's favorite daughter, poet and writer Cora Coralina (1889–1985),

---

Celebrating Pentecost

Pirenópolis is known for its monthlong Festa do Divino e Cavalhadas (Feast of the Divine and Cavalhadas) commemorating Pentecost. The *festa's* date changes according to the church calendar, but it always begins a few weeks after Easter. Various events occur throughout the month, but the main attraction takes place over the last few days: the Cavalhadas, in which costumed figures on horseback reenact cavalry battles of ancient Europe. Open year-round, the **Museu das Cavalhadas** *(Rua Direita 39, Centro Histórico, Pirenópolis, tel 62/3331 1166, $)* displays objects from the festival.

---

much of whose works deals intimately with her hometown (unfortunately, very little of her work has been translated into English). The **Casa de Cora Coralina,** a typical 18th-century house where she lived until she turned 22 and to which she returned to spend the last three decades of her life, has been transformed into a museum. It sits on a bridge astride the Rio Vermelho.

Afterward, simply wander around town. You'll have to climb a hundred stairs to reach the **Igreja de Santa Bárbara** *(Rua Santa Bárbara),* while another church of interest, the **Igreja de São Francisco de Paula** *(Praça Zacheu Alves, Largo de São Francisco),* stands near the river. The **Museu das Bandeiras** (Pioneer Museum; *Praça Brasil Caiado, tel 62/3371 1087, closed Mon., $)* occupies a building that housed both the city jail and city hall until the capital moved to Goiânia. One curiosity is a door that leads from the old courtroom down to the prison—

Pirenópolis

🅰 171 C2

Visitor Information

✉ Centro de Atendimento ao Turista, Rua do Bonfim 1, Centro Histórico

☎ 62/3331 2633

Goiás Velho

🅰 171 C2

Visitor Information

✉ Prefeitura da Cidade de Goiás Velho, Praça da Bandeira 1, Centro

☎ 62/3371 7720

Casa de Cora Coralina

✉ Rua Dom Cândido Tenso 20, Centro, Goiás Velho

☎ 62/3371 1990

🕐 Closed Mon.

💲 $

Parque Nacional da Chapada dos Veadeiros

⛰ 171 C3

✉ GO-239 km 36, Vila de São Jorge, Alto Paraíso de Goiás

☎ 62/3455 1114, 3455 1116, or 9299 8536

💲 $

Alto Paraíso de Goiás

⛰ 171 C3

Visitor Information

✉ Centro de Atendimento ao Turista, Av. Ary Valadão Filho 1100

☎ 62/3446 1159

Suçuarana

✉ Estr. Cavalcante Colinas do Sul km 5.5, Reserva Água do Santo

☎ Local: 62/3494 1536 or 9668 1065 Reservations: 11/7003 7057

Povoado Kalunga do Engenho II

✉ Estr. para São José km 29, Comunidade do Engenho II, 17 miles (27 km) from downtown Cavalcante

a one-way ticket for convicted suspects. There was no other entrance or exit.

Chapada dos Veadeiros

The Chapada dos Veadeiros, 160 miles (260 km) north of Brasília, attracts nature lovers of all stripes, from hard-core trekkers to mellow mystics. Most of this plateau is protected in a national park. A bed of crystal lays the foundation for both the geological formations of the plateau and for much of its attraction for visitors. Numerous rivers crisscross the terrain, and many tumble down rock cliffs in spectacular waterfalls.

The only way to see the **Parque Nacional da Chapada dos Veadeiros's** most imposing rock formations and its most impressive waterfalls is by walking several kilometers. Two trails depart from the park's main entrance, on the southern edge of the park near the village São Jorge. The trails lead to two canyons, Cânion 1 and Cânion 2. You will need a guide to visit the park, and they can inform you about access to the trails, which park officials sometimes close to protect endangered wildlife. Guides can be hired at the Centro de Atendimento ao Turista in nearby São Jorge *(tel 62/3455 1090)* or **Alto Paraíso de Goiás.**

Serious hikers will want to tackle the 11-mile (18 km) round-trip **Sertão Zen** trail, outside the park. It leads to the plateau's highest point (5,499 feet/1,676 m above sea level) and to a 492-foot-tall (150 m) waterfall. You will need

INSIDER TIP:

In Chapada dos Veadeiros, you can appreciate remarkable savanna landscapes and enjoy extraordinary waterfalls, perfect for cooling off in on a hot day.

—FERNANDA WERNECK
National Geographic grantee

a guide, who can be hired in Alto Paraíso de Goiás. There are also opportunities for mountain biking, zip-lining, and other adventure activities in the region.

Another way to experience the region is to stay at the **Pousada Vale das Araras** (see Travelwise p. 294), a guesthouse set on a private nature reserve on the park's northern edge, in the town of Cavalcante. The reserve is crisscrossed by hiking trails and a river. One trail leads past canals built by pioneer gold miners to supply their camps with drinking water. There is also a waterfall.

To further explore the Chapada dos Veadeiros region, consider one of the multiday excursions offered by local firm **Suçuarana,** which visit attractions both inside and outside park limits, including perhaps a visit to the *quilombo* **Kalunga,** a community founded by escaped slaves.

Southern Goiás

The southern part of Goiás state features a national park rife with wildlife-spotting opportunities and a private nature reserve dotted with prehistoric paintings and inscriptions.

Parque Nacional das Emas:

This park offers a glimpse of the subtle differences found in the Cerrado bioregion: grasslands, scrubland, riparian forests, and the greener, lusher *veredas* along the banks of streams. This is also a good place for wildlife spotting, starting with the flightless greater rhea (*ema* in Portuguese), Brazil's largest bird, that gives the park its name—look for it in the open grasslands. You are also likely to see anteaters, tapirs, and deer as you tour the park; the maned wolf and jaguar will be harder to find. Several dirt roads, open to cars and bicycles, wend through a landscape punctuated by reddish dirt termite mounds, which seem to sprout like weeds.

More than 250 miles (400 km) from Goiânia, the park is served by the nearby towns of Chapadão do Céu and Mineiros. You must have a guide (hired through each town's tourist center) to visit some parts of the park.

Serranópolis: Located about 55 miles (90 km) east of Chapadão do Céu, Serranópolis is home to hundreds of prehistoric cave and rock paintings and inscriptions that may date as far back as 11,000 years. Four sites can be visited from your base at the **Pousada das Araras** (see Travelwise p. 294), a guesthouse set in a private nature reserve popular with bird- and wildlife-watchers. The reserve also has short hiking paths with varying degrees of difficulty and a natural pool good for snorkeling. If you don't wish to overnight, day passes are available. ∎

Parque Nacional das Emas
- 171 B2
- GO-206 km 27, Chapadão do Céu
- 64/3929 6000
- $

Serranópolis
- 171 B2

The Rural Beat of *Sertanejo*

When people talk about the divisions between the Two Brazils, they usually mean the chasm between rich and poor. But they might also mean the cultural divide between urban and rural. Nowhere is that split more evident than in popular music, and nowhere is the rural *sertanejo* style, Brazil's rendition of country music, more firmly rooted than in Goiás, a state heavily dependent on agriculture.

The genre customarily features two guitar-wielding front men and traces its roots to a traditional rural style called *caipira*, or hillbilly. Electric instruments were borrowed from the Nashville tradition. Paralleling the transformation of U.S. country music from Jimmy Rogers

and Hank Williams to today's rock/pop–infused model, sertanejo evolved from caipira into a popular, if predictable, commercial formula.

Record companies can attest to the strength and stamina of sertanejo. Top duos like Zezé di Camargo and Luciano (natives of Pirenópolis) and Chitãozinho and Xororó have perennially topped the Brazilian charts for decades. In recent years, however, solo acts have started to push the duos aside: Two albums by Paula Fernandes ranked two and three on the overall Brazilian pop charts in 2011. The popularity of the sertanejo market should hardly be surprising, however: Brazil has a very large rural population.

Mato Grosso do Sul

Mato Grosso do Sul state contains the southern section of the Pantanal wetlands, which are most easily reached via Campo Grande. This state capital also serves as the gateway to the Serra da Bodoquena and the ecotourism attractions of Bonito and neighboring cities, and as the starting point of a popular weekend tourist train that runs through the Pantanal.

Freshwater snorkeling is a popular activity in Bonito, Brazil's ecotourism capital.

Campo Grande

🅰 171 B2

Visitor Information

✉ Centro de Atendimento ao Turista, Av. Duque de Caxias, Aeroporto Internacional

☎ 67/3363 3116

Campo Grande

The capital of Mato Grosso do Sul, Campo Grande has a handful of interesting museums scattered around the city that focus on indigenous Indian culture. The **Memorial da Cultura Indígena** (*Rua Terena, Conj. Marçal de Souza, Tiradentes, tel 67/3314 3544, $*) is a cultural center situated in a village that is home to about a hundred families; it includes an area for exhibitions and a crafts shop. The **Museu de Arte Contemporânea** (*Rua Antônio Maria Coelho 6000, Caranda, tel 67/3326 7449, closed Mon. & a.m.*) boasts a number of works by regional artists—some of them indigenous—in its collection of contemporary art. The natural history museum **Museu das Culturas Dom Bosco** (*Av. Afonso Pena 7000, tel 67/3326 9788, closed Mon., $*), popularly known as the Museu do Índio (Indian Museum), features many Indian artifacts, including headdresses.

If you're interested in taking home indigenous and regional

handicrafts, visit the **Casa do Artesão** *(Av. Calógeras 2050, Centro, tel 67/3383 2633, closed Sun.).* The **Feira Indígena,** held on the square in front of the **Mercado Municipal Antônio Valente** *(Rua 7 de Setembro at Av. Noroeste 5500),* sells mostly agricultural products from Indian farms. Both markets are worth a visit for an insight into local ingredients like *urucum,* red seeds used as food coloring. The **Feira Livre Central** *(Av. Calógeras at Av. 14 de Julho, closed Mon.–Tues. & Thurs.)* is a night market where you'll find produce and crafts stalls tucked in among a lively array of food stands—try two local favorites: Japanese-style soba noodles and mini-skewers of barbecue beef and manioc.

To see where Campo Grande got its start, visit the **Museu José Antônio Pereira** *(Fazenda Bálsamo, Av. Guaicurús, Jardim Monte Alegre, tel 67/3314 3181, closed Mon.),* on the outskirts of town. This museum sits on the former ranch of the man considered to be the founder of Campo Grande. Pereira led a group of settlers who put down stakes here in the 1870s.

Serra da Bodoquena

Astride the Pantanal wetlands in southwest Mato Grosso do Sul, the hilly Serra da Bodoquena region represents an extension of the Atlantic Forest eco-region. Crossed by about a dozen sparkling clear rivers, it is also pockmarked by more than 50 caves and caverns, some with pools of water at the bottom. Visitors can indulge in a range of enticing outdoor activities:

rafting, rappelling, horseback riding, snorkeling, and more. The town of Bonito, widely considered Brazil's most well-organized ecotourism destination, draws the lion's share of visitors, but nearby Jardim and Bodoquena host extraordinary attractions, too, with the added advantage of less hustle and bustle.

Bonito: Bonito, some 194 miles (312 km) southwest of Campo Grande, is so well organized and popular that it sometimes resembles an open-air ecotourism theme park, complete with rules set in place to protect the environment (see sidebar below).

Many of the area's popular attractions involve water somehow. The **Gruta do Lago**

Bonito

  171 A1

Visitor Information

✉ Centro de Atendimento ao Turista, Rod. Bonito/Guia Lopes km 1

☎ 67/3255 1850

Visiting Bonito's Sights

To protect the environment, a "carrying capacity" has been established for each attraction, limiting the daily number of visitors. For most attractions, you purchase a voucher in advance from a local travel agency, such as **Bonito Way** *(Rua General Osório 865, Centro, tel 67/3255 1046, www .bonitoway.com.br).* In general, you must be accompanied by a local guide. Most excursions take the better part of a day and include lunch. It is generally impossible to squeeze in more than one outdoor activity a day.

What isn't very ecological about Bonito, however, is that you'll need a car to get to the attractions. Without one, you need to arrange for transportation with a local travel agency. Sometimes you can share with other visitors to reduce the cost. There are no regular shuttles or other reliable public transportation.

Aquário Natural Reserva Ecológica Baía Bonita

⊠ Rua Coronel Nelson Felício dos Santos 741, Bonito

☎ 67/3255 2160

$ $$

www.aquario natural.com.br

Flutuação on the Rio Sucuri

⊠ Estr. para São Geraldo, 11 miles (18 km) from Bonito

☎ 67/3255 1030

$ $$

Estância Mimosa

⊠ MS-178 km 18, 15 miles (24 km) N of Bonito

☎ 67/3321 3351

$ $$$ for hiking

www.estancia mimosa.com.br

Abismo Anhumas

⊠ Rua General Osório 681, Bonito (cavern 14 miles/23 km from Bonito)

☎ 67/3255 3313

$ $$$$$

www.abismo anhumas.com.br

Projeto Jibóia

⊠ Rua Nestor Fernandes 610, Vila Donária

☎ 67/8419 0313

$ $

Bodoquena

🅰 171 B2

Azul (Estr. para Campo dos Índios, $, children under 5 prohibited), a cave 12.5 miles (20 km) from Bonito, has an intensely blue pool of water at its depths, which you reach by climbing down nearly 300 irregular stairs. The **Aquário Natural Reserva Ecológica Baía Bonita** attracts snorkelers with its clear, natural pond that offers an impressive view of fish and underwater plant life. A **flutuação on the Rio Sucuri** offers a different snorkeling experience: For this activity, you don a wet suit and life jacket and let the river current carry you along as fish swim at your side.

There are also many waterfalls in the area that can be reached via hiking trails. At the **Estância Mimosa,** a former cattle ranch, a trail snakes past seven cascades. Along the way, there is a 19.5-foot-high (6 m) platform for diving into a pool below. You can also bird-watch and go horseback riding here.

For the more adventurous, the **Abismo Anhumas** is a cavern that you visit by rappelling down 236 feet (72 m). **Bote no Rio Formoso** (Rua Coronel Pilad Rebuá 1853, tel 67/3255 1733) runs white-water rafting trips on an exhilarating section of the Rio Formosa. There is also a tubing route on the same river run out of the **Hotel Cabanas** (Rod. Bonito/ Guia Lopes km 6, tel 67/3255 3013 or 9632 5465).

Lobo Guará Bike Adventure (Rua Coronel Pilad Rebuá 2156, tel 67/9235 6954 or 9986 3906) offers novel bicycle tours along back roads, ranging in length from

4 to 80 miles (6–130 km). On the way, cyclists collect seeds that are later delivered to a local nursery. Each rider also plants a seedling along the route.

Bonito also boasts its share of cultural attractions. You can learn all about snakes at the **Projeto Jibóia,** run by a snake-breeding firm. With a boa constrictor draped around his neck, entrepreneur Henrique Naufal makes entertaining presentations. And

INSIDER TIP:

In Mato Grosso do Sul, visiting Bonito is almost mandatory. Its absolutely transparent waters provide an excellent and unique experience for snorkelers.

—DENISE RAMBALDI
Vice President, Instituto Estadual do Ambiente

you can pick up handicrafts at **Bonito Feito à Mão** (Rua Coronel Pilad Rebuá 1956, tel 67/3255 1950), a crafts workshop run by a group of local women.

Bodoquena: Small Bodoquena sits about 50 miles (80 km) north of Bonito. Its flagship attraction is the **Boca da Onça** ranch, located about 22 miles (35 km) south of town on the road to Bonito. Here, two different hiking trails lead to numerous waterfalls, including a 512-foot (156 m) cascade, the

MATO GROSSO DO SUL

state's tallest. If you're feeling adventurous, you can make a 295-foot (90 m) descent from a rappelling platform over the fall.

Jardim: For most attractions in Jardim, some 40 miles (64 km) southeast of Bonito, you must be accompanied by a local guide. The **Buraco das Araras** is a doline, a sinkhole formed when the roof of a cave collapses; at 344.5 feet (105 m) deep, it is one of the biggest such formations in the world. A multitude of scarlet macaws (the *araras* that give the hole its name) and other bird species nest in its craggy walls, and the sight and sound of them can be overwhelming. Part of a private nature reserve, the Buraco das Araras can be experienced in an hour, but you can schedule half- and full-day bird-watching tours through other parts of

the reserve, where more than a hundred bird species have been sighted.

Another remarkable attraction, especially if you're interested in snorkeling or diving (you need a PADI license), is the **Lagoa Misteriosa,** a lake that sits 246 feet (75 m) down another doline sinkhole. The dazzling blue lake reaches 722 feet (220 m) at its deepest point. There is a short hiking trail nearby. Allow at least a couple of hours for this excursion.

Another diving option, this one a river trip, will take you down the Rio da Prata. It is run by the **Rio da Prata Recanto Ecológico** on a private nature reserve. They also offer snorkeling, horseback riding, and bird-watching.

The Lagoa Misteriosa and Rio da Prata Recanto Ecológico are located close to one another. Visits to both must be scheduled *(continued on p. 188)*

(continued on p. 188)

Jardim
🅰 171 A1

Buraco das Araras
✉ BR-267 km 510, Jardim
💲 $$
www.buracodas araras.com.br

Lagoa Misteriosa
✉ BR-267 km 515
💲 $$$
www.lagoa misteriosa.com.br

Rio da Prata Recanto Ecológico
✉ BR-267 km 512, Jardim
💲 $$$
www.riodaprata .com.br

Sunlight from above turns the pool at the bottom of Gruta do Lago Azul a stunning shade of blue.

Refúgio Ecológico Caiman

The 148,000-acre (59,890 ha) Refúgio Ecológico Caiman set in the Pantanal is part benchmark ecolodge and nature reserve, part working cattle ranch. Caimans—the species of alligator for which the refuge is named—sun themselves riverside, and you'll see them as you explore the refuge's open grasslands by horseback, canoe the wetlands, or bike dusty trails. But you'll spot other creatures, too, perhaps even an elusive jaguar.

Hyacinth macaws count among the biggest attractions for bird-watchers in the Pantanal.

A century ago, when passing through this region on his way to the Amazon, Theodore Roosevelt would certainly have taken some potshots at them. "The ugly brutes lay on the sand-flats and mud-banks like logs, always with the head raised and sometimes with jaws open," he wrote in his book *Through the Brazilian Wilderness.* "They are often dangerous to domestic animals and are always destructive to fish, and it is good to shoot them. I killed half a dozen [one morning], and missed nearly as many more—a throbbing boat does not improve one's aim."

Roosevelt could get arrested for that now. A hunting ban that protects Brazil's most vulnerable species has been in place for more than four decades, helping engender a caiman population boom. As a result, some experts defend the return of legalized hunting.

A Ban's Boon

Depending on when you visit, since everything in the Pantanal changes with the rise and fall of the floodwaters, you might spot a group of caimans regularly stationed in a brook at the bottom of some mini-rapids, their mouths agape to catch fish carried over the cascades. A specialized membrane prevents the caiman from drowning while it fishes in such a manner.

The hunting ban has allowed many other species to replenish their numbers as well. One big beneficiary of the no-shooting policy is the jaguar—even though the cat, along with its cousin the puma, is blamed for killing about 400 head of cattle annually at the Caiman Ranch alone. As recently as a generation ago, ranchers employed jaguar hunters to protect their herds. These men were legendary for their cunning and bravery. Roosevelt devotes almost an entire chapter to his adventure in the bush in the company of such men.

But there is more to the Pantanal than jaguars, as Roosevelt notes as he enters the Amazon following a long trek through the Pantanal wetlands: "We did not hear such a chorus of birds and mammals as we had occasionally heard even on our overland journey, when more than once we had been awakened at dawn by the howling, screaming, yelping, and chattering of monkeys, macaws, parrots, and parakeets."

As for birds, not even the most agile and astute bird-watcher can keep track of them all. Hundreds of species of birds inhabit the Pantanal. Visitors to the Refúgio Ecológico Caiman nature reserve might spot a savanna hawk *(Heterospizias meridionalis)* and an Amazon kingfisher *(Chloroceryle amazon)* just before three cobalt blue birds whiz past, followed by two more. Those last ones are hyacinth macaws *(Anodorhynchus hyacinthinus),* beneficiaries of a research-conservation project (see sidebar below) based in the refuge.

Refuge Activities

The Refúgio Ecológico Caiman *(map 171 A2, Estância Caiman, 23 miles/37 km NW of Miranda, tel 67/3242 1450 or 11/3706 1800, www.caiman.com.br)* offers a full-range of wildlife-spotting activities, included as part of your stay at one of the refuge's two lodges or in one of the private villas. And as the refuge area includes a working ranch, you are also encouraged to spend time with the cowboys, getting to understand another aspect of Pantanal culture. During the peak season, June through mid-September, other activities include an astronomy workshop, a Pantaneira local culture day (including a traditional barbecue), and an introduction to the Projeto Onçafari, a jaguar preservation program.

Hyacinth Macaw Project

One of the Pantanal's most magnificent birds is the hyacinth macaw, but disappearing habitat, poaching for the bird trade, and hunting by indigenous Indians who use the bird's feathers in headdresses have all contributed to the bird's endangered status. But since biologist Neiva Guedes launched the **Projeto Arara Azul** (Hyacinth Macaw Project; *head office: Rua Klaus Sthurk 178, Jardim Mansur 79, Campo Grande, tel 67/3341 3331)* in 1990, the hyacinth population has increased fourfold to 6,000 in the project's 1,544-square-mile (4,000 sq km) study area.

The hyacinth is remarkably beautiful, its royal blue feathers contrasting starkly with bright yellow cheeks and eye rings, and it is also the largest macaw, measuring 3.3 feet (1 m) from bill to tail tip and weighing 2.9 pounds (1.3 kg). It is found in parts of the Amazon and northeastern Brazil, but about 70 percent of the bird's population inhabits the Pantanal region.

Using mountain climbing techniques and equipment, Guedes and her team of field-workers hoist themselves up trees to inspect nests and collect data, repairing nests damaged by extended use or storms. They perform emergency rescues and sometimes resort to tricks, like replacing eggs threatened by predators with chicken eggs. The removed eggs are hatched in incubators and later returned to the nests.

Each chick is important because hyacinths reproduce slowly. The birds live in couples, and each pair produces just one or two eggs a year. Both eggs and chicks are vulnerable to predators. Nests, made in cavities in the softwood *manduvi* tree, are at a premium—partly because trees must be at least 60 years old before deemed suitable to a bird. Other bird species also compete for the use of those nests. To help address the housing shortage, Guedes's team studied the characteristics of natural nests and developed a man-made nest acceptable to the birds. The funky looking boxes hang incongruously on high from tree trunks. They may look odd, but they work. Among the rewards: more sightings of hyacinth macaws.

The project maintains a visitor center at its base camp location, the Refúgio Ecológico Caiman.

On the edge of Mato Grosso state, Corumbá sits on the Rio Paraguai, the boundary between Brazil and Bolivia.

Aquidauana

🅰 171 B2

Visitor Information

✉ Prefeitura de Aquidauana, Rua Cassemiro Bruno, Alto Aquidauana

☎ 67/3241 4308

Miranda

🅰 171 A2

Visitor Information

✉ Prefeitura de Miranda, Rua Firmo Dutra, Centro

☎ 67/3242 2471

in advance via an authorized travel agency, such as Bonito Way (see sidebar p. 183) in Bonito.

Pantanal Gateway Cities

Two-thirds of the Pantanal wetlands are located in Mato Grosso do Sul state. The towns of Aquidauana and Miranda are considered gateways to the Pantanal. Many leading ecolodges, offering a variety of outdoor activities, can be found in the surrounding area, including the **Refúgio Ecológico Caiman** (see pp. 186–187), 23 miles (37 km) northwest of Miranda; the **Pousada Aguapé,** 30 miles (50 km) west of Aquidauana; and the **Fazenda San Francisco,** 22 miles (36 km) west of Miranda (see Travelwise p. 294 for the latter two).

Aquidauana: Aquidauana is about 85 miles (136 km) west of Campo Grande. First settled by ex-soldiers discharged after

the 1864–1870 Paraguayan War (see p. 35), Aquidauana was the first town in these parts to have both electricity and later a movie theater. The city has preserved several early 20th-century buildings. The **Museu de Arte Pantaneira** (*Rua Cândido Mariano 462, tel 67/3241 5254*) museum displays artifacts from the above-mentioned war and the city's history. It hosts temporary exhibitions of local artists.

Miranda: Miranda sits roughly 135 miles (218 km) west of Campo Grande, in the direction of Bolivia. The town languished in obscurity until the early 20th century, when it was finally connected to the rest of the country by telegraph and rail (Miranda's train station, built in 1912, is the oldest in Mato Grosso do Sul; it's on Rua Firmo Dutra). It has the second largest indigenous population in the state, with the traditions of the Terena tribe exerting a great deal of influence on local culture. The **Centro Referencial da Cultura Terena** (*Trevo de Miranda, tel 0800 647 6050*) sells pottery and crafts produced by tribe members.

Corumbá

On the banks of the Rio Paraguai, across from Bolivia, Corumbá is one of the oldest cities in central-western Brazil, founded in 1774 when the Portuguese established an outpost and colony here to protect their territory from Spanish forces after the end of the Treaty of Madrid. History buffs can make an excursion to a fort dating from that period, **Forte Coimbra,** 180 miles (292 km) away, with **Canaã Turismo** *(Rua Colombo 245, Centro, tel 67/3231 3667 or 3232 2208)* or other local travel agencies.

After the Paraguayan War— during which the town suffered considerable damage—Corumbá soon became one of the most important ports in South America, shipping goods to and from the heart of the continent via a fluvial network that extended southward to the Rio de la Plata, which sepa- rates Uruguay from Argentina.

By the end of the 19th century, the town was awash with foreign immigrants and was growing quickly. Many of the structures that went up during those boom years in the **Casário do Porto,** the port area, have been declared national heritage sites by the federal govern- ment. One such building, the Prédio Wanderley, Baís, & Cia, has been renovated and now houses the **Museu de História do Pantanal** *(Rua Manoel Cavassa 275, Porto Geral, tel 67/3232 0303, closed Sun.–Mon.),* an interesting museum that tells the history of the region dating back to the original inhabitants. ∎

INSIDER TIP:

When in the Panta- nal, be sure to try the *quebra-torto* breakfast that the *pantaneiros* (cowboys) used to eat in the old days—it's made of rice salad, local corn flour cakes, and biscuits.

—ADRIANA IZZO-ORTOLANO
National Geographic contributor

Corumbá

▲ 171 A2

Visitor Information

✉ Centro de Atendimento ao Turista, International Airport, Av. Santos Dumont, Centro

☎ 67/3907 5329

Forte Coimbra

✉ Av. Tenente Oliveira Melo, Forte Coimbra, Corumbá

☎ 67/3282 1010

EXPERIENCE: Riding the Rails

You can glory in the Pantanal in comfort aboard the **Trem do Pantanal** *(www .serraverdeexpress.com.br; Campo Grande ticket office: Av. Afonso Pena 5140, Morada dos Baís–Mezzanine, tel 67/3043 2233, closed Sun.).* Running though stunning landscape, this train offers a journey into a not-so-distant past when train travel was commonplace in the region.

Though formally called the Pantanal Express, the train is universally known as the Trem do Pantanal, borrowing from a classic popular song of that name. It leaves on Saturday mornings from Campo Grande (see pp. 182–183; *train station: Rua Cascatinha, Vila Entroncamento*) and wends

its way to Miranda (see opposite), 85 miles (136 km) distant, in five hours. It returns on Sunday at 8 a.m. There are a handful of stops along the way, including one at Aquidauana (see opposite). Travel- ers who do not wish to stay overnight in Miranda must return by bus. At BRL150 (US$65), this train trip counts as an outing rather than a mode of transportation.

The train runs along a stretch of rail that comprised part of the run from Bauru to Corumbá until 1996, when the entire Estrada de Ferro Noroeste do Brasil railway was scrapped after serving for most of the 20th century. The weekend tourism excur- sion was inaugurated in 2009.

Mato Grosso

In addition to a swath of the Pantanal, Mato Grosso boasts the Chapada dos Guimarães with its spectacular combination of headwaters, waterfalls, caves, and cliffs in the Cerrado eco-region. Farther east, the Araguaia River region includes the Serra do Roncador, with its stories of missing explorers and UFOs. Remote and largely undiscovered, the region boasts a full-range of outdoor activities. Its clean rivers are excellent for recreational fishing. (The state's northern Amazon region is discussed in the Amazon chapter, p. 242.)

Gateway to the northern Pantanal, Cuiabá boasts a number of good fish restaurants.

Cuiabá

🄰   171 A3

Visitor Information

✉   Inside the Museu do Rio (River Museum), Av. Beira Rio, Porto

☎   65/3027 3269

Cuiabá

An urban outpost surrounded by nature, the state capital functions mostly as a transportation hub, providing access to smaller gateway towns to the state's intriguing interior. But the city does serve up a slice of history.

When in 1892 the leaders of the new Brazilian republic sent a young military engineer named Cândido Mariano da Silva Rondon to lead a mission to extend telegraph connections into the final frontiers of the Brazilian outback,

his initial orders stipulated Cuiabá as the end of the line. Eventually, Rondon and his men strung up more line to even farther-flung destinations, but that story demonstrates how isolated this state capital remained until a century ago. With successive government programs to encourage the occupation of the interior, the population of Cuiabá has exploded to the current 550,000 inhabitants.

If you plan to spend a day or two in town, a handful of attractions will keep you busy.

The **SESC Arsenal,** the old armament depository, built in 1832, now houses a cultural center, its courtyard partly occupied by tables served by the in-house bar and restaurant. Less for the food, more for the ambience, it offers a pleasant place to hang out. Cultural activities and presentations fill its calendar, with a weekly artisans market taking place Thursday evenings. Occupying a historic building that was once a school, the **Casa do Artesão** *(tel 65/3322 2047, closed Sun.)* is a crafts shop organized by theme. It is connected to the **Museu do Artesanato do Mato Grosso,** a museum of articles produced by local and indigenous craftsmakers.

INSIDER TIP:

Pick up either of two Brazilian treats to stave off hunger during long car trips: pizza with creamy *catupiry* cheese or *pães de queijo*—tasty cheese buns.

—PATRICIA H. KELLEY & CHRISTY VISAGGI
National Geographic researchers

Finish your day of sightseeing by sampling some of the local fare, which draws on the eating habits of the area's original inhabitants, meaning lots of fish and manioc. Be sure to try the novel *mojica de pintado,* or catfish stew. The **Peixaria Popular** restaurant (see Travelwise p. 296) is considered the go-to place for fish.

Poconé & the Transpantaneira

Poconé, about 62 miles (100 km) southwest of Cuiabá, is pleasant enough, but the main draw here is the Estrada Parque Transpantaneira, a scenic road that cuts through Mato Grosso's Pantanal region. Poconé's biggest party is June's **Festa de São Benedito,** which culminates in the Cavalhadas, in which costumed riders on horseback reenact a cavalry battle from ancient Europe. Another road from Poconé, the MT-370, leads to the SESC Pantanal Estância Ecológica, a premier ecotourism destination.

Estrada Parque Transpantaneira: The Transpantaneira Highway (MT-060) offers the best way to see Mato Grosso's Pantanal region by car. From Poconé, it stretches south 92.5 miles (149 km) to Porto Jofre, on the Rio Cuiabá at the state border with Mato Grosso do Sul. But be warned: It is a poorly maintained dirt road with more than 120 wooden bridges (many are in sorry shape; you should stop to examine them before crossing).

As you drive, you may spot a variety of animals, such as caimans, capybaras, deer, and a wealth of birds. To ensure creature sightings, travel during the early morning, between dawn and 9 a.m., when the wildlife is more active. Be sure to fill your tank with gas in Poconé and take plenty of water and perhaps some snacks.

A handful of ecolodges are strung along the Transpantaneira.

SESC Arsenal

✉ Rua 13 de Junho, Centro Sul
☎ 65/3611 0550

Museu do Artesanato do Mato Grosso

✉ Rua 13 de Junho 315, Centro Norte
☎ 65/3611 0500
🕑 Closed Sun.

Poconé

🗺 171 A2

Visitor Information

✉ Secretaria Municipal de Turismo e Meio Ambiente (SETMA), Praça da Matriz, Centro
☎ 65/3345 1952
🕑 Closed Sat.–Sun.

Jaguar Ecological Reserve

🗺 171 A2

✉ Estr. Parque Transpantaneira km 110 (3 hours from Poconé)

☎ 65/3646 9679 or 9958 4306

www.jaguarreserve .com

One of the most interesting is the **Pousada Araras Ecolodge** (see Travelwise p. 296) at kilometer 32. The property is named for the hyacinth macaw, and the number of this species in the vicinity grew from 27 in 1993 to 42 by 2012. The surrounding area has served as a location for several feature and documentary films. Lodge activities include hiking, horseback riding, day- and nighttime wildlife-spotting jeep tours, and canoeing.

support from the New Mexico–based Focus Conservation Fund. Its strengths are wildlife-watching and birding excursions, by jeep and boat. The property also has hiking trails.

Set at the confluence of the Rio Paraguai and Rio Cuiabá, the **Parque Nacional Pantanal Matogrossense** protects 520 square miles (1,350 sq km) of Pantanal wetlands. You will need to contact a tour operator

Exploring the wetlands by horseback is just one of many activities offered by Pantanal ecolodges.

Parque Nacional do Pantanal Matogrossense

🗺 171 A2

✉ Estr. Parque Transpantaneira km 147 (3.5 hours from Poconé)

☎ 65/9952 5880

Through its sister company, Pantanal Explorer, you can book additional activities, such as a multiday horse ride through the Pantanal, a multiday photo safari, and a one-day Dia Pantaneiro that will introduce you to the region's rural cowboy culture.

Much farther down the Transpantaneira, at kilometer 110, the **Jaguar Ecological Reserve** is a private nature reserve owned and operated by a local family with

authorized by IBAMA, Brazil's environmental agency, if you wish to visit this national park. Two local operations have authorization: the Pousada Piuval and the Hotel Porto Jofre Pantanal Norte. A ranch that has remained in the same family for 130 years, the **Pousada Piuval** offers lodging and a full range of outdoor activities in addition to park visits. It sits near the beginning of the Transpantaneira. Located on a bank of the Rio Cuiabá, the **Hotel Porto Jofre Pantanal Norte** specializes in fishing expeditions; it only operates from March to October, when fish are not breeding.

SESC Pantanal Estância Ecológica: Running southeast from Poconé for more than 25 miles (40 km), the MT-370 dead-ends at Porto Cercado, where you will find the SESC Pantanal Estância Ecológica. This vast ecological resort comprises a private nature reserve, a scientific research station, and a hotel widely considered the

INSIDER TIP:

While fishing is a Cáceres highlight, birding is also a popular activity. The region's diverse array, which includes the red-necked jabiru and the all-blue hyacinth macaw, is best viewed during Brazil's spring (Sept.–Nov.).

—ROSE DAVIDSON
National Geographic contributor

best equipped in the entire Pantanal. You can sign up for nature hikes, horseback riding, wildlife-spotting jeep safaris, night wildlife spotting, boat trips through rivers and freshwater bays, and more. At the **Borbo-letário,** an enclosed butterfly breeding center, you can delight in the 3,000-plus of these insects, representing more than 20 species, while at the **For-migueiro** you can marvel at the ant colonies held in transparent enclosures and tubes. There's also a **museum** dedicated to the plants and animals of the region.

Cáceres

Cáceres sprawls along the banks of the Rio Paraguai, about 138 miles (220 km) west of Cuiabá. The city has become one of the main centers for recreational fishing in the Pantanal. In fact, it hosts the annual springtime **Festival Internacional de Pesca Esportiva** *(dates vary year to year),* a multiday event that claims to be the biggest sport-fishing tournament in the world.

In town, the narrow streets of Cáceres' historic center feature a handful of interesting buildings, some dating from the 18th century. The **Museu Histórico de Cáceres** displays artifacts from indigenous tribes and includes a space dedicated to Cândido Mariano da Silva Rondon, the military engineer who led missions at the turn of the 20th century to string telegraph lines to improve communication between the state of Mato Grosso and the rest of the country.

Fishing: The Pantanal's annual flooding cycle creates excellent conditions for the reproduction of fish, and sport fishermen tell stories of prize catches of *jaú* (catfish), *pintado* (catfish), and *dourado* ("a fighting fish that is worth the trouble to catch it," as

Pousada Piuval
- ✉ Estr. Parque Transpantaneira km 10, Zona Rural, Poconé
- ☎ 65/3345 1338

Hotel Porto Jofre Pantanal Norte
- ✉ Estr. Parque Transpantaneira km 145
- ☎ 65/3637 1593 or 3637 1263
- **www.portojofre .com.br**

SESC Pantanal Estância Ecológica
- 🗺 171 A2
- ✉ MT-370 km 43, Zona Rural, Poconé
- ☎ 65/3688 2001
- **www.sescpantanal .com.br**

Cáceres
- 🗺 171 A2
- **Visitor Information**
- ✉ Secretaria Municipal de Meio Ambiente e Turismo (SEMATUR), Rua Riachuelo 1, Cavalhada, Centro
- ☎ 65/3222 3455
- 🕐 Closed Sat.–Sun.

Museu Histórico de Cáceres
- ✉ Rua Antônio Maria 244, Centro, Cáceres
- ☎ 65/3223 1500

Parque Nacional da Chapada dos Guimarães

  171 B3

  Rod. Emanuel Pinheiro, MT-251 km 50, Chapada dos Guimarães

☎ 61/3301 1133

one specialized website puts it). All told, the Pantanal is home to more than 200 species of fish.

In the past sport fishermen might have set off in *chalanas*, traditional flat-bottom boats used for transportation in the region. Today, however, you can book a

---

EXPERIENCE:
Search for Jaguars

Cáceres serves as the launching pad for seven-day jaguar-spotting tours run by **Focus Tours** *(Rua Getúlio Vargas 668, Sala 10, Funcionários, Belo Horizonte, tel 31/3309 2060 or 9134 3833 or in U.S. 505/216 7780, www.focustours.com, $$$$$)*. Jaguars are notoriously hard to see in the wild, but one of the best places to find them is in and around the **Estação Ecológica do Taiamã,** a federal nature reserve near Cáceres that is closed to visitors. Lodging on a houseboat near Taiamã, you and your guides head out during the day by boat in search of not only jaguars but also giant river otters and other animals before returning to the houseboat for the evening. Even if the elusive jaguar doesn't make an appearance, you won't soon forget this experience.

---

multiday recreational fishing excursion aboard a modern yacht *(Brazilian fishing license required; arrange through local tour operators)*. The **Barão de Melgaço** *(tel 65/3623 1408)* is a reputable yacht with a capacity of 28 that runs fishing trips out of Cáceres. The season runs from March to October.

Chapada dos Guimarães

The Chapada dos Guimarães, some 43 miles (69 km) northeast of Cuiabá, presents a stunning yet classic example of the savanna-like Cerrado eco-region. This collection of yellowish-red sandstone cliffs, caves, and rock formations is perfect for hiking and other adventure activities—or for relaxing at one of the region's many waterfalls. You'll need to hire a guide in the town of Chapada dos Guimarães for any of these activities.

The 74,000-acre (300 sq km) **Parque Nacional da Chapada dos Guimarães** protects much of the region, which owes its appearance to a complex geological history. Five hundred million years ago, during an ice age, it lay buried under ice. Two hundred million years later, it served as an ocean bed. Then it became a dinosaur-inhabited forest. As tectonic forces pushed the Andes Mountains up, the Pantanal sunk to form the nearby wetlands and the Chapada dos Guimarães was elevated.

Numerous streams run off the plateau, some flowing south to the Rio de la Plata Basin, others north to the Amazon and Araguaia-Tocantins Basins. A popular park outing is the six-hour **Circuito das Cachoeiras** (Waterfall Circuit), a mild hike of waterfall-hopping—swimming in ponds and enjoying natural Jacuzzi-style shoulder massages from gravity-propelled water before heading to the next spot. A car is required, however, to reach the exquisite **Véu da Noiva,** which free-falls 279 feet (85 m) into a sandstone valley; you can see it from a viewing platform accessed via a short trail from a parking lot on Rodovia Emanuel Pinheiro at kilometer 51.

If you're into serious hiking, the challenging 9.25-mile (15 km) trek up 2,743-foot (836 m) Morro de São Jerônimo is a must-do. But you needn't hike that far to find a good vista point. Most of the park's trails lead to spots that offer bird's-eye views.

Serra do Roncador & the Rio Araguaia Basin

Natural beauty, mystery, and mysticism draw visitors to the extreme eastern reaches of Mato Grosso. **Barra do Garças,** about 310 miles (500 km) east of Cuiabá, is the region's central town. It claims to have been the biggest city by area in the world, and technically its jurisdiction, now reduced, does still cover more than 3,475 square miles (9,000 sq km)—a hundred times the size of Paris.

Exploring the region's attractions is difficult to manage on your own. It's best to go on excursions offered by reputable local tour operators, such as **Roncador Expedições.** Activities include floating on the Rio Araguaia, where you can spy freshwater dolphins below and flocks of birds on high. One of its tributaries, the **Rio das Mortes,** ranks among the world's cleanest rivers. During the dry season, you can stop to loll on pristine fluvial beaches along the Rio das Mortes or venture into the fields to spot maned wolves, giant anteaters, and birds like the hoatzin.

The Serra do Roncador highlands top out at 1,969 feet (600 m) and extend for more than 620 miles (1,000 km). English explorer Percy Fawcett and his companions disappeared here without a trace in 1925. The model for the fictional Indiana Jones, Fawcett vanished while searching for the Lost City of Z, which he believed linked to the legend of the El Dorado, the City of Gold. Several trails cut through the area, including one that leads underground (*off-limits to hikers*) and another that mystics believe leads to other dimensions.

Another hike will take you to an oddity: a ***discoporto,*** a landing strip for UFOs, built by the city. The trail to it winds through the **Parque Estadual da Serra Azul,** a state park. UFO believers often maintain nocturnal vigils on the **Platô do Roncador,** at the top of the Serra do Roncador. ■

Barra do Garças

🄰 171 B2

Visitor Information

✉ Prefeitura de Barra do Garças, Rua Carajás 522, Centro

☎ 66/3402 2000

Roncador Expedições

✉ Rua Germano Bezerra, Quadra B, Lote 04, Monte Sinai, Barra do Garças

☎ 66/8121 1151 or 9919 7066

A giant river otter out for a swim. Wildlife spotting ranks as one of the Pantanal's top attractions.

Wild backlands and expansive beaches, prehistoric sites and colonial-era towns, festive celebrations and outdoor adventuring

Northeast

Among the attractions of Salvador's Centro Histórico, known as Pelourinho, is the impressive colonial-era Igreja e Convento de São Francisco.

Northeast

Brasília might be the capital, São Paulo might have the capital, and Rio de Janeiro might be the postcard, but the Northeast is Brazil's heart and soul. This is where the Portuguese first landed in 1500, in Porto Seguro, and it is the site of the old colonial capital, Salvador.

The Northeast engendered Palmares, the most important community of escaped slaves in the 17th century, and Canudos, an alternative community of outcasts at the end of the 19th century. Both brutally squelched by authorities, they continue to fuel the country's popular imagination. Historical parks dedicated to those communities exist in the states of Alagoas and Bahia, respectively. In the 20th century, the region gave Brazil both its most popular musician, Luiz Gonzaga, and its most feared bandit, Lampião. In Sergipe state, you can visit the spot where the latter met his end.

In Bahia, the state capital, Salvador, offers a unique mix of history, Afro-Brazilian culture, and an effervescent party atmosphere. The historic old town of state capital Recife and its sister city, Olinda, mix history and roots cultures that are in dialogue with the rest of the world. Among other things, Recife was home to the first synagogue in the Americas. In Maranhão state, the capital of São Luís—its historic buildings covered by Portuguese tiles—and the ghost town of Alcântara transport you back to earlier times.

The Northeast does not live on history alone. There is also prehistory. In Piauí state, the Serra da Capivara, encompassed within a national park, is an archaeological site that has changed the way paleoanthropologists think about the human settlement of the Americas. It also offers world-class visitor infrastructure. The state of Paraíba is home to one of the world's most important dinosaur archaeological sites, with footprints that have been preserved for thousands of years.

Popular culture surrounds you in the Northeast. In a country of people who truly like their traditional parties, the region offers some of the best. The Carnaval street celebrations in Olinda and Salvador have to be high on any list of the best pre-Lenten festivals. Every winter, there are equally impressive Festas Juninas (June Festivals; three separate festivals, each one honoring one of the three big Catholic saints)—the biggest celebrations taking place in Campina Grande and Caruaru. The latter city, together with nearby Bezerros, is a hotbed of popular art.

Nature's Bounty

Brazil can claim some of the world's best beaches, with many of them found in the Northeast. And if you don't want to just lounge around sipping caipirinhas, there are numerous opportunities for kite surfing, surfing, and diving—including, for the latter, a rich collection of shipwrecks. The

---

NOT TO BE MISSED:

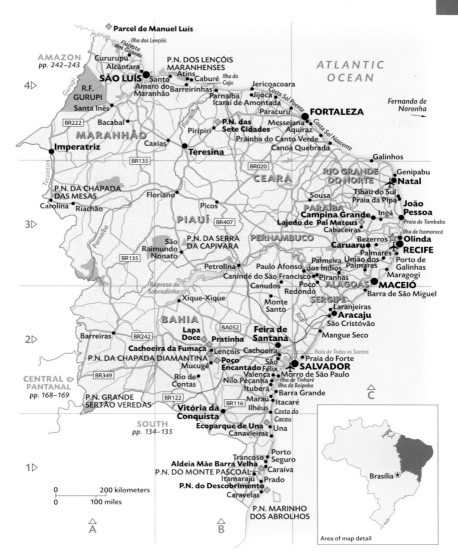

Parcel de Manuel Luís
Ilha dos Lençóis
Floresta
dos Guarás
AMAZON
pp. 242–243
Cururupu
Alcântara
ATLANTIC
OCEAN
P.N. DOS LENÇÓIS
MARANHENSES
SÃO LUÍS
Santo
Atins
Caburé
Ilha do
Caju
Amaro do
Maranhão
Barreirinhas
Jericoacoara
Fernando de
Noronha
R.F.
GURUPI
Parnaíba
Jijoca
Costa Sol Poente
Icaraí de Amontada
Santa Inês
Paracuru
FORTALEZA
BR222
Bacabal
MARANHÃO
Piripiri
P.N. das
Sete Cidades
Messejana
Aquiraz
Costa Sol Nascente
Imperatriz
Caxias
Prainha do Canto Verde
Teresina
Canoa Quebrada
Galinhos
BR135
BR020
Genipabu
RIO GRANDE
DO NORTE
Natal
P.N. DA CHAPADA
DAS MESAS
Floriano
CEARÁ
Sousa
Tibau do Sul
Praia da Pipa
Carolina
Riachão
Picos
PARAÍBA
Inga
João
Pessoa
PIAUÍ
BR407
Campina Grande
Lajedo de Paí Mateus
Praia de Tambaba
Cabaceiras
Ilha de Itamaracá
São
Raimundo
Nonato
P.N. DA SERRA
DA CAPIVARA
PERNAMBUCO
Bezerros
Olinda
Caruaru
RECIFE
BR135
Palmeira
União dos
Palmares
Porto de
Petrolina
Paulo Afonso
dos Índios
Palmares
Galinhas
Canindé do São Francisco
Piranhas
Maragogi
Canudos
Poço
MACEIÓ
Represa de
Sobradinho
Redondo
ALAGOAS
Barra de São Miguel
Xique-Xique
Monte
Santo
SERGIPE
Laranjeiras
Aracaju
São Cristóvão
BAHIA
Lapa
Doce
BA052
Feira de
Santana
Mangue Seco
Barreiras
BR242
Pratinha
Cachoeira
Cachoeira da Fumaça
Lençóis
Baía de Todos os Santos
Praia do Forte
P.N. DA CHAPADA DIAMANTINA
Poço
São
SALVADOR
Mucugê
Encantado
Félix
CENTRAL &
PANTANAL
pp. 168–169
BR349
Rio de
Contas
Valença
Nilo Peçanha
Ilha de Tinharé
Morro de São Paulo
Ilha de Boipeba
Ituberá
Maraú
Barra Grande
P.N. GRANDE
SERTÃO VEREDAS
BR122
Vitória da
Conquista
BR116
Itacaré
Ilhéus
Costa do
SOUTH
pp. 134–135
Ecoparque de Una
Cacau
Canavieiras
Una
Trancoso
Porto
Seguro
Aldeia Mãe Barra Velha
Caraíva
P.N. DO MONTE PASCOAL
Itamaraju
Prado
P.N. do Descobrimento
Caravelas
P.N. MARINHO
DOS ABROLHOS

0   200 kilometers
0   100 miles

Brasília
Area of map detail

Abrolhos region off the coast of southern Bahia is a prime whale-watching area. And a sea turtle conservation group has several outposts along the coast where, in season, you can watch babies hatch on the sand and scramble into the surf.

There are numerous sites for outdoor and adventure activities. In the interior of Bahia, for instance, the Chapada Diamantina is an oasis in the middle of the outback. Nobody ever forgets its caves flooded by sparkling blue water, but it is also a great place for hiking and more.

Nature shows off its beauty and diversity in such places as the Lençóis Maranhenses, with its rain-filled freshwater pools amid desert sand dunes; the Delta do Parnaíba, comparable only to the Mekong and Nile Deltas; and the Cariri region, with the spectacular rock formations of the Lajedo de Pai Mateus set amid the parched *sertão*. ■

Bahia

A hotbed of Afro-Brazilian culture, Bahia's attractions begin with the former colonial capital and world-class party city Salvador. Farther afield, a virtual oasis in the otherwise parched outback, the Parque Nacional da Chapada Diamantina acts as a magnet for outdoor enthusiasts. A long stretch of coast draws everyone from beachgoers to whale watchers.

Salvador's colonial old town, the Pelourinho area is a maze of cobblestone streets lined with interesting architecture and brimming with colorful Bahian culture.

Salvador

 199 C2

Visitor Information

 Serviço de Atendimento ao Turista Salvador, Rua das Laranjeiras 12, Pelourinho

☎ 71/3321 2133 or 3321 2463

www.bahia.com.br

Salvador

Brazil's colonial capital from 1549 to 1763, Salvador offers a unique blend of history and Afro-Brazilian culture. Located almost 1,250 miles (2,000 km) northeast of São Paulo, this is a big (pop. 2.7 million) and sprawling city dotted with points of interest that run from art museums to must-see postcard sites and urban beaches. Most of the main attractions are in

the Cidade Alta (Upper Town), concentrated in the Pelourinho area and north toward the square Largo Santo Antônio Além do Carmo.

Pelourinho: Many of the city's premier sights are concentrated in the Centro Histórico (historic district), known as the Pelourinho, after one of its main squares. **Largo do Pelourinho,** set on a modestly steep incline, peaks at the **Fundação Casa Jorge Amado** (*Largo do*

Pelourinho 51, tel 71/3321 0070, closed Mon., $), with a permanent exhibition about the writer's work and temporary exhibitions. Thanks to Amado (1912–2001), Brazil's best-selling novelist of the 20th century, Salvador holds a special place in the Brazilian popular imagination. Local heroes Olodum (see sidebar below) filmed their appearance in Michael Jackson's video "They Don't Care About Us" here.

Olodum's headquarters and community center, **Casa do Olodum** (Rua Maciel de Baixo 22, tel 71/3321 5010), is south of the square, where you'll find some churches and other points of interest. The **Igreja e Convento de São Francisco** (Largo Cruzeiro de São Francisco, tel 71/3322 6430; try to avoid times when Mass is being held), is an impressive colonial-era baroque church, its interior a riot of gold-leaf paneling. A little east, more colonial churches cluster around the large square known as **Terreiro de Jesus,** as does the **Museu Afro-Brasileiro** (Largo do Terreiro de Jesus, tel 71/3283 5540, www.mafro.ceao.ufba.br), a museum of Afro-Brazilian culture and history. A couple of blocks southwest, the **Fundação Pierre Verger** (Ladeira da Vila América 6, tel 71/3203 8400) features work by a French photographer who dedicated the last five decades of his life to documenting his adopted home of Bahia before dying in 1996.

Before you start walking north from Largo do Pelourinho to Largo Santo Antônio Além do Carmo via Rua do Carmo, detour to the **Museu Tempostal** (Rua Gregório de Matos 33, tel 71/3117 6383, closed Mon.), a quirky museum that celebrates Salvador in postcard form, displaying a century's worth of the mail items.

At the other end of the historic district, on a square known as the Largo de Santo Antônio Além do Carmo, the **Forte de Santo Antônio Além do Carmo** is an old fort that has been transformed into a capoeira (see sidebar p. 21) center where groups train and offer lessons. You can catch a free performance on Saturday evening.

Cidade Baixa & Beyond: Visit the shore-hugging Cidade Baixa (Lower Town) for slightly off-the-beaten-track Salvador treats: a genuine street market, a church that stands as a symbol of religious

---

Olodum

Although it spearheaded the creation of the distinctive sound axé **(described as samba-reggae), Olodum is not a band but rather a community group that includes musical presentations among its activities, along with Carnaval processions and educational work—all with a black pride message. Founded in 1979, Olodum deserves credit for helping to revive the once run-down inner-city neighborhood of Pelourinho, where the group often performs on Tuesday nights. Check with the Casa do Olodum for showtimes.**

GETTING AROUND SALVADOR: A two-line urban railway is being gradually rolled out between 2012 and 2014. Though designed primarily for commuters, it will also ease the lives of visitors. Otherwise, you need to rely on city buses and taxis.

Forte de Santo Antônio Além do Carmo

 Praça Barão do Triunfo, Largo de Santo Antônio

☎ 71/3117 1488 or 3117 1492

NOTE: Forgo shorts and sandals and mimic the way locals dress in Salvador as men wearing long pants and closed shoes are much less likely to be hassled. Also be aware of your surroundings, especially in the Pelourinho area. Malandros (shrewd bad guys) descend on this part of town, expecting to find tourists. Some can be very charming, even speaking a little English. Not everyone you meet is out to get you, but be cautious.

Palácio Rio Branco

- ⊠ Praça Tomé de Sousa, Centro
- ☎ 71/3116 6520 or 3117 6492
- 🕐 Closed Mon.

Mercado Modelo

- ⊠ Praça Visconde de Cayrú, Comércio
- ☎ 71/3241 0242
- 🕐 Closed holidays

Associação Comercial

- ⊠ Praça Conde dos Arcos, Comércio
- ☎ 71/3242 4455
- 🕐 Closed Sat.–Sun.

syncretism, and a 16th-century fort with a view.

An interesting way to get to the Cidade Baixa from the Cidade Alta is via the **Elevador Lacerda** (*Praça Municipal/Praça Tomé de Sousa, Cidade Alta, tel 71/3243 4030, $*). This public elevator on the edge of the Pelourinho district was inaugurated in 1873 to move people up and down the 236 feet (72 m) that separate the two sections of the old town. A 1930 renovation gave it its art deco appearance. Near the elevator's top entrance, you'll find buildings housing the mayor's office and the city council, as well as the **Palácio Rio Branco,** which served as the

The Elevador Lacerda transports citizens between the upper and lower sections of Salvador's Centro Histórico.

INSIDER TIP:

After drinking an *água de coco*, available at almost every Brazilian beach kiosk, ask that the coconut be split in half, so you can eat the coconut flesh.

—ADRIANA IZZO-ORTOLANO
National Geographic contributor

seat of the colonial government when Salvador was the capital.

Opposite the elevator's base, an old customhouse is now the **Mercado Modelo,** a crafts mall. It might seem a bit touristy, but prices can be better here than in Pelourinho stores. Nearby, the district is home to the port and offices like that of the **Associação Comercial,** which is ensconced in a 19th-century English neoclassical building, a rare example of that architecture in Brazil. A little ways farther, the **Museu du Ritmo** (*Av. Jequitaia 1, Comércio, tel 71/3354 2747, www.carlinhosbrown .com.br/universo, closed Sat.–Sun.*) is an arts and cultural center founded by recording star and Salvador native Carlinhos Brown.

Other area attractions lie a bit farther north along the shoreline, so either hail a cab or hop a bus destined for Bonfim or Ribiera. About 1.25 miles (2 km) away, the **Feira de São Joaquim** (*Av. Oscar Pontes, Comércio*) street market spreads out over several blocks, selling everything from produce and meat to traditional munchies, Candomblé articles, and crafts.

Two miles (3 km) farther, the **Igreja do Senhor do Bonfim**

(Praça Senhor Bonfim, Bonfim, tel 71/3316 2196) looms from atop a hill. Dating from 1745 and built in the Portuguese rococo fashion, it is known throughout Brazil as a symbol of Catholic-Candomblé syncretism. At the annual Lavagem do Bonfim, Candomblé women ceremoniously wash its steps on the Thursday before the second Sunday after the Catholic Epiphany (January 6). Outside the church, peddlers press visitors to

the 17th century. In addition to the usual Brazilian modernist suspects, the MAM–BA puts the spotlight on local heroes like Carybé and Mário Cravo. Outside, the sculpture park does the same with the likes of Chico Liberato and Emanoel Araújo. Its Saturday evening jazz jam sessions are popular.

About a mile (1.6 km) away, heading southwest parallel to the shore, the **Museu de Arte Sacra**

Forte de Nossa Senhora de Monte Serrat

- ✉ Rua Santa Rita Durão, Ponta de Humaitá
- ☎ 71/3313 7339

Museu de Arte Moderna da Bahia

- ✉ Av. Contorno, Solar do Unhão
- ☎ 71/3117 6139
- 🕐 Closed Mon.

EXPERIENCE: Understanding Candomblé

You can learn about the Afro-Brazilian religion Candomblé at one of Salvador's *terreiros*. These places of worship are typically found in poor neighborhoods where many of the faithful reside. **Terreiro da Casa Branca do Engenho Velho** *(Av. Vasco da Gama 463, Engenho Velho, tel 71/3018 5899 or 9986 4844)*, **Terreiro de**

Mãe Menininha do Gantois *(Rua Mãe Menininha 23, Federação, tel 71/3331 9231),* and others are open to visitors, but only by appointment or during a feast day service. You don't have to dress up, but you should dress respectably. For safety reasons, it is advised you go with a Brazilian, either someone you know or a tour guide.

---

buy colorful Bonfim ribbons. The tradition is to knot one around your wrist while making a wish; after the ribbon falls off on its own, your desire is realized.

A short distance up the road, you can admire the same view that the old colonial soldiers had of the bay and a nearby island, and of course the Cidade Baixa, from the 1587 **Forte de Nossa Senhora de Monte Serrat.**

Beyond Historic Downtown:

Not far from the Centro Histórico, the **Museu de Arte Moderna da Bahia** (MAM–BA) occupies part of the Solar do Unhão, the former headquarters of a sugar plantation dating from

occupies a 17th-century convent. It is one of Brazil's best museums of Catholic religious art. Another 2 miles (3 km) farther south, you will find in the Graça district the **Palacete das Artes,** a lovely eclectic-style building that serves as a contemporary arts museum.

From here, head farther south still, about 1.25 miles (2 km), to the Barra neighborhood and the **Farol da Barra,** the lighthouse that inspired the song of the same name by the band Os Novos Baianos. No visit to Salvador would be complete without taking in a sunset from here. Come a little beforehand to tour the adjacent fort, **Forte de Santo Antônio da Barra,** which houses the **Museu**

Museu de Arte Sacra

- ✉ Rua do Sodré 276, Dois de Julho
- ☎ 71/3243 6511
- 🕐 Closed Sat.–Sun.

Palacete das Artes

- ✉ Rua da Graça, Graça
- ☎ 71/3117 6987
- 🕐 Closed Mon. & a.m.

Farol da Barra & Forte de Santo Antônio da Barra

- ✉ Av. 7 de Setembro 4442, Barra
- ☎ 71/3331 8039

Museu Náutico da Bahia

- ✉ Largo do Farol da Barra
- ☎ 71/3264 3296 or 3331 8039
- 🕐 Closed Mon.; open daily Jan. & July
- 💲 $

www.museunautico dabahia.org.br

Ferry Boat Terminal Marítimo de São Joaquim

- ✉ Av. Oscar Pontes 1051, Calçada
- ☎ 71/3319 2890, 2105 9700, or 3682 1330

Lancha

- ✉ Terminal Turístico Marítimo de Salvador, Mercado Modelo, Comércio
- ☎ 71/3242 4366

Praia do Forte

- 🄰 199 C2

Náutico da Bahia, a nautical museum with items recovered from a 1668 shipwreck and more. After the sunset, head to **Praia do Rio Vermelho,** 5 miles (8 km) east along the shore, for another Salvador must-do experience: eating *acarajé* (see p. 24), the local street food specialty.

Continuing along the coast you will find mostly residential neighborhoods fronted by urban beaches. Some of the most popular are located on a stretch about 15 to 20 miles (25–30 km) east of downtown: **Piatã, Itapuã,** and **Stella Maris.** Itapuã inspired the bossa nova classic "Tarde em Itapuã" ("Afternoon in Itapuã") by Toquinho and Vinicius de Moraes.

The Recôncavo & Around

Several attractions can be visited on day trips from Salvador: the island of Itaparica; the beach, outdoor activities, and sea turtle conservation center in Praia do Forte; and the historic cities Cachoeira and São Félix in the Recôncavo (the former sugar-cane region surrounding the bay and Salvador).

Itaparica: Several day and evening schooner outings leaving from Salvador's Centro Náutico da Bahia *(Av. da França, Comércio)* explore the **Baía de Todos os Santos,** with many of them calling at Itaparica, the bay's biggest island—and one ringed with many palm-fringed beaches (crowded on weekends). For a longer visit to Itaparica, take the regular car ferry from the **Ferry Boat Terminal Marítimo de São Joaquim.**

The trip takes 1.25 hours (boats leave hourly, early morning to late night). Alternatively, the passenger-only *Lancha* makes the crossing in about 45 minutes. If you need a break from the sand and surf, look for the intriguing **Fonte da Bica** *(Parque da Fonte, Morro de Santo Antônio),* a fountain surrounded by a colorful tile wall dating from 1842. The water is said to have medicinal properties. A legend calls it "fine water that will transform an old lady into a young girl."

INSIDER TIP:

Try to get some beach time at Salvador's Praia do Rio Vermelho to watch the different social scenes develop over the day and early evening. Bring money to buy food and drink, and to rent chairs and umbrellas, but leave valuables in your hotel room safe.

–CHRISTIAN BRANNSTROM
National Geographic grantee

Praia do Forte: A district of Mata de São João, about 50 miles (75 km) northeast of Salvador, Praia do Forte is a stretch of white-sand beaches fronted by a sparkling blue sea and backed by green vegetation and coconut trees. Arriving at the beginning of Brazil's summer,

EXPERIENCE: Enjoying Salvador's Carnaval

Anyone can jump into Salvador's Carnaval street party. For the best results, however, you should pay to join a *bloco* ($$$$$), one of the organized groups that run things. All across Brazil, the big bash spans the long weekend that closes with a crash on Ash Wednesday—except in Salvador, where many carry on with the *ressaca*, literally the "hangover," an opportunity for more merriment and Carnaval parties.

In one sense, Carnaval lasts all summer in Salvador. Already by New Year's Day, the blocos are holding incessant *ensaios* (practices)—basically parties—in preparation for the big event.

Salvador boasts Brazil's biggest street Carnaval. Blocos parade through the streets of the city according to preestablished routes. Each bloco's musicians, mostly favoring the formulaic frenetic pop sound *axé*, play atop a giant sound truck called a *trio elétrico*. People who pay for the privilege parade unhindered inside heavy ropes that surround the truck, carried along by gnarly bouncers. People on the inside wear matching bloco T-shirts and can grab refreshments from an accompanying support vehicle.

Anyone can accompany blocos for free in what's left of the densely crowded streets. These outsiders are called *pipoca* (popcorn). Woe to the pipoca that pops inside the ropes: Remember those bouncers?

Blocos afros generally march to a pounding beat of their drum corps and often carry a message of black pride; the most traditional one is **Ilê Aiyê**, founded in 1974. Not to be missed, if only as a spectator, is the

Revelers jam-pack Salvador's main Carnaval parade routes.

bloco **Filhos de Gandhy**, a group founded in 1949 by dockworkers, inspired by India's Mahatma Gandhi. In white robes and turbans with blue trim, participants parade rather slowly by Carnaval standards and distribute necklaces to fans along the route. If you pay attention, you may spot the Brazilian recording star and former minister of culture Gilberto Gil, who customarily parades with the group.

In one sense, Salvador's Carnaval never ends. The most popular blocos take their shows on the road to towns across the country for off-season Salvador-style Carnaval parades called *micaretas*.

Sign Up With a Bloco

Most blocos are open to anyone willing to pay, though you do need to reserve in advance and places tend to run out. Each group parades at several preset times during the festival.

Choose from any of the following blocos and you're guaranteed a good time during Carnaval:

Afoxé Filhos de Gandhy, Rua Gregório de Matos 53, Pelourinho, tel 71/3321 7073
Bloco Carnavalesco Ilê Aiyê, Rua do Curuzu 233, Liberdade, tel 71/3386 2148
Camaleão, Av. Oceânica 3501, Rio Vermelho, tel 71/3797 6100 or 3535 3000
Grupo Cultural Olodum, Rua Maciel de Baixo 22, Pelourinho, tel 71/3321 5010
Timbalada, Alameda Benevento 113, Pituba, tel 71/3354 2747 or 3355 0680.

Projeto Tamar

✉ Av. Farol Garcia d'Ávila, Praia do Forte

☎ 71/3676 1045

💲 $

Projeto Baleia Jubarte

✉ Av. do Farol, Praia do Forte

☎ 71/3676 1463

www.baleiajubarte .org.br

Cachoeira

🅐 199 B2

Irmanidade Nossa Senhora da Boa Morte

✉ Rua 13 de Maio 32, Centro, Cachoeira

☎ 75/3425 1468

more sea turtles lay their eggs on these beaches than anywhere else in Brazil. The **Projeto Tamar** sea turtle conservation project makes its headquarters here; its visitor center/museum includes a small aquarium. In season (typically January or February), you can view the baby turtles as they hatch.

A full range of outdoor activities are available in Praia do Forte, with the spotlight on a canoe trip down the **Rio Imbassaí** to the ocean, stopping at a deserted beach and a straw handicraft center, **Artesanato de Palha.** From July to October whale-watching excursions set out in search of migrating humpback whales. You can learn more about the baleens at the visitor center of the **Projeto Baleia Jubarte,** a humpback whale conservation group, located in town. For information about

adventure and outdoor activities, contact **Bahia Adventure Ecoturismo** *(Alameda do So, tel 71/3626 1932 or 3676 1231).*

Cachoeira: Roughly a 70-mile drive (112 km) northwest of Salvador, the town of Cachoeira is a jewel. Thanks to its position on the Rio Paraguaçu and the surrounding fertile lands, the town was a prosperous crossroads during colonial times—and its architectural and cultural heritages reflect that. Many Afro-Brazilians come here in search of their ancestral roots, with large numbers coinciding their visit with the annual **Festa da Boa Morte** festival, held in August. Organized by the women's association **Irmanidade Nossa Senhora da Boa Morte,** it highlights the syncretism between Catholicism

São Félix Cigars

Cuba and the Dominican Republic may dominate most Top Ten lists when it comes to cigars, but Bahia has its own long-standing tradition of producing top-notch hand-rolled cigars. The soils of the Recôncavo, the fertile region ringing the Baía de Todos os Santos, grow an especially high-quality tobacco leaf, so in the 19th century many cigar companies located themselves in and around São Félix and neighboring Cruz das Almas.

In 1873, German-born Gerhard Dannemann opened a cigar factory in São Félix and produced superior cigars. His slogan was "A cigar. Don't just smoke it—treat yourself to it." Embracing his new country, Dannemann changed his name to Geraldo and eventually became

mayor of the town. In 1989, the company inaugurated the **Centro Cultural Dannemann** *(Av. Salvador Pinto 29, Centro, São Félix, tel 75/3438 2507, www.centro culturaldannemann.com.br),* a cultural center that, among other things, organizes a biennial international art exhibition. The factory stands next door.

To tour the factory, go to the cultural center first. You will be shown a short video about the company and its operations, then taken to the factory, where a dozen women roll cigars by hand. After watching the process, you can take a stab at rolling your own. When you are done, you will be asked to head out back to plant a tree seedling as part of a company-sponsored reforestation scheme.

and Candomblé. Today, only remnants of the area's vast sugarcane and tobacco plantations survive and support the economy: Five miles (8 km) distant, you can see visit a cigar factory in **São Félix** (see sidebar opposite).

Parque Nacional da Chapada Diamantina

The Chapada Diamantina (Diamond Plateau) is a series of craggy, flat-topped mountains with steep cliffs that lead down into green valleys, much of which is protected in the 587 square mile (1,520 sq km) Parque Nacional da Chapada Diamantina. Most of Bahia's rivers rise in the *chapada,* so the national park features more than 70 waterfalls—including Brazil's highest, the 1,100-foot (340 m) Cachoeira da Fumaça. Lakes and ponds dot the region. Though much of the coastal Northeast is characterized by the parched *sertão,* this inland oasis sits on the edge of the Cerrado bioregion that covers most of central Brazil.

Lençóis, an old diamond- and gold-mining town located just over 250 miles (400 km) west of Salvador, now provides most of the infrastructure for park visitors. Outdoor enthusiasts come in droves to partake in myriad outdoor activities: Rock climbing, caving, trekking, rappelling, mountain biking, canoeing, diving, horseback riding, and zip-lining count among the favorite outdoor activities. And then there are the hiking possibilities.

Outdoor enthusiasts flock to the Chapada Diamantina.

Hiking circuits range from one to ten days, and because the area around the park is well endowed with guesthouses and restaurants, even on the longer trips you can wind down and rest comfortably at the end of the day. The treks are a great way to delve not only into the natural environment but also the local culture.

Many of the shorter walks lead to impressive landmarks like the **Cachoeira da Fumaça** waterfall and another called the **Cachoeira do Mosquito.** There are plenty of caves, too: **Pratinha** and **Lapa Doce** top the list. An old trail leads up the **Morro do Pai Inácio,** rewarding you at the top with one of the region's best views. Other peaks rank as the three highest points in Bahia: **Pico das Almas, Pico do Itobira,** and the **Pico do Barbado;** the last one is the highest point in the whole Northeast at 6,600 feet (2,033 m) above sea

Parque Nacional da Chapada Diamantina

🗺 199 B2

✉ Rua Barão do Rio Branco 25, Palmeiras

☎ 75/3332 2418 or 3332 2310

Morro de São Paulo

199 B2

Ilha de Tinharé

NOTE: Many companies operate boats ($$) to Morro de São Paulo from the Terminal Turístico Marítimo (Av. da França) in Salvador, including **Biotur** (tel 75/3641 3327), **Catamarã Farol do Morro** (tel 71/3319 4570 or 9136 4460), and **IlhaBela TM** (tel 71/3326 7158 or 9195 6744). The trip takes about two hours.

level. The **Poço Encantado** and **Poço Azul** are expansive pools inside caves. When hit by rays of sunlight during certain months of the year, they exude a brilliant neon-blue color.

Guides are important for both short and long hiking excursions or other activities. For more information, contact local operators **Venturas** (Av. 7 de Setembro 22, Lençóis, tel 75/3334 1030) or **Fora da Trilha** (Rua das Pedras 202, Lençóis, tel 75/3334 1326).

Beyond the Park: The surrounding region also has several cities worth a visit. More than 145 miles (233 km) northwest of Lençóis, **Xique-Xique** nearly became a ghost town after the diamond mines ran out in the late 19th century. Almost all its structures are made of stone. About 35 miles (56 km) south of Lençóis, **Mucugê** has a so-called Byzantine cemetery, dating from the 19th century. And **Rio de Contas,** 80 miles (130 km) farther south still, retains important examples of colonial architecture.

South of Salvador

Costa do Dendê: Just south of the Baía de Todos os Santos, the Costa do Dendê is named for the palm oil grown in this region. It offers a mix of beaches, Atlantic Forest, history, and outdoor activities.

First stop, **Morro de São Paulo,** a fishing village and the surrounding northeastern section of the large island **Ilha de Tinharé,** just off the coast from

INSIDER TIP:

Just south of the Parque Nacional da Chapada Diamantina, near Ibicoara, don't miss the beautiful Cachoeira do Buracão. At the head of a canyon, this waterfall drops 262 feet (80 m) into a deep pool.

—RODRIGO NICOLETTE
Professor, University of São Paulo

Valença. It is a popular destination for seekers of sun and sand during the day and a typically Bahian party atmosphere at night. The urban area has recently received a face-lift. Only commercial vehicles are permitted on the island, so you'll need to rely on your feet. At more distant beaches, donkey carts are there to help. The most popular excursions are boat trips that stop at different beaches. The lighthouse is a favorite spot to take in the sunset. The adjacent island, **Ilha de Boipeba,** offers a calmer ambience (you can hire a boat in Morro de São Paulo).

Morro de São Paulo and Boipeba sit just off the coast from the city of **Valença.** Boats link the city to both islands. Valença is an 18th-century colonial town. Among other things, you can find here the ruins of Brazil's first textile factory, **Todos os Santos,** dating from 1844. To reach them, you hike 1.25 miles (2 km) along a riverside trail that parallels the **Rio Una.**

Nearly 20 miles (30 km) south of Valença, tiny **Nilo Peçanha** is surrounded by the Atlantic Forest. Rafting enthusiasts will love the Class III rapids on the **Rio das Almas.** In neighboring **Ituberá,** the **Cachoeira da Pancada Grande,** the biggest waterfall in the region, is sought out for cascading (rappelling). For more information, contact **Ativa Rafting e Aventuras** *(Nilo Peçanha, tel 73/3257 2083 or 9928 1372, www.ativarafting.com.br).*

South of Nilo Peçanha, about 90 miles (140 km) away via roads that double back to get there, the fishing village of **Barra Grande** is the main attraction on the Península de Maraú. Access is still by dirt roads, a fact that helps protect the area and ensures a peaceful atmosphere. If you want to be more energetic, the main activities are boat trips along the coast, including whale-watching trips between July and November, when humpback whales congregate in the warm waters off Bahia state to mate.

Costa do Cacau: The Costa do Cacau (Cocoa Coast) runs south some 130 miles (210 km) from Itacaré to Canavieiras, along Bahia's southeastern edge. This coastal slice combines beaches and sections of the Atlantic Forest with the history of one of the country's most important economic commodity cycles, that of cocoa in the 19th and 20th centuries. Outdoor activities can be combined with visits to cocoa plantations and historical sites.

Itacaré, about 160 miles (260 km) south of Salvador, offers a full-range of outdoor activities, from surfing and canoeing to rafting and trekking. Surfing lessons are available through the **Easy Drop Surfing School** *(Rua João Coutinho 140, Centro, tel 73/3251 3065).* About 18 miles (30 km) west of Itacaré, near the town of Taboquinhas, the **Rio de Contas** forms Class III–IV rapids on a ride that floats past a cocoa plantation, the lush vegetation of the Atlantic Forest, and a freshwater beach. For information, contact Ativa Rafting e Aventuras *(Rua Pé da Pancada, Taboquinhas, tel 73/3257 2083, www.ativarafting.com.br).*

Itacaré
▲ 199 B2

Ilhéus
▲ 199 B2
Visitor Information
✉ Secretária de Turismo de Ilhéus, Av. Soares Lopes 1136, Centro
☎ 73/3634 1977
www.ilheus.ba.gov.br

Casa de Cultura Jorge Amado
✉ Rua Jorge Amado 21, Boa Vista, Ilhéus
☎ 73/3634 8986
🕐 Closed Sat.–Sun.

Morro de São Paulo, a popular beach and party village

Nearly 40 miles (60 km) south of Itacaré, **Ilhéus** is rich in historical attractions. The region provided the setting for *Gabriela, Clove and Cinnamon,* a best-selling novel by Jorge Amado about the cocoa plantation lords. The downtown **Casa de Cultura Jorge Amado** is a house where the writer spent time (what else?)

Mãe da Mata

✉ Estr. Banco da Vitória Maria Jape km 7, Ilhéus

☎ 73/9981 8132, 8816 1318, or 8193 6906

🕐 By appt. only

💲 $

www.rppnmaeda mata.blogspot.com

Ecoparque de Una

🅼 199 B1

✉ Rod. Ilhéus-Una, 28 miles (45 km) S of Ilhéus

☎ 73/3234 3250 or 9983 6363

www.ecoparque .org.br

Porto Seguro

🅼 199 B1

writing. That cultural center anchors an old town that includes the **Bar Vesúvio** *(Praça Dom Eduardo 190, Centro, tel 73/3634 2164)*, a site important to the novel. You can get a taste of the cocoa baron life by visiting one of the area plantations (see sidebar below). There are a couple other interesting attractions outside of town. The private nature reserve **Mãe da Mata** has trails that run through a cocoa forest. You can also visit a *cachaça* distillery and taste tropical fruits grown on the premises. The **Rio do Engenho** *(access by boat from Praça Maramata, in Pontal district, tel 73/3231 9119)* is an old sugar plantation with structures dating from the 16th century.

Some 35 miles (58 km) south of Ilhéus, in the town of Una, the **Ecoparque de Una** is a private nature reserve. It offers guided nature hikes along easy trails, one of which is 1.25 miles long (2 km) and starts in a rubber plantation where visitors learn how that material is harvested. More than 200 species of birds have been identified in the area, and a 65.5-foot-high (20 m) suspension bridge through tree canopies offers a unique perspective.

Canavieiras, 35 miles (58 km) south of Una, is a world-class sportfishing destination given its proximity to the South Atlantic's Royal Charlotte Bank, one of the best places to catch blue marlin.

Costa do Descobrimento: The Costa do Descobrimento (Discovery Coast) is anchored around **Porto Seguro,** a city that marks the spot of the first landing of Portuguese explorers in 1500. The region offers a mix of colonial history, indigenous culture, outdoor attractions, and, of course, beaches. Unfortunately, Porto Seguro has lost much of its charm and little remains of historical or cultural interest. It is now where people go for a good time at the beach, even becoming the Spring Break destination for middle-class Brazilian college students. There is a strip in town called the Passarela do Álcool (Alcohol Catwalk); think of it as New Orleans' French Quarter, without good music or a sense of history.

EXPERIENCE: Visiting a Cocoa Plantation

The area around Ilhéus was a booming center of cocoa plantations until a fungus swept through in the 1980s, wiping out most of the cocoa trees. Despite this, some cocoa farms with small-scale chocolate production still make a go of it. A few of them allow visitors to explore the estate, learn about the cultivation and chocolate-making process, and sample the end product. Both the **Fazenda Yrerê**

(Rod. Ilhéus-Itabuna km 11, tel 73/3656 5054 or 9998 6790, www.fazendayrere .blogspot.com), which offers a two-hour guided tour, and the **Fazenda Primavera** *(Rod. Ilhéus-Itabuna km 20, tel 73/3231 3996 or 9983 1627)* are good choices. For either, you need to schedule your visit ($$) in advance. Reservations can be made through **Cooperbom Turismo** *(tel 73/3231 5563)*, a local travel agency.

Porto Seguro marks the spot where Portuguese explorers first set foot on South America.

Nevertheless, Porto Seguro is the starting and ending point of the **Rota das Aldeias,** a five-day exploration of indigenous Indian settlements and culture in the surrounding region. For more information, contact **Pataxó Turismo** *(Rua Oscar Oliveira 4, tel 73/3288 1256).*

South of Porto Seguro are **Trancoso** and **Arraial d'Ajuda,** two beach resorts that are extremely popular among Brazilians. Trancoso has a Club Med, while Arraial d'Ajuda has an eco-theme park.

Farther south, some 45 miles (74 km) from Porto Seguro, **Caraíva** offers a glimpse of time gone by: It is a carless coastal village only accessible by boat. Electricity only came in 2007, and the locals knew well enough to force officials to put the wires underground. Four miles (6 km) north of Caraíva, the **Aldeia Mãe Barra Velha** is home to about 500 indigenous families. The Indians produce handicrafts that can be purchased at the **Centro Cultural de Tradições Indígenas.**

More than 60 miles (100 km) southwest of Porto Seguro by car is the **Parque Nacional do Monte Pascoal.** Accessed via BR-101 from the town of Eunápolis, this national park has a visitor center and several hiking trails, including the steep 1-mile (1.6 km) ascent up Monte Pascoal to a fantastic vista point. The peak is noteworthy in Brazilian history, having been famously spotted from afar by Pedro Álvares Cabral, the Portuguese explorer who then landed in Brazil at Porto Seguro. Longer treks are possible as well.

Costa das Baleias (Whale Coast): **Caravelas,** some 550 miles (886 km) south of Salvador, is the main gateway town for the marine **Parque Nacional Marinho dos Abrolhos,** the principal attraction along this coastal strip in the extreme south of Bahia state. Tour operators in neighboring towns, including Prado, also offer excursions into this unique park.

Coral reefs abound in a section called the **Parcel dos Abrolhos.**

Caraíva
- 199 B1

Centro Cultural de Tradições Indígenas
- Aldeia Mãe Barra Velha, Caraíva
- 73/3668 5000 or 9931 7610
- $
- Bus from Porto Seguro (Viação Águia Azul bus line, tel 73/3281 3469)

Parque Nacional do Monte Pascoal
- 199 B1
- BR-101 Itamaraju, 18 miles (30 km) S of Eunápolis
- 73/3294 1870

Parque Nacional Marinho dos Abrolhos
- 199 B1
- 73/3297 2258
- $$ (tickets sold via local tour operators)
- 3-hour boat trip from Caravelas

Parque Nacional do Descobrimento

⚠ 199 B1

✉ Off BR-489, 18 miles (30 km) N of Prado

☎ 73/3298 1140

Nearby several volcanic islands form an archipelago. Clear waters provide good visibility for viewing sea turtles, fish, and other marine fauna and flora. There are also shipwrecks: *Rosalina* (1955), *Guadiana* (1885), and *Santa Catharina* (1914). The water temperature varies between 73°F and 80°F (23–27°C), with the air temperature just a little higher. All this makes the area popular with divers. You can get an interesting glimpse into the submarine world (sans shipwrecks) with a mask and snorkel, too. The only island that may be explored is **Ilha Siriba,** home to several bird species, including the

A humpback whale breaches off the Costa das Baleias.

masked booby. Excursions can only be made on boats credentialed by Brazilian environmental officials. Options run from day trips to multiday outings.

Caravelas is also a prime center for humpback whale–watching excursions, which in Abrolhos run from July through November. For more information about excursions into Abrolhos park, including

diving expeditions and whale-watching cruises, contact **Apecatu Expedições** (*Rua Rives Scofield 74, tel 73/3297 1453*) or **Horizonte Aberto** (*Av. das Palmeiras 313, tel 73/3297 1474*).

To explore the area's terrestrial ecology, head to the somewhat nearby **Parque Nacional do Descobrimento.** Expanded in 2012 to nearly 88 square miles (23,000 ha), this national park is served by the city of **Prado,** 30 miles (50 km) north of Caravelas. The area is relatively rich in endangered tree species like brazilwood and Bahian rosewood. Many of the park's trails are former logging roads, blazed before the area became a reserve, and felled trees can still be spotted wayside.

Northern Bahia

Visions of ghosts of a 19th-century dissident community and outdoor activities in the Caatinga (aka sertão) eco-region count among the highlights in northern Bahia.

Canudos: Always in the middle of the parched sertão badlands, the town of Canudos (about 250 miles/400 km N of Salvador) has otherwise bounced around a bit in the last 120 years. In 1897, the army destroyed a congregation of thousands of social and economic outcasts led by messianic religious leader Antônio Conselheiro (see p. 36). The Canudos War consisted of a series of federal incursions against the community. It remains a landmark event in Brazilian history. In the mid-20th century, construction

INSIDER TIP:

When in Mangue Seco, a tour along the Costa Azul, an 18.5-mile-long (30 km) stretch of sand lined with palm trees, wild nature, and a beached shipwreck, is mandatory.

—RODRIGO NICOLETTE
Professor, University of São Paulo

of a hydroelectric dam unceremoniously flooded a second town, rebuilt on the original site. When the dam's water level drops during droughts, the buildings seemingly sprout from the water. A third town of the same name sits a few miles away from the original site.

The **Memorial Antônio Conselheiro** presents artifacts related to the community's members and the war, along with exhibitions on regional natural history. The **Parque Estadual de Canudos,** a state park, covers an area that includes many battlefields. You can visit the burial grounds where federal soldiers buried their dead and see some of the trenches they dug.

Nearby **Monte Santo** (about 60 miles/100 km S of Canudos) served as the setting for the acclaimed 1964 avant-garde film *Black God, White Devil* by Glauber Rocha. It is also where one of the biggest meteorites, the Pedra do Bendegó, was found in the 18th century. Since 1888 it has been on exhibit at Rio de Janeiro's Museu

Nacional (see p. 69), a natural history museum.

Raso da Catarina: The Estação Ecológica Raso da Catarina is a nature reserve in the middle of the sertão near the city of Paulo Afonso, near the state border with Alagoas. It is popular with adventure sports enthusiasts. The region is said to have been a favorite hideout for the backlands bandit Lampião in the early 20th Century. Trekking through the canyons offers views of rock formations and contact with the flora and fauna of the Caatinga bioregion.

Mangue Seco: Set in idyllic surroundings at the extreme northeastern point of Bahia, the coastal village of Mangue Seco is famous in Brazil as the setting of a popular telenovela adaptation *(Tieta)* of a Jorge Amado novel. Despite its notoriety, Mangue Seco remains relatively untouched. Sliced by several rivers making their last drives to the sea, its white-sand dunes come replete with coconut trees. You can take dune buggy excursions. Otherwise the only way around is on foot.

The only convenient way to reach Mangue Seco is from the Sergipe side of the Rio Real. You get dropped there or park your vehicle and take a boat across the river back into Bahia. For more information, contact **Bahia Adventure Ecotourism** *(Alameda do Sol, Praia do Forte, Mata de São João, tel 71/3626 1932, www .bahiaadventure.com).* ∎

Canudos
Ⓜ 199 B3
Visitor Information
✉ Prefeitura de Canudos, Av. Enoque Canário Araújo, Centro
☎ 75/3494 2722
🕐 Closed Sat.–Sun.

Memorial Antônio Conselheiro
✉ Rua São José, Centro, Canudos
☎ 75/3494 2194 or 3494 2000
🕐 Closed Sat.–Sun.

Parque Estadual de Canudos
✉ BR-116, Canudos
☎ 75/3494 2796
NOTE: Authorization needed to visit; inquire at the Memorial Antônio Conselheiro

Estação Ecológica Raso da Catarina
Ⓜ 199
✉ Av. Maranhão 79, Fazenda Chesf, Paulo Afonso, 30 miles (50 km) SW of Paulo Afonso
☎ 75/3281 9999
NOTE: Authorization needed to visit

Mangue Seco
Ⓜ 199 C2

Sergipe & Alagoas

For seekers of sun and sand, the Northeast's two smallest states boast beaches not yet over-run by the masses but with plenty of amenities such as restaurants, bars, and a smattering of historical sites and cultural centers.

The beaches that line the coast around Maceió, Alagoas, attract the sun-and-surf crowd.

Aracaju

⚑ 199 C2

Visitor Information

✉ Centro de Turismo, Praça Olímpio Campos, Centro

☎ 79/3179 1947

Museu da Gente Sergipana

✉ Av. Ivo do Prado 398, Centro, Aracaju

☎ 79/3218 1551

🕓 Closed Mon.

Aracaju & Around

Capital of Sergipe, coastal Aracaju sits roughly equidistant between Salvador to the south (215 miles/ 345 km) and Maceió (150 miles/ 245 km) to the north. This planned city replaced São Cristóvão as the state capital in 1855.

Most of Aracaju's hotels, bars, and other amenities are concentrated around two adjacent beaches: **Praia dos Artistas** and **Praia de Atalaia.** Also along this stretch you will find the **Centro de Arte e Cultura de Sergipe** (Av. Santos Dumont, Praia de Atalaia, tel 79/3255 1413, $), where you can purchase items produced by local artisans, and the **Oceanário de Aracaju** (Av. Santos Dumont,

Praia de Atalaia, tel 79/3243 3214, 79/3243 6126), an aquarium featuring freshwater fish from the Rio São Francisco along with saltwater fish. Headliners are the sharks. A popular kiosk cum restaurant called the **Bar e Restaurante Tia Gleide** (see Travelwise p. 304) serves up regional specialties on the Praia dos Artistas. A few blocks inland from the Praia de Atalaia, **O Miguel** (see Travelwise p. 304) is considered the city's best regional Northeastern joint, using only specially prepared filet mignon for its dried beef, carne de sol.

The must-see cultural and historical attraction in downtown Aracaju is the ultracontemporary **Museu da Gente Sergipana,** where interactive displays allow people to "try on" virtual traditional costumes, bargain for goods at a virtual street fair, and virtually exchange improvised verses with a *repentista*, guitar-wielding expert in the art. Just a few blocks from the museum is the **Mercado Municipal Antônio Franco** *(Rua José do Prado Franco, Centro)*, which has a good selection of local crafts; good street food can be found at the market next door, **Mercado Thales Ferraz.**

Beyond Aracaju, two historic towns and a falcon center are worthwhile destinations. Fourteen miles (23 km) south of Aracaju lies the former state capital of **São Cristóvão,** founded in 1590. In 2010, its central square, **Praça São Francisco,** was declared a World Heritage site; its homogenous ensemble of public and private buildings is an exceptional example of colonial urban planning. Northwest of Aracaju, the town of **Laranjeiras** (18 miles/29 km from Aracaju) lays claim to the **Museu Afro-Brasileiro** *(Rua José do Prado Franco 70, tel 79/3281*

2418, closed Mon., $), with an emphasis on objects from the slavery period. Also northwest of Aracaju, the **Parque dos Falcões** (Falcons Park) is a private conservation and reproduction center for birds of prey. Visits end with a chance to have one of the creatures rest on your arm.

Cânions do São Francisco

Flooded by the Xingó hydroelectric dam in the 1990s (see sidebar below), the canyons of the Rio São Francisco are set in a region of abundant natural beauty and historical significance, more than 130 miles (209 km) northwest of Aracaju. At places reaching as high as 325 feet (100 m) and as wide as 200 feet (60 m), the canyons can be explored via a catamaran tour offered by **MFTur** *(Rod. Náufragos km 9, Aracaju, tel 79/9972 1320).* The town of **Canindé do São Francisco,** near the dam, serves as the gateway to the canyons.

Downriver from the dam, you can also visit the site where Brazil's most notorious bandit of the 20th century met his end. Lampião,

Parque dos Falcões

- ✉ Serra da Itabaina, 28 miles/45 km NW of Aracaju, off BR-235
- ☎ 79/9962 5457 or 9131 3496;
- 🕐 Reservations required
- 💲 $

Canindé do São Francisco
- 🅰 199 C3

Visitor Information

- ✉ Prefeitura de Canindé do São Francisco, Praça Ananias Fernandes do São Francisco
- ☎ 79/3346 9500
- 🕐 Closed Sat.–Sun.

The Diversion of the Rio São Francisco

Called the "river of national integration" because it crosses five states, uniting multiple cultures and climates along its 1,811-mile (2,914 km) course, the Rio São Francisco has suffered multiple indignities: five hydroelectric dams, deforestation at its headwaters, pumping for irrigation, and pollution, as well as being drained by an extensive plumbing operation called a "diversion" project. The 1987–1994 construction of the Xingó hydroelectric dam, near Canindé do São Francisco,

flooded dozens of prehistorical sites found in the area. Archaeologists had to scramble to save what they could; their finds, including rock art and a supposedly 9,000-year-old skeleton, can be seen at the **Museu de Arqueologia de Xingó** *(Rod. Canindé-Piranhas, Trevo da UHE-Xingó, Canindé do São Francisco, tel 79/2105 6448).* The dam itself, the **Hidrelétrica de Xingó** *(Estr. para Piranhas, 4 miles/6 km N of Canindé do São Francisco, tel 82/3686 2193),* is open to visitors.

Piranhas

◭ 199 C3

Visitor Information

✉ Prefeitura de Piranhas, Rua Padre Cícero 9

☎ 82/3686 3078

🕓 Closed Sat.–Sun.

Maceió

◭ 199 C3

Visitor Information

✉ Airport Zumbi dos Palmares, BR-104 km 91, Tabuleiro

☎ 82/3036 5200

his girlfriend Maria Bonita, and members of their gang were killed by federal forces in 1938 at a place called **Grota de Angico.** In the municipality of Poço Redondo, the site is about 18 miles (30 km) southeast of Canindé do São Francisco. MFTur runs a boating excursion that visits this site.

Across the river, which doubles as the state line with Alagoas, lies the town of **Piranhas,** where Lampião's severed head was put on display. The town has been declared a national monument. Its **Museu do Sertão** (*Rua José Martiniano Vasco, tel 82/3628 3013, closed Mon.*) contains objects and images related to Lampião and his gang.

Maceió & the Alagoas Coast

Maceió, a city of almost a million, located more than 160 miles (265 km) south of Recife, is a sun-and-sand destination where the best things to do are go to the beach, go to the beach, and go to the beach. The most popular beaches with the best infrastructure are **Pajuçara, Ponta Verde,** and **Jatiúca.** The primo activity in Maceió is to sail out about a mile (1.6 km) on a *jangada*—a small wooden sailboat traditionally used for fishing—to natural pools formed by coral reefs, where you can swim tranquilly in the middle of the ocean. Floating snack bars, atop jangadas themselves, cater to swimmers' needs. Boats leave at low tide from Praia Pajuçara. Just show up and negotiate with a local fisherman to take you out ($). Also on Pajuçara is the aptly

named **Feira de Artesanato da Pajuçara,** a crafts fair on the strand. Beach kiosks have gone wild on these beaches. Some such as **Kanoa** (*Av. Sílvio Carlos Viana, tel 82/3235 3943, closed Tues., $*) and **Lopana** (*Av. Sílvio Carlos Viana 27, tel/3231 7484, closed Sun.–Thurs., $$*), both in Ponta Verde, even hire DJs, and nightlife revolves around the beaches.

INSIDER TIP:

While in Maceió, try one of the local favorites, the *sururu*. This mussel is often shelled and used to make a hearty stew sold by waterfront vendors.

—ROSE DAVIDSON
National Geographic contributor

At **Barra de São Miguel,** a beach town about 18 miles (30 km) down the coast from Maceió, a reef barrier blocks the waves, making the shoreline perfect for bathers looking for calm waters. Adventure canoeing trips and canoe trips to visit local villages leave from here, organized by the local operator **Gato do Mato** (*Rua Marechal Deodoro, Praia do Frances, tel 82/3033 1040, 9992 6111, or 8815 3078*).

North of Maceió, about 78 miles (135 km) away, **Maragogi** offers natural pools perhaps more impressive than those near the capital. The best pools are 4 miles (6 km) out and are served by boats onshore. Diving, if you have your license, or snorkeling, if you do not, is recommended; contact **Explorer Diving & Adventure** *(tel 82/9361 6449)* in Maragogi.

União dos Palmares

União dos Palmares, about 50 miles (75 km) northwest of Maceió, boasts one of Brazil's most important historical sites. Declared a national park in 2011, the **Memorial Quilombo dos Palmares** (see sidebar p. 35) sits atop a hill called the Serra da Barriga and represents a partial symbolic reconstruction of the community of escaped slaves razed at the end of the 17th century. The population of Palmares, which was founded around the beginning of the 17th century, was at least in the low thousands—not insignificant when compared with the 16,000 to 25,000 who lived in Recife, the nearest major city at the time. Colonial forces destroyed the community's central area in 1694 and captured and killed its leader, Zumbi, in 1695.

About 6 miles (10 km) east of the memorial is the *quilombo* **Muquém,** a community of descendants of escaped slaves. Locals produce ceramic handicrafts that are sold at the **Ateliê Dona Irinéia** *(tel 82/9989 4575),* a crafts showroom that doubles as a point of contact for community visits. For excursions to either the memorial or Muquém, it is probably a good idea to call beforehand and even perhaps hire a local guide. Signage and other tourist information are scanty. For more information, contact the Gato do Mato travel agency

(Loteamento da Garça IV, Quadra G19, Lote 6, Tabuleiro dos Martins, tel 82/3033 1040 or 9992 6111) in Maceió.

In União dos Palmares itself, the **Centro Arqueológico Palmarino** *(Praça Brasiliano Sarmento, Centro, tel 82/3281 1799)* displays artifacts found at the Serra da Barriga. The **Memorial Jorge de Lima,** on the first floor of the museum, preserves the memory of the 20th-century poet born

A fisherman sails a *jangada* in tranquil waters off Maceió.

in União dos Palmares in 1895. The **Casa Cultural Maria Mariá** *(Rua Correia Oliveira 125, Centro, tel 82/3281 2845)* contains artifacts related to the city's history.

About 60 miles (100 km) southwest of União dos Palmares, in the town of **Palmeira dos Índios,** you will find the **Casa Museu Graciliano Ramos** *(Rua José Pinto de Barros 90, Centro, tel 82/8804 5706),* a museum dedicated to one of Brazil's most important novelists of the 20th century (see p. 51), who lived in the house from 1924 to 1930. ∎

União dos Palmares

⚠ 199 C3

Visitor Information

✉ Prefeitura de União dos Palmares, Rua Rui Barbosa 5

☎ 82/3281 3000 or 9657 5789

🕐 Closed Sat.–Sun.

Memorial Quilombo dos Palmares

✉ BR-104, Serra da Barriga, União dos Palmares

☎ 82/3281 1799

Palmeira dos Índios

⚠ 199 C3

Visitor Information

✉ Prefeitura de Palmeira dos Índios, Praça da Independência 34, Centro

☎ 82/3421 3696

🕐 Closed Sat.–Sun.

Pernambuco

Recife doubles as the virtual capital of Northeastern Brazil. Musicians, artists, and writers converge on it, engendering an effervescent roots cultural scene. A colonial town on a hill, Recife's sister city Olinda sports a lively street Carnaval. Top that with the oldest synagogue in the Americas and remnants of the Dutch colonial presence in the 17th century.

A view of Recife from Olinda: The sister cities offer a myriad of cultural activities and roots music.

Recife

🅰 199 C3

Visitor Information

✉ Prefeitura do Recife, Av. Cais do Apolo 925

☎ 81/3355 8000

🕐 Closed Sat.–Sun.

www.recife.pe.gov.br

Recife

The state capital of Pernambuco, Recife is one of Brazil's biggest cities, with a population of 1.6 million. Its historic downtown is a hotbed of regional culture and history, but first take a river tour to get the lay of the land. Many visitors hardly note—maybe because hotels tend to be situated beachside in the Boa Viagem district—that Recife sits at the confluence of the **Rio Beberibe** and the **Rio Capibaribe;** the latter flows to the sea. Other rivers cut through town, too. **Catamaran Tours** (*Rua Coronel Anízio 618, Sala 2903,*

Boa Viagem, tel 81/3424 2845) offers river cruises that will give you a good look at the **Parque de Esculturas** (*Molhes do Porto de Recife),* a grouping of magnificent ceramic sculptures by native son and contemporary artist Francisco Brennand, near the **Marco Zero,** the point around which the city grew. You will also get a good view of the historic buildings of the old downtown area, Recife Antigo, on one of three small islands that hold many of Recife's attractions.

Visitors flock to charming **Recife Antigo** to stroll around its streets, barhop, people-watch, or catch some music amid buildings that date, in some cases, to the 17th century. Standout attractions to see include the **Sinagoga Kahal Zur Israel** (*Rua do Bom Jesus 197, tel 81/3224 2128, www .kahalzurisrael.com*), also known as the Centro Cultural Judaico—the oldest synagogue of the Americas, now a museum; the **Embaixada dos Bonecos Gigantes** (*Rua do Bom Jesus 183, tel 81/3441 5102, $*), a museum of the giant figures that characterize the street Carnaval of neighboring Olinda; and the **Torre Malakoff** (*Praça Artur Oscar, tel 81/3184 3180, closed Sat.–Mon.*), an observatory dating from the 19th century. For crafts, try the **Centro de Artesanato de Pernambuco** (*Av. Alfredo Lisboa, Armazém 11, tel 81/3181 3451*), which occupies a warehouse in the port area. The **Paço do Frevo** cultural center, opened in 2013, occupies an old mansion on the Praça do Arsenal da Marinha. It is dedicated to the memory of the *frevo*, a frenetic style of music and dance popular in the region, especially during Carnaval.

Across a channel, another island holds the São José neighborhood, where you'll find the **Pátio de São Pedro** (*www.patio desaopedro.ceci-br.org*), a square off Avenida Dantas Barreto that is surrounded by historic buildings. Isolated from automobile traffic and downtown hustle and bustle, it is a good place to stop and chill with a beer or your other choice of beverage. The square also tips its cap to some late Pernambucan musicians of different generations: There's the **Memorial Chico Science** (*Casa 21, Pátio de São Pedro, tel 81/3355 3158, closed Sat.–Sun.*), for the godfather of manguebeat (see p. 49), and the **Memorial Luiz Gonzaga** (*Casa*

(continued on p. 222)

Recife Sharks

"DANGER: RISK OF SHARK ATTACK," scream the red-and-white signs in Portuguese and English at Recife's Praia de Boa Viagem. With black profiles of sharks painted in the middle, the placards seem almost comical. But they are dead serious.

A 12.5-mile (20 km) attractive stretch of sand, Boa Viagem unfortunately has earned a reputation as the world's most dangerous beach for swimmers. The crime is arguably no worse than at other urban beaches, but the shark attacks are unparalleled. Between 1992 and 2012, there were 56 reported encounters involving humans and sharks—21 of them fatal. Scientists believe bull and tiger sharks are the likely aggressors in most attacks, but the evidence is only conclusive for a small number of the attacks.

Before 1992, shark attacks were as rare in Recife as anywhere else. Many scientists and ecologists blame the increase in incidents on environmental degradation and habitat loss. Some point accusing fingers at the Porto de Suape, a port located 25 miles (40 km) south of Recife, which began operating in 1984 and was later expanded. Coastal landfill here changed the course of the Rios Ipojuca and Merepe. Denied access to their traditional haunts at the mouths of these rivers, sharks followed the current north along the reefs astride popular beaches like Paiva, Candeias, Piedade, Pina, and, of course, Boa Viagem.

Pernambuco Drive

An excursion into the interior of Pernambuco takes you on a journey that reveals the arts and crafts heritage of the region.

With its colossal erotic sculptures, Várzea's Oficina Brennand is a true must-see attraction.

Begin your trip in **Várzea ❶**, an outlying district of Recife about 9 miles (15 km) west of downtown, where you'll find two art centers of note, both related to the Brennand family. The **Oficina Cerâmica Francisco Brennand** *(Propriedade Santos Cosme e Damião, tel 81/3271 2466, closed Sat.–Sun.)*, Brennand's art studio, occupies an old factory once owned by his father. The grounds have been transformed into a sculpture park for Brennand's giant erotic pagan ceramic figures. Brennand's cousin founded the nearby **Instituto Ricardo Brennand** *(Alameda Antônio Brennand, tel 81/2121 0352, closed Mon.)* to display his art collection. Its highlights are the paintings by 17th-century Dutch artist Frans Post, whose work provides a rare glimpse into the Pernambucan scenery of the era.

From Várzea, take BR-408 northwest. In less than 30 miles (50 km), pass through Carpina and take PE-090 westward to reach the town of **Lagoa do Carro ❷**. Here, the heritage of the old sugarcane plantations that once dominated the region comes alive at the **Museu da Cachaça** *(Chácara Girassol,*

NOT TO BE MISSED:

Instituto Ricardo Brennand • Museu da Cachaça • Feira de Caruaru • Espaço Cultural Tancredo Neves

Lagoa do Carro, PE-090 km 8, tel 81/3621 8208, $), a museum dedicated to the sugarcane alcohol popular throughout Brazil (see sidebar p. 131). The city is also known for its handmade goods, such as the sheep's wool rugs that can be found at the **Associação das Tapeceiras** *(PE-090 km 8, tel 81/3621 8102)*, a weavers association.

Next, return to Carpina and head north on BR-408 to nearby **Tracunhaém ❸**, which is also known as a center of handcrafted goods, namely ceramics. Several local workshops are open to visitors; many of their goods are sold at the **Centro de Produção Artesanal** *(Praça Costa Azevedo, tel 81/3646 1208)*.

Another 4 miles (6 km) north on BR-408, the town of **Nazaré da Mata ❹** is known for its colorful roots, *maracatu* music, and dance groups. The best opportunity to see them strut their stuff is in the town's main square on Monday and Tuesday of Carnaval. Unfortunately, there are no permanent attractions in town dedicated to these groups.

Double back to Carpina, then continue south on PE-050 to BR-232, also known as Rodovia Luiz Gonzaga, named for one of Brazil's most popular musicians of the 20th century, a native of Pernambuco. Follow BR-232 west to **Gravatá ❺**, a hill town whose cooler clime attracts Brazilians fleeing the coastal heat. If it is mealtime, stop in at the **Buchadinha do Gordo** (see Travelwise p. 301) for some delicious Northeastern fare.

Continue west on BR-232 for about 15 miles (25 km) to **Bezerros** ❻, home of the **atelier of J. Borges** (Av. Major Aprigio da Fonseca 420, tel 81/3728 0364 or 8839 0373), a woodcut print artist whose work has been exhibited in the United States and Europe. You can view his vintage mechanical printing machine and perhaps catch the artist carving a new mold. You can purchase chapbooks called *cordel* literature (booklets or pamphlets of ballads, poems, or songs, which almost always have woodcut print covers), prints, and even woodblock molds. Other examples of this kind of art can be seen at Bezerros's **Centro de Artesanato de Pernambuco** (BR-232 km 104).

Caruaru

From Bezerros, drive another 20 miles (35 km) west on BR-232 to **Caruaru** ❼, a veritable hub of popular Northeastern culture. Made famous nationwide by Luiz Gonzaga's song of the same name, the **Feira de Caruaru** (Av. Lourival José da Silva 592, Petrópolis, tel 81/3721 8364) is the largest open-air market in the Northeast. As the lyrics say, "there's everything in the world on sale": local produce, medicinal herbs, leather goods, lacework, cordel chapbooks, and more. Sample the street food and enjoy listening to dueling duos of *repentistas* (guitar-wielding improvisational poets).

In the Alto do Moura district, **Rua Mestre Vitalino** serves as a virtual outdoor mini-mall of shops featuring the miniature clay figurines that depict scenes from daily life, pioneered by Vitalino himself, who died in 1963. Set amid the shops, his house has been turned into a museum, the **Casa-Museu Mestre Vitalino** (Rua Mestre Vitalino 644, tel 81/3721 1257). At the end of the street, the **Memorial Mestre Galdino** (Rua São Sebastião 181, tel 81/3701 1533, closed Mon.) displays the work of another illustrious clay artist.

Don't leave Caruaru without a visit to the **Espaço Cultural Tancredo Neves** (Praça Coronel José de Vasconcelos 100, Nossa Senhora das Dores, tel 81/3721 1257), which encompasses the **Museu de Barro de Caruaru Espaço Zé Caboclo,** a museum of clay art with more than 2,000 pieces; the **Museu Luiz Gonzaga,** a museum dedicated to the musician; and the **Espaço Elba Ramalho,** a space dedicated to the popular singer.

If at all possible, try to be in Caruaru on the winter solstice (June 24), when the town celebrates in grand style the **Festa de São João,** one of the three annual June festivals held to honor three different saints.

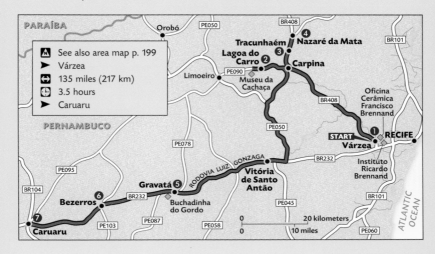

Olinda

199 C3

Visitor Information

Prefeitura de Olinda, Rua São Bento 123, Varadouro

81/3429 0001

Closed Sat.–Sun.

35, Pátio de São Pedro, tel 81/3232 2965 or 3232 2955), for the Rei do Baião (King of the Baião). A few blocks east of the Pátio de São José, the **Mercado de São José** (Praça Dom Vital, tel 81/3424 4681), in an 1875 building, offers a selection of crafts, cordéis (popular chapbooks; see p. 221), and street food.

Farther afield, on the mainland, is the **Museu do Homem do Nordeste** (Av. 17 de Agosto 2187, Casa Forte, tel 81/3073 6340, closed Mon., $), an anthropological museum devoted to the people of the Northeast, founded by sociologist Gilberto Freyre. You can visit the sociologist's home at the **Fundação Gilberto Freyre** (Rua Dois Irmãos 320, Apipucos, tel 81/3441 2883, closed Sat.–Sun.).

Olinda

A calm, historic, colonial-era town on a hillside just 4.5 miles (7 km) north of Recife, Olinda is full of artists, artisans, haute regional cuisine, bars, and a few charming guesthouses—and it has an exceptional Carnaval (see sidebar below). Olinda was founded in 1535, but little remains from those early years, save for a couple of churches that have been fully or partially rebuilt. The Dutch pretty much razed the place in the 17th century, and then made Recife

INSIDER TIP:

Petrolina, 395 miles (636 km) west of Recife, may not be on most lists of must-see sights, but if you're in the area, don't miss its *bododromo*, an outdoor mall of grilled-goat restaurants. The grilled goat is fantastic! Look for the goat statue at the entrance.

—CHRISTIAN BRANNSTROM
National Geographic grantee

their center of operations. When the Portuguese took over again after a couple of decades, they rebuilt the town and revived it as an administrative center.

The best way to tour the Centro Histórico is on foot, but be prepared to trudge uphill now and again. Once at the top, you will find Olinda's emblematic site, the **Igreja da Sé** (Alto da Sé, tel 81/3271 4270), dating from 1537. The view from its square takes in the coastline, including neighboring Recife. Called **Alto**

Olinda's Carnaval

Olinda more than triples in population during Carnaval, as celebrants fill its streets to join in Brazil's most democratic major pre-Lenten festival, which takes place over the four days prior to Ash Wednesday. The town's characteristic oversize *bonecos* (dolls), often representing famous or infamous national or international figures, are paraded through the streets and the crowd dances to the frenetic sounds of *frevo*. In 2012, Bob Marley, Charlie Chaplin, and Gene Simmons of the rock band Kiss counted among the international stars whose likenesses rode head and shoulders above the crowd.

From Olinda's hilltop Igreja da Sé, you can get a great view of the surrounding coastal area.

da Sé, the square is frequented in the late afternoon and evening by street food vendors specialized in tapioca snacks. Close by is another church that dates to the 16th century, the **Igreja e Convento Nossa Senhora das Neves** (*Rua de São Francisco 280, Carmo, tel 81/3429 0517 or 3493 0313*).

Be sure to walk along the **Rua do Amparo,** lined with bars, restaurants, and shops, including the **Oficina do Sabor** (see Travelwise p. 302), which serves up innovative contemporary Northeastern regional cuisine courtesy of chef César Santos. Nearby, the **Museu de Arte Contemporânea de Pernambuco** (*Rua Treze de Maio, tel 81/3184 3153, closed Tues., $*) occupies an 18th-century building first designed as a prison for people accused of crimes against the Roman Catholic Church. The permanent contemporary art collection favors Brazilian modernists like Portinari and Di Cavalcanti, but it also features work by Pernambucan ceramic sculptor Francisco Brennand. Also worth a visit is the **Museu do Mamulengo** (*Rua de São Bento 344, tel 81/3493 2753, closed Mon.*), a museum that features figures from the traditional puppet shows of the Northeast.

Pernambuco Coast

Besides the beaches, colonial history and a manatee conservation project count among the coastal highlights north and south of Recife.

When the Dutch seized this stretch of territory from the Portuguese in the 17th century, they built a fort to defend it on the **Ilha de Itamaracá,** a large island snuggled up against the coast about 28 miles (45 km)

Ilha de Itamaracá

199 C3

Fernando de Noronha

Fernando de Noronha is the largest isle, and the only inhabited one, in a 21-island archipelago in the middle of the Atlantic Ocean off the coast of Northeastern Brazil (it's an hour by plane from Recife). A nature lover's paradise, it boasts crystal-clear waters perfect for diving and snorkeling and endless stretches of white-sand beaches perfect for relaxing.

The visitor count is strictly controlled on Fernando de Noronha, an idyllic Atlantic island.

With much of the island demarcated as part of the nearly archipelago-wide **Parque Nacional Marinho Fernando de Noronha** (Alameda do Boldró, tel 81/3619 1171, $$$), a national marine park, Fernando de Noronha is a wonderful place to get away from it all.

The best scuba diving in Brazil is found here. Visibility can reach 165 feet (50 m), while the water temperature averages 79°F (26°C). Divers will find coral reefs, sea turtles, sharks, spinner dolphins, barracudas, and shipwrecks at places such as **Pedras Secas, Cabeço da Sapata, Baía do Sueste,** and **Porto Santo Antônio.**

If you don't have a PADI license, you can still see much of the underwater world by snorkeling or tow diving. The latter involves holding a small board called a plana sub while a boat slowly tows it. This allows you to "skim" under the surface and view the aquatic flora and fauna for as long as you can hold your breath.

Above the water, wind-surfing is popular, while longboarders can catch good waves between November and March. Beachgoers, meanwhile, rank **Praia do Leão, Praia da Baía dos Porcos,** and **Praia da Baía do Sancho** among the best.

Staying on land, you can spot spinner dolphins, found only here and in the South Pacific, from the vista point **Mirante dos Golfinhos.** The best times are at the end of the day, when they head out to sea to fish, and at daybreak, when they return. To learn more, ask the **Projeto Golfinho Rotador** (Spinner Dolphin Project; tel 81/3619 1295). The **Projeto Tamar** (Alameda do Boldró, tel 81/3619 1171) operates a sea turtle conservation station. Visitors may tour the museum, accompany tag-and-recapture activities, and, in season, watch the laying and hatching of eggs on the beach.

You can explore the island via several trails. Among other things, the trails link ten forts dating from the 18th century.

Know Before You Go

Visitors must pay a daily conservation fee to the government (www.noronha.pe.gov.br), plus the park charges a flat fee for a ten-day permit (for the latter, foreigners pay twice the amount charged to Brazilians). Growth controls help prevent environmental degradation, but also limit the number of beds available. As a result, many people stay in pousadas domiciliares, sections of homes that locals have converted into lodgings. Nearly everything on the island is expensive.

For some activities, you must hire a credentialed guide. To find one, ask the owner of your guesthouse or try the local **Atlantis Travel** (Praça do Cruzeiro, Vila dos Remédios, tel 81/3619 1371 or 3619 1488).

INSIDER TIP:

For a great family outing, go see the captive manatees at Eco-Parque Peixe-Boi. The experience is both educational and entertaining.

—ROSE DAVIDSON
National Geographic contributor

north of Recife. When the Portuguese reclaimed their fort, they refurbished it and formally renamed it. However, more than three centuries later, everybody still calls it **Forte Orange** *(end of Estr. do Forte km 5, Praia do Forte)* rather than Fortaleza de Santa Cruz. The fort, which can be toured, is one of the island's two main attractions. The other is the nearby **Eco-Parque Peixe-Boi & C.I.A.,** the visitor center of a manatee conservation project that also works with other aquatic mammals. Large tanks on the premises hold several manatees, and you can watch them through large glass windows.

South of Recife stretches a string of beaches popular with locals and other Brazilians, but there are other attractions, too. In **Cabo de Santo Agostinho,** about 25 miles (40 km) south of Recife, the 16th-century **Igreja de Nossa Senhora de Nazaré** *(Vila de Nazaré)* sits at the town's highest point. From here, you can see the ruins below of the granite Forte Castelo do Mar, an 18th-century fort, and in the distance, Porto de Suape, Recife's

port. The **Engenho Massangana** *(PE-60 km 10, Vila Massangana, tel 81/3527 4025, closed Mon.)* consists of the plantation house and chapel of an old sugar mill. The Brazilian writer, statesman, and abolitionist Joaquim Nabuco (1849–1910) lived here as a child.

Ten miles (16 km) beyond Cabo de Santo Agostinho, the once tranquil, nearly deserted beach resort of **Porto de Galinhas** has transformed into one of Brazil's leading mass tourism destinations. You can take a *jangada,* a traditional small wooden sailboat, to the natural pools that form offshore at low tide, though the marine life isn't what it used to be. ■

Eco-Parque Peixe-Boi & C.I.A.

- ✉ End of Estr. do Forte km 5, Praia do Forte, Ilha da Itamaracá
- ☎ 81/3544 1056
- 🕐 Closed Mon.
- 💲 $

Porto de Galinhas

- 🄰 199 C3

Animals figure large in locally produced crafts in Olinda.

Paraíba & Rio Grande do Norte

Brazilians flock to the states of Paraíba and Rio Grande do Norte for their beaches, but scrape the surface and you will find plenty of history and culture.

Most people go to João Pessoa for the beaches, but the historic downtown is worth a visit as well.

João Pessoa

🗺 199 C3

Visitor Information

✉ Delegacia de Atendimento ao Turista, Av. Alameda Tamandaré 100, Tambaú

☎ 83/3214 8022

João Pessoa

João Pessoa, the capital of Paraíba state, offers a mix of urban beaches with an attractive historic downtown. Unlike many other beach towns, the city was founded slightly upstream—on the Rio Sanhauá, a tributary of the Rio Paraíba—so the town grew toward the shore instead of away from it. Beachfront buildings are subject to height restrictions, and the city is looking to be more eco-conscious, too: In 2012, city officials pledged to preserve and regenerate sections of the Atlantic Forest that once held forth here.

João Pessoa might not be as "green" as Curitiba down south, but little things add up. Take the "organic cotton" they use in handicrafts and T-shirts. This special breed of "colored cotton" developed in Brazil requires less water to process. You can find articles at the **Mercado de Arte-sanato Paraibano** (*Av. Senador Ruy Carneiro 241, Tambaú, tel 83/3247 3135*), a few blocks inland from the **Praia de Tambaú,** a popular beach. Adjacent to Tambaú, the **Praia do Bessa** is also rated highly by locals.

The **Praia do Jacaré** is a fluvial beach on the Rio Paraíba, just across a slim peninsula from the Praia do Bessa. Head there at day's end to enjoy the sunset while listening to a live rendition of Ravel's "Bolero," played by a saxophonist in a canoe.

Wander around João Pessoa's historic downtown to enjoy its charms, stopping, in particular, at the **Centro Cultural São Francisco** (*Praça São Francisco, Centro, tel 83/3218 4505*), a colonial-era monastery and church, for its baroque architecture and art. A few blocks away, the **Casa do Artista Popular** (*Praça Independência 56, Centro, tel 83/3221 2267, closed Mon.*) features a collection of the ingenious Northeastern popular art.

On the outskirts of town, at the tip of a peninsula 15 miles (25 km) north of downtown, sits a colonial fort, **Fortaleza de Santa Catarina,** you can explore. About 60 miles (100 km) north, you'll find at the Barra de Mamanguape an outpost of the **Projeto Peixe-Boi-Marinho** (*PB-025 off BR-101, Rio Tinto, tel 83/3228 3865*), a manatee preservation center. You can take a boat ride (*$$*) to see animals in the wild. Some 15 miles (25 km) south of João Pessoa, in **Conde,** is the **Praia de Tambaba,** which claims distinction as Brazil's first official nudist beach, authorized by a 2002 law.

Paraíba Interior

The interior of Paraíba is full of sites of historic and prehistoric interest—starting with dinosaurs, moving to prehistoric humans, and then to vestiges of 19th-century sugar production.

Campina Grande & Around: Campina Grande sits 85 miles (135 km) inland from João Pessoa. In June, its **Festa de São João** (St. John, one of the three saints honored with a feast day in June) draws close to one million people (see sidebar below). At other times, the **Museu Assis Chateaubriand** (*Rua João Lélis 581, Catolé, tel 83/3337 3637, closed Sat.–Sun.*) is a main attraction. This museum of modern art was

---

Campina Grande's Festa de São João

Events of the Festa de São João in Campina Grande are concentrated at the **Parque do Povo** (*Rua Major Belmiro*), a 10-acre (4 ha) complex, something of a folkloric movie set with stages, bars, restaurants, and side attractions. Activities include dance competitions, giant bonfires, firework displays, and a marathon of live music, predominantly *forró* (see p. 49). The **Expresso Forrozeiro** train (*tel 83/3066 3300 or 9993 5151, June Sat.–Sun., $$*) makes several special 90-minute party runs, the cars awash in music and dance. It leaves from the Estação Velha de Campina Grande, the old train station that now houses the **Museu de Algodão** (see below).

---

created by Assis Chateaubriand, a 20th-century media mogul born in Paraíba and the driving force in the creation of MASP, perhaps Brazil's most important art museum, in São Paulo. The permanent collection includes works by leading names of Brazilian modernism. The **Museu de Algodão** (*Rua Benjamin Constant, tel 83/3341 0603,*

Fortaleza de Santa Catarina

✉ Rua Francisco Serafim, next to Praia Ponta de Matos, Cabedelo

☎ 83/3228 3959

Campina Grande

🅰 199 C3

Visitor Information

✉ Prefeitura de Campina Grande, Rua Volta Redonda, 3 Irmãs

☎ 83/3310 6127

🕐 Closed Sat.–Sun.

EXPERIENCE: Kite Surfing in Galinhos

If the waves of Santa Catarina pull at serious surfers like riptides, the winds off the Brazilian Northeast work similarly on kite surfers. One of the best spots to kite surf is off-the-beaten-track **Galinhos.** More than 100 miles (160 km) northwest of Natal, its virtually untouched beaches, surrounded by dunes and pyramids of natural salt deposits, are only accessible via boat or a four-wheel-drive vehicle. The only sign of civilization is a fishing village. Many people get around using donkey-drawn buggies. You can also hire a *burro-táxi* (donkey taxi) to tour the area.

Between July and March, you'll find the water here clear and warm, the winds strong, and the waves considerable, perfect for kite surfing. There are good kite-surfing spots for beginners and skilled veterans. Noteworthy is the **Pico das**

Coroas, a sandbank in the open sea, accessible only by boat.

As the name implies, kite surfing involves a plank similar to a small surfboard and a large kite that serves as an airborne sail to provide propulsion. A real kite-surfing ace can take to the air or twist and turn like a gymnast. You will almost certainly need lessons to get started, but the learning curve is similar to that of skiing or snowboarding.

The São Paulo–based **Exbr Kitesurf Travel** *(Rua da Consolação 2710, loja 24, Jardins, São Paulo, tel 11/3506 1822, www .exbr.com.br, closed Sat.–Sun.)* organizes kite-surfing excursions to about a dozen spots in Brazil, including Galinhos (and also offers lessons). Most destinations are concentrated elsewhere in Rio Grande do Norte and in neighboring Ceará state.

Museu da Rapadura

✉ Praça Pedro Américo 76, Solar José Rufino, Areia

☎ 83/8701 0021

Sousa

▲ 199 C3

Visitor Information

✉ Centro de Informação ao Turista, Rua Deputado José de Paiva Gadelha, Gato Preto

☎ 83/3522 2688

🕐 Closed Sat.–Sun.

closed Sun.), a small museum about cotton production in the region, is also worth a visit. If you're hungry, Campina Grande is known for its restaurants that serve up dishes of *carne de sol,* sun-dried beef.

A few sights beyond Campina Grande beckon. In **Ingá,** about 28 miles (45 km) east, the **Sítio Arqueológico Itaquatiara,** also known as the Pedra do Ingá, is a rock 79 feet long and 13 feet high (24 m by 4 m) full of prehistoric carvings dating back thousands of years. It is not easy to find; it's best to go with a local company, such as **Cariri Ecotours** *(tel 84/9660 1818, www.caririecotours .com.br),* based in Natal. In **Areia,** more than 25 miles (40 km) northeast of Campina Grande, the exhibits at the **Museu da**

Rapadura, a museum installed in an old sugar mill, explain how the grainy sugar was made from pure cane juice in the 19th century. And at the **Vale dos Dinossauros** *(Rod. Estadual José de Paiva Gadelha km 5, Sousa, tel 83/3522 1065),* you can marvel at dinosaur footprints preserved for millions of years, including a several-feet-long set of tracks by a plodding iguanodon; the site is in **Sousa,** about 186 miles (300 km) east of Campina Grande.

Cariri Region: When Brazilian location scouts search for places to shoot in the folklore-rich but parched backlands called the *sertão,* the awe-inspiring Cariri region invariably makes the short list. The Cariri's unique geology has left a boulder-strewn landscape highlighted by the expansive **Lajedo de Pai Mateus,** marked by the **Pedra do Capacete** (Helmet Rock, primed to protect the cranium of a giant biker) and the **Pedra Saca de Lã** (Sack of Wool, a formation of granite blocks reminiscent of a warehouse stack of such bags). One can almost imagine the legendary bandits of the Brazilian Northeast roaming these

INSIDER TIP:

Small, laid-back São Miguel do Gostoso (93 miles/150 km N of Natal) has large sand beaches and is extremely favorable to kite and windsurfing.

—RODRIGO NICOLETTE
Professor, University of São Paulo

ranges—as they have many times on the Brazilian big screen. To call attention to their cinematic fame, local boosters have playfully erected their own "Hollywood of the Northeast" sign on a hillside: "Roliude Nordestina" it says, the first term a made-up word that phonetically reflects the way Brazilians pronounce "Hollywood."

Cariri is also home to some of Brazil's most important archaeological artifacts (the most impressive are in Ingá; see opposite). The Lajedo do Pai Mateus has a smattering of primitive paintings, like the one of people roasting a rhea. Descendants of that prehistoric barbecue can be

seen roaming among groves of cacti and bromeliads. Not yet a regular stop on the tourist trail, Cariri is only now beginning to be discovered by Brazilian trekkers and mountain bikers. The latter claim that the region rivals the legendary Slickrock Trail at Moab, Utah, as a place to peddle.

The closest town to the Lajedo de Pai Mateus is **Cabaceiras,** about 45 miles (70 km) southwest of Campina Grande. The town is known for making traditional Brazilian leather cowboy hats—a style made famous in the movies and by musicians Luiz Gonzaga and Dominguinhos.

The easiest way to visit the Cariri region is on an excursion with a local company, such as Cariri Ecotours, mentioned above.

Natal & the North Coast

Most people visit Natal, Rio Grande do Norte's capital, for the area's attractive beaches. As such, most hotels, restaurants, and bars are concentrated around the **Praia de Ponta Negra,** a popular beach. There is, however, a handful of historic and cultural attractions downtown, 8 miles (13 km) away. One highlight is the **Igreja de Santo Antônio, Convento e Museu de Arte Sacra,** an 18th-century church and museum of religious art. There's also the **Instituto Câmara Cascudo,** set in the former home of the 20th-century scholar of Brazilian folk traditions that gives the place its name, plus the nearby **Memorial Câmara Cascudo.** Both feature interesting artifacts from Cascudo's personal collection. Not too far from

Lajedo de Pai Mateus
🗺 199 C3

Cabaceiras
🗺 199 C3
Visitor Information
✉ Prefeitura de Cabaceiras, Rua Coronel Maracajá, 7, Centro
☎ 83/3356 1042 or 3356 1179
🕐 Closed Sat.–Sun.

Natal
🗺 199 C3
Visitor Information
✉ Secretária de Turismo, Rua Hemetério Fernandes 1102, Tirol
☎ 84/3232 2482
🕐 Closed Sat.–Sun.
http://turismo .natal.rn.gov.br

Igreja de Santo Antônio, Convento e Museu de Arte Sacra
✉ Rua Santo Antônio 698, Cidade Alta, Natal
☎ 84/3211 4236

Instituto Câmara Cascudo
✉ Av. Câmara Cascudo 377, Cidade Alta, Natal
☎ 84/3222 3293
🕐 Closed Sun.– Mon.
💲 $

Memorial Câmara Cascudo

✉ Praça André de Albuquerque 30, Cidade Alta, Natal
☎ 84/3342 4912
🕐 Closed Mon.

Fortaleza dos Reis Magos

✉ Av. Praia do Forte, Santos Reis, Natal
☎ 84/3202 9006
💲 $

Parque das Dunas

✉ Av. Alexandrino de Alencar, Tirol, Natal
☎ 84/3201 3985
🕐 Closed Mon.
💲 $

downtown, the **Fortaleza dos Reis Magos** has been faithfully guarding the mouth of the Rio Potengi, the river that skates downtown, since 1598.

The **Parque das Dunas** rivals Rio de Janeiro's Floresta da Tijuca as Brazil's largest urban park. It has three trails; the longest, 2.5-mile (4 km) **Ubaia Doce,** runs through forest cover and rewards you with an ocean view.

Dune Action: "The" thing to do in Natal is an adrenaline-laden buggy trip into the sea of constantly shifting coastal sand dunes. You will pass by the **Lagoa de Jacumã,** a lake that you can slide into from the high-rise dunes, by sitting on a board (known as *esquibunda,* or butt-skiing), via a zip line (*aerobunda,* or air-butt), or on a speed-inducing canvas square. You can either hire a buggy and driver in Natal or at **Genipabu's** beach, about 18 miles (30 km)

Brazilian beaches vary. Rio Grande do Norte's Praia da Pipa will suit those hankering for nightlife; for a quiet beach not frequented by tourists, try scenic Olivença, in Bahia.

—PATRICIA H. KELLEY & CHRISTY VISAGGI
National Geographic researchers

north of downtown. For information, contact the **Associação de Proprietários e Condutores de Buggy** *(Av. Beira Mar 405, Genipabu, tel 84/3225 2077 or 9937 4919).*

In Genipabu, you can also explore the dunes via camel. Camels were first brought to the region around 1860 by a Brazilian scientific expedition to help the

WWII U.S. Military Presence in Natal

During World War II, the United States established a military base in Natal, choosing the then small town for its strategic location. It was the closest point in the Americas to Africa, thus it could both serve as a supply base for the theater in North Africa and defend South America against an eventual Axis invasion. Thousands of U.S. troops were stationed or passed through town during the war.

The main U.S. military base was located astride a civilian facility, which today serves passengers under the name of Augusto Severo International Airport. According to some sources, Parnamirim

Field, as the airstrip was called then, after the Natal suburb where it is located, was one of the busiest airstrips in the world during the war. A military presence still exists at the airport today: The Brazilian Air Force maintains a base here.

The U.S. Navy also had a hydroplane dock near the mouth of the Rio Potengi, in the Santos Reis district. Known locally as Rampa, the old Natal Seaplane Base is the site of the planned **Centro Cultural da Rampa,** a memorial museum set to open in a few years. For more information on the Rampa, visit the website of the **Fundação Rampa** *(www.fundacaorampa.com.br).*

researchers get around. The current group was brought over in recent years. For a ride, you need to make reservations at least two weeks in advance; for more information, contact **Dromedunas** (*Rua Praia de Genipabu, Nova Parnamirim, tel 84/3225 2053*).

Praia da Pipa & the South Coast

Praia da Pipa could be called the beach that ate the township. Ask Brazilians about tiny **Tibau do Sul,** some 53 miles (85 km) south of Natal, and you will be met with blank stares. Ask them about Pipa, and their eyes will light up. Until the 1970s, Praia da Pipa remained a sleepy fishing village. A few hippies started showing up, establishing an aesthetic that continues to this day—though perhaps now more hip than hippie in the original spirit. Once sought out for its tranquillity, Pipa now bustles during vacation periods and holidays. Unless you are coming for the party, it is best to choose an off-peak period to visit.

The main attractions are the beaches. **Praia do Amor** is the happening place. Just a bit farther south is the much more peaceful **Praia das Minas.** Aside from going to the beach, popular activities include excursions by dune buggy, all-terrain vehicle, boat, and a *pau de arara* (a jeep-drawn trailer that borrows its name from the old trucks used by poor Northeasterners to migrate south). There are mountain bike circuits. You can hike in the **Santuário Ecológico de Pipa,** a nature reserve with more than

a dozen mostly easy trails. For more information on outdoor activities, contact **Pipa Aventura** (*Av. Baía dos Golfinhos 654, tel 84/3246 2008*).

Projeto Tamar (*Av. Joaquim Patrício 4000, km 11, Distrito Litoral, Pium, Parnamirim, tel 84/4103 1967*), a sea turtle conservation project, has an outpost here. If you time it right, you can watch the babies as they hatch and scamper

Praia da Pipa
🄰 199 C3

Santuário Ecológico de Pipa
✉ Estr. para Tibau do Sul, Praia da Pipa
☎ 84/3211 6070
🟦 $

www.pipa.com.br/santuarioecologico/english

At play on Rio Grande do Norte's sands

to the sea. The hatching season varies, but it's usually during the first few months of the year.

En route to Pipa from Natal, you can see what locals claim to be the world's largest cashew tree at Pirangi do Norte beach in **Parnamirim,** about 15 miles (24.5 km) south of Natal. In **Nísia Floresta,** another 13 miles (21 km) south, stop to watch craftswomen at their knitting at the **Associação das Labirinteiras de Campo de Santana** (*RN-063, Nísia Floresta, tel 84/3277 8002, call ahead to schedule a visit*). ∎

Ceará, Piauí, & Maranhão

Piauí and Maranhão states combine history and natural beauty with a chance to get off the beaten tourist track. Ceará is best known for its coastline of spectacular beaches.

Fortaleza

Fortaleza has developed into a cross between a mass-tourism destination and a way station for travelers en route to less hectic beach resorts up the coast. Many Brazilians are attracted to

A crafts market, the Feira Noturna, sets up beachside each evening at Fortaleza's Praia do Meireles.

the city's urban beaches that lie within striking distance of decent hotels, reasonably priced bars and restaurants, and lively nightlife. When in doubt, head over to the **Centro Dragão do Mar de Arte e Cultura.** This world-class cultural center includes the **Museu de Arte Contemporânea,** a contemporary art museum; the **Planetário Rubens de Azevedo,** a planetarium; the **Memorial da Cultura Cearense,** an ethnographic museum; the **Cine Dragão do Mar,** a cinematheque; two theaters, the **Teatro Dragão do Mar** and the **Anfiteatro Sérgio Motta;** the **Biblioteca Pública Governador Menezes Pimentel,** a public library; and more. Each of these venues schedules a rich program of events, exhibitions, and perfor-mances. Concerts by leading Bra-zilian musicians are commonplace. The surrounding neighborhood is full of bars and restaurants.

The downtown **Centro de Turismo** is a crafts mini-mall that occupies a converted prison, dating from 1866; the cells have been transformed into little shops. The nearby **Mercado Central** *(Av. Alberto Nepomuceno 199, Centro, tel 85/3454 8586)* also features crafts, but you'll find, too, *cachaça,* cashew nuts, and other items of interest to locals. Also in the downtown Centro district, the **Museu do Ceará** *(Rua São Paulo,*

51, tel 85/3101 2610, closed Mon., $) displays items related to the state's history, with nods to everyone from "saints" like the controversial Padre Cícero (see p. 20) to sinners like the 20th-century backlands bandit Lampião. While in the neighborhood, check out the ornate facade of the belle epoque **Theatro José de Alencar** (Rua Liberato Barroso 525, tel 85/3101 2583, closed Mon., $). It offers a guided tour and a regular program of performances.

During the day, you will find Brazilian tourists on the beach. In the evening many of them will head to the beachside **Feira Noturna** (Av. Beira-Mar at Praia do Meireles) crafts fair starting at 5 p.m.

Ceará Coast

Ceará's coast can be divided into two sections, with the city of Fortaleza the dividing point: The **Costa Sol Poente** (Sunset Coast) to the northwest and the **Costa Sol Nascente** (Sunrise Coast) to the southeast. The main destination along the former coast is **Jericoacoara** (about 185 miles/300 km northwest of Fortaleza; see sidebar above); for the latter, it is Canoa Quebrada (about 100 miles/170 km southeast of Fortaleza).

Activities available for visitors vary little from beach to beach along these coasts. Dune buggy rides are the main attractions at major destinations, including (in order from west to east) Jericoacoara, **Icaraí de Amontada, Lagoinha, Cumbuco,** and **Canoa Quebrada.** The good kite-surfing

Jericoacoara

Many national and international Top Ten lists rank Jericoacoara as one of Brazil's most beautiful beaches. It is relatively well preserved and protected because it is inaccessible to passenger vehicles. To get to there, you take an off-road vehicle from **Jijoca,** the municipality that encompasses the beach. For more information, contact **Jeri Off Road** (tel 88/3669 2268 or 9971 3330, www.jeri .tur.br, closed Sun.). You can also visit Jericoacoara on a multi-day excursion with **EcoAdventure Tour** (Av. Presidente Getúlio Vargas 26, Parnaíba, tel 86/3323 9595, www.ecoadventure.tur.br).

and windsurfing spots are Jericoacoara, Icaraí de Amontada, **Flecheiras, Guajirú, Paracuru, Taíba,** Cumbuco, and Canoa Quebrada. Horseback excursions are also popular in Jericoacoara. For kite-surfing information, contact **Exbr Kitesurf Travel** (Rua da Consolação 2710, loja 24, Jardins, São Paulo, tel 11/3259 1422, www.exbr.com.br).

Costa Sol Nascente: In addition to beaches, the coastal CE-040 highway offers a few interesting attractions. Less than 13 miles (20 km) southeast of downtown Fortaleza, in an outlying district of the capital called **Messejana,** the **Centro das Tapioqueiras**

Fortaleza

A 199 C4

Visitor Information

✉ Prefeitura de Fortaleza, Rua São José 01, Centro

☎ 85/3105 1464

🕐 Closed Sat.–Sun.

Centro Dragão do Mar de Arte e Cultura

✉ Rua Dragão do Mar 81, Praia de Iracema, Fortaleza

☎ 85/3488 8600

🕐 Closed Mon.

Centro de Turismo

✉ Rua Senador Pompeu 350, Centro, Fortaleza

☎ 85/8658 3640

NOTE: Fortaleza has earned a reputation as a sex tourism destination. Prostitution is not illegal in Brazil, whereas pimping and running a brothel are. The age of consent is nuanced, but adults should assume that sexual relations with anyone under 18 are off-limits.

Costa Sol Nascente

A 199 C4

Parnaíba

⚠ 199 B4

Visitor Information

✉ Prefeitura de Parnaíba, Rua Itauna 1434, Boa Esperança

☎ 86/3315 1079

(Av. Washington Soares 10215, tel 85/3274 7565, $) consists of two dozen booths that serve tapioca snacks in sundry flavors. About 20 miles (35 km) southeast of Fortaleza, **Aquiraz** is home to the **Centro das Rendeiras da Prainha** *(Rua Desembargador Péricles Ribeiro, tel 85/3361 6447),* a lacemakers cooperative with about 80 members. You can visit the workshop and purchase their

Though hardly off the beaten track these days, Jericoacoara retains some of its charm because it is so hard to reach.

wares, which include everything from tablecloths to decorative embroidered items. It is a good idea to confirm your visit beforehand.

A few miles farther south, you can visit one of the 20-plus sugar mills in **Pindoretama** to see how *rapadura,* the hard, darkish unrefined sugar that Brazilians eat as candy, is made. The **Complexo Tradição Engenho e Tapiocaria** *(CE-040 km 45, Pindoretama)* and the **Engenho e Museu da**

Rapadura Cana Dá *(CE-040 km 39, tel 85/9713 7798, $),* the latter closer to Aquiraz and featuring a museum, are two good choices.

Northern Piauí

The northern region of Piauí offers beautiful scenery in the form of the delta of the Rio Parnaíba and a small national park known for its archaeological and geological treasures.

The 1,050-square-mile (2,700 sq km) **Delta do Parnaíba,** where the Rio Parnaíba ends its 906-mile (1,458 km) at the ocean, is unique in the Americas and rivaled worldwide only by the Nile and Mekong Deltas. It consists of dozens of river islands replete with sand dunes, mangrove swamps, and abundant bird- and wildlife populations. Even though more than half of the delta is located across the border in neighboring Maranhão, day trips run out of Piauí's second largest city, **Parnaíba.**

On a boat trip down the channels, you may spot caimans and will definitely see a multitude of birds. A separate bird-watching tour heads toward the nesting areas of the spectacular scarlet ibis, a bird that is easier to see near the end of the calendar year—check beforehand to be sure. Jeep tours run off in two different directions. Contact **EcoAdventure Tour** *(Av. Presidente Getúlio Vargas 26, tel 86/3323 9595, www.ecoadventure.tur.br)* in Parnaíba for details. Whichever delta excursion you choose, you will likely see lots of crabs. They are the mainstay of menus at Parnaíba's best eateries.

INSIDER TIP:

For complete isolation in an estuarine wilderness, with crystalline ponds nestled in the hollows of gigantic sand dunes, visit the island of Cajú in the Delta do Parnaíba.

—ROBERT WALKER
Professor of Geography & Scholar of Amazonian Environmental Change, Michigan State University

Parnaíba's EcoAdventure Tour and **Caetés Expedições** *(Av. Brasília 40, Centro, tel 98/3349 0528 or 9158 3349)*, operating out of Barreirinhas, Maranhão, both

offer a multiday, triple-treat trip that takes in the delta, Jericoacoara (in Ceará; see pp. 233–234), and Lençóis Maranhenses (in Maranhão; see pp. 239–240).

Equidistant between Parnaíba (about 110 miles/180 km to the north) and Piauí's capital, Teresina (to the south), is **Piripiri**, the gateway city to the inland **Parque Nacional das Sete Cidades.** The "seven cities" of the national park's Portuguese name refer to seven distinct concentrations of curious rock formations. Trails link the cities, which feature a wealth of prehistoric wall paintings. Best-selling Swiss author Erich von Däniken claims that the paintings, which resemble strands of DNA, provide evidence for

(continued on p. 238)

Piripiri
🅐 199 B4
Visitor Information
✉ Prefeitura de Piripiri, Rua Antônio Alves 747, Centro
☎ 86/3276 1706

Parque Nacional das Sete Cidades
🅐 199 B4
✉ BR-222 km 64, Piripiri
☎ 86/3343 1342

Prainha do Canto Verde

Unlike many fishing villages along the coast of the Brazilian Northeast, Prainha do Canto Verde *(map 199 C4, visitor information, tel 85/3378 2216, closed Sat.–Sun.)*, 70 miles (110 km) down the coast from Fortaleza, has not been overrun by interlopers, sprawl, pollution, drugs, and crime. Residents can still sleep with their doors unlocked.

Instead of moving aside for outsiders, community members have banded together to form a cooperative to promote local ownership and market their special brand of tourism, all the while continuing efforts to combat real estate speculation and illegal, predatory fishing. They run their own guesthouses and excursions and have forged partnerships with outside groups to train themselves and their children as guides and cooks.

They offer a full menu of activities. There are buggy rides across the expanses

of adjacent sand dunes and beaches, visiting lagoons and other points of interest; one trip goes as far as Canoa Quebrada, about 30 miles (50 km) away. You can set sail on either a catamaran or a traditional *jangada*, a small sailboat used by traditional Northeastern fishers. You can accompany fishers as they work, or schedule a sportfishing outing. Three walking trails highlight the natural environment and the community's own history. Guides will show you everything from the old road that led to Fortaleza in the 19th century to the beach where sea turtles lay their eggs. And more than a half dozen beaches lie within easy reach by car.

Lodging options range from individual rooms to a modest house, including a more conventional guesthouse. No five-star luxury, but no matter where you stay, you will enjoy genuine contact with the locals.

Parque Nacional da Serra da Capivara

Piauí's Parque Nacional da Serra da Capivara rivals any archaeological site around the world—not only for its historical relevance and aesthetic splendor but also for its organization and accessibility. It was designated a World Heritage site in 1991.

Floodlights allow nighttime viewing of Serra da Capivara's most impressive prehistoric rock art.

The national park *(map 199 B3, Rua Doutor Luís Paixão 188, Milonga, tel 89/3582 2085)* is situated near **São Raimundo Nonato,** more than 300 miles (500 km) south of Piauí's capital, Teresina. It is more easily reached from Petrolina, 185 miles (300 km) east in neighboring Pernambuco state. This town might seem off the beaten track to us in the 21st century, but beginning as many as 25,000 years ago a group of our ancestors left a rich collection of cave paintings and carvings in the area, along with a number of burial sites. The discovery of these archaeological sites has convinced paleoanthropologists to reevaluate the theory that human beings first colonized the Americas by crossing the Bering Strait from Siberia to Alaska

10,000 years ago. Humans very well may have made that crossing to the north, but it does not explain the presence of people in South America thousands of years before.

Before going to the park, visit São Raimundo Nonato's **Museu do Homem Americano** (Museum of the American Man; *Centro Cultural Sérgio Motta, Campestre, tel 89/3582 1612, $)* to see its well-organized displays. As you look at the skulls and ceramic fragments, read the accompanying texts to build an intellectual basis for what you will see in the field. You may visit the research laboratories at the museum upon request; for permission, contact the **Fundação Museu do Homem Americano** *(tel 89/3582 3684 or 3582 1700),* a

The Parque Nacional da Serra da Capivara features a striking landscape in addition to its rock art.

private foundation that performs archaeological research and supports the national park. The foundation can also provide information about guides for touring the park. You cannot visit the park without a guide.

Rock Art & Landscape

More than 1,000 distinct archaeological sites—about 700 with paintings—have been identified. Roughly 300 are open to the public; about 130 have been prepared for visitation, some with ramps and railings to facilitate access. Numerous trails, or circuits, wind through the park, providing access to the rock-art sites.

The main attraction is a circuit called the **Boqueirão da Pedra Furada,** named after a geological formation that resembles a hole punched through a rock wall. The circuit's highlight is the **Baixão da Pedra Furada,** the park's most extensive, expansive, and well-preserved set of paintings. Animals, especially game like deer, pop up repeatedly in the paintings here and elsewhere in the park. Another recurring theme is sex. It might be worth leaving this circuit as the day's finale: Rangers will illuminate it in the evening, upon request *(ask at ranger station before 4 p.m.)*

Schedule the **Andorinhas** circuit for the late afternoon. Besides seeing the cave paintings, you can watch the swallows that give the

INSIDER TIP:

Bring cash when heading to the Serra da Capivara region. You are truly in the backlands. Few establishments take credit cards, and ATMs are few and far between.

—BILL HINCHBERGER
National Geographic author

site its Portuguese name make their group descent through the narrow canyon into their nests for the night. Hikers should set out for some of the far-flung sites. Nìede Guidon, the octogenarian archaeologist who dedicated her life to exploring the region, suggests the **Alta da Serra circuit** or the **Baixa da Perna trail.**

The Caatinga predominates the rugged terrain. For most of the year, scrubland plants lie practically dormant. Animals trudge around in slow motion. Then come spring showers, and within days the entire landscape turns miraculously green. The Caatinga teems with life for a few months before finally relenting again in the hot sun and dry weather. This sliver of southern Piauí is also a transition region: If you know where to look, you can find vestiges of the neighboring Cerrado and of both Brazil's rain forests, the Amazon and Atlantic.

São Luís
▲ 199 A4

Visitor Information
✉ Secretária de Turismo, Rua da Palma 53, Centro
☎ 98/3212 6200

Alcântara
▲ 199 A4
⛴ Ferries leave from Terminal Hidroviário, São Luís (tel 98/3232 0692)

Parque Nacional dos Lençóis Maranhenses
▲ 199 B4
✉ 1.25 miles/ 2 km N of Barreirinhas
☎ 98/3349 1267
www.parquelencois .com.br

Barreirinhas
▲ 199 B4

Visitor Information
✉ Prefeitura de Barreirinhas, Av. Joaquim Soeiro de Carvalho, Centro
☎ 98/3349 1429
🕐 Closed Sat.–Sun.

the presence of extraterrestrials on Earth.

São Luís

The most interesting thing about the island city of São Luís, the state capital of Maranhão, is its Centro Histórico. Unfortunately lodging in the district is scarce. Note that most attractions close on Monday. And many downtown shops close on the weekend, giving the area a forsaken air that some people find uncomfortable. So schedule your visit between Tuesday and Friday.

Many of the main attractions lie within a block or two of one another, clustered in the Praia Grande neighborhood, where buildings adorned with Portuguese tiles line cobblestone streets. Few, if any, traces remain of the French who founded the city in 1612. The **Museu das Artes Visuais** (Rua Portugal 273, tel 98/3218 9938 or 3218 9939, closed Mon.) is an art museum worth a visit for the colonial tiles. The **Casa de Nhozinho** (Rua Portugal 185, tel 98/3218 9951, closed Mon.) displays the work of traditional artisans. The **Casa do Maranhão** (Rua do Trapiche, tel 98/3218 9955) highlights the folk culture of the state, notably the annual Bumba Meu Boi festival in June. The 19th-century **Casa das Tulhas** (Rua da Estrela 184) shelters a market with booths that sell almost any local item you can imagine, including snacks, shots of manioc-flavored cachaça, and local crafts.

São Luís's other attractions are scattered farther afield in the Praia

Grande neighborhood or just beyond it, but they are still within walking distance. The **Centro de Cultura Popular** (Rua Giz 221, tel 98/3218 9924, closed Mon.), a couple blocks east of the Casa das Tulhas, is a converted old mansion that exhibits artifacts of popular

INSIDER TIP:

Time seems to have stood still in São Luís, Maranhão. In its Centro Histórico, with its perfectly preserved streets and buildings, you step into the 17th century.

—ROBERT WALKER
Professor of Geography & Scholar of Amazonian Environmental Change, Michigan State University

rituals—profane and religious, Catholic and Afro-Brazilian. South of here, an old slave detention center has been converted into a black history museum, the **Museu Cafua das Mercês** (Rua Jacinto Maia 54, tel 98/3218 9920, closed Sat.–Sun., $), which is also known as the Museu do Negro.

Several blocks to the east, the 17th-century **Fonte das Pedras,** on Rua de São João, is one of the two remaining public fountains that once supplied drinking water for the city's residents. Gargoyle heads spout water from their mouths. Returning toward the Centro Histórico, be sure to take a guided tour of the opulent interior of the **Teatro Arthur**

Azevedo *(Rua do Sol, tel 98/3218 9900, $),* an imposing 19th-century theater.

Alcântara: From São Luís, you can visit the former state capital, Alcântara, on the mainland, via a 1.5-hour ferry ride. Founded in 1648, Alcântara saw its economy crumble after the abolition of slavery in the late 19th century, with the town largely abandoned afterward. Now its 22,000 inhabitants mostly live off tourists who visit the ruins. A few buildings have been restored. Alcântara is also home to Brazil's satellite launchpad. The space center is off-limits, but you can visit displays at the **Casa da Cultura Aeroespacial** *(Praça Nossa Senhora do Rosário, tel 98/3216 9263, $).* Inside Alcântara's city limits, the Ilha do Cajual is an island that combines natural beauty with important fossil discoveries, but with little tourism infrastructure.

Lençóis Maranhenses

The Lençóis Maranhenses is like no other place on Earth. Here rainfall creates freshwater lagoons in the valleys between sand dunes in an otherwise barren coastal desert bigger than the city of Los Angeles, California. Even Bollywood came halfway across the globe to use the area as a location. The entire area is protected in the **Parque Nacional dos Lençóis Maranhenses.**

Though the national park dates to 1981, it was only in the 1990s that a smattering of

outsiders began to venture in. The first city in the area to invest in infrastructure was **Barreirinhas,** more than 155 miles (250 km) east of São Luís. If you want a semblance of comfort, Barreirinhas remains the best option for lodging. But the village of **Atins** sits closer to the main attractions within the park, **Lagoa Verde** and **Lagoa do Mário.** The former lagoon provides the best example

Painted tiles adorn the walls of many historic buildings in the old town section of São Luís, Maranhão.

of the area's classic lagoon-surrounded-by-dunes; the latter is uncharacteristically ringed by vegetation. Atins is accessible only by boat or off-road vehicle. Two other small villages offer

The lakes that interrupt the expanse of sand in the Lençóis Maranhenses are formed by rainwater.

Cururupu

 199 A4

Visitor Information

✉ Prefeitura de Cururupu, Av. Getúlio Vargas 20, Centro

☎ 98/3391 1518

🕐 Closed Sat.–Sun.

lodging: Caburé and Santo Amaro do Maranhão.

The sand dunes make it difficult to get around. Most excursions use off-road vehicles. Trekking is possible, but you need to be in pretty good shape to scale the dunes. You will also need a guide. Depending on the route you take, the journey on foot takes two to four days. The days start early, between 5 and 6 a.m., and even with all the walking, you take some stretches in off-road vehicles. Day trips from Barreirinhas into the park seem almost limitless. Most include some combination of hiking, boat ride, and off-road vehicle trip. The boat trip is on the Rio Preguiças, which winds past Barreirinhas, Atins, and Caburé. Also popular is a plane ride over the region. For more details, contact **Caetés Expedições** (Av. Brasília 40, Centro, Barreirinhas, tel 98/3349 0528 or 9158 3349).

Floresta dos Guarás

Western Maranhão is a transition region between the Amazon rain forest and the savanna-like Cerrado that covers most of the state. If you had to draw a line, you would place the Floresta dos Guarás slightly on the Amazon side. Locals claim that the region, also known as the Reentrâncias Maranhenses, contains the world's largest contiguous mangrove forest. The terrain is sliced and diced by numerous rivers, islands, marshlands, swamps, and areas of forest cover. It is rich in fish and shellfish, which attract myriad birds in droves, including several migratory species. The scarlet ibis gets much of the attention—and gives the region its name, *guará* being the Portuguese word for "scarlet ibis." But other species thrive here as well, including the great egret and the wattled jacana.

Cururupu, some 280 miles (450 km) west of São Luís, is the gateway to the region. The federal government has declared more than 715 square miles (1, 850 sq km) of the surrounding area an extractive reserve, a designation that restricts development but allows people who have traditionally inhabited the land to continue to earn a living from it.

Located several hours by boat from the urban center, the **Maiaú archipelago** is the region's main attraction. Its **Ilha dos Lençóis** boasts sand dunes with rainwater-formed freshwater ponds similar to those found in the Lençóis Maranhenses (see pp. 239–240). The island caught the attention of health professionals because of its exceptionally high incidence of albinism among local residents. One result was a nickname: Ilha dos Filhos da Lua (Children of the Moon Island).

Chapada das Mesas

In southern Maranhão, traversed by a half dozen rivers, the Chapada das Mesas presents an odd contrast of abundant water flowing amid the dry landscape of the Cerrado eco-region. The **Parque Nacional da Chapada das Mesas** is one of Brazil's newest national parks, declared such in 2005. The cliffs of the rocky plateau combine with streams and rivers to form waterfalls that are the region's star attractions. Many excursions that take in the top falls are only doable with off-road vehicles and local guides leading the way. For more information, contact the **Cia do Cerrado Ecoturismo** (*Praça José Alcides de Carvalho 236, tel 99/3531 3222 or 8122 0017*), a tour operator in Carolina, the gateway town to Chapada das Mesas.

Topping the list of places to visit is the **Santuário Ecológico da Pedra Caída,** also known as the Balneário da Pedra Caída. Here, the **Cachoeira da Pedra Caída** drops 150 feet (46 m) into a natural pool. Hiking trails lead through canyons and valleys to more waterfalls. Another popular excursion goes to see the waterfalls strung out along the Rio Farinha: Great drapes of water are created by 92-foot-high (28 m), 108-foot-wide (33 m) **Cachoeira de São Romão,** while

not far from the **Cachoeira do Prata** is the **Morro das Figuras,** a rock formation adorned with prehistoric paintings. A third outing takes in the **Cachoeira do Itapecuru,** actually two waterfalls in one. A deactivated hydroelectric dam built in the 1940s stands nearby. The **Ilha dos Botes,** a fluvial island, is a popular hangout for locals.

Parcel de Manuel Luís

Scuba divers should take note of the Parcel de Manuel Luís, a submerged rock formation located about 50 miles (80 km) off the Floresta dos Guarás coast. Encompassing about 175 square miles (450 sq km), it is believed to include the largest coral reef in South America, home to abundant sea life, including parrotfish, barracuda, and sea turtles. It is also a quintessential "shipwreck cemetery," with some 200 vessels littering its depths. Access is difficult. For more information contact a local tour operator or the **Secretaria de Turismo Maranhão** (*Rua Portugal 165, São Luis, tel 98/3231 0822, www.turismo.ma.gov.br).*

In the nearby town of **Riachão,** the **Parque Balneário Santa Barbara** holds yet another waterfall, the **Cachoeira de Santa Barbara,** and the **Poço Azul,** a turquoise pool formed by springs that emerge from adjacent rocks.

Carolina sits on the Rio Tocantins, on the border with Tocantins state. The town enjoyed a brief stint as a regional economic hub during the 20th century, until fluvial transportation lost ground to the trucking industry in the 1960s. The nearest airport is in Imperatriz, 135 miles (220 km) north. ∎

Parque Nacional da Chapada das Mesas

- ⚐ 199 A3
- ✉ Praça Alípio de Carvalho 50, Carolina
- ☎ 99/8122 8977

Carolina

- ⚐ 199 A3

Offering an extraordinary range of experiences, from river tours and jungle stays to indigenous cultures and citywide celebrations

Amazon

Victoria regia, one of the most beautiful plants of the Amazon

Amazon

The Amazon rain forest contains an estimated 10 percent of the Earth's biodiversity and 20 percent of all its freshwater resources. Several countries claim slivers of the Amazon Basin, but Brazil controls the lion's share. Most visitors seek contact with the birds and wildlife that thrive here, but 25 million people inhabit the region and activities featuring local culture and history are just as worthy of attention. Most visitors arrive in one of the two major cities, Manaus and Belém, and strike out from there into the jungle.

Amazonas

Amazonas is Brazil's largest state and its capital, Manaus, the largest city in the region, with a population of about 1.8 million. Located where the Rio Negro and the Rio Solimões meet to form the mammoth Rio Amazonas, Manaus became a bustling metropolis with the late 19th-century rubber boom. Today it is the main jumping-off point for jungle lodges and riverboat tours.

Pará

Second only to Amazonas, Pará state accounts for one-quarter of the territory of the Amazon region. Capital Belém provides access to Ilha de Marajó, the world's largest river-marine archipelago.

North & West of the Amazon

In the far north of Brazil, Amapá consists mostly of rain forest–covered plateaus, though there's also a mountain range, an unusual geological feature in the Amazon. The state boasts interesting natural attractions,

4▷

3▷

NOT TO BE MISSED:

Reliving the rubber boom with a city tour of Manaus   246–247

The Carnavalesque Festival Folclórico do Boi-Bumbá in Parintins   250

Boating the Parque Nacional de Anavilhanas   253–254

Embarking on a multiday river excursion up the Rio Negro and deep into the jungle   255

Joining the world's largest Catholic celebration   259

Alter do Chão, considered the most spectacular beaches in Brazil   262

Riding the *pororoca*, the longest wave on the Rio Amazonas   265

Hanging for a few days in Cristalino Jungle Lodge, one of Brazil's benchmark ecolodges   271

Jalapão, where waterfalls, rivers, and lakes mix with the sand dunes of the Cerrado   272

Pico da Neblina
2,994m
R.B.E. DO MORRO
DOS SEIS LAGOS
São Gabriel
da Cachoeira   P.N. DO
PICO DA
NEBLINA

COLOMBIA
Japurá   R.D.S.
MAMIRAUÁ

Tef

Tabatinga
Carauari

AMAZONAS

2▷
Eirunepé

Cruzeiro
do Sul   F.N.
PURUS

P.N. DA   BR364
SERRA DO   ACRE
DIVISOR

Rio Branco

R.E. CHICO   Xapuri
MENDES   Guajará-
Caminhos de   Mirim
Chico Mendes

1▷

△
A

PERU

△
B

many of them in protected areas like Parque Nacional do Viruá, but infrastructure for visitors is scanty. Farther north still, Roraima, Brazil's least populated state, is home to the Yanomami, one of the country's best known surviving Indian tribes, whose territory extends into neighboring Venezuela.

South & East of the Amazon

Set in the extreme western end of the Brazilian Amazon, the state of Acre is best known as the home of assassinated rain forest activist Chico Mendes. Much of Acre's original forest cover remains intact. Neighboring Rondônia's rampant

deforestation has pretty much shoved the state off the radar for leisure travelers. More promising is the biologically rich northern region of Mato Grosso state. Tocantins features the world's largest river island and Jalapão, with abundant water-falls, rivers, dunes, and lakes. ∎

Amazonas

With its bounty of natural riches and storied history, Amazonas looms large in the global imagination. The river basin and surrounding jungle remain primary attractions, but increasing numbers of visitors come to experience the state's bustling cities and indigenous communities. In the far west, Amazonas also boasts the country's highest mountain peak, Pico da Neblina.

Imported piece by piece from Europe, Manaus's Teatro Amazonas symbolizes the rubber boom.

Manaus

◪ 245 C3

Visitor Information

✉ Centro de
Atendimento
ao Turista, Av.
Eduardo Ribeiro
666, Centro

☎ 92/3182 6250

🕐 Closed Sat. p.m.
& Sun.

Teatro Amazonas

✉ Praça do
Congresso,
Centro

☎ 92/3622 2420

💲 $ (30-min.
guided tour)

Manaus & Around

Most visitors to the rain forest begin their trip in sprawling Manaus, the largest city in the region and home to 1.8 million people. Once one of the world's richest cities, this former rubber boomtown boasts a number of impressive turn-of-the-20th-century monuments, including its must-see opera house, **Teatro Amazonas.** Inaugurated in 1896, the belle epoque theater features ornate interior furnishings and a spectacular tiled dome. The theater closed in the early 20th century, when

the rubber boom dwindled, and it remained closed until 1990. Since then it has been splendidly restored. Today it stages world-class performances and is home to the Orquestra Amazonas Filarmônica (Amazonas Philharmonic Orchestra) as well as the annual Festival Amazonas de Ópera (Amazonas Opera Festival).

South of the Teatro Amazonas the **Palacete Provincial** *(Praça Heliodoro Balbi, Centro, tel 92/3622 8387, closed Mon.),* a former police station built in 1874, now houses exhibits on subjects ranging from money and archaeology to regional law enforcement and firefighting. Don't miss the display of contemporary Brazilian art.

Other period landmarks line the shore of the Rio Negro, including the **Porto de Manaus** (*Rua Marquês de Santa Cruz 25, Centro, tel 92/2123 4350, www .portodemanaus.com.br*), a floating dock, and the neighboring **Alfândega e Guardamoria** (*Rua Marquês de Santa Cruz, Centro, tel 92/2125 5577*), the city's customhouse. Inaugurated in 1882, the **Mercado Municipal Adolfo Lisboa** (*Rua dos Barés 46, closed for renovations*), long the port of entry for regional fish and produce, recalls the art nouveau design of the Les Halles markets in Paris.

For a more intimate sense of life during the rubber boom, visit the delightful **Palácio Rio Negro** (*Av. Sete de Setembro 1546, Centro, tel 92/3232 4450, closed Sat.–Sun.*), east of downtown. Built in 1903 as the home of a rubber baron, this eclectic building later served as the governor's mansion and state administrative headquarters. Today it is a cultural center, with sumptuous period furnishings and displays of art and sculpture.

Indigenous Culture: Like most major cities in Brazil, Manaus is ethnically diverse. Yet the heritage of the region's original inhabitants is the one felt most keenly here. A handful of attractions dedicated to indigenous peoples and their traditions and culture allow visitors to soak up the atmosphere.

Founded by Catholic missionaries in 1952, the excellent **Museu do Índio,** located downtown, features thousands of artifacts, including artwork, ornamental objects, musical instruments, weapons, tools, and more. Interpretive text is given in Portuguese and English.

About 2.5 miles (4 km) east of downtown, the **Centro Cultural Povos da Amazônia** (Amazon Peoples Cultural Center) is a huge exhibition area, covering nearly 750,000 square feet (70,000 sq m), dedicated to the indigenous peoples of the region. It hosts exhibitions and cultural presentations by people not only from Brazil, but also from countries that share the rain forest: Bolivia, Colombia, Ecuador, French Guiana, Guyana, Peru, Suriname, and Venezuela. Permanent exhibitions include reproductions of the traditional living quarters of the

Museu do Índio
- ✉ Av. Duque de Caxias 296, Centro
- ☎ 92/3635 1922
- 🕓 Closed Sun.

Centro Cultural Povos da Amazônia & Museu do Homem do Norte
- ✉ Praça Francisco Pereira da Silva
- ☎ 92/2123 5301

NOTE: You can take in most of the sites in Manaus from aboard the **Amazon Bus** (tel 92/3633 6708, $$), which also passes the Ponte Rio Negro, the longest river bridge in Brazil. Pick up the bus next to the tourist office on Rua Marquês de Santa Cruz or next to Teatro Amazonas.

Manaus Luthier

Luthiers are master artisans of handmade string instruments who can trace their tradition back to the Middle Ages. (The term originally meant "lutemaker.") Today the tradition thrives in modern Manaus. Using discarded wood from logging companies certified as environmentally friendly, the **Oficina Escola de Lutheria da Amazônia** (OELA; *Av. do Turismo, DIMPE Rua Angelim Galpão 20, Tarumã, Manaus, tel 92/3232 9950, www.oela.org.br*) teaches poor kids from the city's outskirts how to make acoustic guitars and other instruments. This is not just an experiment. An executive at Nashville-based Gibson Guitar Corporation placed multiple orders for instruments made by students, and top-notch Brazilian musicians like Lenine use OELA axes. The workshop welcomes visitors.

Arawak and Yanomami peoples. In 2012, the **Museu do Homem do Norte** (Museum of the Northern Man), inaugurated downtown in 1985, reopened on the site. It contains more than 2,000 articles related to the lives and livelihoods of people in the region, including items recovered from archaeological expeditions, indigenous cultural artifacts and art, and displays of contemporary regional culture.

Several shops and markets sell indigenous handicrafts. Located about 2.5 miles (4 km) north of downtown Manaus, **Central de Artesanato Branco & Silva** (Av. Mário Ypiranga Monteiro, Adrianópolis, tel 92/3236 1241) houses about two dozen stores that feature articles produced by indigenous and river-dweller communities. Nearby, **Arte Indígena** (Av. Mário Ypiranga Monteiro 2305, Adrianópolis, tel 92/3236 1229) sells articles made by the Waimiri Atroari people.

Back downtown, **Galeria Amazônica** (Rua Costa Azevedo 272, Térreo Largo do Teatro, Centro, tel 92/3233 4521, www.galeriama zonica.org.br) has a more upscale feel and offers items from various indigenous groups. **Ecoshop** (Rua Dez de Julho 509, Centro, tel 92/3234 8870) also sells a wide range of items.

The **Feira de Artesanato e Produtos do Amazonas** (Av. Eduardo Ribeiro, Centro), an open-air fair, occupies Avenida Eduardo Ribeiro, a downtown street, every Sunday morning.

Meeting of the Waters:

Manaus is where the Rio Negro and the Rio Solimões merge to create the colossal Rio Amazonas. Take a boat trip out to where the

---

EXPERIENCE: Survive in the Jungle

Jeffson Araújo dos Santos, a career military officer, believes that basic jungle survival training is worthwhile for anyone who intends to fully explore the Amazon rain forest. And as you might expect, the Brazilian army is pretty good at jungle survival training. During his military career, Araújo dos Santos served at several Amazonian frontier outposts, mostly in Roraima state, and eventually became the commander of an elite unit that included a Manaus-based search and rescue group. In addition to his military background, Araújo dos Santos holds a degree in literature and speaks English and Spanish.

For more than a decade he has also been imparting his jungle survival techniques to visitors. Based on the left bank of the Rio Negro, some 22 miles (36 km) upriver from Manaus, his company, **Jaguar Jungle Tour** (Rua 17, Quadra A 16, No. 9, Conjunto Jardim de Versalles II, Manaus, Igarapé do Arara, tel 92/3651 2003 or 9128 3852, www.jaguarjungletour .com.br), leads regular day and overnight wilderness treks into the jungle.

During the trip, Araújo dos Santos will teach you how to make a fire and also how to obtain salt and safe drinking water. He will also explain the uses of different plants, how to trap animals, how to build a shelter, and more. Depending on the excursion, there may even be time to see some of the area's pink dolphins or learn about the legends of the Amazon. Some itineraries take in waterfalls and local villages.

INSIDER TIP:

Wander through the riverside fish market in Manaus. It's just as exciting as watching the rivers—and it's totally free.

—ROBYN BURNHAM
National Geographic grantee

rivers meet but, for reasons of density and speed, do not mix. The swirling sight inspired the wavy mosaics in the square in front of the opera house—later copied in Rio de Janeiro. For tour details, contact Swallows and Amazons Tours *(Av. Ramos Ferreira 922, tel 92/3622 1246, www .swallowsandamazonstours.com)* or Viverde Turismo *(Rua Guariúbas 47, tel 92/3248 9988, www.amazon astravel.com.br).*

Gateway to the Rain Forest:
Manaus sits incongruously in the middle of the Amazon rain forest, and it is the primary jumping-off point for longer explorations of the surrounding region. If you don't have much time but want to get a taste of the Amazon, you will find several ways to do so in and around town.

Located about 4 miles (6 km) northeast of downtown, the **Bosque da Ciência** (Science Forest) serves as a cross between an open-air natural history museum and a zoo. Run by the Instituto Nacional de Pesquisas da Amâzonia (National Institute for Research in the Amazon/INPA), one of Brazil's leading scientific

research centers, it features trails, a tank with Amazonian manatees, an area for giant otters, another for caimans, and an exhibition space, all on 32 acres (13 ha) of land.

Created in 2009 on 247 acres (100 ha) of the Reserva Adolfo Ducke, the **Museu da Amazônia,** about 4.5 miles (7 km) east of downtown, is billed as a "living museum," where you can accompany one of the guided tours through the forest. The area is also home to the **Jardim Botânico de Manaus** *(Rua Uirapuru, Cidade de Deus, tel 92/3582 2929, closed Mon., www.jardimbotanicodemanaus .org),* a botanical garden that also has a butterfly-breeding center and exhibitions on natural history and regional culture. Scientists make regular evening presentations about their research.

Less than 12.5 miles (20 km) from downtown, the **Parque Municipal do Mindu** is a nature reserve that covers about 100 acres (41 ha). Founded in 1993 to protect part of the habitat of the endangered pied tamarin, the park is traversed by several trails, which run through preserved forest and areas that were degraded before the park was established. At the **Zoológico do CIGS,** a zoo operated by the Brazilian army, don't miss the star attraction: jaguars.

Escape the concrete jungle and experience the rain forest firsthand by traveling about an hour out of town by boat to the **Parque Ecológico do Lago Janauari.** Many tour operators run excursions that include canoe trips through the park's

Bosque da Ciência
- ✉ Av. Otávio Cabral s/n
- ☎ 92/3643 3192
- 💲 $
- **www.inpa.gov.br/ bosque**

Museu da Amazônia
- ✉ Rua Uirapuru, Cidade de Deus
- ☎ 92/3236 3079 or 3236 9197
- **www.museuda amazonia.org.br**

Parque Municipal do Mindu
- ✉ Av. Grande Circular 600, Cidade Nova
- ☎ 92/3236 7702

Zoológico do CIGS
- ✉ Estr. Ponta Negra 750, São Jorge
- ☎ 92/3625 2044
- 🕐 Closed Mon.

Parque Ecológico do Lago Janauari
- 🄰 245 C3
- ✉ Av. Brasil 2971, Novo Airão

Parintins
◭ 245 D3
Visitor Information
✉ Secretaria Municipal de Turismo, Av. Nações Unidas, Sala 2, Centro
☎ 92/3533 3109

Presidente Figueiredo
◭ 245 C3
Visitor Information
✉ Centro de Atendimento ao Turista, BR-174 km 107 (behind Igreja Municipal)
☎ 92/9144 1158

streams. The highlight has to be the giant *Victoria* lily pads, some of which measure 6.5 feet (2 m) in diameter. You'll also be introduced to the local wildlife. For more information, contact Swallows and Amazons Tours or Viverde Turismo (see p. 249).

Parintins & Itacoatiara

Located more than 310 miles (500 km) east of Manaus by boat along the Rio Amazonas, Parintins sits on **Ilha Tupinambarana,** an island almost at the state border with Pará. Depending on your boat and the direction you are heading, the river journey takes about 24 hours.

Amazonian Waterfalls

Brazil is blessed with waterfalls, except in the Amazon. If you're set on seeing some, however, the place to go is **Presidente Figueiredo.** In this region 78 miles (125 km) north of Manaus there are an estimated 150 waterfalls, most in private or public nature reserves. Among the most popular are: the **Complexo Turístico Iracema Falls** (*BR-174 km 115, Presidente Figueiredo, tel 92/9250 4370*), with one of the area's biggest waterfalls; the **Reserva Ecológica Cachoeira Santuário** (*AM-240 km 12, Presidente Figueiredo, tel 92/3324 1741 or 8855 5826*), which also has a guesthouse; and the **Parque Urubuí** (*Estr. Municipal da Choeira Parque Urubuí, Centro, Presidente Figueiredo*), with a natural pool for bathing.

Once you've cooled off, head about 50 miles (80 km) northeast of Manaus to the **Etnotrilha do Selvagem** (*AM-010, Aldeia Beija-Flor, Rio Preto da Eva, tel 92/9382 8759 or 9297 2982, www .beijaflorrpe.blogspot.fr*), a guided trail that introduces you to the indigenous peoples of the rain forest.

Parintins hosts an annual operatic extravaganza called the **Festival Folclórico do Boi-Bumbá** (Ox Folklore Festival). The 100,000-strong town roughly doubles in size during the three-day event in June, as rivals Garantido, in red, and Caprichoso, in blue, do battle for crosstown bragging rights. Set to a characteristically Brazilian beat, both groups run through a choreographed enactment of the same legend. According to the story, Francisco, a young husband, kills an ox belonging to his employer to satisfy the hunger of his pregnant wife. When the boss finds out and threatens to kill him, Francisco appeals to a medicine man who resurrects the ox. The performances are held in a specially built stadium popularly called the **Bumbódromo** (Centro Cultural e Esportivo Amazonino Mendes; *Praça Eduardo Ribeiro 2052, Parintins*). Starting in late April, both groups begin public *ensaios* (rehearsals) in their respective headquarters: Curral do Garantido (*Rua Gomes de Castro 685, Parintins*) and Caprichoso's Curral Zeca Xibelão (*Rua Gomes de Castro 685, Centro, Parintins, tel 92/3533 4676*).

Beyond the festival and related activities, many visitors to Parintins like to hang out at nearby beaches or go for a boat ride on **Lago Macurany,** a nearby lake. The town's **Vila Amazônica** is a district noteworthy for being founded by Japanese immigrants.

About 168 miles (270 km) east of Manaus and accessible by both road and water, Itacoatiara sits on the banks of the Amazon.

Seek out **Pep & Jo's Amazon Adventure** *(tel 92/9136 2204 or 608/698-9655 in U.S., www.pepjo amazon.net)*, a guesthouse cum tour operator run by an American who married a local, for the kind of low-key but personalized service that allows you to settle in like a local. Its fishing expeditions are more like Sunday outings with friends, in a small boat on a pristine lake, accompanied by a local fisherman who knows all the best spots. The company also offers day and overnight boat trips.

protected area run by the non-profit Instituto Mamirauá and located 1.5 hours by boat from Tefé. As a flooded rain forest, this nature reserve attracts more wildlife than most other parts of the Amazon: Seasonal ebbs and flows of floodwaters that can rise by as much as 33 feet (10 m) contribute to the abundance of wildlife in this region.

Mamirauá is less noted for its diversity than for its endemism: the appearance of species restricted to a particular area.

Itacoatiara
🔼 245 D3
Visitor Information
✉️ Prefeitura Itacoatiara, Av. Parque 1452
☎️ 92/3521 1576

Reserva de Desenvolvimento Sustentável Mamirauá
🔼 244 B3
Visitor Information
✉️ Instituto Mamirauá, Estr. do Bexiga 1584, Fonte Boa, Tefé
☎️ 97/3343 9700 or 92/3584 4475 (local Tefé number)
www.mamiraua.org .br

Bird-watchers flock to the forests of Presidente Figueiredo.

The region around Itacoatiara has a long history, and archaeologists have discovered ancient petroglyphs here. But this is not a major tourist destination so restaurants and bars are simple and have a distinctly local flavor.

Reserva Mamirauá
The **Reserva de Desenvolvimento Sustentável Mamirauá** (Mamirauá Sustainable Development Reserve) is a state

Some animals, like the white uacari monkey, are rarely if ever spied elsewhere. Wildlife here is also remarkable in its sheer volume. Immobile and serene, caimans line the edges of long, narrow lagoons that look like rivers. Less well-behaved, pink dolphins leap about, sometimes in tandem, sometimes freestyle. Deep inside the forest, howler monkeys announce their presence with waves of eerie calls.

The sky often fills with birds, the cormorant and great egret leading the way. Cormorants perch on the half-submerged branches of fallen trees. Egrets stalk the water's edge, craning elongated necks at odd angles and snapping up fish with their long beaks. Casual bird-watchers might spy a hoatzin, notable because their young have a prehistoric remnant "wing claw" that allows them to climb rocky surfaces. At the right time of year you might

EXPERIENCE:
Sample *Guaraná*

Discovered centuries ago by the indigenous people of the Amazon, tiny red *guaraná* berries pack more than twice as much caffeine as coffee beans. Today you can enjoy guaraná in its diluted form as a popular soft drink. For a real jolt, however, visit **Casa do Guaraná Saterê** *(Rua Marcílio Dias 257, Centro, Manaus, tel 92/3233 8113, closed Sun.),* which serves a sweet and potent concoction of powdered guaraná mixed with local fruits and guaraná syrup.

even glimpse an osprey down for the season from New Jersey.

The presence of so many birds is supported by abundant aquatic life, the birds' main source of food. In fact, about 300 species of fish make Mamirauá home. With leaping abilities that earned it the nickname "water monkey," the *aruanã*—known to jump into small boats—can snatch insects above the surface. Another species, the pirarucu, considered the world's largest freshwater fish species, weighs as much as 300 pounds

(136 kg); a single scale might be larger than the screen on your cell phone. Outside the water, the pirarucu, which always surfaces, can survive for as long as 24 hours, but death can be measured in minutes if it isn't able to come up for that gulp of air. Its gills are essentially redundant. An innovative fisheries management program in Mamirauá works to protect this endangered species.

Pousada Uacari: For a truly intensive experience of all that Mamirauá has to offer, visit Pousada Uacarí (see Travelwise p. 305), a floating ecolodge run by Instituto Mamirauá and set on a calm lagoon in the middle of the reserve. Considered a landmark worldwide, Uacari is located on a tributary of the Rio Solimões about an hour by speedboat from the city of Tefé, which lies about 435 miles (700 km) west of Manaus.

With its five floating cabins, the lodge and its menu of excursions are partly managed by local riverside dwellers called *caboclos.* Many of them are descendants of immigrants from the Northeast who first arrived here to collect sap from the rubber trees in the forest. Today they live mostly from fishing and small-scale agriculture.

The program for visitors includes trips to local villages, led by a resident. Visitors are also introduced to some of the many scientists who carry out research in the area. Arrive at the right time and you might be able to watch biologists snag, weigh, and identify pink dolphins.

The Amazon's expansive wetlands are a magnet for birds, like the hoatzin.

Fourteen trails, averaging 2 miles (3 km) in length, run through the area surrounding the lodge. During the peak of the high water period *(May–July),* you will be led along them in a canoe. Otherwise you can walk through the forest, perhaps spotting howler monkeys, squirrel monkeys, sloths, and more. The lodge also offers excursions to **Lago Mamirauá,** a lake where you are most likely to spot the pirarucu and pink dolphin. On nighttime excursions, you are sure to see caimans and probably bats; if you are really lucky, a jaguar might even turn up.

Parque Nacional de Anavilhanas

Consisting of about 400 islands and hundreds of lakes, rivers, and streams, must-see Parque Nacional de Anavilhanas is located upriver from Manaus on the Rio Negro and offers an accessible introduction to the Amazon rain forest. A protected area since 1981, and one of the world's largest river archipelagos, it was upgraded to national park status in 2008.

The archipelago is best explored by boat. During the low water period, from September to January, the receding river reveals sandy beaches along the edges of its islands. This is also a good time to explore the channels in small craft and observe the park's wildlife. Mammals that inhabit the region include the giant anteater, the giant armadillo, and the giant otter. Jaguars are also around, though they are notoriously difficult to spot. More likely you will spy Amazonian manatees and pink dolphins. As you move along, the landscape shifts continually from densely covered forest to sparsely wooded grasslands. During periods of high water, tree trunks seem to grow right out of the water. The park's caves, **Grutas do Madadá,** are open to visitors.

Getting to Anavilhanas:

The park's gateway city is **Novo Arião,** about 112 miles (180 km) by paved road northwest of Manaus. By road, the trip takes

Parque Nacional de Anavilhanas

🅰 245 C3

✉ Rua Antenor Carlos Frederico 69, Novo Arião

☎ 92/3365 1345 or 3365 1197

Novo Arião

🅰 245 C3

Visitor Information

✉ Centro Atendimento ao Turista, Av. Ajuricaba s/n (next to police station)

☎ 92/3365 1391

Museu do Seringal Vila Paraíso

✉ Igarapé São João (access by boat only)

☎ 92/3234 8755

🕐 Closed Mon.– Tues.

demus@cultur amazonas.am.gov.br

Parque Nacional do Jaú

▲ 245 C3

☎ 92/3365 1345

about 2.5 hours. From Novo Arião, speedboats and larger vessels are available for excursions into the archipelago.

It is also possible to take a boat directly from Manaus. (Depending on the type of vessel, a boat trip can take anywhere from three to nine hours.) Day-trip boat excursions often stop at the **Museu do Seringal Vila Paraíso,** something of a mini-theme park dedicated to the history of rubber production in the Amazon. The museum consists of a film set–style re-creation of a village to illustrate the techniques and lives of rubber tappers. For more information on excursions, contact Swallows and Amazons Tours (see p. 249).

Novo Arião was founded in the 1940s after the rubber export cycle lost steam and the inhabitants of Arião (see opposite) decided to leave en masse. The nearby **Anavilhanas Jungle Lodge** (see Travelwise p. 304), just outside the park, has luxurious cottages and bungalows for rent and offers bilingual guided tours.

Parque Nacional do Jaú

Covering nearly 5.9 million acres (2.4 million ha), Parque Nacional do Jaú represents one of the largest sections of officially protected rain forest in the world. It is located between the cities of Novo Arião and Barcelos (see opposite), both of which offer lodging and customary urban amenities, so either makes a good base for exploring. The park is six hours by boat from Manaus, and about one hour by plane or helicopter.

The best way to visit the park is by motorboat. Following the park's rivers, you are likely to see macaws and parrots flying above the streams and animals moving along the riverbanks. In calm stretches, notice how the mirror-like water below you reflects images of the orchids and other plants growing along the shore. There are waterfalls, hiking trails, and bright reflecting pools—though some attractions become inaccessible due to seasonal flooding and drainage. An on-site archaeological dig has uncovered prehistoric carvings.

Parque Nacional do Jaú is often visited as part of a multiday river excursion from Manaus

INSIDER TIP:

For the experience of a lifetime, swim with the pink dolphins in the Rio Negro. In Anavilhanas they are free in the wild.

—NIVEA ATALLAH
Terra Brazil

(see sidebar opposite). For more information, contact Swallows and Amazons Tours (see p. 249) or Maia Expeditions *(Rua Badajo 62, Parque Shangrilá 1, Bairro de Flores, Manaus, tel 92/9983 7141 or 3613 4683, www.maiaexpeditions .com).* Packages include meals and bilingual guides.

Arião Velho: Along the way to the park, your boat tour may

EXPERIENCE: Explore the Rain Forest

There are basically three ways to really experience the Amazon rain forest firsthand. The first is to lace up your boots, put on your backpack, and follow the footsteps of the old explorers into the mosquito-infested jungle. It might be worth it, but be prepared to suffer. The second is to set up shop at an ecolodge like Pousada Uacari in the Reserva de Desenvolvimento Sustentável Mamirauá (see pp. 251–252) and take day trips into the jungle from your base.

The third, and perhaps the most interesting, is to take what is known in the business as an expedition cruise up the Rio Negro. The boats that leave from Manaus are upgraded versions of the medium-size riverboats regularly used for transportation in the waterlogged Amazon. With a capacity of about 18 people, they are remarkably comfortable. During a weeklong excursion, with three outings per day into the jungle, you will experience everything there is to experience in the Amazon. You will see monkeys, caimans, and birds, and you'll watch the sun set or rise from the bow of your very own boat. Better than that, you will leave all your stress behind in the rain forest.

For itineraries and pricing, contact **Amazon Nature Tours** (*Av. Sete de Setembro 188, Centro Antigo, Manaus, tel 401/423 3377 in U.S., www.amazon-nature-tours.com*).

---

stop at Arião Velho. The first village established along the Rio Negro, Arião Velho was founded by Christian missionaries in the 17th century but has been a ghost town since the 1940s. Its original name, Santo Elias do Jaú, was later changed to Arião. It added "Velho" (Old) when the townspeople abandoned it en masse, reestablishing in today's Novo Arião. According to legend, the residents were forced out by an invasion of ants. Coincidentally or not, they made the move as the rubber export cycle petered out, forcing people to change how they earned their livelihoods. If ants ever had the run of the place, they got fed up and left as well. You won't see many of them, though you can visit some remaining 18th-century structures, including a cemetery, a church, and a school.

Barcelos

This quaint river town prides itself as a leading supplier of ornamental fish. Every year it also hosts the **Festival do Peixe Ornamental** (Ornamental Fish Festival). Though the name might suggest otherwise, this is not an aquarium trade show. Held in late January or early February, this three-day festival is a spectacular Carnavalesque celebration akin to the better known extravaganza in Parintins (see p. 250), involving music, art, and dance performances.

Barcelos also offers opportunities for sportfishing. The nonprofit organization **Projeto Piaba** (*www.opefe.com/piaba.html*) has been working since 1989 to promote sustainable harvesting practices that help protect the Amazon rain forest and the people who live there. Customized tours last from two to eight days and include jungle camping.

Barcelos

 245 C3

Visitor Information

✉ Prefeitura Municipal, Rua Tenreiro Aranha 204, Centro

☎ 92/3321 1796

EXPERIENCE: Sportfishing on the Rio Negro

Mountain climbers chase peaks, surfers chase waves, and sportfishermen chase trophy peacock bass. At least that's what they do along the Rio Negro, a river that attracts hard-core anglers from across the globe.

Sportfisherman in the Amazon displays the supreme prize for any visitor: a peacock bass.

Home to more than 2,000 species of fish, the inky black water of the Rio Negro is a prime location for catching peacock bass. Here you can fish for three species of this giant fish and maybe even chase a world record. After all, it's been done before: Three record-setting peacock bass have been caught by fishermen along the Rio Negro. Other species in this region include catfish and piranha, as well as freshwater tropical fish like tetras and rainbow bass.

History of Fishing Along the Rio Negro

Today's sportfishermen are just the most recent in a long line of Amazon anglers that has included such famous figures as Theodore Roosevelt, who visited the Amazon in 1914. But the tradition goes back much further.

For centuries, the indigenous people of this region subsisted on fish. Their traditional tackle consisted of bows and arrows (with specially designed arrows for specific fish), spears, and an array of ingenious nets, baskets, and bizarre traps. Europeans introduced hooks, which locals soon became very proficient in using.

These days sportfishermen rely on bait casting and spinning equipment to catch the fish here, though fly fishing is growing in popularity.

Sportfishing Tours

Serious fishers waste little time with anything beyond snagging a peacock bass, be it barred, speckled, or butterfly. Anglers head out at dawn with local guides for 12 hours on the water, returning to the mother ship for some shut-eye before repeating the drill the next day. The boat moves around to get to the most promising spots—often hidden lagoons.

From September to March, **Capt. Peacock Yachts & Expeditions** (tel 817/471 2716 in U.S., $$$$$, www.captpeacock.com) offers weeklong fishing trips on the Rio Negro. The excursion begins in Manaus, where you catch a charter flight to Barcelos (see p. 255) or another city along the river. Your "hotel" for the duration is the company's 125-foot (38 m) luxury yacht, with a capacity of 14–22 anglers. The number of peacock bass caught each day varies, but the average is usually around 30. Other side trips available include visits to nearby indigenous villages and wildlife hikes through the Amazon rain forest. Fishing equipment is provided. A return flight to Manaus is included in the tour price.

Other tour operators with regular Amazon fishing trips include **Acute Angling** (tel 866/832 2987, www.acute angling.com), Florida-based **HighRoller Adventures** (tel 877/205 1764 in U.S., www .highrolleroutdooradventures .com), and **Pescamazon** (www.pescamazon.com).

Western Amazonas

São Gabriel da Cachoeira

sits about 525 miles (850 km) northwest of Manaus, upriver on the Rio Negro. With an estimated 90 percent of inhabitants of tribal origin, it has earned a reputation as Brazil's most indigenous town. Along with Portuguese, three native tongues have been raised to the status of co-official languages in the surrounding municipality.

INSIDER TIP:

In October, don't miss seeing the indigenous people of São Gabriel de Cachoeira in their element as they hold Festibral, which includes traditional music and dance.

—ROSE DAVIDSON
National Geographic contributor

The Federação das Organizações Indígenas do Rio Negro, known best by its acronym FOIRN, has its headquarters downtown and runs the **Wariró Casa de Produtos Indígenas do Rio Negro** (Wariró House of Rio Negro Indigenous Products; *Av. 31 de Março, Centro, tel 97/3471 1450*), which sells crafts made by the ethnic groups of the region.

The area's river beaches, notably **Ilha do Sol** and **Ilha da Brigada,** are popular with locals. You can also take several short hikes from town, including to

Serra da Bela Adormecida, a hill that offers a great vantage point for watching the sunset.

Just 34 miles (55 km) northeast of gateway city São Gabriel da Cachoeira, **Parque Nacional do Pico da Neblina** (Peak of the Mists National Park) is one of Brazil's largest national parks, covering about 8,500 square miles (22,000 sq km). Together with the adjacent Venezuelan national park across the border to the north, Pico da Neblina comprises part of one of the largest stretches of contiguous protected areas of the Amazon rain forest. The park is marked by the Serra do Imeri mountain range, which boasts Brazil's two highest peaks: **Pico da Neblina** (9,823 feet/2,994 m) and **Pico 31 de Março** (9,751 feet/2,972 m). Like the rest of the area, dense vegetation covers the mountainsides.

The park is open to nature aficionados, adventure enthusiasts, and trekkers, but only if accompanied by a licensed guide. Hiking to the top of Pico da Neblina does not require special rock- or mountain-climbing skills, but you do need to be in good physical shape to make the ascent.

Also located inside Parque Nacional do Pico da Neblina is the **Reserva Biológica Estadual do Morro dos Seis Lagos,** a state nature reserve that doubles as an indigenous reserve. One of the region's most beautiful areas, it contains six lakes—each a different tone of greenish blue due to the minerals that are present. Indeed, a major deposit of valuable niobium has been discovered here. ∎

São Gabriel da Cachoeira

🅜 244 B3

Visitor Information

✉ Prefeitura São Gabriel da Cachoeira, Av. Dom Pedro Massa s/n, Centro, São Gabriel da Cachoeira

☎ 97/3471 1769 or 3471 1460

Parque Nacional do Pico da Neblina

🅜 244 B3

Visitor Information

✉ Rua Dom José 51, Centro, São Gabriel da Cachoeira

☎ 97/3471 1617 or 3638 3495

Pará

Like neighboring Amazonas, Pará—Brazil's second largest state—serves as a gateway to exploring the Amazon. It counts among its attractions a number of parks and protected natural areas as well as the traditional ceramics and dances of the ancient Marajó people. Brazilians flock to capital city Belém every October for what may be the world's largest Catholic procession.

Vessels moored in Belém: Most long-distance travel in the Amazon is done by boat.

Belém

 245 E3

Visitor Information

✉ Praça Maestro
Waldemar
Henrique s/n,
Reduto

☎ 91/3212 0575

Complexo Ver-o-Peso & Mercado Municipal de Carnes Francisco Bolonha

✉ Blvd. Castilhos
França, Cidade
Velha

Belém

Set on the Rio Guamá, Belém has several interesting attractions in its historic old town, with a spotlight on the lively **Complexo Ver-o-Peso.** With a name that warns "check the weight," the Ver-o-Peso is a riverside fish and produce market with hundreds of stalls selling just about everything that can be culled, extracted, or pulled from the Amazon Basin. The market's highlight is the myriad fish, which begin to arrive in the wee hours. The building's hodgepodge architecture reflects a series of additions and expansions that date to the 18th century. In the same area, the ironworks

of the **Mercado Municipal de Carnes Francisco Bolonha** hosts a meat market.

Next door to the markets, the **Estação das Docas** (Docks Station; *Blvd. Castilhos França, tel 91/3212 5525*) has benefited from a downtown urban-renewal scheme and features a strip of fashionable restaurants. The traditional restaurant **Lá em Casa** (see Travelwise p. 306), which some argue has the best Amazonian cuisine anywhere, has a branch here, as does the famed **Cairu** (see Travelwise p. 306) ice-cream shop. If you are looking for nightlife, the Docas, with its concentration of bars, is a good choice.

From the market and docks, you can walk to the historic old town. Most of what the city has to offer visitors can be found within a few square blocks. The **Casa das Onze Janelas** is a cultural center and modern art museum (with works by Tarsila do Amaral and Lasar Segall) that occupies an old mansion. From the **Forte do Presépio,** a 17th-century fort, you can get a view of the river and Ver-o-Peso. It also has a museum with regional and historical artifacts. The **Corveta Museu Solimões** (*Praça Dom Frei Caetano Brandão, Cidade Velha*) is an old Brazilian navy vessel dating to the 1950s that has been converted into a museum. Just a few blocks away, the **Museu de Arte de Belém** occupies part of the Palácio Antonio Lemos, also known as the Palacete Azul, and features objects and artwork from the 18th and 19th centuries.

The old trolley car, called the **Bondinho da Cidade Velha,** has been reactivated for Sunday fun rides through the historic downtown. Now powered by biodiesel fuel rather than electricity, it nevertheless runs along the same old tracks as it used to. Departures are from the **Museu de Arte Sacra.**

Exploring the Amazon:

Several attractions within reach of downtown Belém remind visitors that they are on the cusp of the rain forest. A few blocks from downtown, occupying 10 acres (4 ha) astride the river, the **Mangal das Garças** (Mangrove of the Herons) complex was inaugurated in 2005 as a way to bring the rain forest to the city. Its attractions include the Viveiro das Aningas, an area with dozens of bird species; the Reserva José Márcio Ayres, which claims to be the world's largest butterfly nursery;

Casa das Onze Janelas
- Rua Siqueira Mendes, Cidade Velha
- 91/4009 8823

Forte do Presépio
- Praça Dom Frei Caetano Brandão, Cidade Velha
- 91/4009 8828

Museu de Arte de Belém
- Praça Dom Pedro, Cidade Velha
- 91/3114 1028

Mangal das Garças
- Passagem Carneiro da Rocha, Cidade Velha
- 91/3242 5052
- www.mangalpa.com.br

Círio de Nazaré & Belém's Religious Attractions

Brazil is one of the world's largest Catholic countries and the Círio de Nazaré on the second Sunday of October is reputed to be the biggest Catholic celebration in the world. More than two million people flood the streets of Belém, taking part in a procession to honor the miracle-working Virgin Mary. Many come to "pay back" debts to the Virgin whom they believe has performed a miracle on their behalf.

The procession begins in the city's historic downtown at the 18th-century **Cathedral da Sé** (*Praça Frei Caetano Brandão, Cidade Velha, tel 91/3223 2362*) and proceeds about 2.5 miles (4 km) east to the **Basílica de Nazaré**

(*Av. Nazaré 1300, Praça Justo Chermont, tel 91/4009 8400*). Both are open year-round. The latter dates from 1909 and was built on the spot, as the story goes, where a poor *caboclo* (person of mixed white-indigenous heritage) found a statue of the Virgin Mary in 1700.

To learn about the history of the Círio de Nazaré procession in Belém's old town, visit the **Museu do Círio** (*Al Quartel Nazaré, tel 91/3224 9614*). Another must-see, the **Museu de Arte Sacra** (*Praça Frei Caetano Brandão, Cidade Velha*), a collection of religious art, sits next to **Igreja de São Francisco Xavier** (*Passagem Hortinha 207, Marco, tel 91/3283 3052*), a 17th-century church.

Parque Ecológico Zoobotânico do Museu Paraense Emílio Goeldi

- ✉ Av. Magalhães Barata 376, São Braz
- ☏ 91/3219 3358
- 🕐 Closed Mon.

Jardim Botânico Bosque Rodrigues Alves

- ✉ Av. Almirante Barroso 2305, Marco
- ☏ 91/3276 2308

Parque Ambiental do Utinga

- ✉ Av. João Paulo II, Utinga

Parque Ecológico de Gunma

- ✉ Rod. Augusto Meira Filho km 18, Santa Bárbara do Pará

Ilha de Marajó

- ⛰ 245 E3

Salvaterra

- ⛰ 245 E3

Soure

- ⛰ 245 E3

Visitor Information

- ✉ Prefeitura de Soure, Travessa 16 s/n, Centro
- ☏ 91/3741 1275

the Farol do Belém, a lookout tower; an orchid nursery and a conventional nursery; and the Museu Amazônico da Navegação (Amazon Sailing Museum).

Located in the same direction, about 1 mile (1.6 km) from downtown along the riverside, the **Portal da Amazônia** (access via Rua Doutor Assis & Rua do Arsenal) provides 1.25 miles (2 km) of waterfront with refreshment stands and other amenities. Inaugurated in 2012, the urban renewal project ejected the poor slum dwellers who used to live here on houses built on stilts to resist flooding. They protested their ousting to no avail.

Less than 3 miles (5 km) east of downtown, the open-air **Parque Ecológico Zoobotânico do Museu Paraense Emílio Goeldi,** run by one of Brazil's leading research institutions, offers an education in Amazonian flora and fauna. The area open to visitors presents a cross between a park and a zoo.

About 4.5 miles (7 km) northeast of downtown, the 19th-century **Jardim Botânico Bosque Rodrigues Alves** contains more than 2,000 species of plants from the Amazon region. Stroll along the garden's nature trails or go canoeing on an artificial lake.

Other attractions slightly farther afield include **Parque Ambiental do Utinga,** a state park covering more than 3,200 acres (1,300 ha) with nature trails in the Utinga district of Belém east of downtown. **Parque Municipal da Ilha do Mosqueiro** (44 miles/70 km

N of Belém), a municipal nature reserve, comprises three of the five dozen islands that surround Belém. In neighboring **Santa Bárbara do Pará,** about 30 miles (50 km) northeast of Belém, **Parque Ecológico de Gunma** covers 1,334 acres (540 ha), most of which is covered by primary growth forest. All of these reserves have hiking trails.

INSIDER TIP:

No visit to Belém is complete without a stop at the Ver-o-Peso market, the largest in South America. Buy yourself a love potion or fillet of red snapper.

—ROBERT WALKER
Professor of Geography & Scholar of Amazonian Environmental Change, Michigan State University

Ilha de Marajó

At 15,480 square miles (40,100 sq km), Ilha de Marajó is the world's largest river-marine island in the world's largest river-marine archipelago. A dozen small towns, marked by concentrations of colonial buildings, dot the landscape. The port town of **Salvaterra,** about three hours by boat north of Belém, and **Soure,** just north across the Rio Paracauari, provide the best infrastructure.

Most visitors to Majaró arrive by boat, but it is also possible to arrive by air. Ferries can carry vehicles. During the high water period *(Jan.–June),* many fields are flooded, lending a spectacular air to the island landscape. The second half of the year, however, is better for wildlife spotting and outdoor activities.

Small streams—populated by a curious four-eyed fish known locally as *tralhoto*—cut through the island, which is noted for calm beaches backed by sand dunes. Wildlife lovers delight in the island's flocks of scarlet ibises. Others come for the local pottery, which draws on the tradition of the region's prehistoric inhabitants, the Marajoara. As for lounging on the sand, you have your choice of ocean beaches or river ones. One of the most popular is **Praia do Pesqueiro,** along the ocean in Soure.

The island's buffalo are raised for meat, cheese, and even transportation, and many of the working buffalo farms offer lodging and a menu of outdoor activities. The island's down-home eateries—often a wing of the cook's house—are legendary, featuring both fish and buffalo meat. Typical activities at the farm-lodges might include nature walks, buffalo-led cart rides, "buffalo-back" riding, canoeing, horseback riding, birdwatching, wildlife spotting, boat excursions, and bicycle rides. To find a farm-lodge with the right activities for you, visit Hidden Pousadas Brazil *(www.hiddenpousadasbrazil.com).*

Majaró is also known for its traditional dances like the *dança do vaqueiro de Marajó* (Marajó cowboy dance), the *carimbó* (which simulates courtship), the *siriá,* and

The Ilha de Marajó region is known for its high-quality ceramics.

the sensual *lundu.* Some farmlodges offer dance presentations as part of their programs, or you can make separate arrangements to see them.

Ilha Caviana, another of the archipelago's islands, offers the best view of the *pororoca,* a tidal phenomenon that also occurs in other parts of the Amazon, such as Amapá (see sidebar p. 265).

Santarém & Alter do Chão

In economic terms, Santarém is the second most important city in Pará and the third in population, but there is no direct or easy road access. The city lies west of Belém, more than 500 miles (800 km) by boat (three days) and 935 miles (1,500 km) by road. The trip is worth it, however, for the area boasts one of the world's most stunning river beaches, a national forest, and superb traditional and local crafts.

Downtown **Museu Dica Frazão** displays more than a hundred articles produced by

Santarém
📍 245 D3
Visitor Information
✉ Prefeitura de Santarém, Av. Doutor Anysio Chaves 853, Aeroporto Velho
☎ 93/2101 5100

Museu Dica Frazão
✉ Rua Floriano Peixoto 281, Santarém
☎ 93/3522 1026

**Floresta
Nacional de
Tapajós**
🏛 245 D3
✉ Av. Tapajós
2267, Santarém
(road access is
difficult)
☎ 93/3523 2815

Belterra
🏛 245 D3

In the outback of the Amazon, many people still get much
of their sustenance from small-scale fishing.

Fordlândia
🏛 245 D3

Salinópolis
🏛 245 E3
Visitor Information
✉ Prefeitura
Salinópolis, Rua
João Pessoa
406, Centro,
Salinópolis
☎ 91/3423 5333

Santarém's best known crafts-
woman, Dica Frazão, who uses
local fibers like *buriti* and açai to
produce clothing and decorative
objects. A few blocks away, the
Centro Cultural João Fona (*Rua
Adriano Pimentel*) is dedicated to
the ceramic legacy of the Tapajós
Indians, who once populated the
region. Another popular attraction
in town is the **Encontro das
Águas,** a phenomenon similar
to the one found near Manaus
(see pp. 248–249), where the
waters of the Rio Tapajós and Rio
Amazonas meet without merg-
ing, sometimes referred to as a
"dance." To see it, hire a boat at
the Terminal Fluvial Turístico (*on
strand near Praça do Pescador*).

About 22 miles (35 km)
west of Santarém, **Alter do
Chão** began to receive national
attention in Brazil after the British
newspaper *The Guardian* ranked
its river beaches along the Rio
Tapajós as the best beaches of

any kind in the country, and
this in beach-crazed Brazil. The
beaches are best visited during the
low-water period from August to
February. In addition to the usual
lounging around, they are popular
for windsurfing and kayaking.

Multiday guided kayak excur-
sions into **Floresta Nacional de
Tapajós** depart from Alter de
Chão. For more information about
cost and sample itineraries, con-
tact Rumo Norte Expedições (*Av.
Serzedêlo Corrêa 895, casa 59, 2 piso,
Belém, tel 91/3225 5915*).

Every September thousands
of Brazilians descend on Alter do
Chão for the **Festa do Çairé,** a
religious and secular celebration
whose dances and processions
reveal a mixture of Portuguese
and indigenous influences.

About 30 miles (48 km) southwest of Santarém, **Belterra** is one
of the sites where Henry Ford
tried to establish his Amazonian
rubber plantations. The other,
several hours away by boat, is
appropriately named **Fordlândia.**
Offering a strangely out-of-place
vision of 1930s America in the
middle of the rain forest, both
places can be visited—though
tourism infrastructure is sparse.

Atlantic Amazon

Although not much talked about,
the long stretch of Brazilian
coast that runs from Amapá
to Maranhão marks the place
where the Amazon and Atlantic
meet. The mouths of the Rio
Amazonas (Amazon River) takes
up a large part of Pará's 350-mile
(562 km) coast, and the region is
a mishmash of islands, bays, coves,

channels, streams, and swamp-land. Indeed more than 62 miles (100 km) worth of swampland extend inland by an average of 12.5 miles (20 km). The organic material swept toward the sea by the river feeds fish and other aquatic life, which in turn attract birds—notably the scarlet ibis. Rumo Norte Expedições (see opposite) offers three-day guided kayaking excursions though parts of this region.

Algodoal is the name of the largest fishing village on an island officially called Ilha de Maiandeua, but hardly anybody uses the formal name. Everyone calls it Algodoal. By whatever name, the island remains mostly wilderness. Electricity was introduced only in 2005, and freshwater comes from wells drilled by residents. Bicycles, boats, and horse-drawn carriages provide transportation. There are no cars, and access is only by boat from Marudá, about 100 miles (160 km) northeast of Belém.

Residents of Belém and other larger cities are attracted by the beaches in places like **Salinópolis,** about 125 miles (200 km) north-east of the state capital. Just off the coast, **Ilha Itaranajá** serves as an island nesting area for herons, scarlet ibises, woodpeckers, jaca-mars, and garganey ducks.

Located about 130 miles (210 km) east of Belém, **Bragança** is one of the oldest cities in Pará. Outside of town you can find ruins of the **Belém-Bragança railway** that was completed in 1908 and operated until 1965. Sportfishing and scuba diving are also popular here. Evident

throughout the region, the scarlet ibis has a nesting area on **Ilha das Canelas,** off the coast of Bragança. Migrating birds also use it as a way station.

Urumajó is a protected area in the town of **Augusto Corrêa,** which is located about 140 miles (225 km) east of Belém. Besides its abundant vegetation and animal life, it serves as a nesting place for sea turtles. The entire coastal region, extending up to French Guiana and Suriname, also serves as an important habitat for the manatee. ■

Bragança

 245 E3

Visitor Information

✉ Prefeitura Bragança, Rua 09 de Setembrom

☎ 91/3425 3020

Augusto Corrêa

◢ 245 E3

Visitor Information

✉ Augusto Corrêa Prefeitura, Praça São Miguel 30

☎ 91/3482 1215

Using Games to Educate Local Communities

As its name suggests, the **Projeto Saúde e Alegria** (Health and Fun Project; *Av. Men-donça Furtado 3979, Liberdade, Santarém, tel 93/3067 8000, www.saudeealegria.org.br*) is a health program run by a Brazilian nonprofit group that also adds a playful element to its otherwise serious agenda.

Based in Santarém, the group has been visiting far-flung communities in western Pará by boat since 1987, bringing basic medical attention along with participa-tory games and activities—among them the Circo Mocorongo, which helps locals produce their own community circus.

The group offers an opportunity for travelers to accompany a three- to five-day excursion to villages up and down the Tapajós, Arapiuns, and Amazon Rivers. They are also opening up a small chain of com-munity guesthouses in some villages. The first of the batch, the **Pousada Encanto do Arapiuns** in the village of Atodi, opened its doors in 2012. This is not luxury; the first guests slept in hammocks, but the group's plan is to add six rooms with beds. And future guests will enjoy fully functioning community guesthouses.

North & West of the Amazon

In the far north of Brazil, Amapá state consists mostly of rain forest–covered plateaus, though the region also has a mountain range, a fairly unusual geological feature in the Amazon. While using the capital Macapá as a base, visitors will find that the region offers numerous outdoor activities—from jungle hikes to canoe river excursions.

The restored 18th-century fort is one of the main attractions in Macapá.

Macapá

 245 E3

Visitor Information

✉ Macapá Prefeitura, Av. Fab 840

☎ 96/8136 9325

Fortaleza de São José do Macapá

✉ Av. Cândido Mendes, Centro

☎ 96/3212 5118

Macapá & Around

Situated right on the Equator, Amapá state capital Macapá also sits astride Brazil's illustrious Rio Amazonas. Almost 1,350 miles (2,200 km) north of Brasília, Macapá cannot be reached overland from other parts of Brazil. The closest connection from a major town is via Belém (see pp. 258–260): about two hours by air or 24 hours by boat.

The city offers a handful of attractions, including the **Fortaleza de São José do Macapá,** a restored 18th-century fort. Twice a year during the equinox, crowds converge in celebration on the **Marco Zero do Equador** *(Rod. Juscelino Kubitschek km 2),* which marks the spot where the Equator runs through town. Inaugurated in 1945, the **Trapiche Eliezer Levy** *(Av. Beira-Rio),* a pier that extends 1,181 feet (360 m) into the Rio Amazonas, offers a nice view of the river. The nearby riverside strand concentrates most of Macapá's nighttime activity.

To learn more about the region's culture and history, head to the **Museu Sacaca** *(Av. Feliciano Coelho 1509),* a natural history and cultural museum focused on the region and its people. Also worth-while are the **Museu Histórico do Amapá Joaquim Caetano da Silva,** an archaeological museum, and the **Centro de Cultura Negra** *(Rua General Rondon, Laguinho),* which is dedicated to Afro-Brazilian culture and includes a theater and a museum. The **Casa do Artesão** exhibits and sells local crafts.

About 6 miles (10 km) north of Macapá, the town of **Curiaú** is surrounded by a nature reserve called the **Area de Proteção Ambiental Curiaú.** Among other things, the village includes a *quilombo,* a community of descendants of escaped slaves. This area is considered the birth-place of the state's emblematic

cultural traditions, Marabaixo and Batuque—two distinct styles of Afro-Brazilian music and dance.

About 13 miles (21 km) south-west of Macapá, Santana is home to **RPPN Revecom** *(Rua D28 422, Vila Amazonas, tel 96/3281 3849),* a private nature reserve that encompasses 42 acres (17 ha) of riverside rain forest. Take a walk to observe the local fauna and flora, including the harpy eagle, one of the world's largest eagles. An open-air museum includes reconstructions of a river dweller's hut, a rubber tapper's hut, and a *maloca* (indigenous dwelling).

Parque Nacional do Viruá

Located 93 miles (150 km) south of **Boa Vista,** Parque Nacional

Museu Histórico do Amapá Joaquim Caetano da Silva
- ✉ Rua Cândido Mendes Perpétuo Socorro
- ☎ 96/3212 5120

Casa do Artesão
- ✉ Rua Francisco Furtado Central
- ☎ 96/3223 5444

Parque Nacional do Viruá
- ▲ 245 C3
- ✉ By boat via Rivo Branco
- ☎ 95/3624 3712

Boa Vista
- ▲ 245 C4

EXPERIENCE: Surfing the Amazon

Every surfer's dream is to catch an endless wave. Though there is no such phenomenon in reality, the *pororoca* comes pretty close. Billed by one surf documentary as the "longest wave ever," the pororoca is a massive wave on the Rio Amazonas that offers one of the world's most unique surfing experiences. But beware: The pororoca is swift and dangerous and is best attempted by experienced surfers only.

In the native Tupi language, "poro-roca" translates as something like "the roaring." The phenomenon represents the sea's ability to briefly resist the surge of the river. When the ocean gets its shot, it comes with a vengeance. The force of the waves onshore can be brutal, knock-ing off slabs of the riverside and sending the shock reverberating back into diverse tributaries. Usually the force of the river current is sufficient to keep the sea at

bay. But when high tides combine with a full or new moon, conditions shift in favor of the ocean, which reverses the flow of the river, creating marathon waves.

Over land, the region where the poro-roca can be viewed—or surfed—is reached via an access road that leaves from the town of **Ferreira Gomes** *(visitor informa-tion, Prefeitura Ferreira Gomes, Av. Costa e Silva 158, tel 96/3326 1228),* 87 miles (140 km) north of Macapá. By water, the trip can take upward of 15 hours on the small riverboats customarily used for transportation in the region.

Pororoca season generally lasts from January to May and returns again during September. Waves reach heights upward of 16.5 feet (5 m), last about 40 minutes, and travel at a speed of 12 miles an hour (20 kph) or so. When surf's up, a wave appears once every 12 hours. **Rio Surf n Stay** *(www.riosurfnstay.com)* offers tours.

Caracaraí

◮ 245 C3

Visitor Information

✉ Prefeitura Caracaraí, Av. Dr. Zany 100

☎ 95/3532 1225

do Viruá was founded in 1998 to protect nearly 89,000 square miles (225,000 sq km) of habitat. Trails traverse a 10-square-mile (25 sq km) section, but much of the park has yet to be explored—even by rangers. Nevertheless, tourism officials are braced for an influx of visitors. With more than 500 identified bird species, the park is likely to become a bird-watcher's paradise. When the current identification effort began in 2001, only about 100 different species had been recorded in the area. But a team of ten ornithologists claims to have set a world record by identifying 225 bird species here in a single 24-hour period. Researchers have also catalogued more than 400 species of fish (including a few new ones),

more than 100 mammals, and dozens of reptiles and amphibians.

Though park access is relatively easy, lodging in the area is sparse. Within the park limits, there are two structures with accommodations for about 30 people. As of early 2013, only a select group of tour operators were allowed access to the park, so check before heading out.

The park's gateway town, **Caracaraí,** which has little history of receiving outside visitors, sports an indigenous reserve as well the Estação Ecológica de Caracaraí, which is open to authorized scientists. The **Corredeiras do Bem Querer** (BR-174 km 136, Caracaraí), a set of rapids on the Rio Branco, is popular with locals for canoeing and kayaking. ∎

EXPERIENCE: Visiting Indigenous Communities

Spend just one night in the jungle—your tired limbs tucked up in a gently swaying hammock—and the experience will more than make up for lack of conveniences. Having lived among the local indigenous people, having seen how they interact with their environment, and having joined them in celebration, you will come away with a better understanding and appreciation of the traditional way of life in the Amazon.

To visit an indigenous village is notoriously difficult in Brazil. Not only are many reservations located far from major centers, but Brazilian legislation creates legal barriers. It is almost impossible for an average traveler to obtain the required permission from FUNAI, Brazil's version of the Bureau of Indian Affairs. However, a few specialized tour operators work with indigenous communities and can navigate the process for you.

Based in Boa Vista, **Roraima Adventures** (Rua Coronel Pinto 86, Sala 106, Edificio Manoel Nabuco, Centro, Boa Vista, tel 95/3624 9611, email: adventures@roraima-brasil.com.br, www.roraima-brasil.com.br) provides access to a handful of different communities, including: an Ingarikó village in northern Roraima, a Maruwai community 87 miles (140 km) from Boa Vista, and a Yanomami community across the border in Venezuela. Excursions last between two and nine days, depending on the distance covered and difficulty of access. The nine-day Yanomami expedition must be booked at least two months in advance.

These excursions are for travelers who want to experience the jungle intimately, including all the discomfort you can handle. Come prepared with sunscreen and insect repellent, swimming clothes, a hat, a flashlight, and durable hiking shoes.

South & East of the Amazon

Off the beaten tourist path, this region rich in natural attractions was also home to noted rain forest activist Chico Mendes.

A local fisherman demonstrates cast-net fishing on the Río Purus near Acre.

Acre

Set in the extreme western end of the Brazilian Amazon, the state of Acre is perhaps best known as the home of Chico Mendes (see sidebar p. 269), the rain forest activist assassinated in 1988, and his protégé, Marina Silva, who went on to become a senator, minister of the environment, and presidential candidate. The state's connections to the rest of the country are primarily by air and river. Only one highway, BR-364, provides a link by land, running into the central western region.

Rio Branco: Founded in 1882 by rubber tappers, pleasant state capital Rio Branco sits 310 miles (500 km) east of Porto Velho, capital of the neighboring state of Rondônia (see p. 270). Running along the bank of the Rio Acre, the river that runs through town, **Rua da Gameleira** (which means "strangler fig road") marks the spot where the original community was founded. The fig tree remains rooted there, now measuring 65 feet (20 m) in height and 8 feet (2.5 m) in diameter. Bars, restaurants, and cultural centers have commandeered the street's old houses, making this the place to be at night.

During the day, head for **Parque da Maternidade,** Rio Branco's "central park," which offers recreational areas as well

Rio Branco
🅰 244 B1
Visitor Information
✉ Centro de Atendimento ao Turista, Praça Povos da Floresta
☎ 68/3223 3998

as several cultural institutions including **Casa dos Povos da Floresta** *(Via Parque Setor B, Aviário, tel 68/3227 6584)*. Built in the style of an indigenous *maloca*, Casa dos Povos features crafts and other articles from local Indian tribes and non-native peoples. **Biblioteca da Floresta** is a library that also serves as a natural history, archaeological, and anthropological museum dedicated to the Amazon. It includes a section dedicated to the memory of Chico Mendes. More local crafts are on display at **Casa do Artesão** *(Rua Coronel João Donato, Parque da Maternidade, tel 68/3223 0010)*.

A few blocks from the park you'll find the **Museu da Borracha Governador Geraldo Mesquita** *(Av. Ceará 41, Cadeia Velha)*. The name might translate literally as "rubber museum," but this eclectic collection also includes much more. You'll find displays of prehistoric fossils, indigenous artifacts, and other archaeological objects, as well as items related to the rubber-boom colonizers. Walk along a few blocks more to the **Memorial dos Autonomistas** *(Praça Eurico Dutra, tel 68/3224 2133)*, a museum for the political heroes of Acre's "autonomy." Here you will find the remains of Senator Guiomar Santos, a leader of the statehood movement, and his wife.

In Rio Branco's old town, the **Fundação de Cultura Elias Mansur e Galeria de Arte Juvenal** *(Rua Eduardo Assmar 1291, Centro Histórico, tel 68/3223 9688)* displays temporary exhibitions of work by local artists and others from around Brazil.

Dating from the 1920s, the **Novo Mercado Velho** *(Av. Epaminondas Jacome)*, a renovated old market building on the left bank of the Rio Acre, serves as a crafts market and also has food stalls, vendors of medicinal plants, and more. It is a nice place for a beer at the end of the afternoon.

Workers have been harvesting latex from rubber trees in the Amazon for more than a century.

Rubber Tappers Movement

The modern history of Acre began in 1882, when Brazilian rubber tappers founded the town of Seringal Empresa (later established as the capital and renamed Rio Branco). They were followed in the late 19th and early 20th centuries by migrants eager to capitalize on the rubber boom. At the time, this region was part of Bolivia, but beginning in 1893, Brazilians engineered a series of armed revolts against Bolivian rule. A 1903 treaty gave Brazil control of the territory in exchange for cash and the promise to build a railway that would allow the Bolivians to access the river transportation network through the Amazon.

The rubber boom ended in the early 20th century due to competition from Asia. During World War II, the United States and Brazil wanted to boost rubber production, and a new wave of immigrants from Brazil's Northeast converged on Acre, which won statehood in 1962.

In the 1970s the Brazilian government encouraged logging, cattle ranching, and other large-scale endeavors in the Amazon that threatened local livelihood. In Acre small-scale rubber tappers, led by activist Chico Mendes, fought back. Using a tactic called *empate*, they physically occupied areas targeted for deforestation. In 1988 Mendes was gunned down by local landowners, but his protégé, Marina Silva, went on to become a senator, environmental minister, and presidential candidate.

Eventually, the rubber tappers movement was instrumental in convincing state authorities in Acre, and later the federal government, to create "extractive reserves," protected areas from which products can be taken only in a sustainable manner. Andrew Revkin's nonfiction account, *The Burning Season: The Murder of Chico Mendes and the Fight for the Amazon Rain Forest*, is essential reading.

Located on the way to the airport, the **Usina de Arte João Donato** (Av. das Acacias 1, Distrito Industrial, tel 68/3229 6892) is an art school named after the bossa nova legend who was born in Rio Branco. A former chestnut processing facility, it also hosts exhibitions and performances.

Beyond the City: Tourism officials and private tour operators have developed a circuit called the **Caminhos de Chico Mendes** (Chico Mendes Trails) that follows in the footsteps of the deceased rain forest activist. Located 118 miles (190 km) southwest of Rio Branco, the first stop in the circuit is **Xapuri,** a town of 14,000 and Mendes's hometown.

The activist's house—which is also the place where he was killed—has been declared a national monument. Like many others in the region, **Casa Chico Mendes** (Rua Batista de Moraes 10, Setor 1, Distrito 1, Lote 290, Centro) is a simple wooden structure. Today it operates as a museum, displaying articles related to the leader's life.

A little way out of town, the **Assentamento Agroextrativista Chico Mendes** (Ramal Cachoeira km 15, take BR-317 toward Rio Branco, turn left at km 143 and go 10.5 miles/17 km, tel 68/3901 3023) marks the area that served as the stage for the most dramatic episodes of the anti-deforestation movement led by Mendes. It is now an "extractive reserve," where

Xapuri

🅰 244 B1

Visitor Information

✉ Prefeitura Xapuri, Coronel Brandão 156

☎ 68/3542 2272

Porto Velho

⚞ 245 C2

Visitor Information

✉ Centro de
Atendimento
ao Turista,
Aeroporto
Internacional
Jorge Teixeira,
Av. Jorge
Teixeira s/n,
Nova Esperança

☎ 69/3219 7450

only traditional economic activities are allowed. For more information about the Chico Mendes Trails, contact Morais'Tur *(Rua Marechal Deodoro 825, Centro Histórico, Rio Branco, tel 68 3223 6161)*.

Unrelated to Chico Mendes, but also in Xapuri, the **Museu da Casa Branca** *(Rua 17 de Novembro 287, Centro)*, situated in a structure dating from 1910, once served as the seat of Bolivian authority in the region and is an important landmark to the Brazilian victory. The museum features artifacts from the period.

INSIDER TIP:

To see wolves, oases, and Sahara-size sand dunes in the Amazon Basin, visit Jalapão. Owls live in the ground in tiny burrows, and flocks of emu-like rhea will race your jeep.

—ROBERT WALKER
Professor of Geography & Scholar of Amazonian Environmental Change, Michigan State University

A large part of the state's primary forest remains intact. Occupying the remote far northwestern edge of the state, **Parque Nacional da Serra do Divisor** *(373 miles/600 km from Rio Branco via BR-364, a dirt road; admin. headquarters: Rua Jamináuas Cruzeirão, Cruzeiro do Sul, tel 68/3322 7851 or 3322 1203)*, founded in 1989,

unites the biodiversity of the Amazon and the Andes. State and federal officials have periodically stated their intentions to open the park to visitors, but as of early 2013 it remained closed.

Acre is also known for its centuries-old geoglyphs, large-scale patterns, geometrically shaped or representing figures, that can be seen from the air. If you do any flying in the area, look for them on the way to Porto Velho (see below).

Rondônia

In the middle of the South American continent, Rondônia state is off the beaten path. Sharing a border with Bolivia to the southwest, Rondônia probably represents one of the least attractive regions of Brazil for a leisure traveler. Although set wholly inside the Amazon region, you see very little forest when you crisscross the state. The ravages of deforestation are so extensive that they can be identified in satellite photographs.

The emblematic symbols of its capital city, **Porto Velho,** are the **Três Caixas d'Água** *(bet. Av. Carlos Gomes & Rua Euclides da Cunha)*, three prefabricated water towers imported from the United States to provide water for railway workers. The building that once housed the headquarters of the railway is an architectural curiosity. Inaugurated around 1950, it was designed to resemble a locomotive. The building is known by locals as the **Prédio do Relógio** (Clock Building; *Av. Sete de Setembro 237)* for the timepiece that tops it.

The **Ponte de Jaci-Paraná** in the town of Jaci-Paraná, 50 miles (80 km) southwest of Porto Velho, is an iron railway bridge made from materials imported from the United States.

Northern Mato Grosso

The Amazon extends southward into the northern part of Mato Grosso state. This biologically rich region is popular with bird-watchers, wildlife spotters, and sportfishermen.

The 50,000-person city of **Alta Floresta**, about 500 miles (800 km) north of Cuiabá, is the gateway to **Cristalino Jungle Lodge** (see Travelwise p. 305), located in the middle of a private nature reserve that covers nearly 30,000 acres (12,141 ha), twice the size of the island of Manhattan. The reserve offers the only way for visitors to explore the region at length. It is crossed by about 22 miles (35 km) of trails, including several easy ones that are popular with birders. More strenuous hikes, canoeing, swimming, butterfly observation walks, and boat trips (including one to the nesting area of a legendary "prehistoric" bird called the hoatzin), overnight forest hikes, and jungle survival lessons complete the menu of excursions. A tree house provides cover to help you observe mammals below, while a canopy tower serves as a vista point for sunsets and sunrises, and for spotting topside dwellers like monkeys and toucans.

About 30 miles (50 km) northwest of Alta Floresta, the small town of **Paranaíta** is home

---

Madeira-Mamoré Railway

Rondônia is perhaps best known as the starting point for disastrous efforts to build the Madeira-Mamoré Railway in the late 19th and early 20th centuries. Intended to give landlocked Bolivia a way to export its rubber via the Atlantic, the railroad was plagued with disasters as laborers were harassed by tropical diseases and indigenous tribes. A 224-mile (360 km) stretch between Porto Velho and Guajará-Mirim was completed in 1912 and operated until 1972. Five miles (8 km) near Porto Velho have been listed as a national heritage site. The **Museu da Estrada de Ferro Madeira-Mamoré** *(Av. Sete de Setembro & Av. Farquar, next to Praça Madeira-Mamoré, Rondônia, tel 69/3901 3651)* displays period railway artifacts.

---

to **Pedra Preta,** an archaeological site covering an area of several acres with large-scale, prehistoric carvings of animal figures and symbols. The municipality is reportedly studying how to better structure visitation to the site.

The river that runs through town, the Rio Teles Pires, abounds in fish species, making Paranaíta and neighboring Alta Floresta popular destinations for sportfishing. However, the impressive **Cachoeira Sete Quedas** waterfall threatens to be swallowed up by the Teles Pires hydroelectric dam. The dam has been the subject of legal challenges by local indigenous populations who claim that the project impinges on sacred lands. Water enthusiasts shouldn't miss **Lagoa Azul,** a lake surrounded by jungle, or the **Andradas,** river rapids sought out for rafting and canoe trips.

Alta Floresta
- 245 D2

Visitor Information
- Prefeitura Alta Floresta, Av. Ariosto da Riva 3391
- 66/3903 1000

Paranaíta
- 245 D2

Visitor Information
- Prefeitura Paranaíta, Via L 12
- 66/3563 1166

Parque Estadual do Jalapão

🏔 245 E1

✉ TO-255 km 14, Mateiros

☎ 63/3534 1072

Tocantins

Tocantins state is located in a transition region where the Amazon rain forest meets the savanna-like Cerrado. Another of Brazil's one-of-a-kind places, Tocantins features a mix of waterfalls, rivers, lakes, and sand dunes. You can even take a multiday white-water rafting trip through this distinctive landscape.

Jalapão: With the closest gateway city, Ponte Alta do Tocantins, about 125 miles (200 km) southeast of state capital Palmas, Jalapão sits barely but firmly over the edge on the Cerrado side. It is popular with nature and adventure lovers because of its abundant waterfalls, rivers, lakes, and sand dunes.

Jalapão is not a town or place but a region that extends beyond **Parque Estadual do Jalapão**, a state park that alone is larger than nine U.S. states. The area is largely uninhabited: The four anchor towns of Mateiros, Ponte Alta do Tocantins, Novo Acordo, and São Félix have a combined population of less than 15,000.

The dunes lend parts of the region a desert-like quality. Some press reports have actually referred to it as such, and you can take an excursion through the dunes that will give you that desert feel. But if you take to the water, you will see that on one side there might indeed be dunes but on the other extensive, if not lush, vegetation. The region boasts several impressive waterfalls, notably **Cachoeira da Velha,** true to its nickname "little Iguaçu Falls." Another unique attraction is the **Fervedouro,** a pool surrounding a spring. The force of the water from below makes it impossible for swimmers to sink.

Word about Jalapão's natural attractions has spread more quickly than infrastructure for visitors can be built. Don't expect luxury accommodations, or anything near it. You may even have to camp. But fame does not mean that the place is overrun. Not even the Tocantins state capital, Palmas, is on the way to anywhere, so there are plenty of logistical barriers. Because of the scanty infrastructure, most people visit Jalapão as part of a package. There are several good operators that organize circuits around the region or offer specific activities like multiday white-water rafting excursions. (For information on outfitters, see Travelwise p. 312.)

Unique Farm Stay

Near Lagoa da Confusão, 125 miles (200 km) southwest of Palmas, **Fazenda Praia Alta** (see Travelwise p. 307) is a working farm that has reserved an area for ecotourism. Open to individuals as well as families, the farm's hostel-style accommodations feature clean bathrooms, large, comfortable beds, and air-conditioning. Regular organized activities include bird-watching and wildlife-spotting excursions, nature hikes past backwater lakes, horseback riding, visits to Ilha do Bananal and nearby indigenous villages, and sportfishing. A typical farm stay lasts three days and two nights. Pousada Fazenda Praia Alta also runs Projeto Quelônio, an Amazon turtle conservation project.

Ilha do Bananal & Western Tocantins: Measured at 4.9 million acres (2 million ha), Ilha do Bananal holds two federal reserves: **Parque Indígena do Araguaia,** an Indian reservation, and **Parque Nacional do Araguaia** *(Santa Terezinha, Mato Grosso, tel 63/3219 8437),* a national park that covers roughly one-quarter of the northeastern part of the island.

Nudged up against the northeasternmost edge of Mato Grosso state, Ilha do Bananal joins vegetation of three different eco-regions: the Amazon rain forest, the savanna-like Cerrado, and the Pantanal wetlands. Animals here include the endangered marsh deer. To explore the region, base yourself in Lagoa da Confusão (37 miles/60 km E of the park), Pium (80 miles/130 km E) or Paraíso do Tocantins (127 miles/205 km E).

The town of **Santa Terezinha** sits just on the other side of the **Rio Araguaia,** the river that marks the state border. Visitation is allowed, but you need to request permission beforehand from park rangers. Once inside you can hike trails or take canoe trips along streams.

Just north of Ilha do Bananal, **Parque Estadual do Cantão** *(tel 63/3379 1438)* is a state park that officials want to promote as a tourist destination. Like its island neighbor, the park mixes aspects of the Amazon and the Cerrado. The region is home to dozens of mammals, more than 300 species of birds, and sundry reptiles, amphibians, and fish. It is also a

Crafts woven from the local *capim dourado* (golden grass) are popular in Jalapão, Tocantins.

breeding area for the man-size pirarucu and bass. The town of **Caseara** makes a good base for exploring the park and the surrounding region.

Fishing is prohibited within park limits, but **Rio Araguaia** and the almost parallel **Rio Formoso** are considered prime destinations for sportfishermen, especially those after the prized peacock bass (see sidebar p. 256). The rivers' beaches are especially popular during the low-water season *(June–Sept.).*

Lagoa da Confusão *(TO-230),* the lake that gives the nearby town its name, is more than 2.5 miles (4 km) in diameter, with a surface that looks like a mirror. A large rock sits in the middle and appears to change position, depending on the angle from which it is viewed. Named for the abundance of birds that frequent its shores, neighboring **Lagoa dos Pássaros** (Lake of the Birds) is also home to caimans, capybaras, and other animals. ■

Santa Terezinha
🄼 245 E1
Visitor Information
✉ Prefeitura Santa Terezinha, Rua 25, Centro
☎ 66/3558 1119

Caseara
🄼 245 E2
Visitor Information
✉ Prefeitura Municipal de Caseara, Av. Trajano Almeida 264, S Central
☎ 63/3379 1376

Lagoa da Confusão
🄼 245 E1
Visitor Information
✉ Prefeitura Lagoa da Confusão, Av. Vitorino Panta Q Área, S Central
☎ 63/3364 1228

TRAVELWISE

Estação da Luz, a train station in the Luz neighborhood of São Paulo

PLANNING YOUR TRIP

When to Go

Before deciding when to go, consider what you want to do. Brazil offers myriad cultural and historical attractions that can, for the most part, be visited any time of the year. The tropical climate in most of the country makes outdoor activities possible year-round. However, visitors to the Amazon rain forest and the Pantanal wetlands should pay attention to the seasonal shifts, as rainfall and flooding will affect what's possible to do and to see.

The pre-Lenten Carnaval festivities in many cities rank as world-class parties. The most famous take place in Rio de Janeiro, Salvador, and Olinda, but you can find a party anywhere in Brazil during this period. Check the festival calendars for other notable times including: the Northeast's São João festivals in June; the Amazon's Festival Folclórico de Parintins, in late June; Bumba Meu Boi festival in São Luís.

Roads, airports, and resorts tend to get congested during holidays and school vacation periods.

Climate

About 90 percent of Brazilian territory falls within the tropics, so—aside from blazing summers in some places—it is welcoming year-round most everywhere. Only the southern part of the country experiences cold that requires winter coats, and even then extremes are rare. Yet Brazil is a big country, and weather conditions vary.

It goes without saying that the seasons are flip-flopped in the Southern Hemisphere in relation to the Northern, but—instead of hot versus cold—much of the country alternates between rainy and dry periods. In many places, rainy-season tropical storms last just a few hours, generally vacating the premises in favor of sunshine. However, in the Amazon and the Pantanal, greater care is required.

What to Take

Except your passport, and your visa if you need one, don't sweat it. If you forget anything else, you can buy it in Brazil. People's biggest mistake is to forget a jacket. Although a tropical country, it can get chilly in the south.

Insurance
Make sure that you have adequate insurance to cover medical treatment and expenses.

Passports & Visas
See sidebar p. 10.

HOW TO GET TO BRAZIL
Airlines and Airports
Two-thirds of international passengers arrive in São Paulo. Rio de Janeiro ranks second.

São Paulo International Airport (GRU), commonly referred to as Guarulhos or Cumbica, is located about 19 miles (30 km) northeast of São Paulo. Taxi fares are prepaid at a kiosk outside the arrivals area: around US$50, depending on the destination. A shuttle service runs between the airport and six points in São Paulo, including the domestic airport. For most destinations, the fare is BRL 35 (US$18, *www.airportbusser vice.com.br*). Tickets for the shuttle can be purchased outside arrivals. Travel time averages an hour. If you have connecting domestic flights from São Paulo, they might leave from Congonhas (CGH) or even Viracopos in the city of Campinas, 37 miles (60 km) away. Most of Viracopos's flights are operated by Azul, a domestic carrier that operates a shuttle bus from Congonhas.

Rio de Janeiro International Airport (GIG), still commonly called Galeão, is about 9 miles (15 km) from Rio. Real Auto Ônibus runs shuttles into town for BRL 12 (US$6). Taxis cost between BRL 45–80 (US$23–41) depending

on the destination. The time to the beach area is about 45 minutes. The domestic airport Santos-Dumont (SDU) is located in Centro.

About three dozen companies operate international flights to Brazil including:

Air Canada—www.aircanada.com
Air France—www.airfrance.com
American—www.aa.com
Avianca—www.avianca.com.br
Azul—www.voeazul.com.br
Copa Airlines—www.copaair.com
Delta Airlines—www.delta.com
Gol—www.voegol.com.br
KLM—www.klm.com
Lufthansa—www.lufthansa.com
TAM—www.tam.com.br
United—www.united.com

By Bus
Several bus companies offer service from Chile, Argentina, and Uruguay to Brazil, but given the distances they can take more than two days.

GETTING AROUND
By Air & Bus
Three major carriers fly to the country's main airports: Azul, Gol, and TAM. Colombia's Avianca flies to about two dozen places. Smaller domestic carriers, Pantanal (*www.voepantanal.com.br*) and Passaredo (*www.voepassaredo .com.br*) serve 15–20 destinations each. Until recently, you could not purchase tickets online with any of these companies without a Brazilian tax number, called a CPF. This is changing, but it might be easier to use a travel agent.

Itapemirim (*www.itapemirim .com.br*) offers Brazil's most extensive bus network, covering more than two-thirds of the country. Another, Cometa (*www.viacaocometa.com .br*), offers good service in the South Central states of Minas Gerais, Rio de Janeiro, and São Paulo, along with runs south to Florianópolis

and Curitiba. A plethora of smaller companies can be found for regional travel. For the bus companies, you must go physically to the station to buy your tickets.

By Subways, Commuter Trains, & City Buses
The cities with subways or metropolitan rail systems are São Paulo, Rio de Janeiro, Brasília, Recife, Porto Alegre, and Belo Horizonte. Many cities also have suburban commuter trains. Even though most lines are designed for commuters, they can be useful for visitors, but don't expect them to go to all the major tourist sites. For more on the São Paulo subway, see page pp. 104–105.

Some cities have dedicated surface bus lines with subway-style stations. In some places the suburban commuter trains are not recommended for foreign visitors unless you speak fluent Portuguese.

By Taxis & Chauffeurs
Cabs can be the best option for many tourists. However, English-speaking drivers are rare, and few speak Spanish. An option is to hire an English-speaking guide and have him/her handle the cab arrangements.

Taxis are regulated by municipal codes so fares and customs change from place to place. Generally the best place to catch cabs is at a taxi stand. In most cities, there is a surcharge called *Bandeira 2* for night, weekend, and holiday runs.

Fares in Rio de Janeiro: For Common Cabs—with a Portuguese-speaking driver—the meter starts at BRL 4.70 (US$2.40) and adds BRL 1.70 (US$0.87) per km. The fee for waiting (*tempo parado*) is BRL 20.42 (US$10.60) per hour. Higher fares (roughly 20 percent more) apply between 9 p.m. and 6 a.m. on Sundays and holidays.

Special Taxis—The prices for special taxis are roughly 80 percent higher than those for common cabs. **Rádio-Táxi Coopertramo** (www.radio-taxi.com.br) is a cooperative that has English content on its website and offers bilingual drivers.

Chauffeur Services—These services are usually available through the concierge at five-star hotels. In Rio, prices start at about BRL 80 (US$41) per hour.

Driving in Brazil

Chaotic driving and congested streets can upset visitors, so generally driving is not recommended. However, all you need to drive in Brazil is your license and passport. You will need to have your license translated by an official translator (tradutor juramentado), or get an international license, which can be obtained from AAA (www.aaa.com).

It goes without saying: Do not drive under the influence of alcohol or other controlled substances. A campaign against drunk driving is enforced partially by frequent, unannounced roadblocks.

Renting a Car

Airports are the best places to rent cars. Many international companies operate in Brazil, including Alamo, Avis, Budget, Hertz, and Thrifty and domestic firms, such as Localiza and Unidas. A credit card with an overall limit greater than the total cost of the rental is required. Rentals in Brazil are expensive, around US$200 a day for a budget car.

PRACTICAL ADVICE
Accessible Travel

Although Brazil has made efforts to improve, it is not particularly advanced in terms of accessibility. In many places people with disabilities and mobility problems face some barriers. On the plus side, the city of Socorro

(www.socorro.tur.br) in São Paulo state is a world leader in terms of accessible adventure tourism.

Communications
Internet: Many bars and cafés offer complimentary Wi-Fi. A Brazilian franchise operation called Fran's Café has nationwide penetration and generally offers Wi-Fi. So do many McDonald's.

Phones: Making phone calls in Brazil can be confusing. Here is a rundown of what to do by type of call:

Local calls: To a number within same area code—dial only the eight digit phone number.

Long distance: Domestic long distance—dial 0 + operator code + area code + phone number.

Operator codes—Brasil Telecom 14, Claro 36, Embratel 21, Intelig Telecom 23, Sercomtel 43, Telefónica 15, Telemar 31, Claro 36, and TIM 41.

International calls—dial 00 + operator code + country code + area code + phone number. When calling Brazil, the country code is 55.

Area codes—To find an area code (called DDD in Brazil), check www.embratel.com.br. (Although the website is in Portuguese, the tool is intuitive.)

Collect calls: For local collect calls, dial 9090 + phone number. For long distance collect calls, dial 90 + operator code + area code + phone number.

Exception: Whenever you call a mobile phone in São Paulo (area code 11), you need to add a 9 before the phone number. If calling from outside São Paulo, you insert the number 9 between the area code and the phone number.

Mobile Phones: You can purchase prepaid SIM cards at any of the kiosks—including the TIM kiosk on the first floor of

Terminal 1 at the Rio airport—and shops of Brazilian phone companies around the country. Minutes can be added at newsstands or kiosks. A SIM card usually costs about BRL 15 (US$7). A recharge ranges from BRL 13–100.

Using a Brazilian phone line for sending texts or calling internationally tends to be expensive, but your carrier might offer vacation packages that cover Brazil. SMS messages sent within Brazil cost BRL 0.50 (US$0.25) apiece and BRL 9 (US$4.62) for overseas.

Public Phones: Most public telephones (orelhão or big ear) have all but disappeared. To use a working one, purchase a phone card from a newsstand.

Post Offices: Post offices can be found all over, but opening hours vary. Detailed information about the locations of post offices and their services can be found in English on the official website: www.correios.com.br. Although there are yellow plastic mailboxes on many streets, it might be best to just drop your letter off at the post office.

Conversions
1 kilo = 2.2 pounds
1 liter = 0.26 U.S. gallons
1 mile = 1.6 kilometers

Corruption
Stories of traffic police are legendary. They often stop motorists without cause, and if they look hard enough they can usually find some minor infraction. These things are difficult for foreigners to navigate, so if you are traveling with Brazilians, let them take the lead. If not, phone a Brazilian friend or contact, such as a tour operator, for orientation. Do make sure that all of your travel documents, including your driver's license, are in order, and

double-check required safety gear, such as the mini-fire extinguisher. Do not assume that "this is Latin America and I can just bribe my way out of anything."

Etiquette & Local Customs

The biggest problem visitors have is with personal greetings. The rules can vary from region to region, but generally: women greeting women or men—two kisses on alternate cheeks; and men greeting men, a handshake and/or quick hug with maybe a pat on the back.

Punctuality can also be a major issue. In most cases, if you show up on time you are early. However, for a business meeting, you should be there on time because the Brazilians might show up "early" (on time) if they are meeting with a foreigner. For parties, show up at least an hour late.

Events and Festivals

See sidebar p. 52.

GLBT

Compared to most places, Brazil is relatively tolerant. São Paulo hosts what might be the world's biggest gay pride parade. (The dates vary from year to year, but it is usually in early June.) However, hate crimes are not unheard of. There has also been a rise of fundamentalist Christian sentiment in the country. Based in Salvador, the Grupo Gay da Bahia claims to be the country's oldest organization dedicated to combating homophobia.

Health

Generally no special precautions are necessary—except some extra sunscreen. If you plan to spend time in the Amazon rain forest, a yellow fever shot is recommended. Some also take antimalarials when they visit the Amazon. Elsewhere anti-malaria pills are unnecessary.

Unless off the beaten path, tap water is safe to drink. Sanitary conditions in restaurants in major Brazilian cities are as good as anywhere else in the world. In São Paulo, a municipal law requires eateries to allow patrons to visit their kitchens upon request.

You should check to make sure that you have adequate medical coverage before arriving in Brazil. Expatriate groups in some cities, such as the American Society of São Paulo (www.americansociety .com.br) maintain lists of English-speaking physicians.

Liquor, Drugs, & Smoking

The drinking age is 18. Other than that, and the obvious ban on drunk driving, there are few restrictions on alcohol use. Federal legislation prohibits smoking in closed public spaces. Marijuana and other drugs are available, but most such substances are illegal.

Media

Aside from the monthly *Time Out São Paulo,* there is no widespread English-language media in Brazil. Cable television packages available in upscale hotels usually include a number of international channels with foreign programming in several languages.

A few interesting English blogs for general information about Brazil include:

Foreign correspondent Andrew Downie: www.andrewdownie .wordpress.com

Deep Brazil by Brazilian journalist Regina Scharf: www.deepbrazil .com

Time Out Saõ Paulo and Time Out Rio de Janeiro: www .timeout.com

For Rio de Janeiro, RioReal by former foreign correspondent Julia Michaels: www.riorealblog.com.

Money Matters

See sidebar p. 11.

Opening Hours

Banks are generally open from 10 a.m. to 4 p.m.; shopping malls from 10 a.m. to 10 p.m.; and business offices from 9 a.m. to 6 p.m. Some restaurants close between lunch and dinner. Attractions like museums often close on Monday, so check your local listings.

Pets

To bring a dog or cat into Brazil, consult your veterinarian to obtain a vaccination certificate and an animal health certificate. You must then take those to your government's health office (in the United States, that would be the USDA) to obtain an international health certificate. You take that document to the nearest Brazilian consulate to have it "authenticated." The international health certificate is valid for entry for ten days after it is issued.

Places of Worship

Brazil is religious. Well-known as one of the world's largest Catholic countries, it is also home to other faiths. The best sources for information are the churches' respective offices. For the Afro-Brazilian Candomblé faith, the best contact is in Salvador. For the positivist religion, it is in Rio de Janeiro.

Restrooms

Public restrooms are virtually nonexistent in Brazil. Usually you can enter a bar or *boteco* to use the restroom. To be nice, you might want to buy a drink or something to compensate them for the trouble, but generally they will not mind, if you ask first. The only exception would be bars near open-air fairs, frequented by large numbers of people. Beware: Some restrooms can be a little icky.

Security

Security usually tops the list of concerns for foreign travelers to Brazil, especially first-timers. The generic advice for cities like Rio de Janeiro and São Paulo is to take the same precautions that you would in any crime-prone major city in the world. However, given the level of concern, this issue deserves more detailed attention.

Jim Wygand, an American security expert who has lived in Brazil for more than 40 years, has written *The Secure Urbanite: Personal Security in the Asphalt & Concrete Jungle*, a book on personal security in urban environments. He notes, "The greatest threat to individuals is from the drug users who routinely approach cars stuck in Brazil's horrendous traffic jams or pedestrians caught unawares on the street." Basically, be aware of your surroundings, and don't act like a tourist.

Pay careful attention when using an ATM. Try to use them only during the day and in relatively well-secure areas, when there are other people nearby, in bank branch offices, inside supermarkets, or shopping malls.

Time Zones

The country has three time zones, but most places are in sync with the capital, Brasília, with a standard time that is three hours behind Greenwich Mean Time (one hour earlier than New York City). Daylight Savings Time runs from mid-October until mid-February. In general, the states of the South and South-Central switch, and those of the Northeast and North do not.

Tipping

In restaurants and bars, a 10 percent gratuity is generally included in the bill. For small-scale services, a good rule of thumb is to tip the price of a normal beer, say, BRL 7 (US$3.60).

Tourist Information Abroad

For information about travel to Brazil, contact the nearest Brazilian consulate or embassy or visit: www.visitbrasil.com.

Lost Property

A police report is called a Boletim de Ocorrência (B.O.). To file one, you need to visit the nearest police station, called a Delegacia de Polícia.

Voltage & Electrical Outlets

Depending on the city, the electrical current in Brazil is 110 or 220 volts, or both. Because of the number of different types of outlets, an adaptor is advisable. Do check before plugging in.

Women

Many women express concerns about traveling in Brazil alone. The country is certainly not devoid of sexism, but neither is it a place where women are likely to be unduly harassed, though attacks are reported. Many states and cities have special police stations for women, staffed by female officers. They generally go by the name of Delegacia da Mulher.

EMERGENCIES

102 Operator Tel
190 Police Tel
192 Ambulance Tel

However, do not expect the operator to speak English at these emergency phone numbers. Many places have established special police stations to attend to the needs of visitors; they go by the name of Delegacia do Turista.

Embassies & Consulates

United States
brazil.usembassy.gov
Brasília: Embassy, SES—Av. das Nações, Quadra 801, Lote 03; tel 61/3312 7000
Rio de Janeiro: Consulate General, Av. Presidente Wilson 147, Castelo; tel 21/3823 2000
São Paulo: Consulate General, Rua Henri Dunant 500, Chácara Santo Antônio; tel 11/5186 5000
Recife: Consulate, Rua Gonçalves Maia 163, Boa Vista; tel 81/3461 3050

United Kingdom
ukinbrazil.fco.gov.uk
Rio de Janeiro: Consulate General, Praia do Flamengo 284, 2 andar; tel 21/2555 9600
São Paulo: Consulate General, Rua Ferreira de Araujo 741, Pinheiros; tel 11/3094 2700

Australia
www.brazil.embassy.gov.au
Brasília: Embassy, SES—Av. das Nações, Quadra K, Lote 07; tel 61/3226 3111
São Paulo: Consulate General, Alameda Santos 700, 9th fl., Cj. 92, Jardim Paulista; tel 11/2112 6200

What to Do in a Car Accident

If there are no serious injuries, traffic officials should be called to the site to fill out a report (*ocorrência*). Register a report that reflects your point of view about what happened. If there are serious injuries or fatalities, the Polícia Militar (Military Police) must be called. Make sure that they get down your version. Try to obtain the contact information of any witnesses.

Hotels & Restaurants

Lodging in Brazil is less inspiring than the surrounding landscape. Brazil's hotels tend to be over-priced and underwhelming even at the four-star level, but a new crop of small boutique hotels and guesthouses predict a bright future. Meanwhile the restaurants are both traditional and innovative. The local specialties tend to reflect the regional diversity of the residents from the indigenous peoples to the immigrants of Europe, Africa, and Asia.

HOTELS

Things are slowly improving, and in cities like Olinda, Rio de Janeiro, Salvador, and São Paulo you can find quality lodgings with character. There are also interesting properties scattered around the country, including wonderful world-class guesthouses. Do not assume, however, that everyone will speak English.

Beyond the listings below and the usual array of international websites, there are two Brazilian resources that are useful. Roteiros de Charme (www.roteirosdecharme .com.br) is a self-policing association of distinctive properties. As of 2013, it included 59 members in 16 states, covering 51 destinations. Also useful is a website called Hidden Pousadas (www.hiddenpousadasbrazil.com), an English-language lodging website run by a group of gringos.

Many Brazilian lodging establishments go by the name pousada. Literally meaning "landing place" in Portuguese, the term refers to operations that are smaller than hotels. The range of quality, comfort, and pricing is enormous.

Brazil launched a new government-run star classification system in September 2012. After six months, only 33 of the country's 6,000-plus registered lodging establishments had signed up for the program. The bottom line: Do not consider star rankings when choosing a hotel or guesthouse.

RESTAURANTS

A boteco, or botequim, is a down-home neighborhood bar. Invariably botecos serve food in addition to drink. Popular throughout the country, they can come in both upscale and down-scale versions and are generally a neighborhood hangout, especially for men.

For a quick, easy, and relatively cheap lunch, try one of the many by-the-weight per "kilo" buffet restaurants. Fill your plate and weigh it at the end of the line. Ubiquitous at lunchtime and catering to employees of nearby businesses, they rarely stay open for dinner.

In general, restaurants automatically add a 10 percent service charge to the bill. This is supposed to be given to waiters, and that rule is generally—though not always—followed. The 10 percent surcharge should appear as a separate line item on your bill; if included, no additional tip is needed.

Brazil is adopting the portable credit card machines that allow waiters to swipe your card at your table. However, many establishments still use the old system, meaning that waiters must take your card back to the register. Although hardly at epidemic proportions, it is not uncommon for unscrupulous employees to record data for the later cloning of cards. Do keep an eye on your online statements.

Entries here are organized by chapters, states, alphabetically by neighborhoods or cities, and then by price ranges.

Abbreviations used are: AE (American Express), DC (Diners Club), MC (MasterCard), and V (Visa).

PRICES

HOTELS

An indication of the cost of a double room in the high season is given by **$** signs.

$$$$$	Over $400
$$$$	$300–$400
$$$	$200–$300
$$	$100–$200
$	Under $100

RESTAURANTS

An indication of the cost of a three-course meal without drinks is given by **$** signs.

$$$$$	Over $60
$$$$	$45–$60
$$$	$30–$45
$$	$15–$20
$	Under $15

■ RIO DE JANEIRO

BARRA

⊞ TUAKAZA
$$$–$$$$

ESTR. DA CANOA 2600, SÃO CONRADO
TEL 21/3322 6715
www.tuakaza.com
It doesn't get more back to nature than Tuakaza, whose tropically hued, rustic chalets on stilts are plunged into a lush junglescape. Refuge here necessitates a car (or taxis).
🛈 6 🅿 🚭 🛜 🌊 🐾 All major cards

BÚZIOS

🏨 CACHOEIRA INN
$$$$-$$$$$
RUA E-1, LOTE 18,
PRAIA DA FERRADURA,
ARMAÇAO DOS BÚZIOS
TEL 22/2623 2118
www.cachoeirainnbuzios.com
This inspired American-
owned guesthouse boasts
nine waterfalls.
🛏 4 🅿 🚫 🌀 🏊 📺
🕙 MC, V

🏨 POUSADA CASA BÚZIOS
$$-$$$
RUA MORRO DA HUMAITÁ,
CASA 1, ORLA BARDOT,
ARMAÇÃO DE BÚZIOS
TEL 22/2623 7002
www.pousadacasabuzios.com
This casual French-owned
pousada possesses a wonder-
fully relaxed vibe. Very good
value.
🛏 6 🅿 🚫 🌀 🏊 🕙 AE,
MC, V

CENTRO

🏨 HOTEL OK
$$$
RUA SENADOR DANTAS 24
TEL 21/3479 4500
www.hotelok.com.br
Wedged onto a noisy little
street behind Cinelândia, within
spitting distance of Lapa, this
is one of Centro's most conve-
nient and best value options.
🛏 155 🚫 🌀 🏊 📺 🕙 All
major cards

🏨 HOTEL BELAS ARTES
$$
AV. VISCONDE DO RIO BRANCO 52
TEL 21/2252 6336
www.hotelbelasartes.com.br
Tucked away in the heart of
Centro, the rooms within this
gracious historic building are
very basic, but spotless.
🛏 65 🅿 🌀 🕙 All major
cards

🍴 RIO MINHO
$$$$
RUA DO OUVIDOR 10
TEL 21/2509 2338
Brazil was still an empire when
Rio's oldest restaurant still in
existence opened in 1884.
🍽 108 🕙 Closed Sat.–Sun.
🚫 🌀 🕙 All major cards

🍴 CONFEITARIA COLOMBO
$–$$
RUA GONÇALVES DIAS 32
TEL 21/2505 1500
Do as Cariocas do and order
Portuguese pastries (sweet or
savory) along with strong shots
of *cafezinho*. Then sit back and
pretend you're a 19th-century
Brazilian aristocrat.
🍽 400 🕙 Closed Sun.
🚫 🌀 🕙 All major cards

CORCOVADO & PAO DE AÇÚCAR

🏨 CASA 32
$$$$
LARGO DO BOTICÁRIO 32,
COSME VELHO
TEL 21/3289 9999
www.casa32.com
This mid-19th-century house
has been converted into
an exclusive B&B with two
impeccably decorated apartments that mingle antiques
with modern conveniences.
🛏 2 🚫 🌀 🏊 🕙 AE, MC, V

🏨 O VELEIRO
$$
RUA MUNDO NOVO 1440,
BOTAFOGO
TEL 21/2554 8980
One of Rio's pioneering
B&Bs, this restive home sits
perched on a residential street
halfway up to Corcovado,
which means that the Tijuca
Forest—and its chattering
inhabitants—share the garden
with guests. The Canadian-
Carioca hosts are warm and
very knowledgeable.

🛏 3 🅿 🚫 🌀 🏊 🕙 All
major cards

ILHA GRANDE

🏨 POUSADA ASALEM
$$$
PRAIA DA CRENA
TEL 24/3361 5602
www.asalem.com.br
Set into a jungly hillside
overlooking the sea, the spacious guest rooms combine
comfort with splendid seclusion—25 minutes by foot (or
15 minutes by boat) from
Vila Abraão.
🛏 8 🚫 🌀 🕙 AE, MC, V

🏨 POUSADA NATURÁLIA
$$
RUA DA PRAIA 149
TEL 24/3361 9583
www.pousadanaturalia.net
Squeezed between lush jungle
and a diaphanous bay, the
suites—all with verandas and
hammocks staring out to sea—
make this extremely well-run
pousada one of Ilha Grande's
best value options.
🛏 12 🚫 🌀 🕙 MC, V

AROUND LAGOA

🏨 LA MAISON
$$$
RUA SÉRGIO PORTO 58,
GÁVEA
TEL 21/3205 3585
www.lamaisonario.com
Perched on a residential hillside,
this villa owned by Frenchman
Jacques Dussol offers stylish
lodgings in thematically (and
dramatically) decorated suites.
The seclusion is such that a car
or taxi is necessary.
🛏 5 🚫 🌀 🏊 📺 🕙 All
major cards

🍴 ROBERTA SUDBRACK
$$$$$
AV. LINEU DE PAULA MACHADO
916, JARDIM BOTÂNICO,
TEL 21/3874 0139
Roberta Sudbrack, one of

🏨 Hotel 🍴 Restaurant 🛏 No. of Guest Rooms 🍽 No. of Seats 🅿 Parking 🕙 Closed 🔲 Elevator

Brazil's most innovative contemporary chefs, got her auspicious start as cook to then president Fernando Henrique Cardoso. Tasting menus are devised daily (lofty prices are reduced on Tues.).
🔲 62 🕐 Closed Sun.–Mon. 🅂 🅰 🅲 MC

🍴 BRASEIRO DA GÁVEA
$$
PRAÇA SANTOS DUMONT 116, GÁVEA
TEL 21/2239 7494
The former "bar across from the racetrack" is a ritual gathering spot for Zona Sul young blood, particularly on weekends and Monday evenings.
🔲 120 🅂 🅲 🅰 All major cards

🍴 DRI CAFÉ
$
RUA JARDIM BOTÂNICO 414, PARQUE LAGE, JARDIM BOTÂNICO
TEL 21/ 2226 8125
This café overlooks a turquoise swimming pool and, in turn, is overlooked by Cristo Redentor.
🔲 40 🅂 🅰 All major cards

LAPA & AROUND

🏨 HOTEL SANTA TERESA
🍴 $$$$$
RUA ALMIRANTE ALEXANDRINO 660, SANTA TERESA
TEL 21/3380 0200
A luxurious hotel that occupies a 200-year-old coffee plantation. The **Térèze** restaurant draws on tropical ingredients.
ⓘ 44 🔲 80 🅂 🅲 🅰 🅰 All major cards

🏨 CASA COOL BEANS
$$
RUA LAURINDA SANTOS LOBO 136, SANTA TERESA
TEL 21/2262-0552
www.casacoolbeans.com
Enjoy the bright, cheery chalets and rooms—each

decorated by a local artist—at this welcoming B&B.
ⓘ 10 🅂 🅲 🅰 🅰 None

🏨 HOTEL REGINA
$$
RUA FERREIRA VIANA 29, FLAMENGO
TEL 21/3289 9999
www.hotelregina.com.br
Few vestiges remain of this formerly grand 1920s-era hotel, but rooms are comfortable and nicely priced.
ⓘ 117 🅿 🔁 🅂 🅲 🔽 🅰 All major cards

🏨 RIAZOR
$
RUA DO CATETE 160 , CATETE
TEL 21/2225 0121
www.hotelriazor.com.br
The impressive 1890 facade is deceptive; the rooms are clean but threadbare. How much you enjoy the atmosphere of retro down-and-outness will depend on your frame of mind. Strongest selling points are the location (across from the Parque do Catete and next to the Metrô) and the low price.
ⓘ 50 🅿 🅂 🅲 🅰 V

🍴 ESPÍRITO SANTA
$$$$
RUA ALMIRANTE ALEXANDRINO 264, SANTA TERESA
TEL 21/2507 4840
Chef Natacha Fink draws on the exotic produce of her native Amazon in surprising and seductive ways. Reservations recommended.
🔲 70 🕐 Closed Tues. 🅂 🅲 🅰 AE, MC, V

🍴 PORCÃO RIO'S
$$$$
AV. INFANTE DOM HENRIQUE, PARQUE DO FLAMENGO, FLAMENGO
TEL 21/3461 9020
The main event at this popular chain of *churrascarias* (barbecue houses) is the *rodízio*, a system

whereby, every two minutes, a waiter arrives at your table brandishing a succulent cut of meat.
🔲 800 🅿 🅂 🅲 🅰 All major cards

🍴 COSMOPOLITA
$$
TRAVESSA DO MOSQUEIRA 4, LAPA
TEL 21/2224 7820
This retro 1920s restaurant-bar is the birthplace of one of Rio's most iconic dishes: the Filé á Oswaldo Aranha.
🔲 90 🕐 Closed Sun. 🅂 🅲 🅰 All major cards

PARATY

🏨 VIVENDA
$$
RUA BEIJA FLOR 9, CABORÉ
TEL 24/3371 4272
www.vivendaparaty.com
A ten-minute walk from Paraty's Centro Histórico, the tastefully appointed modern bungalows are unbeatable in terms of the level of comfort and pampering guests receive.
ⓘ 3 🅿 🅂 🅲 🅰 🅰 None

🏨 SOLAR DOS GERÂNIOS
$
PRAÇA DA MATRIZ, CENTRO
TEL 24/3371 1550
www.paraty.com.br/geranio
One of the Centro Histórico's most affordable options, this rambling old mansion is a wonderfully atmospheric place. Rooms are small, but homey.
ⓘ 12 🅂 🅰 All major cards

🍴 CASA DO FOGO
$$$
RUA COMENDADOR JOSÉ LUIZ 390
TEL 24/3371 3163
Casa do Fogo takes its name (House of Fire) quite seriously by setting many of its main dishes aflame with the fragrant aid of regionally produced *cachaça*.

🅂 Nonsmoking 🅲 Air-conditioning 🅰 Indoor Pool 🅰 Outdoor Pool 🔽 Health Club 🅰 Credit Cards

🍴 50 🕐 Closed Wed.
📵 📵 📵 All major cards

🍴 SABOR DA TERRA
$
AV. ROBERTO SILVEIRA 180,
PATATIBA
TEL 24/3371 2384
Located a few steps beyond
the Centro Histórico, this modest per kilo restaurant compen-
sates for the lack of decor with
the wealth of freshly prepared
salads, grilled fish and meats,
and seafood dishes.
🍴 40 📵 None

PETRÓPOLIS

🏨 HOTEL SOLAR DO
🍴 IMPÉRIO
$$$
AV. KOELER 376, CENTRO
TEL 24/2103 3000
www.solardoimperio.com.br
This 1875 mansion is only
one of many lavish summer
abodes built by vacationing
counts and barons. Afternoon
tea—served in the exquisite
Leopoldina restaurant—is
included in the rate.
🛏 24 📵 📵 📵 📵 📵
📵 All major cards

🏨 POUSADA 14 BIS
$
RUA BUENOS AIRES 192, CENTRO
TEL 24/2231 0946
www.pousada14bis.com.br
Nicely priced and centrally
located with modest, warm,
and comfortable rooms.
🛏 16 📵 📵 📵 📵 📵 DC,
MC

🍴 BORDEAUX
$$
RUA IPIRANGA 716, CENTRO
TEL 24/2242 5711
This atmospheric wine bar/
emporium is located in the
coach house of the historic
Casa de Petrópolis. Aside from
1,200 vintages, delicious gourmet sandwiches and appetizers

are available to munch on.
🍴 180 📵 📵 📵 DC, MC

THE ZONA SUL BEACHES

HOTELS

🏨 COPACABANA PALACE
$$$$$
AV. ATLÂNTICA 1702,
COPACABANA
TEL 21/2548 7070
www.copacabanapalace.com
A landmark and a legend.
🛏 243 📵 📵 📵 📵 📵 📵
📵 All major cards

🏨 ARPOADOR INN
$$
RUA FRANCISCO OTAVIANO 177,
ARPOADOR
TEL 21/2523 0060
www.arpoadorinn.com.br
Mere feet away from the surf-
ista mecca of Praia do Arpoa-
dor, this uninspiring address is
Rio's only hotel that's actually
right on the beach.
🛏 50 📵 📵 📵
📵 All major cards

🏨 HOTEL SANTA CLARA
$$
RUA DÉCIO VILLARES 316,
COPACABANA
TEL 21/2256 2650
www.hotelsantaclara.com.br
Five blocks from the beach but
close to the Metrô, this is a
modest but cozy hotel in the
traditional Bairro Peixoto part
of Copa.
🛏 25 📵 📵
📵 All major cards

🏨 IPANEMA INN
$$
RUA MARIA QUITÉRIA 27,
IPANEMA
TEL 21/2523 6092
www.ipanemainn.com.br
The half block that separates
this hotel from Ipanema's
famous sands makes for lack-
luster views, but cheap prices
for this neck of the beach.

Rooms are smallish and unin-
spiring, but clean, functional,
and affordable.
🛏 56 📵 📵 📵 📵 📵 All
major cards

🏨 SESC COPACABANA
$$
RUA DOMINGOS FERREIRA 160,
COPACABANA
TEL 21/2548 1088
www.sescrio.org.br
This modernist building was
designed by Oscar Niemeyer
only one block from the beach.
Good value rooms are airy
and minimalist.
🛏 120 📵 📵 📵 📵 All
major cards

RESTAURANTS

🍴 BRASILEIRINHO
$$
RUA JANGADEIROS 10, LOJA A,
IPANEMA
TEL 21/2513 5184
Oozing with a rusticity typical
of rural Brazil, Brasileirinho
serves up robust portions of
country cooking with a predi-
lection for the heady cuisine of
Minas Gerais.
🍴 54 📵 📵 📵 All major
cards

🍴 FELLINI
$$
RUA GEN. URQUIZA 104, LEBLON
TEL 21/2511 3600
One of Rio's most high-
quality per-kilo banquets.
There are offerings for
vegetarians and diabetics.
🍴 140 📵 📵 📵 DC, MC, V

🍴 MARKET IPANEMA
$$
RUA VISCONDE DE PIRAJÁ 499,
IPANEMA
TEL 21/3283 1438
Market is a relaxing oasis where
both carnivores and herbivores
in search of fresh, yet flavorful
sustenance can find it.
🍴 80 📵 📵 All major cards

🏨 Hotel 🍴 Restaurant 🛏 No. of Guest Rooms 🍴 No. of Seats 📵 Parking 🕐 Closed 📵 Elevator

▮ **BRACARENSE**

$-$$

RUA JOSÉ LINHARES 85-B,
LEBLON

TEL 21/2294 3549

This deliciously unpretentious neighborhood *boteco* is a
favorite haunt of Leblon's after-
beach and happy-hour crowd.

🍴 88 🅂 🅒 None

▮ **BIBI SUCOS**

$

AV. ATAULFO DE PAIVA 591-A,
LEBLON

TEL 21/2259 4298

This hard-core juice bar is
frequented by Leblon's body-
conscious residents as well as
the jiujitsu crowd who pack on
the protein with acai fortified
with honey and tapioca.

🍴 25 🅂 🅒 All major cards

■ SOUTH-CENTRAL

ESPÍRITO SANTO

DOMINGOS MARTINS

▣ **POUSADA RABO DO**
▮ **LAGARTO**

$$$

ES-164 KM 70, SÃO PAULO
DO ARACÊ

TEL 27/3248 2383 OR 9942 6121
www.rabodolagarto.com.br

A well-designed and
attractive eco-conscious
guesthouse at the edge of the
Pedra Azul State Park and a
view of the outcropping.

ℹ️ 17 🍴 30 🅿 🅒 None

LINHARES

▣ **HOTEL DA RESERVA**
▮ **NATURAL VALE**

$$

BR-101 KM 120

TEL 27/3371 9797

Owned and managed by one
of the world's largest mining
companies, Brazil's Vale, this
guesthouse with sauna sits
inside an important protected

area of the Atlantic Forest.

ℹ️ 35 🍴 58 🅿 🅒 🏊
🅒 AE, MC, V

MINAS GERAIS

BELO HORIZONTE

▣ **IBIS BH LIBERDADE**

$$

AV. JOÃO PINHEIRO 602,
LOURDES

TEL 31/2111 1500
www.accorhotels.com

A branch of the international
budget chain owned by
France's Accor group.

ℹ️ 30 🅿 🛎 🅒 🏊 🅒 All
major cards

▣ **MY PLACE SAVASSI**

$$

RUA PROFESSOR MORAES 674,
SAVASSI

TEL 31/3311 2191

A good business-style hotel.

ℹ️ 42 🅿 🅒 🏊 🅒 All
major cards

▣ **OURO MINAS**
▮ **PALACE**

$$

AV. CRISTIANO MACHADO 4001,
PALMARES

TEL 31/3429 4001
www.ourominas.com.br

Bills itself as the only five-star
hotel in Belo Horizonte. Has
handicap facilities.

ℹ️ 346 🍴 250 🅿 🛎 🅒 🏊
🏊 🚣 🅒 All major cards

▮ **FOGO DE CHÃO**

$$$$

RUA SERGIPE 1208, SAVASSI

TEL 31/3227 2730

The local branch of one of
Brazil's top all-you-can-eat
rodízio steakhouses.

🍴 280 🅂 🅒 🅒 All major
cards

▮ **HERMENGARDA**

$$$

RUA OUTONO 314, CARMO

TEL 31/3225 3268

Brazilian contemporary cuisine
in an atmosphere designed to
remember grandma's house in
Minas Gerais.

🍴 70 🕐 Closed Mon. 🅒
🅒 AE, MC, V

▮ **DONA LUCINHA**

$$

RUA PADRE ODORICO 38,
SÃO PEDRO

TEL 31/3227 0562

Traditional *mineiro* food from
Minas Gerais, with both buffet
and à la carte options.

🍴 100 🕐 Closed Sun. 🅂
🅒 🅒 All major cards

▮ **XAPURI**

$$

RUA MANDACARU 260,
BRAÚNAS

TEL 31/3496 6198

In the Pampulha district, at
arm's length from downtown,
Xapuri offers local *mineiro*
fare in an atmosphere
designed to recall a farm
in the countryside.

🍴 480 🅂 🅒 🅒 AE, MC, V

DIAMANTINA

▣ **POUSADA DO**
▮ **GARIMPO &**
RESTAURANTE O
GARIMPEIRO

$

AV. DA SAUDADE 265

TEL 38/3532 1040

Small hotel, near the local market, with a nice restaurant. The
chef, Vandeca, is considered
one of the best in the state. The
son of a local diamond miner,
Vandeca is a staunch believer in
authentic down-home *comida
mineira*, as the state's characteristic fare is known.

ℹ️ 57 🍴 10 🅿 🕐 Mon.–
Fri. D; Sat.–Sun. L & D
🅂 🅒 🏊 🅒 🅒 All major
cards

🅂 Nonsmoking 🅒 Air-conditioning 🏊 Indoor Pool 🏊 Outdoor Pool 🚣 Health Club 🅒 Credit Cards

MARIANA

🏨 POUSADA DA
🍴 SERRINHA
$
RUA DONA YOLANDA
GUIMARÃES 370
TEL 31/3557 5071
www.pousadaserrinha.com.br
A tranquil setting, surrounded
by an orchard and vegetable
gardens. Pets allowed.
ⓘ 13 🛏 20 🅿 🚭 None

🍴 RANCHO DA PRAÇA
$
PRAÇA GOMES FREIRE 108
TEL 31/3558 1060
Self-service buffet known for
its soups.
🛏 110 🚭 All major cards

MONTES CLAROS

🏨 POUSADA DO SESC
🍴 $
AV. DEPUTADO ESTEVES
RODRIGUES 1124
TEL 38/3221 1018
A reputable property in north-
ern Minas Gerais. A good base
for exploring the region.
ⓘ 58 🛏 100 🅿 ⊟ 🚭 🏊
🚭 MC, V

OURO PRETO

🏨 POUSADA DO
MONDEGO
$$–$$$
LARGO DE COIMBRA 38,
CENTRO HISTÓRICO
TEL 31/3551 2040
A renovated building dating
from 1747 situated near the
Igreja de São Francisco de Assis
downtown. Modern comfort
with historical charm.
ⓘ 24 🅿 🚭 DC, MC, V

🏨 SOLAR DA ÓPERA
🍴 $–$$
RUA CONDE DE BOBADELA 75,
CENTRO HISTÓRICO

www.hotelsolardaopera.
com.br
TEL 31/3551 6844
Occupying a renovated 18th
century mansion, just 300 feet
(100 m) from Praça Tiradentes.
Handicap facilities available.
ⓘ 16 🛏 40 🅿 🚭 🚭 DC,
MC, V

🍴 RESTAURANTE CONTOS
DE RÉIS
$$
RUA CAMILO DE BRITO 21,
CENTRO HISTÓRICO
TEL 31/3551 5359
A buffet of traditional Minas
Gerais fare served in an 18th-
century mansion.
🛏 220 🚭 DC, MC, V

SANTA BÁRBARA

🏨 FAZENDA DO
ENGENHO & POUSADA
DO CARAÇA PBCM
FAZENDA DO ENGENHO
$
ESTRADA DO CARAÇA KM 9,
BARÃO DE COCAIS
TEL 31/3809 4004
www.santuariodocaraca
.com.br
Located in an old mansion,
surrounded by farmland.
Perfect locale for hikers.
ⓘ 50 in *pousada* & 27 in
fazenda 🚭 🚭 None

SERRA DA CANASTRA
(SÃO ROQUE DE MINAS)

🏨 HOTEL CHAPADÃO
🍴 DA CANASTRA
$
RUA BEIJAMIN CONSTANT 10,
SÃO ROQUE DE MINAS
37/3433 1267 OR 3433 1440
Situated on a local stream,
in an area with few options.
Abundant birds, monkeys,
and other small creatures.
Pets welcome.
ⓘ 24 🛏 120 🅿 🏊 🚭 All
major cards

TIRADENTES

🏨 POUSADA SOLAR
🍴 DA PONTE
$$$$
PRAÇA DAS MERCÊS
TEL 32/3355 1255
The first guesthouse estab-
lished in Tiradentes, back in
1974, by an Englishman and
his wife. (No children ages 12
or younger.)
ⓘ 18 🛏 40 🅿 ⊟ 🚭
🚭 🏊 🚭 All major cards

SÃO PAULO

ÁGUAS DE SÃO PEDRO

🏨 BALNEÁRIO DO
🍴 GRANDE HOTEL SÃO
PEDRO
$$$$$
PARQUE DOUTOR OTÁVIO DE
MOURA ANDRADE, ÁGUAS DE
SÃO PEDRO
TEL 19/3482 7600

🏨 Hotel 🍴 Restaurant ⓘ No. of Guest Rooms 🛏 No. of Seats 🅿 Parking 🚭 Closed ⊟ Elevator

The Grande Hotel maintains some of the glamour of its heyday as a mineral water spa in the mid-20th century. Thermal baths and massages are on the menu. Golf course.

① 112 P Ⓢ Ⓐ Ⓢ ☎ ⌚
▼ Ⓒ All major cards

BARRETOS

▥ **BARRETOS**
▯ **COUNTRY HOTEL**
$$$–$$$$
VIA PEDRO VICENTINI 111,
JARDIM AEROPORTO
TEL 17/3321 2323
www.barretoscountryhotel
.com.br
Family-oriented lodging occupy part of a recreational area that includes a water park, a restaurant, and a bar. Horse riding activities available.

① 72 ✚ 100 P ⊖ Ⓢ ☎
Ⓒ AE, MC, V

BRAGANÇA

▯ **BAR DO ROSÁRIO**
$
RUA BARÃO DE JUQUERI 6,
BRAGANÇA PAULISTA
TEL 11/4032 8579
Bragança bills itself as the Sausage Capital: This is the place to go to see if they are right.

✚ 40 Ⓒ MC, V

CUNHA

▥ **POUSADA DOS**
▯ **ANJOS**
$$
SP-171 KM 57.8, APARIÇÃO,
TEL 12/3111 5115
www.pousadadosanjos.com.br
Three chalets, three suites, and a historic main building in a rural setting on the banks of the Rio Paraibuna. Horse-riding facilities.

① 9 ✚ 20 P ⊖ ☎
Ⓒ MC, V

ILHABELA

▥ **POUSO SAMBAQUIS**
$$
RUA POSSIDÔNIO GOMES DA
SILVA 111, PEREQUÊ
TEL 12/3896 5202 OR 9193 9741
www.sambaquis.com.br
An informal *pousada* popular with people looking for outdoor and adventure sports activities. Suites connected by garden.

① 7 P Ⓢ Ⓢ ☎ Ⓒ DC,
MC, V

MARESIAS
(SÃO SEBASTIÃO)

▥ **POUSADA DOS CONDES**
$$$
RUA DAS MARITACAS 4
TEL 12/3865 6322
www.pousadadoscondes
.com.br
With decor inspired by Bali and a menu of spa services, this is a relaxing place to come back to after a day of adventure sport activities or lounging at the beach.

① 30 P Ⓢ Ⓢ ☎
Ⓒ All major cards

SÃO LUIZ DO
PARAITINGA

▥ **FAZENDA CATUÇABA**
$$$$$
FAZENDA SANTA HELENA,
CATUÇABA
12/3671 6158 OR 11/2495 1586
www.catucaba.com
Set on a 1000-acre working organic farm. Site includes church and school for employees. A new spa opened in 2013. Breakfast and dinner included.

① 10 ✚ 50 P Ⓢ ☎
Ⓒ All major cards

SÃO PAULO CITY

HOTELS

▥ **EMILIANO**
▯ **$$$$$**
RUA OSCAR FREIRE 384,
JARDIM PAULISTA
TEL 11/3069 4369
www.emiliano.com.br
Luxury that includes a spa and all the amenities and a high employee-to-guest ratio. Kids activities provided.

① 57 ✚ 46 P ⊖ Ⓢ
Ⓒ All major cards

▥ **FASANO**
$$$$$
RUA VITORIO FASANO 88,
JARDIM PAULISTA
TEL 11/3896 4000
www.fasano.com.br
A luxury hotel with spa and panoramic views. Spawned by one of São Paulo's most impressive restaurants (see p. 287). Handicap facilities.

① 60 P ⊖ Ⓢ ☎ ▼
Ⓒ All major cards

▥ **HILTON MORUMBI**
▯ **$$$$$**
AV. DAS NAÇÕES UNIDAS 12901,
BROOKLIN NOVO
TEL 11/2845 0000
A branch of the international chain in the Berrini district with good service. Handicap accessible. Pets allowed.

① 487 ✚ 120 P ⊖ Ⓢ ☎
▼ Ⓒ All major cards

▥ **TIVOLI SÃO PAULO**
▯ **MOFARREJ**
$$$$$
ALAMEDA SANTOS 1437,
JARDIM PAULISTA
TEL 11/3146 5900
www.tivolihotels.com
Near the Trianon Park, this 23-story tower, opened in 1988, was recently renovated. Spa treatments include a

tropical rain mist. Handicap facilities.

ℹ 220 🔀 90 🅿 ⬄ 🚭 ≋ 🍷 ⬢ All major cards

SOMETHING SPECIAL

🏨 **UNIQUE**
🍴 **$$$$$**

AV. BRIGADEIRO LUIS ANTÔNIO 4700, JARDIM PAULISTA
TEL 11/3055 4700
www.hotelunique.com
This upscale property near the Ibirapuera Park has become an architectural landmark with its half-watermelon shape rounded on the bottom. (**Skye** restaurant see p. 287.)

ℹ 95 🅿 ⬄ 🚭 ≋ ⬢ All major cards

🏨 **TRANSAMÉRICA**
🍴 **$$$$–$$$$$**

AV. DAS NAÇÕES UNIDAS 18591, SANTO AMARO
TEL 11/5693 4511
This place may seem remote, but good if you have business or appointments in the southern Santo Amaro district or if you are in town for the Formula 1 race.

ℹ 396 🔀 90 🅿 🚭 ≋ ⬢ All major cards

🏨 **L'HOTEL PORTO BAY**
🍴 **$$$–$$$$**

ALAMEDA CAMPINAS 266, BELA VISTA
TEL 11/2183 0500
www.portobay.com.br
A European-style upscale boutique hotel with spa.

ℹ 83 🔀 48 🅿 🚭 ⬢ All major cards

🏨 **BLUE TREE PREMIUM**
🍴 **MORUMBI CONVEN-TION CENTER**
$$$

AV. ROQUE PETRONI JÚNIOR 1000, BROOKLIN NOVO
TEL 11/5187 1200
www.bluetree.com.br

The Brazilian Blue Tree chain caters to business travelers, especially businesswomen. Handicap facilities and a spa.

ℹ 398 🔀 100 🅿 🚭 ≋ ≋ ⬢ All major cards

🏨 **MARRIOTT AIRPORT**
🍴 **$$$**

AV. MONTEIRO LOBATO, GUARULHOS
TEL 11/2468 6999
www.marriott.com.br
A good alternative for passengers in transit and others who find themselves stuck near the airport in Guarulhos. Shuttle service.

ℹ 314 🔀 150 🅿 ⬄ 🚭 ≋ 🍷 ⬢ All major cards

🏨 **CAESAR PARK &**
🍴 **CAESAR BUSINESS**
$$–$$$

ROD. HÉLIO SMIDT, GUARULHOS (AIRPORT ACCESS ROAD)
TEL 11/2124 5800
www.accorhotels.com
Good accommodations, handicap accessible, near the international airport in Guarulhos.

ℹ 385 🔀 82 🅿 🚭 ≋ ⬢ All major cards

🏨 **CAESAR PARK**
🍴 **FARIA LIMA**
$$–$$$

RUA OLIMPÍADAS 205, VILA OLÍMPIA
TEL 11/3049 6622
www.accorhotels.com
One of the best choices in the Vila Olímpia neighborhood. Though part of a chain, tries to provide boutique hotel–style service.

ℹ 129 🔀 90 🅿 ⬄ 🚭 🍷 ⬢ All major cards

🏨 **ESTANPLAZA BERRINI**
🍴 **$$–$$$**

AV. ENGENHEIRO LUIS CARLOS BERRINI 853
TEL 11/5509 8900
www.estanplaza.com.br

A Brazilian option among the upscale chains in the thriving Berrini business district.

ℹ 130 🔀 120 🅿 ⬄ 🚭 🚭 ≋ ⬢ All major cards

🏨 **COMFORT SUITES**
🍴 **OSCAR FREIRE**
$$

RUA OSCAR FREIRE 1948, JARDIM PAULISTA
TEL 11/2137 4700
www.comfortsuites.com
A good choice if you want to stay in the Pinheiros district. Pets allowed. Handicap facilities.

ℹ 150 🔀 100 🅿 ⬄ 🚭 ≋ 🍷 ⬢ All major cards

🏨 **GOLDEN TULIP**
🍴 **PAULISTA PLAZA**
$$

ALAMEDA SANTOS 85, PARAÍSO
TEL 11/2627 1000
www.paulistaplaza.com.br
Standard accommodations within reach of Paulista Avenue and Ibirapuera Park. Spa facilities. Restaurant with sushi bar.

ℹ 368 🔀 120 🅿 ⬄ 🚭 🍷 ⬢ All major cards

🏨 **CITYLIGHTS HOSTEL**
$

RUA PADRE GARCIA VELHO 44, PINHEIROS
TEL 11/2364 4231
www.citylightshostel.com
One of the best of a growing number of affordable guesthouses in town. Kitchen facilities available.

ℹ 7 🚭 ⬢ All major cards

🏨 **NIKKEY PALACE**
🍴 **$**

RUA GALVÃO BUENO 425, LIBERDADE
TEL 11/3207 8511
www.nikkeyhotel.com.br
Mainly catering to Japanese travelers, the best choice in the Liberdade neighborhood.

ℹ 96 🔀 60 🅿 ⬄ 🚭 ⬢ All major cards

🏨 POUSADA ZILÁH
🍴 $

ALAMEDA FRANCA 1621,
JARDIM PAULISTA
TEL 11/3062 1444
www.zilah.com
A charming guesthouse not far
from the Avenida Paulista. Home
of the Ziláh Gourmet restaurant.
🚪 14 🛏 28 🅿 🐾 AE, MC, V

RESTAURANTS

🍴 A FIGUEIRA RUBAIYAT
$$$$$

RUA HADDOCK LOBO 1738,
JARDIM PAULISTA
TEL 11/3087 1399
A top-notch, à la carte steakhouse, with outdoor seating
under the gigantic fig tree that
gives the place its name.
🛏 350 🅿 🚭 🐾 All major
cards

🍴 BARBACOA
$$$$$

RUA DOUTOR RENATO PAES DE
BARROS 65, ITAIM BIBI
TEL 11/3168 5522
One of the best all-you-can-
eat (rodízio) places in town.
🛏 220 🚭 🅰 🐾 All
major cards

🍴 D.O.M
$$$$$

RUA BARÃO DE CAPANEMA 549,
JARDIM PAULISTA
TEL 11/3088 0761
A Brazilian contemporary from
Chef Alex Atala, it regularly
appears on upscale global "best
of" lists.
🛏 350 🅿 🕐 Closed Sun. D
🚭 🐾 All major cards

🍴 DON CURRO
$$$$$

RUA ALVES GUIMARÃES 230,
JARDIM PAULISTA
TEL 11/3062 4712
Best Spanish food in town.
🛏 150 🅿 🕐 Closed Mon. D
🚭 🐾 AE, DC, MC

🍴 FASANO
$$$$$

RUA VITORIO FASANO 88,
JARDIM PAULISTA
TEL 11/3062 4000
Upscale Italian dining with
panoramic views.
🛏 90 🅿 🚭 🐾 All major
cards

🍴 KINOSHITA
$$$$$

RUA JACQUES FÉLIX 405, VILA
NOVA CONCEIÇÃO
www.restaurantekinoshita
.com.br
São Paulo is known for its excellent Japanese restaurants. This
is one of the best of the bunch.
🛏 72 🅿 🕐 Closed Sun.
🚭 🚭 🐾 All major cards

🍴 SKYE
$$$$$

AV. BRIGADEIRO LUÍS ANTÔNIO
4700, JARDIM PAULISTA
TEL 11/3055 4702
Set on the roof of the upscale
and fashionable Hotel Unique
(see p. 286), Skye is a bar that
mixes a luxurious atmosphere
with an exuberant view.
🛏 150 🚭 🅰 🐾 All
major cards

🍴 ACRÓPOLES
$$$

RUA DA GRAÇA 364, BOM
RETIRO
TEL 11/3223 4386
Nothing fancy, but serving good
hearty Greek food for lunch and
dinner since 1959.
🛏 72 🚭 🐾 All major cards

🍴 ANDRADE
$$$

RUA ARTUR DE AZEVEDO 874,
PINHEIROS
TEL 11/3085 0589
São Paulo's premiere Northeast-
ern restaurant, with live traditional
forró. Live music after 7 p.m.
🛏 180 🕐 Closed Mon.
🚭 🚭 🐾 All major cards

🍴 ARABIA
$$$

RUA HADDOCK LOBO 1397,
JARDIM PAULISTA
TEL 11/3061 2203
The best Lebanese food in
town.
🛏 120 🅿 🚭 🐾 All
major cards

🍴 CANTINA CAPUANO
$$$

RUA CONSELHEIRO CARRÃO 416,
BELA VISTA
TEL 11/3288 1460
Founded in 1907, this Italian
cantina remains a mainstay of
the Bexiga neighborhood.
🛏 68 🕐 Closed Mon.
🚭 🐾 All major cards

🍴 DIE MEISTER STUBE
$$$

RUA BARÃO DO TRIUNFO 1213,
CAMPO BELO
TEL 11/5536 4982
The best German place in
town in a neighborhood that
once welcomed large numbers
of immigrants from Germany.
🛏 809 🅿 🕐 Closed Sat.–
Sun. 🚭 🚭 🐾 All major
cards

🍴 RESTAURANTE
CORRIENTES 348
$$$

RUA COMENDADOR MIGUEL
CALFAT 348, ITAIM BIBI
TEL 11/3849 0348
Authentic Argentinean parrilla
(barbecue).
🛏 120 🅿 🕐 Closed Mon. D
🚭 🐾 All major cards

🍴 RESTAURANTE GIGETTO
$$$

RUA AVANHANDAVA 63,
CENTRO
TEL 11/3256 6530
Founded in 1938, once a hang-
out for intellectuals and artists,
now enjoying a comeback.
🛏 180 🅿 🕐 Closed Mon.
🚭 🚭 🐾 All major cards

🚭 Nonsmoking 🅰 Air-conditioning 🏊 Indoor Pool 🏊 Outdoor Pool 🏋 Health Club 🐾 Credit Cards

🍴 ASTOR
$$
RUA DELFINA 163,
VILA MADALENA
TEL 11/3815 1364
An upscale *boteco* that harkens
back to the bohemian era of
the 1950s.
🔲 150 🅿 🚫 🔳 🚫 All
major cards

🍴 BAR BRAHMA
$$
AV. SÃO JOÃO 677,
CENTRO
TEL 11/3367 3601
One of São Paulo's traditional
establishments with menu that
harkens back to its golden era.
🔲 490 🚫 🔳 🚫 All major
cards

🍴 BAR DO BIU
$$
RUA CARDEAL ARCOVERDE 776,
PINHEIROS
TEL 11/3081 6739
Home-style Northeastern food
in a simple setting. Popular
with artists, intellectuals, and
other local notables.
🔲 60 🚫 🚫 All major cards

🍴 CERVEJARIA NACIONAL
$$
AV. PEDROSO DE MORAIS 604
PINHEIROS
TEL 11/3628 5000
São Paulo's only brew pub
opened in 2001. Occupying
three floors, it offers several dif-
ferent styles of fresh draft beer.
🔲 160 🕐 Closed Sun.
🚫 🔳 🚫 All major cards

🍴 CONSULADO MINEIRO
$$
PRAÇA BENEDITO CALIXTO 74,
PINHEIROS
TEL 11/3088 6055
The place to go for *mineiro* cui-
sine from Minas Gerais state.
Extensive cachaça menu.
🔲 130 🕐 Closed Mon.
🚫 🔳 🚫 All major cards

🍴 FILIAL
$$
RUA FIDALGA 254,
VILA MADALENA
TEL 11/3813 9226
The Filial's decor recalls that
of a down-home *botequim*
eulogized by old-time samba
composers like Zé Keti and
Noel Rosa. Caters to the
over-30 demographic. Open
until 3 a.m.
🔲 150 🚫 All major cards

🍴 MONTECHIARO
$$
RUA SANTO ANTÔNIO 844,
BELA VISTA
TEL 11/3257 4032
Still one of the best Italian
cantinas in Bexiga.
🔲 150 🕐 Closed Mon.
🚫 All major cards

🍴 PIZZARIA A
ESPERANÇA
$$
AV. MORUMBI 8185, BROOKLIN
TEL 11/5533 5743
Serving some of the best
pizza in São Paulo since
1957.
🔲 96 🚫 🔳 🚫 All
major cards

🍴 ROPERTO
$$
RUA TREZE DE MAIO 634,
BELA VISTA
TEL 11/3288 2573
This Italian cantina has been a
Bexiga mainstay since 1942.
🔲 340 🅿 🚫 🚫 All
major cards

🍴 TUBAÍNA
$$
RUA HADDOCK LOBO 74,
CONSOLAÇÃO
TEL 11/3129 4930
In the heart of the Baixo
Augusta, Tubaína takes its
name from the generic name
for cheap, popular soft drinks.
Childhood nostalgia mixed
with contemporary flair.

🔲 80 🕐 Closed Sun.
🚫 DC, MC, V

🍴 VELOSO
$$
RUA CONCEIÇÃO VELOSO 56,
VILA MARIANA
TEL 11/5572 0254
A newfangled, old-style *boteco*
with award-winning munchies
and legendary caipirinhas.
🔲 180 🕐 Closed Mon.
🚫 🚫 All major cards

UBATUBA

🏨 HOTEL RECANTO
🍴 DAS TONINHAS
$$$$$
ESTR. RIO-SANTOS KM 55.5,
PRAIA DAS TONINHAS UBATUBA
TEL 11/3288 2022
www.recantodastoninhas
.com.br
An upscale beachside hotel
with a good fitness center.
🚪 54 🔲 100 🅿 🚫 🏊 📺
🚫 All major cards

🏨 POUSADA
🍴 PICINGUABA
$$$$
RUA G VILA DA PICINGUABA
TEL 12/3836 9105
www.picinguaba.com
A beach hideaway with private
balconies in a natural setting.
Breakfast and lunch included.
🚪 11 🔲 25 🅿 🚫 🔳 🏊
🚫 All major cards

🔳 SOUTH

PARANÁ

CURITIBA

🏨 LA DOLCE VITA
🍴 $$$
R-376 KM 635, RIO DO UNA,
TIJUCAS DO SUL
TEL 41/3634 8900
www.hotelladolcevita.com.br
Set on a lake outside of town,
it offers spa facilities and
outdoor activities like cycling,

🏨 Hotel 🍴 Restaurant 🚪 No. of Guest Rooms 🔲 No. of Seats 🅿 Parking 🕐 Closed 🔳 Elevator

fishing, and rowing.

(i) 33 **☐** 150 **P** **☺** **☒** **☒**
☒ AE, MC, V

🏨 FOUR POINTS BY
🍴 SHERATON
$$–$$$

AV. 7 DE SETEMBRO 4211,
ÁGUA VERDE
TEL 41/3340 4000
www.fourpoints.com/curitiba
The local property of the
international Sheraton chain
with handicap facilities.

(i) 165 **☐** 102 **P** **☺** **☺** **☒**
☒ **☒** All major cards

🏨 BOURBON CURITIBA
🍴 $$

RUA CÂNDIDO LOPES 102,
CENTRO
www.bourbon.com.br
TEL 41/3221 4600
A centrally located branch of
a Brazilian chain that offers
accommodations, three restaurants from a brasserie
to a sushi bar, and services
similar to better-known
international chains. Handicap
facilities available.

(i) 174 **☐** 40 **P** **☺** **☺** **☒**
☒ **☒** **☒** All major cards

🍴 MADALOSSO
$$

AV. MANOEL RIBAS 5875,
SANTA FELICIDADE
TEL 41/3372 2121
Santa Felicidade, Curitiba's
Little Italy, is known in part
for cavernous trattorias that
serve all-you-can eat, set menu,
Italian meals. Madalosso also
ranks among the world's larg-
est eateries.

☐ 4,000 **P** **☺** **☒** DC,
MC, V

🍴 RESTAURANTE VENEZA
$$

AV. MANOEL RIBAS 6860,
SANTA FELICIDADE
TEL 41/3372 2626
Veneza is Madalosso's neigh-
borhood rival, with a similar

all-you-can-eat menu, set
menu, Italian meals. This one
was founded in 1965.

☐ 780 **P** **☺** Closed Mon.
D **☺** **☒** All major cards

🍴 COSTELÃO CURITIBANO
$

RUA CHILE 1746, REBOUÇAS
TEL 41/3332 3563
Costelões are set-price budget
barbecues that specialize
in all-you-can-eat beef ribs
accompanied by self-service
buffet of potato salad, green
salad, fried polenta, and more.
Open 24 hours, including the
Costelão Curitibano.

☐ 150 **P** **☺** **☒** All major
cards

🍴 COSTELÃO DO HAVANA
$

RUA SILVEIRA NETO 144,
ÁGUA VERDE
TEL 41/3243 2262
A costelõe, open 24/7 with
eight types of carved meats
served for lunch on Sat. and Sun.

☐ 192 **P** **☒** DC, MC, V

FOZ DO IGUAÇU

🏨 HOTEL DAS
🍴 CATARATAS
$$$$$

BR-469 KM 32, PARQUE
NACIONAL DO IGUAÇU
TEL 45/2102 7000
www.hoteldascataratas.com
Located inside the park, this is
the most upscale option available at Foz. It also offers the
only way to see the falls in the
evening or at dawn, when the
park gates are closed. Night
excursions available for guests.
Handicap facilities.

(i) 180 **☐** 280 **P** **☺** **☺**
☒ **☒** **☒** All major cards

🏨 HOSTEL PAUDIMAR
🍴 CAMPESTRE
$

ALAMEDA CAIBI 201,
REMANSO GRANDE

TEL 45/3529 6061
www.paudimar.com.br/
Albeit a hostel, part of the
Hostelling International
network, this is about the
only place in town with any
character or charm.

(i) 27 **☐** 50 **P** **☺** **☒**
☒ MC, V

ILHA DO MEL

🏨 POUSADA FIM DA
🍴 TRILHA
$$

PRAIA DE ENCANTADAS
TEL 13/3426 9017
www.fimdatrilha.com.br
One of the best guesthouses
on the island, with one of the
best restaurants.

(i) 8 **☐** 60 **☺** **☒** **☒** DC,
MC, V

LAGAMAR

🏨 LAGAMAR ECOHOTEL
🍴 & RESTAURANTE
TEMPERO DE CATAIA
$$

ESTR. MUNICIPAL DO ARIRI
KM 6
TEL 11/9 8145 5317
A new guesthouse and restaurant owned and operated by a
former foreign correspondent
from Italy. One room equipped
for handicap access.

(i) 13 **☐** 40 **P** **☺** **☒** MC, V

LAPA

🍴 RESTAURANTE LIPSKI
$$

AV. DOUTOR MANOEL PEDRO
1855, CENTRO
TEL 41/3622 1202
Mule-train hands (*tropeiros*)
founded the city in about
1730 as a way station, and
the culinary traditions of their
grub are maintained by the
Restaurante Lipski. The main
dish is *quirera lapeana*, made of
corn and pork ribs.

☐ 90 **☒** MC, V

MORRETES

🏨 RESTAURANTE MADALOZO
$$
RUA ALMIRANTE FREDERICO DE
OLIVEIRA 16, CENTRO
TEL 41/3462 1410; 994 2192
www.madalozo.com
Morretes bills itself as home
of *barreado*, Paraná's most tra-
ditional dish, a thick beef stew
accompanied by rice, bananas,
manioc meal, and banana-
flavored *cachaça*. The riverside
Madalozo Restaurante special-
izes in this dish.
🪑 600 🅿 🕒 Closed Mon.
◈ All major cards

RIO GRANDE DO SUL

BENTO GONÇALVES

🏨 SPA DO VINHO
🏨 CAUDALIE
$$–$$$
RS-444 KM 21,
VALE DOS VINHEDOS
TEL 54/2102 7200
www.spadovinho.com.br
Hotel with carefully selected
antiques and spa that
specializes in vinotherapy.
🛏 128 🪑 130 🅿 🛗 ◈
◈ ◈ ◈ ◈ All major cards

🏨 CASA BUCCO
$$
RSC-470 KM 194.3, TUIUTY,
VALE DO RIO DAS ANTAS
TEL 54/3504 2026
www.casabucco.com.br
Guesthouse and good restaurant set astride a family-run
cachaça distillery.
🛏 4 🪑 50 🅿 ◈ ◈ None

🏨 DALL'ONDER
🏨 GRANDE HOTEL
$$
RUA HENRY HUGO DREHER 197
TEL 54/3455 3555
www.dallondergrandehotel
.com.br
A standard hotel in town

that hosts the offices of the
Associação Caminhos de Pedra
and serves as the starting point
for visits there.
🛏 264 🪑 70 🅿 ◈ ◈ ◈
◈ All major cards

🏨 POUSADA DON
🏨 GIOVANNI
$$
LINHA AMADEU KM 12
TEL 54/3455 6293
www.dongiovanni.com.br
Seven apartments located in a
1930s mansion on a winery 7
miles (11 km) outside of town.
🛏 7 🪑 60 🅿 ◈ ◈ ◈
◈ All major cards

🏨 POUSADAS VILLA
🏨 VALDUGA
$$
VIA TRENTO 2355, VALE DOS
VINHEDOS
TEL 54/2105 3154
www.villavalduga.com.br
Separate guesthouses set
on the premises of a winery
located just 4 miles (6 km)
outside of town.
🛏 24 🪑 80 🅿 ◈ ◈ DC,
MC, V

🏨 MARIA VALDUGA
$$$
VIA TRENTO,
LINHA LEOPOLDINA,
VALE DOS VINHEDOS
TEL 54/2105 3154
Italian fare accompanied
by wines made by the Casa
Valduga winery where the
restaurant is located.
🪑 350 🅿 ◈ ◈ All
major cards

🏨 CANTINA SALVATI &
SIRENA
$$
RUA LINHA PALMEIRO,
CAMINHOS DE PEDRA
TEL 54/3455 6400
Inside the octagon-shaped
structure, wine casks line the
walls. By appointment, groups
can partake of a traditional

immigrant Sunday meal: not
spaghetti, but rather bean
soup, polenta (fried cornmeal),
chicken stew, and frittata (an
Italian-style omelet akin to a
Spanish tortilla).
🪑 80 ◈ None

🏨 CASA BERTARELLO &
RESTAURANTE NONA
LUDIA
$$
RUA LINHA PALMEIRO 120,
CAMINHOS DE PEDRA
TEL 54/3455 0157
An Italian restaurant that
occupies a stone structure
built by immigrants in 1880.
🪑 180 🕒 Closed Mon.–
Tues. ◈ MC, V

🏨 CASA VANNI
$
LINHA PALMEIRO 795,
CAMINHOS DE PEDRA
TEL 54/3455 6383
Traditional Italian food in a
wooden structure built by

locals in 1935.
🔲 120 🅿 ⬢ DC, MC, V

GRAMADO & CANELA

⊞ VARANDA DAS
🍴 BROMÉLIAS
$$$–$$$$$
RUA ALARISCH SCHULZ 158–198,
PLANALTO, GRAMADO
TEL 54/3286 6653
www.varandadasbromelias
.com.br
Charming establishment with
fireplaces and balconies.
ℹ 17 🔲 100 🅿 ⬢ ⬛
⬢ AE, MC, V

⊞ HOTEL POUSADA
QUINTA DOS MARQUES
$$$
RUA GRAVATAÍ 200, CANELA
TEL 54/3282 9812
In a renovated house dating
to the 1930s, this property is
uniquely designed and is surrounded by the 4,000 square
miles of forest.
ℹ 18 🅿 ⬢ ⬢ ⬛ ⬢ AE,
MC, V

🍴 CAFÉ COLONIAL BELA
VISTA
$$$
AV. DAS HORTÊNSIAS 4665,
CARNIEL, GRAMADO
TEL 54/3286 1608
A *café colonial* is an abundant
"more-than-you-can-eat" late-
afternoon "snack" consisting
of cakes, pies, sweets, jams
and jellies, cold cuts, cheese,
sausages, and more. The Café
Colonial Bela Vista is the place
to go for these treats.
🔲 96 🅿 ⬢ ⬢ ⬢ AE,
MC, V

🍴 GASTHOF EDELWEISS
$$
RUA DA CARRIERI 1119,
PLANALTO, GRAMADO
TEL 54/3286 1861
German and Swiss food served
on a veranda.
🔲 100 ⬢ ⬢ All major cards

PORTO ALEGRE

⊞ SHERATON PORTO
🍴 ALEGRE
$$$$
RUA OLAVO BARRETO VIANA 18,
MOINHOS DE VENTO
TEL 51/2121 6000
www.sheraton-poa.com.br
Located steps from Moinhos
shopping center, this is a
local branch of the international chain.
ℹ 169 🔲 370 🅿 ⬢ ⬢ ⬢
⬛ ⬢ All major cards

⊞ BLUE TREE PREMIUM
🍴 $$$
AV. CORONEL LUCAS DE
OLIVEIRA 995, BELA VISTA
TEL 51/3019 8000
www.bluetree.com.br
A local branch of the national
Brazilian chain. Popular with
business travelers.
ℹ 132 🔲 80 🅿 ⬢ ⬢ ⬢
All major cards

⊞ PLAZA SÃO RAFAEL
🍴 $$$
AV. ALBERTO BINS 514,
CENTRO
TEL 51/3220 7000
www.plazahoteis.com.br
A good standard hotel with
handicap facilities.
ℹ 283 🔲 100 🅿 ⬢ ⬢ ⬢
⬛ ⬢ All major cards

🍴 GALPÃO CRIOULO
$$$
PARQUE MAURÍCIO SIROTSKY
SOBRINHO, RUA OTÁVIO
FRANCISCO CARUSO DA ROCHA,
CENTRO
TEL 51/3226-8194
Locals might find it a bit over
the top, but many foreigners
enjoy this typical all-you-
can-eat *rodízio* steakhouse
that offers presentations of
traditional dance and music.
🔲 600 🅿 ⬢ ⬢ MC, V

🍴 BARRANCO
$$
AV. PROTÁSIO ALVES 1578,
PETRÓPOLIS
TEL 51/3331 6172
A steakhouse popular with
local politicians, artists,
intellectuals, and football
fans—especially at night and
on weekends. Large enough to
meet the demand, in general,
though reservations are recommended for Sunday lunch.
🔲 700 🅿 ⬢ ⬢ DC, MC, V

🍴 SANTO ANTÔNIO
$$
RUA DOUTOR TIMÓTEO 465,
FLORESTA
TEL 51/3222 3130
A family-run steakhouse with a
kids area, in the same location
since 1935.
🔲 260 🅿 ⬢ All major cards

🍴 STEINHAUS
$$
RUA CORONEL PAULINO
TEIXEIRA 415, RIO BRANCO
TEL 51/3330 8661
German restaurant opened in
1979 and is still family run.
🔲 50 🕐 Closed Sun.
⬢ ⬢ All major cards

SANTA CATARINA

BALNEÁRIO
CAMBORIÚ

⊞ FELISSIMO
🍴 EXCLUSIVE HOTEL
$$$$$
RUA ALLES BLAU 201,
PRAIA DOS AMORES
TEL 47/3360 6291
www.felissimoexclusivehotel
.com.br
An upscale guesthouse favored
by celebrities overlooking
Amores Beach.
ℹ 10 🔲 30 🅿 ⬢ ⬛ ⬢
⬢ All major cards

⬢ Nonsmoking ⬢ Air-conditioning ⬛ Indoor Pool ⬛ Outdoor Pool ⬢ Health Club ⬢ Credit Cards

FLORIANÓPOLIS

🏨 POUSADA COSTÃO DO SANTINHO
$$$$$

ESTR. VEREADOR ONILDO
LEMOS 2505, PRAIA DO
SANTINHO
TEL 48/3261 1000
www.costao.com.br
Upscale beachside lodging
surrounded by sand dunes,
with hiking trails, and a modest archaeological site. Tennis,
horse riding, and playground
for children.
🛈 695 🅿 🔁 💺 🌊 🏊 🎾
🆔 All major cards

🏨 POUSADA DA VIGIA
$$$

RUA CÔNEGO WALMOR CASTRO
291, CACHOEIRA DO BOM JESÚS
TEL 48/3284 1789
www.pousadavigia.com.br
Comfortable beachside
lodgings designed to make
you feel like you are at home.
🛈 10 🅿 🔁 🌊 🆔 AE,
MC, V

🏨 POUSADA NATUR CAMPECHE
$$

AV. PEQUENO PRÍNCIPE 2196,
CAMPECHE
TEL 48/3237 4011
www.naturcampeche.com.br
Themed suites and a beach
area option that accepts small
animals. Has handicap facilities
and laundry services.
🛈 21 🔁 🌊 🆔 All
major cards

🏨🍴 POUSADA ILHA DO PAPAGAIO
$

ILHA DO PAPAGAIO,
PRAIA DO SONHO
TEL 48/3286 1242
www.papagaio.com.br
An upscale guesthouse with
bungalows and a tranquil beach
surrounded by a preserved section of the Atlantic Forest.

🛈 21 🔁 60 🌊 🎾 🆔 All
major cards

🍴 OSTRADAMUS
$$$

BALDICERO FILOMENO 7640,
ROD. RIBEIRÃO DA ILHA
TEL 48/3337 5711
One of Floripa's top spots for
fresh oysters located along the
waterfront.
🔁 140 🅿 🕐 Closed Mon.
🆔 DC, MC, V

SOMETHING SPECIAL

🍴 BOX 32
$$

MERCADO PÚBLICO MUNICIPAL
DE FLORIANÓPOLIS, BOXE 32,
RUA CONSELHEIRO MAFRA,
CENTRO
TEL 48/3224 5588
An animated *boteco* inside the
Mercado Municipal that prides
itself as the "most democratic
bar in the country," serving
everyone from minimum-wage
errand boys (called "office
boys" in Brazil) to hotshot
politicians and celebrities.
🔁 80 🕐 Closed Sun. 🆔 All
major cards

🍴 RESTAURANTE BEIRA D'ÁGUA
$$

RUA GILSON DA COSTA XAVIER,
SAMBAQUI
TEL 48/335 0194
Family-run place specializing
in oysters. Owned by some of
the pioneers in oyster farming
on the island.
🔁 20 🆔 DC, MC, V

LAJES & REGION

🏨 RIO DO RASTRO ECO RESORT
$$–$$$

SC-438 KM 130,
BOM JARDIM DA SERRA
TEL 48/9931 6100
www.riodorastro.com.br

Chalets with fireplaces,
Jacuzzis and views of the
surrounding countryside.
Boating, fishing, horse riding.
🛈 18 🅿 🔁 💺 🎾 🆔 All
major cards

🏨🍴 CASCATA VÉU DA NOIVA & RESTAUR-ANTE E POUSADA
$$

ESTR. GERAL MORRO DA IGREJA,
SANTA TEREZINHA, URUBICI
TEL 49/9134 3029
Brightly painted cabins and a
restaurant near a waterfall that
serves local fare.
🛈 1 cabin, 13 houses 🔁 160
🅿 🔁 🆔 None

🏨🍴 FAZENDA DO BARREIRO
$$

SC-438 KM 42, LAJES
TEL 49/3222 3031
www.fazendadobarreiro
.com.br
Founded in 1782, the farm is
run by the eighth generation
of the founding family. The
main house, a stone building,
features a kitchen with a wood
fire that remains lit throughout
the cold winter days. Activities
include hiking, fishing, helping
with the chores (from milking
cows to caring for the stable
of horses), and, of course,
horseback riding.
🛈 19 🔁 60 🅿 🔁 💺
🆔 None

🍴 CAFÉ COLONIA SABOR DA ROÇA
$

COMUNIDADE SÃO PEDRO
TEL 49/3278 2078 EXT. 21
Have an enormous afternoon
"snack" of cakes, jams, and
more at the Café Colonia
Sabor da Roça. Reservations
required.
🔁 100 🆔 None

LAGUNA

🏨 LAGUNA TOURIST
🍴 $$
AV. CASTELO BRANCO
PRAIA DO GI
TEL 48/3647 0022
www.lagunatourist.com.br
There aren't many options
in Laguna. This one faces
the water.
🛏 92 🔲 220 🅿 🚭 🖈 🏊
🏊 🎽 🅲 All major cards

🍴 ARRASTÃO
$$$
AV. SENADOR GALOTTI 629,
MAR GROSSO
TEL 48/3647 1900
Specializes in seafood, and
new wine cellar.
🔲 130 🚭 🅲 All major cards

PRAIA DO ROSA

🏨 QUINTA DO BUCANERO
$$$–$$$$$
ESTR. GERAL DA PRAIA DO ROSA
TEL 48/3355 6056
www.bucanero.com.br
Ten rooms with panoramic
views, amenities that run from
Jacuzzis to a fitness center and
exclusive access to the beach
by boat via a saltwater lake.
🛏 10 🅿 🚭 🖈 🅲 All major
cards

🏨 POUSADA FAZENDA
🍴 VERDE DO ROSA
$$$
ESTR. GERAL DA PRAIA DO ROSA
TEL 48/3355 7272
Fourteen exclusive cabins. Just
a 22-yard walk to the beach.
🛏 14 🔲 30 🅿 🚭 🖈 🅲
All major cards

🏨 THE ROSEBUD POUSADA
🍴 & RESTAURANTE
$$
CAMINHO DO REI 515
TEL 48/3355 6101
Small, relaxed, and comfort-
able. Rooms have hammocks
on balconies.

🛏 6 🔲 18 🅿 🚭 🖈 🎽
🅲 All major cards

🏨 POUSADA VILLA
AGRIFOGLIO
$$
ESTR. GERAL DA PRAIA DO ROSA,
IBIRAQUERA, IMBITUBA
TEL 48/3354 0299
www.villagrifoglio.com.br
Rooms are just 275 yards from
the beach.
🛏 18 🅿 🖈 🎽 🅲 AE,
MC, V

◼ CENTRO & PANTANAL

FEDERAL DISTRICT

BRASÍLIA

With nearly all lodging located
in dedicated hotel ghettos,
Brasília offers a series of business
hotels that cater to politicians
and lobbyists. There is little that
distinguishes them.

🏨 ROYAL TULIP ALVORADA
🍴 $$$$
SHTN, TRECHO I CONJ. 1B,
BLOCO C
TEL 61/3647 0022
www.royaltulipbrasiliaalvo
rada.com
Cosmopolitan architecture,
designed by Ruy Ohtake.
🛏 395 🔲 350 🅿 🚭 🖈 🅲
🖈 🎽 🅲 All major cards

🏨 KUBITSCHEK PLAZA
🍴 $$$
SHN, Q2, BLOCO E
TEL 61/3329 3333
www.kubitschek.com.br
This place is especially popular
with movers and shakers.
Located minutes away from
stadium and government
buildings.
🛏 250 🔲 40 🅿 🚭 🖈 🖈
🎽 🅲 All major cards

🏨 NOBILE LAKESIDE
🍴 CONVENTION &
RESORT
$$–$$$
SHTN, TRENCHO 1, LOTE 2,
PROJETO ORLA 3
TEL 61/3035 1100
www.nobilehoteis.com.br
One of the few options out-
side the dedicated hotel area.
Lakeside on Lago Paranoá.
Offers spa facilities.
🛏 109 🔲 100 🅿 🚭 🖈 🖈
🎽 🅲 All major cards

🏨 SAINT MORITZ PLUS
EXPRESS
$$
SHN, QUADRA 1, ÁREA
ESPECIAL A BLOCO B
TEL 61/3433 3888
www.saintmoritzhotel.com.br
Provides a view of Brasília's
monumental architecture from
the roof.
🛏 436 🅿 🚭 🖈 🖈 🎽
🅲 DC, MC, V

🍴 TREM DA SERRA
$$
NÚCLEO RURAL SOBRADINHO II
CHÁCARA 46
TEL 61/3387 0304
About 18 miles (30 km) outside of town, this restaurant
relies on local ingredients.
Founded by a couple who
decided to branch out from
their pork-raising business into
the culinary arena.
🔲 144 🕐 Closed Mon.–
Thurs. 🅲 DC, MC, V

🍴 DONA EVILÁSIA AT THE
FEIRA DE ARTESANATO
DA TORRE DE TV
$
EIXO MONUMENTAL NORTE/
SUL R584
TEL 61/3257 2866
www.feiradatorredf.com.br
Serving street food from
Evilásia's native Bahia at the
Fair Tower.
🔲 300 🕐 Closed Mon.–
Thurs. 🅲 DC, MC, V

🍴 FEIRA PERMANENTE DO GUARÁ
$

ÁREA ESPECIAL DO CAVF, GUARÁ II
TEL 61/3382 2323
Street food offering flavors of the Northeastern backlands.
🕐 Closed Mon.–Wed.
🚫 None

🍴 FEITIÇO MINEIRO
$

CLN 306 BLOCO B LOJAS 45/51, ASA NORTE
TEL 61/3272 3032
Features down-home grub of Minas Gerais, the basics cooked over a wood stove.
🪑 150 🚫 DC, MC, V

🍴 SABORELLA
$

SCLN 112,B LOCO C, LOJA 38, ASA NORTE
TEL 61/3340 4894
Ice cream shop with Brazilian fruit flavors.
🪑 65 🚫 DC, MC, V

GOIÁS

CHAPADA DOS VEADEIROS (ALTO PARAÍSO & CAVALCANTE)

🏨 POUSADA MAYA
$–$$

RUA DAS CURICACAS, QUADRA 11, LOTE 4/5, ESTÂNCIA PARAÍSO, ALTO PARAISO
TEL 62/3446 2062
www.pousadamaya.com.br
Suites in a tranquil rural setting not far from the national park.
ℹ️ 8 🚣 🚫 MC, V

🏨 POUSADA VALE DAS ARARAS
$

ESTRADA CAVALCANTE COLINAS DO SUL KM 3, CAVALCANTE

TEL 62/3459 0007
www.valedasararas.com.br
Set in a private nature reserve that offers hiking trails. The reserve is popular with bird-watchers.
ℹ️ 9 🅿️ 🚫 🚣 🚫 AE, MC

🍴 RANCHO DO VALDOMIRO
$

GO-239 KM 18, ALTO PARAÍSO
TEL 62/9802 4419
Simple Brazilian fare.
🪑 200 🚫 None

GOIÁS VELHO

🏨 CASA DA PONTE
$

RUA MORETTI FOGGIA QUADRA 10 LOTE 1, CENTRO HISTÓRICO
TEL 62/3371 4467
On the margin of the Rio Vermelho, the river that traverses the town, across the way from the Casa Cora Coralina.
ℹ️ 38 🅿️ 🚫 🚫 DC, MC, V

🍴 FLOR DE IPÊ
$

RUA BOA VISTA 32A, CENTRO HISTÓRICO
TEL 62/3372 1133
In a natural setting, which keeps the area cool no matter what the temperature, this restaurant features local Goiás fare—buffet at lunch, à la carte in the evening.
🪑 200 🅿️ 🕐 Closed Mon. D
🚫 DC, MC, V

PIRENÓPOLIS

🏨 POUSADA VILLA DO COMENDADOR
$$

GO-431 KM 1
TEL 62/3331 2424
www.villadocomendador.com.br
A charming, rustic guesthouse in a charming, rustic town.
ℹ️ 31 🪑 80 🅿️ 🚫 🚣
🚫 None

🏨 POUSADA ARVOREDO
$

AV. ABÉRCIO RAMOS, QUADRA 7, LOTE 15, ALTO DA LAPA
TEL 62/3331 3479
www.arvoredo.tur.br
Built using recycled bricks and other materials. Seedlings were planted in the surrounding area to compensate for the wood used in construction.
ℹ️ 14 🅿️ 🚫 🚣 🚫 MC, V

🏨 POUSADA O
🍴 CASARÃO
$

RUA DIREITA 79, CENTRO HISTÓRICO
TEL 62/3331 2662
www.ocasaraopirenopolis.com.br
This guesthouse occupies a renovated old colonial structure.
ℹ️ 11 🪑 130 🅿️ 🚫 🚣
🚫 All major cards

SERRANÓPOLIS

🏨 POUSADA DAS
🍴 ARARAS
$$$

GO-184 KM 70, ZONA RURAL
TEL 64/9988 8436
www.pousadadasararas.com
In some of the chalets, nature has been integrated into the design. Others have small indoor gardens or gardens on the veranda.
ℹ️ 23 🪑 60 🅿️ 🚫 🚫 V

MATO GROSSO DO SUL

AQUIDAUANA

🏨 FAZENDA SAN
🍴 FRANCISCO
$$$

23 MILES FROM MIRANDA
TEL 67/3242 1088 OR 3242 3333
www.fazendasanfrancisco.tur.br
Learn about conservation

efforts at this ecolodge run by California expats.

🛈 18 ⚏ 100 🅿 ⚟ 🅴 MC, V

🏨 POUSADA AGUAPÉ
$$$

RUA MARECHAL MALLET 588, CENTRO

TEL 67/3258 1146

www.aguape.com.br

Ecolodge set on cattle ranch 30 miles from town and owned by the same family for 150 years.

🛈 15 ⚟ 🅴 All major cards

BONITO & SERRA DA BODOQUENA

🏨 🍽 HOTEL SANTA ESMERALDA
$$–$$$

ESTR. BONITO GUIA LOPES KM 17

TEL 67/3255 2683

www.hotelsantaesmeralda .com.br

Located on a bank of the Rio Formoso, near natural pools and waterfalls.

🛈 18 ⚏ 60 (guests only) 🅿 🆂 ⚟ 🅴 AE, MC, V

🏨 HOTEL CABANAS
$$

ESTR. BONITO GUIA LOPES KM 6

TEL 67/3255 3013

Choice of staying in regular or cabins on stilts.

🛈 17 🅿 🆂 ⚟ 🅴 DC, MC, V

🏨 POUSADA GALERIA ARTES
$$

RUA LUIZ DA COSTA LEITE 1053, VILA DONÁRIA

TEL 67/3255 4843

www.pousadagaleriaartes .com.br

A *pousada* with character amid an abundance of green space.

🛈 5 🅿 🆂 ⚟ 🅴 MC, V

🏨 🍽 POUSADA OLHO D'ÁGUA
$$

ROD. BONITO TRÊS MORROS KM 1

TEL 67/3255 1430

www.pousadaolhodaqua .com.br

Surrounded by 25,000 square miles of forest and nature about 2 miles from downtown Bonito. No noise, traffic, or pollution.

🛈 20 ⚏ 48 🅿 🆂 ⚟ 🅴 All major cards

🍽 RESTAURANTE SANTA ESMERALDA
$$

RUA CORONEL PILAD REBUA 1838, CENTRO

TEL 67/3255 1943

Specializing in local dishes from Mato Grosso do Sul.

⚏ 60 🆂 🅴 All major cards

🍽 CASA DO JOÃO
$

RUA CORONEL NELSON FELICIO DOS SANTOS, 664A, CENTRO

TEL 67/3255 1212

Restaurant specializing in regional fish dishes, notably *traíra* (wolf fish) and other local catches.

⚏ 180 🕐 Closed Tues. D 🅴 DC, MC, V

CAMPO GRANDE

🏨 🍽 GRAND PARK HOTEL CAMPO GRANDE
$$

AV AFONSO PENA 5282, CHÁCARA CACHOEIRA

TEL 67/3044 4444

www.grandparkms.com

Opened in 2011, this hotel is centrally located and comes with all the amenities.

🛈 129 ⚏ 100 🆂 🆂 ⚟ 🅴 All major cards

🍽 FOGO CAIPIRA
$$

RUA JOSÉ ANTÔNIO 145,

VILA GATÃO

TEL 67/3324 1641

Sun-dried beef prepared on the premises is a favorite at this restaurant that features dishes straight from the farmhouse.

⚏ 50 🕐 Closed Mon. 🆂 🅴 All major cards

CORUMBÁ

🏨 NACIONAL PALACE HOTEL
$$

RUA AMÉRICA 936, CENTRO

TEL 67/3234 6000

www.hnacional.com.br

Considered one of the best hotels in Corumbá.

🛈 134 🅿 🆂 🆂 ⚟ 🆂 🆅 🅴 All major cards

ESTRADA PARQUE PANTANAL

🏨 POUSADA XARAÉS
$$$

MS 184, ZONA RURAL

TEL 67/9906 9272

www.xaraes.com.br

Bird watchers haven on the banks of the Abobral River.

🛈 17 🅿 🆂 ⚟ 🅴 MC, V

🏨 PASSO DO LONTRA PARQUE HOTEL & POUSADA SÃO JOÃO
$$

MS-184 KM 8, ZONA RURAL, PASSO DO LONTRA

TEL 67/3231 6569

www.passodolontra.com.br

Located in Pantanal, with full services.

🛈 26 🅿 🆂 🅴 MC, V

MATO GROSSO

BARRA DO GARÇAS & NOVA XAVANTINA

🏨 ESPLANADA PALACE HOTEL
$$

RUA WALDIR RABELO 1009, CENTRO

BARRA DO GARÇAS

TEL 66/3401 2515
www.esplanadahotel.net
Operating since 1977 in a place otherwise short of lodging infrastructure.
🏨 42 🅿 🔄 ≋ MC, V

🏨 **HOTEL FAZENDA ENCANTOS DO RONCADOR**
$$
ESTRADA DO ARAÉS KM 10, NOVA XAVANTINA
TEL 66/3438 1348
www.hotelroncador.com.br
On the bank of the Rio Manso, near two freshwater beaches and a mineral water pool.
🏨 7 🅿 🔄 ≋ 🔄 None

🍴 **CHURRASCARIA PANELÃO**
$$
AV. MINISTRO JOÃO ALBERTO 678, CENTRO
TEL 66/3401 2273
A pay-by-the-pound buffet.
🍴 120 🔄 AE, MC, V

CACERÉS

🏨 **BARÃO DE MELGAÇO BARCO-HOTEL**
$$$
RIO PARAGUAI
TEL 65/3623 1408
www.barcobarao.com.br
A "boat hotel" for fishing and ecoexcursions.
🏨 9 🔄 All major cards

CHAPADA DOS GUIMARÃES

🏨 **POUSADA DO PARQUE**
🍴 **$$**
MT-251 KM 52
TEL 65/3391 1346
www.pousadadoparque.com.br
Located strategically near the park for quick and easy access. Caters to outdoor enthusiasts.
🏨 8 🍴 10 🅿 🔄 ≋
🔄 None

🏨 **POUSADA SOLAR DO INGLÊS**
$$
RUA CIPRIANO CURVO 142, CENTRO
TEL 54/3301 1389
www.solardoingles.com.br
As the name says, owned by an Englishman—a former jaguar hunter at that. Comfortable in a home-like atmosphere.
🏨 8 🅿 🔄 ≋ 🔄 DC, MC, V

🍴 **MORRO DOS VENTOS RESTAURANTE**
$$$
AV. RIO CASCA 1
TEL 65/3301 1030
Local fare served with spectacular bird's-eye view.
🍴 100 🔄 None

CUIABÁ

🏨 **HOLIDAY INN EXPRESS CUIABÁ**
$$
AV. MIGUEL SUTIL 2050, JARDIM LEBLON
TEL 65/3055 8500
www.holidaycuiaba.com.br
The local representative of the international chain.
🏨 128 🅿 🔄 🔄 ≋ 🔄
🔄 All major cards

🍴 **BIBA'S PEIXARIA**
$$
RUA GENERAL JOÃO SEVERIANO DA FONSECA 508, ARAÉS
TEL 65/3322 3174
Founded in 1991 by Ademyr Alves, the restaurant is now run by his son-in-law. One of the best fish restaurants in a town full of them.
🍴 80 🔄 None

🍴 **PEIXARIA POPULAR**
$$
AV. SÃO SEBASTIÃO 2324, GOIABEIRAS
TEL 65/3322 5471
Another of the city's best fish restaurants.
🍴 100 🅿 🔄 🔄 DC, MC, V

POCONÉ

🏨 **JAGUAR ECOLOGICAL RESERVE**
$$$
ESTR. PARQUE TRANSPANTANEIRA KM 110
TEL 65/3646 9679
www.jaguarreserve.com
Ecolodge surrounded by Pantanal habitat. Porches with hammocks. On-site shop sells local artisanal crafts.
🏨 9 🔄 🔄 All major cards

🏨 **POUSADA ARARAS**
🍴 **ECOLODGE**
$$
ESTR. PARQUE TRANSPANTANEIRA KM 32, ZONA RURAL
TEL 65/3682 2800
www.araraslodge.com.br
Ecolodge located within a biosphere reserve. Activities include birding, canoeing, and trekking.
🏨 19 🍴 40 🅿 🔄 ≋
🔄 All major cards

🏨 Hotel 🍴 Restaurant 🏨 No. of Guest Rooms 🍴 No. of Seats 🅿 Parking 🔄 Closed 🔄 Elevator

SESC PANTANAL ESTÂNCIA ECOLÓGICA
$$
MT-370 KM 43,
PORTO CERCADO
TEL 65/3688 2001
www.sescpantanal.com.br
Located on banks of the Rio Cuiaba, this guesthouse provides ample opportunities to discover Pantanal.
🛏 138 P 🅿 ⊠ 🅰 DC, MC, V

■ NORTHEAST

ALAGOAS

MACEIÓ

KENOA EXCLUSIVE BEACH SPA & RESORT
$$$$$
RUA ESCRITOR JORGE DE LIMA 58, BARRAMAR, BARRA DE SÃO MIGUEL
TEL 82/3272 1285
www.kenoaresort.com
A beachfront design hotel just an hour north of Maceió.
🛏 23 🍴 46 P 🅿 🅿 ⊠ 🅵 🅰 All major cards

RADISSON HOTEL MACEIÓ
$$
AV. DOUTOR ANTÔNIO GOUVEIA 925, PAJUÇARA
TEL 82/3202 4900
www.atlanticahotels.com.br
The local branch of the international chain.
🛏 195 🍴 200 P 🅿 ⊠ 🅰 All major cards

RITZ CORALLI
$$
RUA ENGENHEIRO MÁRIO DE GUSMÃO 126, PONTA VERDE
TEL 82/3177 6400
A boutique hotel with minimalist modern architecture.
🛏 62 P 🅿 ⊠ 🅰 All major cards

DIVINA GULA
$$
AV. ENGENHEIRO PAULO BRANDÃO NOGUEIRA 85, JATIÚCA
TEL 82/3235 1016 OR 3235 1262
Grew from a hole-in-the-wall in the 1980s to Maceió's favorite restaurant, featuring Brazilian cuisine with a nod to the founders' home state, Minas Gerais.
🍴 400 ⊘ Closed Mon. 🅰 DC, MC, V

KANOA BEACH BAR
$$
AV. SÍLVIO CARLOS VIANA 25, PONTA VERDE
TEL 82/3235 3943
A popular beach kiosk-bar.
🅰 MC, V

RESTAURANTE O PEIXARÃO
$$
AV. ALÍPIO BARBOSA DA SILVA 532, PONTAL DA BARRA
TEL 82/3351 9090
Seafood and fish on the beach.
🍴 350 P 🅰 DC, MC, V

PALMEIRA DOS ÍNDIOS

VERDE HOTEL
$$
RUA JOSÉ PINTO DE BARROS 164
TEL 82/3421 2328
www.verdehotel.com.br
Simple lodgings but an attentive staff.
🛏 50 🍴 30 P 🅿
🅰 All major cards

PIRANHAS

HOTEL PEDRA DO SINO
$
RUA ALTO DO MIRANTE CENTRO HISTÓRICO 1600
TEL 82/3686 1365
www.pedradosino.com.br
Inaugurated in 2010 in the historic downtown. Located in Alagoas but on Sergipe side of river.

🛏 16 🍴 80 P 🅰
🅰 All major cards

BAHIA

BOIPEBA, ILHA DE BOIPEBA

POUSADA A MANGUEIRA
$$
PRAIA DE MORERÉ
TEL 75/3653 8915
www.pousadamangueira.com
Individual bungalows set amid a tropical garden in a fishing village.
🛏 4 🅰 None

POUSADA MANGA-BEIRAS
$$
RUA DA PRAIA BOCA DA BARRA
TEL 75/3653 6153 OR 3653 6214
www.pousadamangabeiras.com.br
Comfortable lodgings next to the beach and surrounded by 18,000 square miles of Atlantic Forest.
🛏 9 🍴 40 🅿 ⊠ 🅰 AE, V

CACHOEIRA

FAZENDA VILLA RIAL
$$
ESTR. SANTO AMARO KM 42
TEL 75/3602 4600
www.villarial.com.br
Simple but comfortable accommodations on a working farm. Horse riding and tennis.
🛏 41 🍴 15 🅿 ⊠ 🅰 MC, V

CARAVELAS

MARINA PORTO ABROLHOS
$$
RUA DA BALEIA 333, BARRA DE CARAVELAS
TEL 73/3674 1060
www.marinaportoabrolhos.com.br
The bungalows sit between

the beach and an ample swimming pool.

ℹ️ 32 🪑 20 🅿️ ⛄ 🏊
♨️ DC, V

CHAPADA DIAMANTINA & LENÇÓIS

🏨 **HOTEL CANTO**
🍴 **DAS ÁGUAS**
$$
AV. SENHOR DOS PASSOS 1
TEL 75/3334 1154
www.lencois.com.br
On the banks of the Rio Lençóis near downtown, with architecture and interior design in harmony with the colonial era surroundings.

ℹ️ 44 🪑 112 ⛄ 🏊 🍹
♨️ All major cards

🏨 **POUSO DA TRILHA**
$
RUA DOS MINEIROS 60, CENTRO
TEL 75/3334 1192
www.pousodatrilha.com.br
Located downtown, in an old colonial house, a good option if you want to interact with the locals.

ℹ️ 10 ⛄ ♨️ DC, MC, V

ILHÉUS

🏨 **POUSADA PARAÍSO**
🍴 **VERDE**
$$
BA-001 KM 30
TEL 73/9971 7371
www.casaparaisoverde.com
Accepts small dogs, hammocks. Hiking, horse riding, kayaking, surfing, walking, waterfalls, windsurfing, and yoga. Rustic but stylish beachside bungalows decorated by the late American artist Keith Haring.

ℹ️ 4 🪑 15 🏊 ♨️ None

🍴 **BAR VESÚVIO**
$$
PRAÇA DOM EDUARDO 190, CENTRO
TEL (73) 3634 2164
Founded in 1910 and made

famous by Jorge Amado's novel *Gabriela*.

🪑 210 🅿️ ⛄ ♨️ All major cards

ITACARÉ

🏨 **ART JUNGLE ECO LODGE**
$$
ROD. ILHÉUS–ITACARÉ KM 62, ALTO DA BOA VISTA
TEL 73/9929 3487
artjungle.com.br
Hidden in the hills just five minutes from downtown on a riverbank, with an ocean view and surrounded by a sculpture park.

ℹ️ 8 ⛄ 🏊 ♨️ None

🏨 **POUSADA LAGOA**
🍴 **DO CASSANGE**
$$
LAGOA DO CASSANGE, MARAÚ
TEL 73/3255 2348
www.lagoadocassange.com.br
Occupies ten hectares on a peninsula, 15 km from Itacaré. Bungalows provide privacy with ocean views.

ℹ️ 14 🪑 40 🅿️ ♨️ MC, V

MANGUE SECO

🏨 **POUSADA O FORTE**
🍴 **$$**
PRAIA DA COSTA
TEL 75/3445 9039
pousadaoforte.com
Twelve bungalows in a natural beachside setting near the main square.

ℹ️ 12 🪑 15 🅿️ ⛄ 🏊
♨️ AE, MC, V

MORRO DE SÃO PAULO

🏨 **VILA DOS ORIXÁS**
BOUTIQUE HOTEL
$$
PRAIA DO ENCANTO
TEL 75/3652 2055
www.hotelviladosorixas.com
Located on the Praia do Encanto, the last beach in Morro de São Paulo, this place

prides itself as the most exclusive hotel in the vicinity.

ℹ️ 10 ⛄ 🏊 ♨️ MC, V

PORTO SEGURO & REGION

🏨 **POUSADA PITINGA**
🍴 **$$$**
PRAIA DE PITINGA 1633, ARRAIAL D'AJUDA
TEL 73/3575 1067
www.pousadapitinga.com.br
A stylish guesthouse located on an area of 3,500 square miles decorated with works by local artists.

ℹ️ 19 🪑 40 ⛄ 🏊 ♨️ All major cards

🍴 **CABANA GOIANIA**
RESTAURANTE
$$
BR-367 KM 75.5, PRAIA DO MUTÁ
TEL 73/3677 1378
Beach kiosk known for its fresh crabs and octopus with rice.

🅿️ 🕐 Closed mid-May–June
♨️ All major cards

PRAIA DO FORTE (MATA DE SÃO JOÃO)

🏨 **TIVOLI ECO RESORT**
🍴 **PRAIA DO FORTE**
$$$$
AV. DO FAROL
TEL 71/3676 4000
www.tivolihotels.com
Large upscale award-winning resort with multiple tennis courts and pools.

ℹ️ 287 🪑 500 🅿️ ⛄ 🏊 🍹
♨️ All major cards

🏨 **POUSADA REFÚGIO**
🍴 **DA VILA**
$$$–$$$$
LOTE ALDEIA DOS PESCADORES 6–8, QUADRA 39
TEL 71/3676 0114
www.refugiodavila.com.br
Rustic but upscale guesthouse just 110 yards from the beach.

🏨 Hotel 🍴 Restaurant ℹ️ No. of Guest Rooms 🪑 No. of Seats 🅿️ Parking 🕐 Closed ⬆️ Elevator

⏱ 30 ⊞ 50 🅿 🄰 🏊 🏋
🄲 All major cards

🍽 **RESTAURANTE TERREIRO BAHIA**
$$$
AV. ACM
TEL 71/3676 1754
Seafood restaurant that uses exclusively fish caught locally.
⊞ 70 🄲 AE, MC, V

SALVADOR

🏨 **HOTEL VILLA BAHIA**
🍽 $$$
LARGO DO CRUZEIRO DE SÃO FRANCISCO 16–18 PELOURINHO
TEL 71/3322 427
Occupies two colonial mansions from the 17th and 18th centuries in the central Pelourinho neighborhood.
⏱ 17 ⊞ 30 🄰 🏊 🄲 All major cards

🏨 **HOTEL CATHARINA PARAGUAÇÚ**
$$
RUA JOÃO GOMES 128, RIO VERMELHO
TEL 71/3334 0089
www.hotelcatharinapara guacu.com.br
A charming guesthouse that occupies a 19th-century mansion in the Rio Vermelho neighborhood.
⏱ 31 🅿 🄰 🄰 🄲 All major cards

🏨 **POUSADA CASA DA VITÓRIA**
$$
RUA ALOÍSIO DE CARVALHO 95, VITÓRIA
TEL 71/3013 2016, 9955 4404, OR 3015 2017
www.casadavitoria.com
A small guesthouse with a family atmosphere in the Vitória neighborhood close to museums.
⏱ 7 🄰 🄲 MC, V

🍽 **YEMANJÁ**
$$$$
AV. OTÁVIO MANGABEIRA 4665, JARDIM ARMAÇÃO
TEL 75/3461 9010
A good place for Bahian cuisine.
⊞ 520 🄲 DC, MC, V

🍽 **A PORTEIRA**
$$$
AV. DOM EUGÊNIO SALES 96, BOCA DO RIO
71/3461 3328
Good Northeastern food.
⊞ 380 🅿 🄲 Closed Mon. D 🄲 DC, MC, V

🍽 **O PICUÍ**
$$
RUA MELVIN JONES 91, JARDIM ARMAÇÃO
TEL 75/3461 9000
Top-notch Northeastern food.
⊞ 380 🅿 🄲 DC, MC, V

CEARÁ

AQUIRAZ

🏨 **POUSADA VILA**
🍽 **SELVAGEM**
$$
RUA ERNESTINA PEREIRA 401, PONTAL DE MACEIÓ
TEL 88/3413 2136 OR 3413 2031
www.vilaselvagem.com
All units have verandas with ocean views.
⏱ 15 ⊞ 40 🅿 🄰 🏊
🄲 AE, MC, V

FORTALEZA

🏨 **GRAN MARQUISE**
🍽 **HOTEL**
$$$
AV. BEIRA MAR 3980, MUCURIPE
TEL 85/4006 5000
granmarquise.com.br
A beachfront hotel popular with both business and leisure travelers.
⏱ 230 ⊞ 80 🅿 🄰 🏊 🏋
🄲 AE, MC, V

🏨 **MARINA PARK HOTEL**
🍽 $$–$$$
AV. PRESIDENTE CASTELO BRANCO 400, PRAIA DE IRACEMA
TEL 85/4006 9595
www.marinapark.com.br
Centrally located on a popular urban beach.
⏱ 315 ⊞ 60 🅿 🄰 🄰 🏊
🏋 🄲 All major cards

🍽 **CANTINHO DO FAUSTINO**
$$
RUA FREI MANSUETO 1560, ALDEOTA
TEL 85/3267 5864
Northeastern fare, barbecue, and seafood.
⊞ 150 🅿 🄲 All major cards

ICAPUÍ

🏨 **HOTEL CASA DO MAR**
🍽 $$$
CE-261 3597, PRAIA DE TREMEMBÉ
TEL 88/3432 4155 OR 3432 4149
www.hotelcasadomar.com.br
All rooms have their own balconies with hammocks.
⏱ 19 ⊞ 50 🄰 🏊
🄲 MC, V

JERICOACOARA

🏨 **MY BLUE HOTEL**
🍽 $$
RUA ISMAEL
TEL 85/3263 4765
www.mybluehotel.com.br
Bills itself as offering simple sophistication. Indoor Jacuzzi.
⏱ 80 ⊞ 150 🄰 🏊 🏋
🄲 All major cards

PRAINHA DO CANTO VERDE (BEBERIBE)

🏨 **POUSADA SOL E MAR**
🍽 $
PRAINHA DO CANTO VERDE, BEBERIBE
TEL 85/3378 2219 OR 9621 1668

🄰 Nonsmoking 🄰 Air-conditioning 🏊 Indoor Pool 🏊 Outdoor Pool 🏋 Health Club 🄲 Credit Cards

Simple but functional family-run place 19 miles North of Beberibe.

ⓘ 6 ➕ 40 ⬛ None

TRAIRI

🏨 **ORIXAS HOTEL**
🍴 **$$$$$**

AV. BEIRA MAR 574,
PRAIA DE FLECHEIRAS
TEL 85/3351 3114
www.orixashotel.com.br
Rustic but sophisticated coastal property with decor inspired by Afro-Brazilian culture.

ⓘ 20 ➕ 60 🅿 🅢 ⬛
⬛ All major cards

MARANHÃO

CHAPADA DAS MESAS (CAROLINA)

🏨 **POUSADA DO LAJES**
$

BR-230 KM2, SUCUPIRA
TEL 99/3531 3222
www.pousadadolajes.com.br
The best lodging option near Cachoeira do Itapecuru.

ⓘ 50 🅿 ⬛ ⬛ DC, MC, V

🍴 **RESTAURANTE K-FUNÉ**
$

RUA JOSÉ AUGUSTO DOS SANTOS 90, CENTRO, CAROLINA
TEL 99/3531 2468
Perhaps the best dining in Carolina.

➕ 40 ⬛ None

CURURUPU

🏨 **POUSADA TRAVÉS'CIA**
$

RUA HERCULANA VIEIRA 29, CENTRO
TEL 98/3391 1169
Simple but clean in colonial house with gazebo.

ⓘ 14 🅿 🅢 🅢 ⬛ None

LENÇÓIS MARANHENSES (BARREIRINHAS)

🏨 **POUSADA DO BURITI**
$$

RUA INÁCIO LINS, CENTRO
TEL 98/3349 1802
www.pousadadoburiti.com.br
A comfortable place to relax after a full day of outdoor activities.

ⓘ 33 🅿 🅢 ⬛ ⬛ MC, V

🍴 **A CANOA**
$$

AV. BEIRA RIO 300, CENTRO
TEL 98/3349 1724
Varied and basic menu featuring dishes like salmon and Parmesan steak.

➕ 95 ⬛ All major cards

SÃO LUÍS

🏨 **POUSADA PORTAS**
🍴 **DA AMAZÔNIA**
$$

RUA 28 DE JULHO 129, CENTRO
TEL 98/3222 9937
www.portasdaamazonia.com.br
A stylish guesthouse that occupies a restored 17th-century mansion.

ⓘ 36 ➕ 70 🅢 ⬛ All major cards

🍴 **RESTAURANT BASE DA LENOCA**
$$

AV. LITORÂNEA 9 SÃO LUÍS
TEL 98/3235 8971
Bases are local joints that started out serving lunch to workers in the neighborhood, specializing in regional cuisine. This is one of the best of the bunch.

➕ 50 ⬛ MC, V

🍴 **RESTAURANT BASE DO RABELO**
$$

RUA PROJETADA 267,
OLHO D'ÁGUA
TEL 98/3226 7171

Proud of its warm hospitality, this *base* serves up regional specialties using fresh ingredients.

➕ 98 ⬛ DC, MC, V

PARAÍBA

CABACEIRAS (PAI MATEUS)

SOMETHING SPECIAL

🏨 **HOTEL FAZENDA PAI**
🍴 **MATEUS**
$$$

ESTR. BOA VISTA-CABACEIRAS,
LAJEDO DO PAI MATEUS
TEL 83/3356 1250
www.paimateus.com.br
Rustic but comfortable with good regional food.

ⓘ 28 ➕ 100 🅿 🅢 🅢
⬛ ⬛ None

CAMPINA GRANDE

🏨 **HOTEL VILLAGE**
🍴 **PREMIUM CAMPINA GRANDE**
$$

RUA OTACÍLIO NEPOMUCENO 1285
TEL 83/3310 8000
www.hotelisvillage.com.br
A decent option located in the heart of Catolé.

ⓘ 86 ➕ 100 🅿 🅢 ⬛
⬛ MC, V

🏨 **GARDEN HOTEL**
🍴 **$**

RUA ENGENHEIRO JOSÉ BEZERRA 400, MIRANTE
TEL 83/3310 4000
www.gardenhotelcampina.com
Built with local craftsmanship, this hotel is next to a major convention center. Has indoor thermal pool.

ⓘ 192 ➕ 250 🅿 🅢 🅢 ⬛
⬛ 🅥 ⬛ MC, V

🍴 **CAMPINA GRILL**
$$

83/3341 6464

AV. MANOEL TAVARES 1900, ALTO
BRANCO
A good Northeastern-style
place in town.
🔳 600 🅿 🕒 Closed Mon. D
🔄 🔷 All major cards

🍴 **MANOEL DA CARNE DE
SOL**
$$
RUA FÉLIX ARAÚJO 263, CENTRO
TEL 83/3321 2877
Campina Grande is known
for restaurants that serve up
dishes of *carne de sol*, sun-dried
beef. This is the most tradi-
tional of the bunch.
🔳 170 🔷 MC, V

🍴 **TÁBUA DE CARNE**
$$
AV. MANOEL TAVARES 1040,
ALTO BRANCO
TEL 83/3341 1008
More than 20 years serving
traditional Northeastern food.
🔳 480 🅿 🔄 All
major cards

JOÃO PESSOA

🏨 **POUSADA DO CAJÚ
PRAIA MAR**
$$
AV. ALMIRANTE TAMANDARÉ
864, TAMBAÚ
TEL 83/2107 8700
www.pousadadocaju.com.br
A comfortable guesthouse
located across from a popular
beach. More character than you
will get anywhere else in town.
🚪 11 🅿 🔄 🌊 🔷 AE, DC, V

🍴 **BADIONALDO**
$$
RUA VITORINO CARDOSO 196,
PRAIA DO POÇO, CABEDELO
TEL 83/3250 1299
A beachside seafood place
popular since 1959.
🔳 640 🔷 MC, V

SOUSA

🏨 **JARDINS PLAZA
HOTEL**
$
AV. JOÃO BOSCO MARQUES
DE SOUZA
TEL 83/3522 4212
Older hotel with large rooms,
nearby bus station.
🚪 50 🔳 60 🅿 🔄 🔄 🌊
🔷 DC, MC, V

PERNAMBUCO

CARUARU

🏨 **VILLAGE HOTEL
CARUARU**
$$
BR-232, PETRÓPOLIS
TEL 81/3722 5544
www.hotelvillagecaruaru.com.br
Nearby the business center of
Caruaru, this hotel has a read-
ing room and cybercafe.
🚪 80 🔳 50 🅿 🔄 🌊 🎯
🔷 All major cards

🍴 **BODE ASSADO DO
LUCIANO**
$
RUA MESTRE VITALINO 511,
ALTO DO MOURA
TEL 81/3722 0413
Traditional Northeastern
country fare.
🔳 180 🅿 🕒 Closed Mon.
🔷 All major cards

FERNANDO DE NORONHA

🏨 **DOLPHIN HOTEL**
$$$$$
BR-363, VACARIA
TEL 81/3366 6601
dolphinhotel.tur.br
Surrounded by the Atlantic For-
est astride the island's postcard
image, the Morro do Pico.
Great view from the restaurant.
🚪 11 🔳 64 🕒 Closed Sun.
🔷 All major cards

🏨 **POUSADA
MARAVILHA**
$$$$$
BR-363, BAÍA DO SUESTE
TEL 81/3619 0028
www.pousadamaravilha.com.br
Exclusive Japanese-style
guesthouse.
🚪 8 🔳 30 🅿 🔄 🌊 🔷 AE,
MC, V

🏨 **POUSADA SOLAR
DOS VENTOS**
$$$$$
BR-363, VILA DO SUESTE
TEL 81/3619 1347
Bungalows with private veran-
das and ocean views.
🚪 9 🔳 26 🔄 🔷 AE, MC, V

🏨 **POUSADA ZÉ MARIA**
$$$$–$$$$$
RUA NICE CORDEIRO 1,
FLORESTA VELHA
TEL 81/81 3619 1258
www.pousadazemaria.com.br
Bungalows with verandas near
the Morro do Pico.
🚪 21 🅿 🌊 🎯 🔷 MC, V

GRAVATÁ

🍴 **BUCHADINHA DO
GORDO**
$
RUA 7 DE SETEMBRO 594
TEL 81/3533 0995
Traditional Northeastern
fare.
🔳 100 🔷 MC, V

ILHA DE ITAMARACÁ

🏨 **POUSADA VENTO LESTE**
$$
ESTR. DO FORTE, PE-1 KM 4,
FORTE ORANGE
TEL 81/3544 1699
Basic but decent lodgings. The
manager has been known to
take guests on excursions.
🚪 33 🔳 60 🅿 🔄 🌊
🔷 MC, V

RESTAURANTE DA IRMÃ GICÉLIA

$

FINAL DA ESTRADA DO FORTE KM 5, FORTE ORANGE
TEL 81/3544 2971
Simple food but varied menu.
120 MC, V

RECIFE & OLINDA

HOTEL 7 COLINAS

$$-$$$

LADEIRA DO SÃO FRANCISCO 307, CARMO, OLINDA
TEL 81/3493 7766
www.hotel7colinas.com.br
An attractive guesthouse in a colonial-style building.
44 50 All major cards

CULT HOTEL

$$

AV. CONSELHEIRO AGUIAR 755, BOA VIAGEM, RECIFE
TEL 81/2123 2777
culthotel.com.br
An artistically designed hotel near the Boa Viagem beach.
60 None

POUSADA DO AMPARO

$$

RUA DO AMPARO 199, OLINDA
TEL 81/3429 6889
www.pousadadoamparo.com.br
A charming and comfortable guesthouse that evokes the 18th century.
18 50 AE, MC, V

SOMETHING SPECIAL

POUSADA DOS 4 CANTOS

$$

RUA PRUDENTE DE MORAIS 441, CARMO OLINDA
TEL 81/3429 0220
www.pousada4cantos.com.br
Occupies a large 19th-century colonial building.
18 AE, MC, V

SOMETHING SPECIAL

OFICINA DO SABOR

$$$

RUA DO AMPARO 335, AMPARO, OLINDA
TEL 81/3429 3331
Northeastern contemporary cuisine from Chef César Santos.
120 Closed Mon. DC, MC, V

RECANTO DO PICUÍ

$$

RUA RIBEIRO DE BRITO 1197, BOA VIAGEM, RECIFE
TEL 81/3325 5901
A good spot for Northeastern food.
300 D

RESTAURANTE LEITE

$$

PRAÇA JOAQUIM NABUCO 147, SANTO ANTÔNIO, RECIFE
TEL 81/3224 7977
Around for more than one hundred years, offering traditional Brazilian dishes.
160 Closed Sat. DC, MC, V

CALDINHO DO DOGÃO

$

PRAÇA DO FORTIM 27, CARMO OLINDA
TEL 81/3439 4499
A bar that offers regional munchies and meats.
650 DC, MC, V

EDMILSON DA CARNE DE SOL

$

AV. MARIA IRENE 311, JORDÃO
TEL 81/3082 6481
One of Recife's best places for traditional Northeastern food.
300 None

PRICES

HOTELS

An indication of the cost of a double room in the high season is given by $ signs.

$$$$$	Over $400
$$$$	$300–$400
$$$	$200–$300
$$	$100–$200
$	Under $100

RESTAURANTS

An indication of the cost of a three-course meal without drinks is given by $ signs.

$$$$$	Over $60
$$$$	$45–$60
$$$	$30–$45
$$	$15–$20
$	Under $15

RIO GRANDE DO NORTE

GALINHOS

AMAGALI POUSADA

$$

AV. BEIRA RIO 17, CENTRO
TEL 84/3552 0083
www.amagali.com
Chalets set amid an area of 7,800 square miles dotted with coconut trees.
18 All major cards

NATAL

MANARY PRAIA HOTEL

$$$

RUA FRANCISCO GURGEL 9067, PRAIA DE PONTA NEGRA
TEL 84/3204 2900
www.manary.com.br
Neocolonial architecture set on the beach at the Praia de Ponta Negra.

ⓘ 23 🛏 32 🚭 🏊 🏋️
💳 MC, V

🏨 CORAIS DE
🍴 MARACAJAÚ
$
RUA DA IGREJA 8,
CORAIS DE MARACAJAÚ
TEL 84/3261 6313
www.coraisdemaracajau.com
An attractive beachside
guesthouse.
ⓘ 20 🛏 50 🚭 🏊
💳 AE, MC, V

🍴 CAMARÕES
RESTAURANTE
$$$
AV. ENGENHEIRO ROBERTO
FREIRE 2610, PONTA NEGRA
TEL 84/3209 2424
Serving regional-style
seafood since 1989.
🛏 200 🅿️ 🚭 💳 AE, MC, V

🍴 PAÇOCA DE PILÃO
RESTAURANTE
$$
AV. DEPUTADO MÁRCIO
MARINHO 5708, PRAIA DE PI-
RANGI DO NORTE, PARNAMIRIM
TEL 84/3238 2088
As of 2012, at the age of 75,
Adalva Dias Rodrigues was
still holding court over the
kitchen at this traditional
Northeastern-style restaurant.
🛏 200 🅿️ 💳 MC, V

PRAIA DA PIPA
(TIBAÚ DO SUL)

🏨 POUSADA TOCA DA
🍴 CORUJA
$$$$
AV. BAÍA DOS GOLFINHOS 464
TEL 84/3246 2095
www.tocadacoruja.com.br
An upscale guesthouse surrounded by 9,750 square miles
of vegetation.
ⓘ 28 🛏 50 🅿️ 🚭
💳 AE, MC, V

🍴 RESTAURANTE O
CRUZEIRO PESCADOR
$$$
RUA DOS CONCRIS 1, CHAPADÃO
TEL 84/3246 2026
Born as a hole-in-the-wall in
1996, this place has evolved
into the epicenter of slow
food in town. Reservations
required for special occasions
and big groups.
🛏 20 🅿️ 💳 None

PIAUÍ

PARNAÍBA

🏨 HOTEL POUSADA
🍴 DOS VENTOS
$$
AV. SÃO SEBASTIÃO 2586,
PINDORAMA
TEL 86/3322 2177
www.pousadadosventos.com.br
Good-quality lodgings located
near Atalaia Beach.
ⓘ 50 🛏 60 🅿️ 🚭 🏊
💳 AE, MC, V

🍴 RESTAURANTE LA
BARCA
$
AV. NAÇÕES UNIDAS 200
TEL 86/3322 2825
Specializes in seafood.
🛏 70 🚭 💳 AE, MC, V

SERRA DA CAPIVARA
(SÃO RAIMUNDO
NONATO)

🏨 POUSADA ZABELÊ
$
PRAÇA MAJOR TOINHO 280,
CENTRO
TEL 89/3582 2726
www.pousadazabele.com.br
Basic, simple, and clean, where
rooms are named after birds.
ⓘ 16 🅿️ 🚭 💳 All major
cards

🍴 BODE ASSADO LUIS
TANGA
$
RUA FRANCISCO ANTUNES DE
MACEDO 449, SANTA FÉ
TEL 89/3582 2128
Specializes in barbecue
goat meat.
🛏 48 💳 None

🍴 RESTAURANTE DA
RAIMUNDA E DO JOÃO
PIU
$
RUA ANTÔNIO DE CASTRO
MARQUES 279, GAVIÃO
TEL 89/3582 2175
Ample portions of home-
cooked Northeastern staples
like Baião de Dois. Serves 24
hours. If it looks closed, just
knock; the owners live out
back and will open in a minute.
It is something of a tradition
for partiers to hit the place
after the local dance, but the
hearty fare is probably best
for lunch.
🛏 50 💳 None

🍴 RESTAURANTE E CON-
FEITARIA SABOR E ARTE
$
RUA AVELINO FREITAS 517,
CENTRO
TEL 89/3582 2835 OR 9922 2115
Buffet lunches and award-
winning snacks adorned with
images inspired by archaeological wall paintings.
🛏 50 💳 None

SERGIPE

ARACAJU

🏨 ARUANÃ HOTEL
🍴 ECO PRAIA
$
ROD. PRESIDENTE JOSÉ SARNEY
1000, ARUANÃ
TEL 79/2105 5200
www.aruanahotel.com.br
An attractively landscaped
beachside property.
ⓘ 54 🛏 110 🅿️ 🏊 🏋️
💳 DC, MC, V

⚟ O MIGUEL
$$

AV. ANTÔNIO ALVES 340,
ATALAIA VELHA
TEL 79/3243 4142
www.restauranteomiguel
.com.br
Traditional Northeastern food
that attracts Brazilian celebri-
ties when they are in town.
🪑 240 🅿 🎦 All
major cards

⚟ BAR E RESTAURANTE
TIA GLEIDE
$

AV. SANTOS DUMONT, ATALAIA
TEL 79/3248 8434
One of the city's most popular
beach kiosks, serving good
regional fare.
🎦 None

CANINDÉ DE SÃO FRANCISCO

⌂ XINGÓ PARQUE
⚟ $$

SE-206, SERRA DO CHAPÉU DE
COURO
TEL 79/3346 1245
Perhaps the best of few
options in the area.
ⓘ 60 🪑 20 🅿 🎦 🛉
🎦 All major cards

■ AMAZON

ACRE

RIO BRANCO

⌂ IMPERADOR GALVEZ
⚟ $$

RUA SANTA INÊS 401, AVIÁRIO
TEL 68/3223 7027
www.hotelimperador.com.br
Where Brazilian politicians
and celebrities stay when they
are in town.
ⓘ 42 🪑 60 🅿 🎦 🛉
🎦 AE, MC, V

⚟ POINT DO PATO
$

PRAÇA JOSÉ BISTENI, JARDIM

TROPICAL III
TEL 68/3224 8009
Specializes in local fare.
🪑 100 🕒 Closed Sun.
🎦 All major cards

AMAPÁ

MACAPÁ

⌂ HOTEL IBIS MACAPÁ
$

RUA TIRADENTES 303, CENTRO
TEL 96/2101 9050
www.accor.com.br
Located near the Amazon, an
internationally owned hotel.
ⓘ 96 🅿 🎦 🎦 🎦 All major
cards

OIAPOQUE

⌂ CHÁCARA DO PARAÍSO
$

RUA AZARIAS NETO BAIRRO,
PLANALTO
TEL 96/3521 1761
www.chacaradoparaiso.com
With architecture inspired by
Amazon Indians, you'll find
chalets in a park-like setting.
ⓘ 10 🎦 None

AMAZONAS

JUNGLE LODGES

The state of Amazonas boasts a
full slate of jungle lodges. As a
general rule, these are full-service
ecolodges that offer menus of
outdoor activities along with
unique accommodations.

⌂ AMAZON JUNGLE
PALACE
$$$$$

RIO NEGRO, MARGEM DIREITA
LAGO DO TATU, MANAUS
TEL 92/3212 5600
amazonjunglepalace.com.br
Floating on a barge on the
left back of the Río Negro,
this luxury lodge just outside
Manaus is completely
surrounded by water. Relax

by the pool or join one of the
wildlife-spotting, boating,
or hiking excursions in the
jungle.
ⓘ 69 🎦 🎦 🎦 🛉
🎦 All major cards

⌂ AMAZON TURTLE
⚟ LODGE
$$$$$

PARANÁ DO MAMORI, LAGO
DO TRACAJÁ, CAREIRO DO
CASTANHO, MANAUS
TEL 92/3877 9247
www.amazonturtlelodge
.com.br
Socially and ecologically
responsible, the lodge runs
specialty bird-watching and
kayaking/camping expeditions
for guests. Accommodations
are in comfortable but sparse
apartments and bungalows on
Lake Tracajá.
ⓘ 18 🪑 56 🎦 🎦 🎦 None

⌂ ANAVILHANAS
⚟ JUNGLE LODGE
$$$$$

AM-352 KM 1, NOVO AIRÃO
TEL 92/3622 8996
www.anavilhanaslodge.com
Probably the best upscale
choice in jungle lodges, these
cottages and bungalows
nestled in the forest offer
minimalist decor and modern
amenities.
ⓘ 20 🪑 44 🎦 🎦 🛉
🎦 All major cards

⌂ ARIAÚ AMAZON
TOWERS
$$$$$

PARANÁ DO RIO ARIAÚ,
IRANDUBA, ARIAÚ
TEL 92/2121 5000
www.ariauamazontowers
.com
Miles of treetop canopy
walkways and a spectacular
location near the Anavilhanas
archipelago are just two of the
draws. The lodge offers suites
with balconies and private
canopy-level treehouses.

🔢 240 🔲 🏊 🔲
🔲 All major cards

🏨 **CRISTALINO JUNGLE LODGE**
$$$$$
AV. PERIMETRAL OESTE 2001, ALTA FLORESTA
TEL 66/3521 1396
www.cristalinolodge.com.br
This top-notch ecolodge is located on the southern end of the Amazon rain forest in the middle of its own private nature reserve. Topped by thatched roofs in the tradition of the region's Kayabi tribe, cabins are basic but comfortable. A floating deck in the middle of the river makes a good spot for swimming and bird-watching. The restaurant serves regional dishes, or head to the bar for a caipirinha.
🔢 16 🔲 All major cards

🏨 **JUMA LODGE**
$$$$$
LAGOA DO JUMA, FAZENDINHA, AUTAZÉS
TEL 92/3232 2707
www.jumalodge.com
Completely integrated into the Amazon, the lodge's bungalows perch on stilts, some with forest views, others overlooking the lake. Take in an opera of jungle sounds from the open-air Hammock House or your own private veranda, or sign up for a full range of outdoor activities and personalized excursions. Three miles by boat from Manaus.
🔢 20 🔲 MC, V

🏨 **AMAZON ECOPARK JUNGLE**
$$$$–$$$$$
RIO TARUMÃ ACU, MANAUS
TEL 92/9146 0594
www.amazonecopark.com.br
A two-hour boat ride from Manaus, this is a good option

if you want to stay in a jungle lodge but don't have time to stray further afield.
🔢 84 🔲 🏊 🔲 DC, MC, V

SOMETHING SPECIAL

🏨 **POUSADA UACARÍ RESERVA DE MAMIRAUÁ**
$$$$
RESERVA DE MAMIRAUÁ, MÉDIO SOLIMÕES, TEFÉ
TEL 97/3343 4160
www.pousadauacari.com.br
This floating ecolodge set on a calm lagoon within the reserve may be far-flung but it's worth the effort. Each of the bungalows features two rooms and two bathrooms, and every room has a balcony with a view.
🔢 10 🔲 AE, MC, V

🏨 **MALOCAS JUNGLE LODGE**
$$$
BAIXO RIO PRETO DA EVA, PRESIDENTE FIGUEIREDO
TEL 92/3648 0119
www.malocas.com
The architecture at this lodge on the Rio Preto, a tributary of the Amazon, copies the traditional indigenous huts that give the place its name. It offers a range of outdoor activities.
🔢 12 🔲 None

MANAUS

🏨 **TROPICAL HOTEL**
🔲 $$–$$$
AV. CORONEL TEIXEIRA 1320, PONTA NEGRA
TEL 92/2123 5000
www.tropicalhotel.com.br
A cross between a real hotel and a Club Med–style activity spa, the Tropical has long been the default choice for travelers to a city with few options.
🔢 556 🔲 180

🔲 🔲 🔲 🏊 🔲 All major cards

🏨 **BOUTIQUE HOTEL CASA TEATRO**
$
RUA 10 DE JULHO 632, CENTRO
TEL 92/3633 8381
www.casateatro.com.br
Located in the heart of Manaus's historic downtown, this new hotel near the old opera house has small but bright, modern rooms.
🔢 23 🔲 🔲 All major cards

SOMETHING SPECIAL

🍴 **CANTO DA PEIXADA**
$$
RUA EMÍLIO MOREIRA 1677, PRAÇA 14 DE JANEIRO
TEL 92/234 3021
www.cantodapeixada.com
Regional fish prepared every way you can imagine. A Manaus institution for over three decades, it was chosen by Pope John Paul II for lunch during his visit.
🔢 160 🔲 Closed Sun. 🔲 🔲 V

🍴 **BAR DO ARMANDO**
$
RUA 10 DE JULHO 593, CENTRO
TEL 92/3232 1195
A downscale *boteco* popular with local intellectuals and bohemians. The coldest beer in town.
🔢 60 🔲 None

NOVO AIRÃO

🏨 **POUSADA BELA VISTA**
$
AV. PRESIDENTE GETÚLIO VARGAS 47, CENTRO
TEL 92/3365 1023
www.pousada-belavista.com
Set on a 1,500-square-mile property within reach of the national park.
🔢 22 🔲 🔲 🔲 🏊 🔲 MC, V

🔲 Nonsmoking 🔲 Air-conditioning 🏊 Indoor Pool 🏊 Outdoor Pool 🔲 Health Club 🔲 Credit Cards

PARINTINS

🏨 AMAZON RIVER
🍴 RESORT HOTEL
$

RUA JOAQUIM DE FREITAS
VIEIRA, 697, SANTA RITA
TEL 92/3533 1342
The most comfortable among
a sparse offering of local
lodgings. Visitors to the town's
annual festival often sleep on
the boats that brought them.
🛏 61 🍽 100 🅿 🛗 🏊 All
major cards

PRESIDENTE FIGUEIREDO

🏨 POUSADA CACHOEIRA
🍴 DO SANTUÁRIO
$

AM-240 KM 12, ZONA RURAL
TEL 92/3324 1741
Set on a private nature reserve,
this guesthouse features both
ample man-made amenities
along with three waterfalls,
natural pools, and streams.
🛏 40 🍽 30 🅿 🛗 🏊
🏊 All major cards

PARÁ

ALGODOAL

🏨 POUSADA ABC
$

TRAVESSA ELIAS SARAIVA 25,
PRAIA DA CAIXA D'ÁGUA
TEL 91/8190 3226
Small and simple like the other
establishments here.
🛏 7 🛗 🏊 None

ALTER DO CHÃO

🏨 BELOALTER HOTEL
$$

RUA PEDRO TEIXEIRA, 500
TEL 92/3527 1230
www.beloalter.com.br
The best option in an area
not blessed with good
lodging alternatives.
🛏 29 🅿 🛗 🏊 🏊 MC, V

BELÉM

🏨 RADISSON HOTEL
🍴 BELÉM
$$$

AV. COMANDANTE BRÁS DE
AGUIAR 321, NAZARÉ
TEL 91/3205 1399
www.radisson.com
Found in Nazaré neighbor-
hood, this is a new branch of
the international chain.
🛏 78 🍽 80 🅿 🛗 🏊
🏊 All major cards

🍴 BOTECO DAS ONZE
$$

PRAÇA FREI CAETANO BRANDÃO
CIDADE VELHA
TEL 91/3224 8599
Enjoy lunch or dinner—and
nightly live music—at this
upscale boteco.
🍽 350 🅿 🛗 🛗 🏊 DC,
MC, V

🍴 LÁ EM CASA
$$

BLVD. CASTILHOS FRANÇA
ESTAÇÃO DAS DOCAS GALPÃO
2 LOJA 4
TEL 91/3212 5588
Boasting an outdoor patio
overlooking the Río Guamá,
this award-winning restaurant
offers superb regional fare
with international flair. Don't
miss the local favorite, *pato no
tucupi* (roast duck served in a
broth with *jambu* leaf).
🍽 230 🅿 🏊 DC, MC, V

🍴 REMANSO DO PEIXE
$$

TRAVESSA BARÃO DO TRIUNFO
2590 CASA 64, MARCO
TEL 91/3228 2477
For some of the best contem-
porary Amazonian cuisine
around head for this hidden
gem tucked in a residential
area. Dishes featuring local fish
are not to be missed.
🍽 130 ⏰ Closed Mon.
🛗 🏊 All major cards

PRICES

HOTELS
An indication of the cost of
a double room in the high
season is given by **$** signs.

$$$$$	Over $400
$$$$	$300–$400
$$$	$200–$300
$$	$100–$200
$	Under $100

RESTAURANTS
An indication of the cost of
a three-course meal without
drinks is given by **$** signs.

$$$$$	Over $60
$$$$	$45–$60
$$$	$30–$45
$$	$15–$20
$	Under $15

🍴 CAIRU
$

BLVD. CASTILHOS FRANÇA 707,
CAMPINA
TEL 91/3212 5595
Belém's most famous ice-
cream chain specializes in rain
forest flavors like açai and
cupuaçu. Experiment by mixing
and matching flavors, or try
one of the 20 kinds of *picolés*
(popsicles).
🍽 100 🏊 None

🍴 TACACÁ DA DONA
MARIA
$

AV. NAZARÉ 902, NAZARÉ
TEL 91/9142 0433
The go-to sidewalk stand
for *tacacá* soup, traditional
Amazonian street food.
🏊 None

MARAJÓ/SOURE

HOTEL CASARÃO AMAZÔNIA
$–$$
RUA QUARTA 6226, SÃO PEDRO
TEL 91/3741 1988
Occupies a converted 18th-century Portuguese-style colonial mansion.
ⓘ 10 ⬛ 50 ₱ ⓢ ⓢ ⓐ
ⓢ AE, MC, V

DELÍCIAS DA NALVA
$
RUA QUARTA 1051,
MACAXEIRA,
TEL 91/8229 9678
One of the best of Marajó's unique local eateries.
⬛ 40 ⓢ None

RONDÔNIA

PORTO VELHO

HOTEL VILA RICA
$$
AV. CARLOS GOMES 1616,
SÃO CRISTOVÃO
TEL 69/3224 3433
www.hotelvilarica.com.br
A good choice in a town where there aren't many.
ⓘ 115 ⬛ 50 ₱ ⓢ ⓢ
ⓐ ⓢ All major cards

CARAVELA DO MADEIRA
$
RUA JOSÉ CAMACHO 104,
ARIGOLÂNDIA
TEL 69/3221 6641
Serving fresh fish with a panoramic view.
⬛ 120 ₱ ⓒ Closed Mon.
ⓢ ⓢ MC, V

RORAIMA

AMAJARI

ESTÂNCIA ECOLÓGICA SESC TEPEQUÉM
$$
GLEBA TEPEQUÉM 3775,
VILA DO PAIVA
TEL 95/3621 3942
Complete with tree-climbing facilities.
ⓘ 4 cabins ⬛ 100 ₱ ⓥ
ⓢ AE, MC, V

BOA VISTA

BOA VISTA ECO HOTEL
$$
AV. GLAYCON DE PAIVA 1240,
MECEJANA
TEL 95/3621 7100
www.boavistaecohotel.com
Centrally located and good standard lodging. Just don't let the "eco" in the name fool you. This property is in the city.
ⓘ 106 ⬛ 60 ₱ ⓢ ⓢ
ⓢ All major cards

TOCANTINS

LAGOA DA CONFUSÃO

FAZENDA PRAIA ALTA
$$
TO-255 KM 121, ZONA RURAL
TEL 63/3364 1112
www.fazendapraioalta
.com.br
This working farm in a natural setting caters to sport fishers and ecotourists.
ⓘ 11 ⬛ 80 ⓢ ⓢ MC, V

JALAPÃO (MATEIROS & PONTE ALTA DO TOCANTINS)

POUSADA SANTA HELENA
$
AV. MARANHÃO,
CENTRO MATEIROS
TEL 63/3534 1050
www.pousadasantahelenajal
apao.com.br
Basic accommodation, but there are not many options in Jalapão. People often camp out.
ⓘ 18 ₱ ⓢ ⓐ ⓢ All major cards

PLANALTO POUSADA
$
PRAÇA CAPITÃO ANTÔNIO MASCARENHA 436, CENTRO, PONTE ALTA DO TOCANTINS
TEL 63/3378 1141
A reasonable place to sleep during your visit to Jalapão.
ⓘ 10 ₱ ⓢ None

PALMAS

POUSADA DOS GIRASSIÓS
$$
103 SUL, CONJUNTO 03, LOTE 39B & 39C, CENTRO
TEL 63/3212 0202
pousadadosgirassois.com.br
A reasonably comfortable hotel if you need somewhere to stay in the capital on either end of your trip to Jalapão.
ⓘ 70 ⬛ 70 ₱ ⓢ ⓐ ⓥ
ⓢ MC, V

PORTAL DO SUL RODÍZIO
$
102 N AV. TEOTÔNIO SEGURADO CJ 1, LOTE 4
TEL 63/3225 8744
A traditional Brazilian all-you-can-eat steakhouse. Includes a salad buffet.
⬛ 300 ⓢ All major cards

ⓢ Nonsmoking ⓢ Air-conditioning ⓐ Indoor Pool ⓐ Outdoor Pool ⓥ Health Club ⓢ Credit Cards

Shopping

Brazil may not be not a good place for shopping given that the Brazilian real is ranked among the most overvalued currency. The exceptions are for distinctly Brazilian products. Besides crafts, the top three on that list are: Brazilian soccer jerseys, especially national team shirts; Havaianas-brand flip-flops; and the local spirit *cachaça*. Soccer jerseys can be found in any sporting goods shop. Havaianas can be found in most department stores. Cachaça can be purchased in any supermarket.

Each region of the country has its own distinct kinds of handmade craft goods.

▥ RIO DE JANEIRO

The most interesting purchases you can make in Rio (as opposed to elsewhere) include beachwear, musical recordings by classic and contemporary artists, jewelry wrought from Brazil's dazzling array of precious and semi-precious stones, and traditional arts and crafts culled from around the country.

Rio Sul
Rua Lauro Müller 116, Botafogo,
Tel 21/2122 8070
www.riosul.com.br
One of the oldest *shoppings* (social gathering place with shops) in town.

Shopping Leblon
Av. Afrânio Melo Franco 290,
Leblon
Tel 21/2430 5122
www.shoppingleblon.com.br
The biggest and glitziest mall in the Zona Sul with more than 200 stylish stores.

São Conrado Fashion Mall
Estrada da Gávea 899,
São Conrado
Tel 21/2111 4444
www.fashionmall.com.br
Skylit, chic, and rarefied.

Brasil & Cia
Rua Maria Quitéria 27, Ipanema
Tel 21/2267 4603
www.brasilecia.com.br
Original decorative objects from materials such as sisal, clay, fabric, papier mâché, and *capim dourado*

(golden grass), harvested from the stems of a rare flower from the Amazonian state of Tocantins.

Novo Desenho
Museu de Arte Moderno, Av. Infante Dom Henrique 85, Parque do Flamengo
Tel 21/2524 2290
www.novodesnho.com.br
The Museu de Arte Moderno's airy design shop showcases some of the best of Brazilian modern and contemporary design. Closed Monday.

Bossa Nova & Companhia
Rua Duvivier 37, Copacabana
Tel 21/2295 8096
www.bossanovaecompanhia
.com.br
Tucked away in the Beco das Garrafas, the legendary alleyway in which bossa nova sprouted to life, this music store is actually a treasure trove for samba aficionado.

Casa Oliveira de Música
Rua da Carioca 70, Centro
Tel 21/2508 8539
www.casaoliveirademusica.com.br
One of the few surviving music stores that once littered Rua da Carioca, this is recommended for those in search of Brazilian string and percussion instruments.
Closed Sunday.

Garapa Doida
Rua Carlos Góis 234, Loja F,
Leblon
Tel 21/2274 8186
Rio's first and only store devoted exclusively to *cachaça*.
Closed Sunday.

Livraria Argumento
Rua Dias Ferreira 417, Leblon
Tel 21/2239 5294
www.livrariaargumento.com.br
Cozy neighborhood *livrarias* (bookstore) that feels like a second home for Leblon residents.

Livraria da Travessa
Rua Visconde de Pirajá 572,
Ipanema
Tel 21/3205 9002
www.travessa.com.br
There are several branches of this mellow, well-stocked bookstore around town, but this Ipanema outpost has a particularly warm vibe (in addition to a great café).

Maracatu Brasil
Rua Ipiranga 49, Laranjeiras
Tel 21/2557 4754
www.maracatubrasil.com.br
This combination music school/recording studio sells a terrific array of used and new Brazilian string and percussion instruments.
Closed Sunday.

▥ SOUTH-CENTRAL

MINAS GERAIS

BELO HORIZONTE

Centro de Arte Popular Mineira
Rua Rio de Janeiro 1046, Centro
Tel 31/3214 5354
Crafts center.
Closed Sun.

Centro de Artesanato Mineiro
Av. Afonso Pena 1537,
Palácio das Artes, Centro
Tel 31/3274 9434

Crafts center.
Closed Sat. & Sun. p.m.

Feira Mineira de Arte e Artesanato
Av. Antônio Abrahão Caram 1001, Pampulha
Tel 31/3491 2798
www.feiramineira.com.br
Crafts fair.
Open Thurs. p.m. & Sun. 8 a.m.–6 p.m.

Mercado Central
Av. Augusto de Lima 744, Centro
Tel 31/3274 9434
www.mercadocentral.com.br
Municipal market with local goods and crafts.

SÃO PAULO

SÃO PAULO CITY

Feira da Liberdade
Praça da Liberdade
Tel 11/3208 5090
www.feiraliberdade.com.br
Weekend crafts fair.

Feira da Praça Benedito Calixto
Praça Benedito Calixto 112, Pinheiros
www.pracabeneditocalixto.com.br
Crafts fair (see p. 108)
Open Sat. only.

Havaianas
Rua Oscar Freire 1116, Jardim Paulista
Tel 11/3079 3415
br.havaianas.com
A store dedicated to flip-flops.
Closed Sun. a.m.

Livraria da Vila
Alameda Lorena 1731, Jardim Paulista
Tel 11/3062 1063
www.livrariadavila.com.br
Bookstore.

Mercado Municipal de São Paulo
Rua da Cantareira 306, Centro
Tel 11/3313 7456
www.mercadomunicipal.com.br
Municipal market with food stalls and more.

Mercado das Flores
CEAGESP (Flower Fair)
Av. Doutor Gastão Vidigal 1946, Vila Leopoldina
www.feiradeflores.com.br
Flower market (see p. 109).
Closed Tues. & Fri.

Rua 25 de Março
Rua 25 de Março, Centro
Open-air mall.

◼ SOUTH

PARANÁ

CURITIBA

Feira do Largo da Ordem
Bet. Praça Garibaldi & Rua Barão do Serro Azul São Francisco
www.feiralargodaordem.com.br
Traditional downtown Sunday crafts fair.

Feirinha Praça da Espanha
Praça Central do Batel, Batel
A Saturday antiques fair.

Mercado Municipal
Av. 7 de Setembro 1865, Centro
Tel 41/3363 3764
www.mercadomunicipaldecuritiba.com.br
Food and crafts market.

RIO GRANDE DO SUL

GRAMADO

Chocolates Prawer
Av. das Hortências 4100, Gramado
Tel 54/3286 1580
www.prawer.com.br
Small-scale chocolate maker.

PORTO ALEGRE

Brique da Redenção
Av. José Bonifácio, Parque Farroupilha, Bom Fim
www.brinquedaredencao.com.br
Sunday antique and crafts fair in the park.

Mercado Público
Largo Jornalista Glênio Peres, Centro
Tel 51/3289 4800
www.mercadopublico.com.br
Good for *chimarrão* and other local products.
Closed Sun.

SANTA CATARINA

FLORIANÓPOLIS

Casa Açoriana
Rua Cônego Serpa 30, Santo Antônio de Lisboa
Tel 48/3235 1268
www.casaacoriana.com.br
Experience the culture of immigrants from Portugal's Azores islands at this crafts shop and art gallery with a café and restaurant out back.

Casa da Alfândega
Rua Conselheiro Mafra 141, Centro
Tel 48/3028 8100
www.fcc.fc.gov.br/casadaalfandega
Crafts center.
Closed Sun.

◼ CENTRO & PANTANAL

FEDERAL DISTRICT

BRASÍLIA

BSB Mix
Pontão do Lago Sul, SHIS Q1, Cj. 10, Lago Sul
Tel 61/3364 2761
www.bsbmix.com
A weekend fair that includes booths selling fashion items.

Feira de Artesanato da Torre de TV

Eixo Monumental Norte/Sul
Tel 61/3226 6719
www.feiradatorredf.com.br
Crafts fair with good street food.
Closed Mon.–Wed.

Feira Permanente do Guará

Área Especial do CAVF Guará II
Tel 61/3382 2323
Traditional crafts fair with good street food.
Closed Mon.–Wed.

MATO GROSSO

CUIABÁ

Casa do Artesão
Rua 13 de Junho 315, Centro Norte
Tel 65/3611 0500
Crafts center.
Closed Sun.

MATO GROSSO DO SUL

BONITO

Bonito Feito a Mão
Rua Pilad Rebuá 1956, Centro
Tel 67/3255 1950
Hand-sewn items including pillows and handbags featuring locally inspired images.

CORUMBÁ

Casa de Massa Barro
Rua Cacimba de Saúde
Tel 67/3231 0518
Clay items adorned with images of animals from the region and religious figures.
Closed Sun.

Cooperativa Vila Moinho
Rua Domingos Sahib 300,
Beira Rio
Tel 67/3232 9981
A cooperative that features the work of more than three dozen local artisans.
Closed Sat. & Sun.

MIRANDA

Centro Referencial da Cultura Terena

Trevo de Miranda
Clay pots and animal sculptures and more from the Terena ethnic group.

◼ NORTHEAST

ALAGOAS

UNIÃO DOS PALMARES

Atêlier Dona Irinéia
Bet. Vale do Paraíba & Mundaú,
3 km from União dos Palmares
Tel 82/9989 4575
Locally produced ceramics.

BAHIA

SALVADOR

Feira de São Joaquim
Bet. Cidade Baixa & the Baía de Todos os Santos & the Av. Engenheiro Oscar Pontes, Comércio
Street fair with a little bit of everything.

Mercado Modelo
Praça Visconde de Cairu,
Comércio
Tel 71/3241 2893
www.mercadomodelobahia.com.br
A touristy crafts center.

CEARÁ

FORTALEZA

Feira Noturna
Av. Beira-Mar, Praia do Meireles
An evening beachside crafts fair.

Mercado Central
Av. Alberto Nepomuceno 199,
Centro
Tel 85/3454 8586
www.mercadocentraldefortaleza
.com.br
A local market with crafts and more.

MARANHÃO

SÃO LUÍS

Casa das Tulhas
Largo do Comércio, Rua da Estrela 184, Praia Grande
A market with booths that sell almost any local item you can imagine, including snacks, shots of manioc-flavored cachaça, and local crafts.

PARAÍBA

JOÃO PESSOA

Mercado de Artesanato Paraibano
Av. Senador Rui Carneiro 241
Brisamar
Tel 83/3247 8288
www.mercadoartesanatopb.com.br
Crafts market.

PERNAMBUCO

BEZERROS

Atêlier J. Borges
Av. Major Aprigio da Fonseca 420,
BR-232, Bezerros
Tel 81/3728 0364 or 8839 0373
The artist's atelier.

Centro de Artesanato de Pernambuco
BR-232 KM 101
Tel 81/3728 6650
Crafts center.
Closed Mon.

CARUARU

Feira de Caruaru
Av. Lourival José da Silva 592,
Petrópolis
Tel 81/3721 3490
The fair made famous by a Luiz Gonzaga song.

LAGOA DO CARRO

Associação das Tapeceiras
PE-90 KM 8
Tel 81/3621 8315

The city is also known for its handmade goods, like the rugs made of sheep wool that can be found at this weavers association.

Centro de Produção Artesanal
Praça Costa Azevedo, Tracunhaém
Tel 81/3646 1208
Tracunhaém is known for its ceramics. Several local workshops can be visited. The Centro de Produção Artesanal is a shop that sells their works.

RECIFE

Centro de Artesanato de Pernambuco
Av. Alfredo Lisboa, Armazém 11, Recife Antigo
Tel 81/3181 3450
Crafts center.

Mercado São José
Praça Dom Vital, São José
Tel 81/3232 2319
A market that occupies a building dating to 1875, offering a selection of crafts, *cordel* (popular chapbooks), and street food.

PIAUÍ

SERRA DA CAPIVARA (SÃO RAIMUNDO NONATO)

Cerâmica Serra da Capivara
Rua Ângelo Acelino 682
Tel 89/3582 1949
www.ceramicacapivara.com.br
Ceramics inspired by the nearby archaeological finds.

RIO GRANDE DO NORTE

NATAL

Alma Brasileira
Rua Senador Theotônia Vilela 4, Ponta Negra
Tel 84/3219 3174

Crafts center.
Closed. Sun.

Associação das Labirinteiras de Campo de Santana
RN-063 KM 45, Nísia Floresta
Tel 84/3277 8002
Watch craftswomen at their knitting and purchase their wares. Call to schedule an appointment

SERGIPE

ARACAJU

Centro de Arte e Cultura de Sergipe
Av. Santos Dumont, Praia de Atalaia
Tel 79/3255 1413
www.ceramicacapivara.com.br
Crafts center.

▦ AMAZON

ACRE

RIO BRANCO

Casa do Artesão
Rua Coronel João Donato
Parque da Maternidade
Tel 68/3223 0010
Local crafts center.
Closed Sun.

Casa dos Povos da Floresta
Via Parque Setor B Aviário, Parque da Maternidade
Tel 68/3227 6584
Features indigenous crafts.
Closed Sun.

AMAZONAS

MANAUS

Ecoshop
Rua Dez de Julho 509, Centro
Tel 92/3234 8870
www.ecoshop.com.br
Sells only goods made in Manaus.
Closed Sun.

Feira de Artesanato e Produtos do Amazonas
Av. Eduardo Ribeiro, Centro
Sunday crafts fair, with stands that serve local delicacies.

Mercado Municipal Adolfo Lisboa
Rua dos Barés 46, Centro
Tel 92/3231 8441
The municipal market has crafts but also local medicinal herbs, produce, and more.

SÃO GABRIEL DA CACHOEIRA

Wariró–Casa de Produtos Indígenas do Rio Negro
Av. 31 de Março, Centro
Tel 97/3471 1450
www.foirn.org.br
Features products from the tribes that inhabit the surrounding region.
Closed Sat. & Sun.

PARÁ

BELÉM

Complexo Ver-o-Peso & Mercado Municipal de Carnes Francisco Bolonha
Blvd. Castilhos de França, Cidade Velha
Working fish, produce, and meat markets—local crafts are also available.
Closed Mon.

RORAIMA

BOA VISTA

Centro de Artesanato da Praça das Águas
Praça das Águas, Centro
Crafts from indigenous tribes in the region.

Outdoor Activities

Almost every leisure activity, except winter sports, is available in Brazil. There are few national or statewide organizations that unite practitioners of different activities. Here are a few business groups, practitioner associations, and nongovernmental organizations that might be of use as you plan your trip.

Adventure & Ecological Tourism

The **Associação Brasileira das Empresas de Ecoturismo e Turísmo de Aventura** (Brazilian Association of Ecotourism and Adventure Tourism Companies, ABETA, *www.abeta.tur.br*) is a business group of small local operators around the country. Its website is only in Portuguese, but you can click through to the websites of companies, many of which have English versions.

Birding

Avistar—This group organizes an annual birding conference in São Paulo in May. It is the best resource for bird watching at the national level in Brazil. www.avistarbrasil.com.br

Climbing

Rio is a climber's paradise, not just due to the fact that it boasts around a thousand climbing routes—the largest of any city on the planet—but because the scalable topography (including the celebrated peaks of Sugarloaf, Corcovado, and Morro Dois Irmãos) is so breathtaking. A couple of outfitters that offer outings as well as courses for beginners:
Climb in Rio *(tel 21/2557 7299, www.climbinrio.com)* and **Companhia da Escalada** *(tel 21/2567 7105, www.companhiadaescalada .com.br)*.

Community Tourism

Small-scale tourism projects organized by local communities are on the rise in Brazil. Unfortunately, there is no viable national organization to represent these groups. The best organized community tourism group can be found in the northeastern state Ceará, with its **Cearense Network of Community Tourism** *(Tucum, www.tucum.org)*. An NGO called **Projeto Bagagem** (Baggage Project; *www.projetobagagem.org*) works with several groups.

Cycling

The **Clube de Cicloturismo do Brasil** (Brazilian Cycling Club; *www .clubedecicloturismo.com.br*) is a nationwide volunteer organization of cycling aficionados.

Rural Tourism

The **Instituto de Desenvolvimento do Turismo Rural** (Institute for the Development of Rural Tourism; *www.turismorural .org.br*) promotes rural tourism in Brazil.

Scuba Diving

The coast of Brazil offers some of the best diving opportunities. The **Professional Association of Diving Instructors** (PADI; *www .padi.com/brasil/list.asp*) has affiliates in Brazil.

Surfing

Surfrider Foundation Brasil *(www.surfrider.org.br)*—Brazil has a chapter of the California-based international coastal conservation group made up of surfers.

INDEX

Bold page numbers indicate illustrations.
CAPS indicates thematic categories.
NP stands for National Park.

ILLUSTRATIONS CREDITS

National Geographic
TRAVELER
Brazil

◀125▶
YEARS

Published by the National Geographic Society
John M. Fahey, *Chairman of the Board and Chief Executive Officer*
Declan Moore, *Executive Vice President; President, Publishing and Travel*
Melina Gerosa Bellows, *Executive Vice President; Chief Creative Officer, Books, Kids, and Family*
Lynn Cutter, *Executive Vice President, Travel*
Keith Bellows, *Senior Vice President and Editor in Chief, National Geographic Travel Media*

Prepared by the Book Division
Hector Sierra, *Senior Vice President and General Manager*
Janet Goldstein, *Senior Vice President and Editorial Director*
Jonathan Halling, *Design Director, Books and Children's Publishing*
Marianne R. Koszorus, *Design Director, Books*
Barbara A. Noe, *Senior Editor, National Geographic Travel Books*
R. Gary Colbert, *Production Director*
Jennifer A. Thornton, *Director of Managing Editorial*
Susan S. Blair, *Director of Photography*
Meredith C. Wilcox, *Director, Administration and Rights Clearance*

Staff for This Book
Caroline Hickey, *Managing Editor*
Kay Kobor Hankins, *Art Director and Photo Editor*
Jennifer Siedel, Jane Sunderland, Mary Stephanos, Olivia Garnett, and Alison Kelman, *Editors*
Carl Mehler, *Director of Maps*
Michael McNey, Nicholas Rosenbach, and Mapping Specialists, *Maps*
Ernest White II, *Research*
Rose Davidson, Michael O'Connor, and Lise Sajewski, *Contributors*
Marshall Kiker, *Associate Managing Editor*
Galen Young, *Rights Clearance Specialist*
Katie Olsen, *Production Design Assistant*

Production Services
Phillip L. Schlosser, *Senior Vice President*
Chris Brown, *Vice President, NG Book Manufacturing*
Nicole Elliott, *Director of Production*
George Bounelis, *Senior Production Manager*
Rachel Faulise, *Manager*
Robert L. Barr, *Manager*

The information in this book has been carefully checked and to the best of our knowledge is accurate. However, details are subject to change, and the National Geographic Society cannot be responsible for such changes, or for errors or omissions.

The National Geographic Society is one of the world's largest nonprofit scientific and educational organizations. Founded in 1888 to "increase and diffuse geographic knowledge," the Society works to inspire people to care about the planet. National Geographic reflects the world through its magazines, television programs, films, music and radio, books, DVDs, maps, exhibitions, live events, school publishing programs, interactive media and merchandise. National Geographic magazine, the Society's official journal, published in English and 33 local-language editions, is read by more than 60 million people each month. The National Geographic Channel reaches 435 million households in 37 languages in 173 countries. National Geographic Digital Media receives more than 19 million visitors a month. National Geographic has funded more than 10,000 scientific research, conservation and exploration projects and supports an education program promoting geography literacy. For more information, visit www.nationalgeographic.com.

For more information, please call 1-800-NGS LINE (647-5463) or write to the following address:

National Geographic Society
1145 17th Street N.W.
Washington, D.C. 20036-4688 U.S.A.

For information about special discounts for bulk purchases, please contact National Geographic Books Special Sales: ngspecsales@ngs.org

For rights or permissions inquiries, please contact National Geographic Books Subsidiary Rights: ngbookrights@ngs.org

ISBN: 978-1-4262-1164-5
Printed in Hong Kong
13/THK/1